PICTURE HISTORY OF
JEWISH CIVILIZATION

PICTURE HISTORY OF JEWISH CIVILIZATION

Editor-in-Chief:

DR. BEZALEL NARKISS

Co-Editors:

DR. SAMUEL ABRAMSKY

PROF. DAVID FLUSSER

PROF. ABRAHAM C. SCHALIT

DR. MICHAEL ZIV

Tudor Publishing Company   New York

Published in association with Massada Press Ltd. Ramat Gan, Israel

© 1970 by Massada Press Ltd. Israel
1974 © Revised Edition Tudor Publishing Company, New York

PRINTED IN ISRAEL BY PELI PRINTING WORKS LTD.

Library of Congress Catalogue Card Nubmer: 70-117513

ISBN Number: 0-8148-0587-6

CONTENTS

THE HEBREWS
IN THE
BIBLICAL PERIOD

A Semitic prisoner painted on terra cotta. From the period of the XIXth Dynasty. The Louvre, Paris

The ancestors of the ancient Hebrews were Semitic nomads wandering across the sun-baked plains of the upper Euphrates in the vicinity of Haran in search of grazing lands and water. But they were not alone. Other peoples seeking similar means of subsistence, as well as men who lived by the sword, forced them farther and farther away from their original terrain in what is now north-central Syria. The relentless struggle for survival in the Land of the Two Rivers—Mesopotamia—thrust them far to the south. Eventually, they came in sight of the great city of Ur of the Chaldees, 550 miles southeast of Haran. Living on the outskirts of Ur, with its vast temples and palaces, these wanderers from the north slowly absorbed the outlook and customs of this mighty center of Sumerian culture. The roughness of their nomadic ways had been gradually mellowed by the ideas and practices of other great Mesopotamian cities as well. They had walked through the streets of Mari, on the central Euphrates, and Haran, in the north, mingled with the inhabitants—people from western Semitic tribes who were their kin racially and culturally—and sharpened their wits in conversations about events which were discussed in the market places.

For these were the years of some of the biggest folk migrations in history. From the Caucasus in the north to the marshes of the Egyptian delta, whole tribes and entire nations were plodding across the face of the earth, taking with them their possessions, their livestock, and their gods. During the first half of the second millennium B.C.E., elders would search their memories for the traditions they had heard from their fathers in their youth, and would pause in the cool shade of a wayside tree to debate the pros and cons of a site for their tribe's new home with the warriors of the tribe and an occasional, inquisitive, widely traveled merchant.

During this period, the greatness of the city of Ur began to decline. No longer the dynamic center of a growing culture, it began to lose its hold over the many peoples who dwelt there. Among the families who packed their belongings and set out on the long journey back to their ancestral homeland was that of Terah, Abraham's father.

Terah was going home. Naturally he took his family with him. In the turmoil of peoples of strange races and different speech, Terah struggled fiercely to maintain his family's and his own identity. At a time of constant movement of peoples and powers, which was remaking old boundaries and creating new empires, he could leave no one behind. So he took Abraham his son and Sarah his daughter-in-law with him. By night, the small group camped by the wayside, which was dotted with similar knots of people on the move, headed for what is now Asia Minor, and northern Syria. In modern Iraq, which includes most of the ancient Land of the Two Rivers, stone tablets inscribed in cuneiform—a writing that looks like a series of tiny pegs and wedges—have been unearthed recording the way stations along the routes

from southern Mesopotamia to the region of the upper Euphrates. Letters written at Mari on the middle Euphrates in the eighteenth century B.C.E. corroborate these Babylonian records.

Terah and his family were traveling to the city of Haran, but only as a way station on the road to the land of Canaan. Haran (Haranu in Assyrian) means "way." A turbulent, colorful, cosmopolitan city like a latter-day Rome, Paris, or London, it lay athwart the principal crossroads from Mesopotamia to Asia Minor and the teeming cities of the Mediterranean coast. All the wares of the Orient were proclaimed in its market places; musical instruments from Sumer sent waves of nostalgia through new arrivals from Ur. Everywhere, men marveled at the city's buildings, representing half a dozen different styles, which varied from the opulent gold-sheathed pillars of the south to the simple sun-baked brickwork of the east. Here, too, men and women sang hymns to the moon god and gathered in dark groves for worship of a kind which Terah and his family knew well from Ur.

Terah's family was deeply rooted in this country. The names of cities near Haran bring to mind the names of Terah's family recorded in the Bible, in the Book of Genesis: Tell Torahu—the city of Terah; Tell Nahori—the city of Nahor (Nahor was Abraham's brother who stayed behind in Haran); Sarugi—Serug, the city of Terah's grandfather. These cities had been named for the nomadic tribes which lived in or near them. Mesopotamian cities frequently had quasi-permanent populations of nomads and seminomads living in special suburbs. They were looked down upon by the settled, well-established, propertied classes. Nevertheless the nomads—the gypsies of those days—lived in peace with the rest of the population.

Thus, Terah's people grazed their livestock, culti-

Stone mold for casting the figurine of a goddess, with a modern cast. Discovered in the 1954–55 excavations of a Canaanite temple (17–16th centuries B.C.E.) at Nahariya, Israel. Excavations of Israel Department of Antiquities and Museums

Clay figurine resembling an ox. Discovered in a Late Bronze Age tomb in Jerusalem. Courtesy Israel Museum

vated the soil seasonally, and even engaged in crafts and trade. Some—those who were specially gifted, with quick wits and a talent for succeeding in business affairs in the cutthroat struggle for survival in a changing civilization—might achieve considerable wealth. With what satisfaction they watched their livestock increase, their hoard of precious metals grow! For with wealth came respect and distinction. In this way, in the Haran district, the family of Bethuel attained prominence while, in the land of Canaan, the name of Abraham the Hebrew came to be spoken with increasing approval and admiration. For, while his brother remained to bask in his wealth at Haran, Abraham had moved on toward the southwest to Canaan. It was there he was dubbed "the Hebrew" *(ha-Ivri)*, the man who had crossed the River, the man from beyond the Euphrates.

Scrupulously honest, hard-working, and a friend to every man, Abraham was the embodiment of a self-made man achieving success in a new land. His wealth grew and, with it, his fame. He was rich in cattle, camels and asses, gold and silver. He lived in grand style, waited upon by both menservants and maidservants, and all who knew him judged him great. Local people addressed him with the title "Mighty Prince."

Canaan was a thickly populated land in Abraham's time. With his extensive possessions and numerous retainers, the Hebrew Patriarch preferred to range through the more sparsely inhabited areas. At first, he kept mostly to the mountain regions and the wide open spaces of the Negev desert in the south. Later, he pitched his camp near towns on the outskirts of which there were local sanctuaries and sacred places. Trees were generally associated with divinities, and Abraham became familiar with the best-known cult

Clay jug with its neck in the form of a monkey. Discovered in the 1954–55 excavations of a Canaanite temple (17th–16th centuries B.C.E.) at Nahariya, Israel. Excavations of Israel Department of Antiquities and Museums

Two Egyptian scarabs engraved with the names of Hyksos kings. (Left) Y'q(b)-Har; (right) Ozer-n-Ra. British Museum, London

The thousands of war captives who were transformed into slaves made it possible for the Egyptian kings to implement their feats of engineering. Chained captives are shown on these painted clay facing plaques from a building erected by Ramses II in honor of the king's brave warriors. From the period of the XIXth Dynasty. The Louvre, Paris

The upper row of the painting from the tomb of Naht at Thebes shows workmen gathering and pressing grapes. The wine was stored in tapered jugs, which bore inscriptions indicating the year, kind of wine, vineyard, proprietor of the vineyard, and the vinedresser. The bottom row shows a hunter with a snare

centers in Canaan. He visited the terebinth of Moreh near Shechem, in the central hill region, and the terebinths of Mamre near Hebron and of Beersheba. On the high, flat prominence of Beth El, he erected an altar to God and watched the cool north wind waft the smoke of his sacrifice up to heaven.

And at night, as he gazed up through the clear mountain air into the low-hanging sky of southwest Asia, where the stars seem to shine much more brightly and to be so much more numerous, he would ponder his God and his own personal destiny.

Man of the spirit, man of affairs, and deeply concerned with his fellow human beings, Abraham was also a man of action. To survive and flourish in the protean world of the eighteenth century B.C.E., one had to be all these, and more.

From out of Mesopotamia, an army led by a coalition of kings bent on plunder and conquest swept through Transjordania, leaving a trail of burning tents and sacked villages behind them. From the Arabah, south of the Dead Sea, through the Negev, they pushed into Sinai beyond Kadesh Barnea, sending the troops of the kings of Sodom and Gomorrah reeling in ignominious defeat. Turning back then, they thrust northward as far as Dan.

At the head of his own warriors, the "trained servants" who were attached to his large household, Abraham set out in pursuit of the invaders, overtook them in the region of Damascus, and defeated them in

(Opposite page) Model of a granary. Taxes were paid in produce, and the wheat collected in this way was stored in state granaries scattered throughout Egypt. At the right, the taskmaster, stick in hand, stands over the people to supervise their work. At the lower right, a clerk records the number of sacks of wheat being stored in the granary. National Museum, Copenhagen

The Egyptians became familiar with the horse and wagon after the victory of the Hyksos and the beginning of the long period (1730–1580 B.C.E.) of the rule of Asiatic peoples in the land of the Pharaohs. This painting on a coffin shows Tutankhamon shooting his enemies from a war chariot. From the tomb of Tutankhamon. Egyptian Museum, Cairo

Painting from a tomb at Thebes from the period of the XVIIIth Dynasty. The hieroglyphics contain instructions such as "Load a large ship... with barley and wheat." Later on, the inscription notes that the grain has been earmarked for a temple. The Louvre, Paris

battle. With the enemy dead or in flight, Abraham and his men gathered up the property plundered from the kings of Sodom and Gomorrah and returned everything to them.

The essential characteristic of Canaan's geographical position was already apparent in Abraham's time. Forming as it did a land bridge between Asia and Africa, it was a battleground for the contending armies of Mesopotamia and Africa, each one bent on engulfing or obliterating the other. Flame and the sword made short shrift of many towns and villages such as Ham and Ashteroth Karnaim, mentioned in the Bible, and

at the beginning of the second millennium B.C.E., the advanced material culture of the central Negev was destroyed. A forbidding stillness hung over the dust-covered ruins of dwellings, temples, and cisterns, and over the plundered stalls of the market places.

Yet, in spite of all the upheaval of wars and clashes and the shifting of populations, the people of the land continued their commercial ties with the metropolitan centers of the ancient world, particularly with the flourishing, rich culture of the land of the Pharaohs on the banks of the Nile.

Abraham the Hebrew, whose early life had been shaped by the advanced Mesopotamian civilization, observed the manifestations of Egyptian culture in Canaan. But he was moved to admiration neither by the military expeditions which thrust down into black Africa, nor by the luxuries of a newly created middle class. For him, the many gods of the Nile kingdom of the XIIth Dynasty aroused only revulsion. He had no eye for the statues or wall paintings at which later generations marveled. Abraham's wanderings through the silence of vast expanses, which even the jackals' shrill cries never pierced, only strengthened his belief in the existence of a single all-powerful God.

In outward appearance, Abraham and his household resembled the well-to-do class of Canaan. He wore colorful clothes and sandals on his feet. On his leisurely journeys from one place to another, he rode a small, sturdy donkey which, rather than the camel, deserved the name of "ship of the desert." Usually, a young serving boy would lead the little animal by a rope while another walked behind to regulate its speed with a stick.

The Father of the Hebrew People, so different in his outlook from the inhabitants of Canaan and the Semitic tribes of the region, fearlessly proclaimed his faith wherever he went. He erected altars to his God for all to see, thereby planting the germ of skepticism in the hearts of some of the followers of other cults.

One of the early converts to the faith of Abraham was Melchizedek, King of Salem—the city of Jerusalem, which is mentioned in contemporary Egyptian documents as Ashmem. Melchizedek had heard of the foreigner from beyond the Euphrates, for the fame of his hospitality, generosity, love for his fellow man, and devotion to his God had reached Jerusalem.

The city of Jerusalem, standing high on its hilltops, was a major crossroads on the road to Shechem. There was something in the mellow glow of its sunsets, in its brilliantly hued sunrises which ladled molten gold over the Mount of Olives, and in its heady refreshing summer air, which made people feel that, here, they were closer to the Creator of the Universe. Roads led up to its heights from all points of the compass and all were welcome inside its strong walls.

Returning from his victory over the invading kings, Abraham came to Jerusalem on his way to the Dead Sea. At the city's outskirts, Abraham was surprised to meet a group of people chanting a song of welcome. At their head, mounted on a caparisoned donkey, sat Melchizedek, the king of the city. The monarch greeted

Tomb paintings. (Above) Baboons worshiping the Sun Boat. The soul of the deceased is pictured in the form of a bird. (Below) The jackal god Anubis bringing the deceased to Osiris. Isis, Nephthys, Horus, and Hathor stand behind Osiris. Egyptian Museum, Turin

Abraham, tired and dusty from his long journey, with bread and wine. "Blessed be Abram [Abraham] of God Most High, Maker of heaven and earth." The king received the Hebrew as a man who worshiped the same divinity as he himself. In his turn, Abraham presented the king with a tenth of his war booty.

It was during the dark, cool nights that Abraham meditated on the universe about him and acquired his unshakable faith. It was on such a night that the Father of the Hebrew Nation made his first covenant with God. A deep sleep fell upon him and filtering through the mist of a great distance he heard the voice of his God telling him that his descendants would live as strangers in a foreign land where they would remain in bondage for four hundred years. "And in the fourth generation they shall come back hither," God promised, assuring the land of Canaan to his offspring.

Life for the Hebrews in Canaan was fraught with all the hardships which must assail a minority group trying to found a new home in an alien environment. It was a common occurrence for brothers to be separated from one another. People who had grown up together, had experienced the same harrowing adjustments to life in a new land together, and had grown to depend on each other for companionship, communion, and material aid found themselves forced to live in diverse parts of their new country. While some took up their abode on the fringe of the austere,

Model of a bakery. Bread was a staple in Egypt. There were bakeries in which one man milled the flour, another kneaded, and a third brought the bread to the oven. The entire operation was directed by the man sitting in the rear. Egyptian Museum, Turin

(Opposite page) In the Sinai desert. The Jews wandered in the wilderness for forty years until they reached the borders of the land promised to them since the days of Abraham. According to the Bible, the people wandered in the desert for a long time because of the sin of the spies sent out by Joshua who brought back an evil report of the land. Moses, the Israelite leader, saw the Promised Land only from the summit of Mount Nebo

Mount Sinai, on which, according to Jewish tradition, God gave Moses the Law while the people waited at the foot of the mountain, looms up out of the forbidding terrain of the Sinai Peninsula

clenched his fists in impotent rage. Calling his sons to him, he shouted, his eyes flashing, "Ye have troubled me, to make me odious unto the inhabitants of the land.... and I, being few in number, they will gather themselves together against me and smite me; and I shall be destroyed, I and my house."

Like all aliens living in a land where they form a minority dependent on the precarious goodwill of the native population, the Patriarchs maintained close ties with their "old country," with the families of Nahor in northern Mesopotamia. The Hebrews were of Aramean descent and they observed a strict prohibition against intermarrying with the local inhabitants, the Canaanites or Hittites. Instead, they took wives from their own people, undertaking the long arduous journey through plain and valley to Mesopotamia. The memory of the Hebrew nation's original home remained engraved on the people's hearts forever. Much later, whenever a Jew brought the first fruits of his agricultural produce to the priest in the Temple at Jerusalem, he would always preface his offering of them with a statement which summed up his people's hazy but ineradicable memory of the dawn of their history, "A wandering Aramean was my father...."

Among the Mesopotamian customs current during the first half of the second millennium B.C.E., which the Hebrews brought with them to Canaan was the practice of a childless wife giving her maidservant to her husband to bear him children. The code of laws of Hammurabi and various documents discovered in the town of Nuzi, east of the Euphrates, describe this rule which Sarah, Abraham's wife, followed when she gave Hagar to her husband for a wife. Hagar's son, Ishmael, was the progenitor of a clan of Hebrews which took up a Bedouin existence in the desert. Fierce, withdrawn men, trusting no one, they lived by the sword.

Abraham's respected position was transmitted to his son Isaac and his grandson, Jacob. Rich in livestock and worldly goods, they enjoyed the same respect as had been paid to the first Hebrew. They, too, moved with the seasons through the hills of Ephraim and Judah, roamed across the Negev, and pitched their tents on the coastal plain of the Philistines and the southern foothills between Beersheba and Gerar. Nomads recognized them and greeted them as the believers in the One God. Around their campfires, the Hebrew men would exchange experiences and opinions with members of other Semitic clans. Listening attentively, their eyes gazing dreamily into the flickering embers of a fire they were too tired to replenish, the Hebrews heard of the great cities in Egypt, of the way of life of the towns of the Nile kingdom, and of the wanderings of other tribes.

Many of the people made the long, hazardous trip to Egypt, taking local produce with them—balm, honey, pistachio nuts, and almonds. Selling these, they purchased grain, and had money left over to pay for the pleasures of the large Egyptian cities. Some of the Semites discovered that they had a sense for trading and made the journey often, selling and buying for profit. Others found jobs on the construction of

dun-colored desert, others pitched a more or less permanent camp high on the central hills. Life, hard and exacting as it was, sometimes kept them apart for long periods of time.

Canaan never enjoyed an abundance of water. In a region where every drop was precious, possession of a well or the rights to a spring was frequently the cause of bloody conflicts. The Hebrews, too, often had to lead their wives, children, and livestock to safety in the wilderness, far up in the hills or deep inside some hidden cave, while they sharpened their swords and went off to give battle to the usurpers of their rights to a well or a grazing area. And there were times when other tribes took a fancy to their camp sites and tried to wrest the land from them by force of arms. There were also instances in the history of the early Hebrews when wise counsel prevailed and they were able to conclude treaties with their warlike neighbors.

Family honor played a central part in the life of all the peoples of Canaan. To avenge the rape of their sister, Dinah, Jacob's sons Simeon and Levi put the town of Shechem to the sword, and avenged themselves particularly against Shechem son of Hamor, prince of the town. When Jacob heard of this, he the magnificent buildings which aroused the awe of all visitors to Egypt. There were no such structures in Canaan, and nomads who had been to the land of the Nile never tired of describing the huge blocks hoisted into place by hundreds of heaving and panting men. With their fingers, they would try to draw in the sand in imitation of the paintings that graced the walls of these buildings. Some people from "Retenu," as the Egyptians called Canaan, even worked in the mines of Sinai.

"And men of our flesh have also achieved high office in the land of the Nile and south in Sinai and the people honor them and defer to their opinions," someone would always put in with breathless pride. What impelled the people of Canaan to undertake the fatiguing, sometimes dangerous, trek across a seemingly endless expanse of unknown territory? Canaan produced too little food for its large, mainly pastoral, population. The need to seek out new sources of food forced the Hebrew clans, too, to split up and go their diverse ways. The Ishmaelites and Children of the East became desert dwellers and established themselves in the Negev and Sinai. Some of them, consumed by a burning curiosity to see what was beyond the next dune, the next hill, and, fired by a belief that beyond the broad plain stretching before them there were hills with better grazing, people with tastier food to sell, and wells with more and sweeter water, pushed on as far as the Arabian peninsula. Moab and Ammon, the descendants of Lot, the son of Abraham's brother, Haran, spread their encampments across Transjordania. The sons of Jacob's brother Esau—the Edomites or Idumaeans—took up their abode on Mount Seir in the rugged mountain fastness south of the Dead Sea.

Jacob's sons, driven by the gnawing anxiety of a famine which seemed interminable, slowly made their way to Egypt, where they settled in the region of Goshen. Living close together, they preserved a way of life of their own. By choice, they remained alien to the culture which surrounded them. Fervently, they kept alive the faith of their fathers, spoke their own language, and refused to adopt Egyptian names.

During this period, Semitic tribes enjoyed a favored position in Egypt. For these were the times of the Semitic Hyksos, the so-called Shepherd Kings, who had swept down from somewhere beyond Syria to make themselves masters of the land of the Nile. The Hyksos ruled Egypt from the end of the eighteenth century B.C.E. until the beginning of the sixteenth century B.C.E. Scarabs (seals) from this period bear Egyptian inscriptions naming rulers and distinguished persons of Semitic origin. One of the Semites to rise high during this period was Joseph, one of Jacob's sons. Attaining the rank of viceroy, he drew up an economic program to help Egypt overcome the effects of a severe famine and instituted measures to consolidate the country's social structure. Revealing his true identity to his brothers, who many years before had sold him into bondage, Joseph surprised them with details of his exalted position, and told his wide-

One of the oases in the Wilderness of Sinai. The oases served as way stations for the people on the long journey out of Egypt

eyed audience, "God hath made me a father to Pharaoh, and lord of all his house, and ruler over all the land of Egypt."

As long as the Semitic Hyksos ruled Egypt, they allowed the Hebrews in Goshen to live apart and to follow their own customs. But once the Hyksos were expelled, at the end of a series of savage wars, the fortunes of all other Semites in Egypt were reversed. The Hebrews, too, regarded as a potential fifth column and a threat to the new regime, found themselves mercilessly suppressed and forced into slavery. The Egyptian Pharaohs made use of Hebrew slaves in the fields and on their grandiose construction schemes. Slave labor was expendable and the rulers of the kingdom of the Nile made lavish use of it. Egyptian inscriptions tell of a people called the 'Apiru or Habiru wearily toiling in Egypt.

The basic building material in Egypt has always been sun-dried bricks made of mud. To this day, the countless villages of Egypt are constructed of these bricks, made from mud mixed with straw to make it cohere. Learning of a movement among the Hebrews to liberate themselves, the Pharaoh ordered them henceforth to gather their own straw for their bricks,

(Above) Decorated pot found in a Late Bronze Age tomb in Jerusalem. Courtesy Israel Museum

Beads discovered in the 1954–55 excavations of a Canaanite temple (17th–16th centuries B.C.E.) at Nahariya, Israel. Excavations of Israel Department of Antiquities and Museums

in order to punish them and also to leave them neither time nor energy for thoughts of freedom.

The Habiru mentioned in Egyptian documents appear to have been identical with the Hebrews. In the fourteenth century B.C.E., they slashed through Canaan stirring up revolts against the Egyptians, who had made themselves masters of the country in the second half of the second millennium. The Egyptian governors lived in dread of the mounting reports of new raids, rebellions, and disputes in the areas under their administration. Unable to maintain their authority against the successive blows of the alien invaders, the officials in Canaan sent letters to Egypt begging for help.

Such letters found at Tel el-Amarna tell of the Habiru devastating villages, plundering caravans, and sparking off insurrections against the power of the Pharaohs and their representatives. Instead of presenting a common front against the migrants from across the river, the petty kings of Canaan quarreled with one another, sought to seize control of adjacent territories, concluded alliances against one another. Each one cried to Pharaoh to send help against the others.

One of the powerful monarchs of the period was Labaya (Lavi), King of Shechem, who joined forces with the Habiru, conspired against Pharaoh, and made himself master of considerable areas of Mount Ephraim and the Jezreel valley. Labaya's descendants, together with the Habiru, are said to have helped the Israelites–Habiru who had been living in Egypt—to take Shechem without a fight. In Egypt, the Israelites perpetuated characteristics which in the course of time made them distinctive from the other Habiru or Hebrew whom they resembled in economic status and in certain social practices. However, they rigorously preserved their racial purity and stubbornly clung to their own religious traditions and their faith in the God of the Patriarchs.

But the shaky Egyptian government at home could send no aid to its officials in Canaan. Reeling from the body blows delivered by the Habiru in the fourteenth century, Egyptian power in Canaan began to crumble. And soon a more terrifying force appeared to melt the

(Opposite page) The spot where the Jordan River flows into the Dead Sea, the Scriptural Salt Sea. The sea, 51 miles long and 11 miles wide, is located in a deep depression. Its surface lies more than 1,300 feet below the level of the Mediterranean. The high concentration of salt in the water precludes the possibility of any kind of life in it

20

hearts of the Canaanite peoples as the desert sun makes dew vanish. As Egyptian power in Canaan began to wane, the Israelites had left Goshen and were now emerging from the wilderness to advance into the Promised Land with the irresistible drive of a people imbued with a mission.

What had unleashed this group to brave the formidable expanses of desert, human foes, and the rigors of the elements? How, from a mob of subservient slaves, had these people been welded into a power so strong that the mere mention of their name struck terror into the hearts of the inhabitants of Sinai, Transjordania, and Canaan?

The Pharaoh who reduced the Hebrews of Goshen to slavery is believed to have been Ramses II. During his reign, the capital of Egypt was once more transferred to Zoan, in Lower Egypt, and given the name of *Par-Raamses*, the House of Ramses. This was the storage city built by Hebrew slaves.

The Hebrew slaves apparently left Egypt about 1280 B.C.E., and headed for the Sinai desert in an effort to steer clear of Egyptian garrisons and marauding Bedouins. In the dead of night, the Hebrews made a determined break for freedom. In Jewish tradition, this night is called "A night of watching," and the Exodus from the land of the Nile under the leadership of Moses, the lawgiver and the greatest of the Hebrew prophets, became the central event in the memory of the people down the ages, in the conception of Jewish history, and as a turning point in the cultural pattern of the whole Western world.

The Israelite spirit was forged in the deserts of Sinai and the Negev. Trudging on day after day across trackless wastes stretching in all directions as far as the eye could see, past massive mountain ranges that seemed to hold up the sky, and lying down exhausted and footsore under the still, clear, low-hanging skies at night, brought the Hebrews nearer to the concept of the existence of a single Supreme Being.

In Sinai, also, the basis of their legal system was laid down and a firm foundation established for relations between men. But the greatest impact was made by the unequivocal adoption of a monotheistic faith. In the ancient East, belief in powerful gods and goddesses with varying responsibilities and human traits had been part of the lives of all peoples for centuries. No religion before had achieved the concept of a single, unseen, ubiquitous, omniscient God — not even the faith of the Egyptian King Ikhnaton, who attributed supreme power to the sun disc, Aton. Jewish tradition ascribes the revelation of God to Moses at various times during the wandering in the desert. It was on a tall, imposing peak called Mount Sinai that the God of Israel is said to have bestowed His sacred Law on the Hebrews. Here, the Lord of Creation gave the Jews and the world the Ten Commandments, embodying ethical standards which have become the basis of civilized life everywhere.

The journey through the Sinai, the Negev, and the plains of Moab in Transjordania seemed to drag on interminably, yet, as time slowly wore on, the Hebrews underwent a radical transformation. They themselves were not always aware of the change they were undergoing in the crucible of their solitary wanderings. Not only did their skins become tough and burnt by the sun and wind; not only did their bowed backs—accustomed to the lashes of an overseer—straighten up and pull their heads erect; not only did their legs and thighs acquire hard, sinewy muscles capable of enduring long hours of uninterrupted strain; but by the time they reached the banks of the River Jordan, having fought and conquered the kings of the Amorites and marched across the kingdoms of the Moabites and Ammonites, their spirits were as tough, as proud, and as tenacious as their bodies. Gilead and the slopes of the Jordan valley were theirs, and they had begun to feel the glow of victory pulsing in their veins. They stood and stared long and hard at the green, shimmering oasis of Jericho in the distance. Behind Jericho lay jagged hills and, beyond them, the places their fathers and their fathers' fathers had spoken of longingly—the hills of Judah and Ephraim. The time had come to reconquer what was theirs.

Moses, their leader, also surveyed the Promised Land from afar. His tired eyes followed the line which ran down from Mount Nebo, on which he stood, to the distant bluish-green of the Dead Sea, the plain of Jericho, and the hills beyond. In his mind, he saw, with amazing clarity, across the breadth of the land to the surf-edged shore of the Mediterranean and snow-capped Hermon in the far north. He let his glance drop to the vista below and his people waiting for a word from him. His task had been far from easy. But he was satisfied with his accomplishment. He had stalked out of Egypt at the head of a mob of slaves and had delivered them, a nation, to the gateway to their land. His duty was completed and he could now relinquish the leadership to a man of the sword, his faithful servant Joshua.

Joshua was a young man, confident of his mission and clearly aware of the odds against him. He knew that the material culture of the Canaanites was far superior to that of his Israelites who were still essentially nomads. The Canaanites had fortified cities surrounded by high walls and massive towers manned by soldiers skilled in the arts of defensive war against ragtag mobs storming their gates. The Hebrew fighting men could not take the Canaanite cities by direct assault, nor did they have the equipment or techniques for overcoming a walled city by siege. And Joshua's men certainly could not stand up to the swift-moving cavalry and sweeping chariots of the Canaanites.

An astute strategist, Joshua wisely adopted tactics which have always proved effective against armies with superior equipment and weapons—surprise attacks, night raids, ambushes, deceptions, and encounters with the enemy in hills where war chariots could not be employed successfully, if at all.

Once the Canaanites heard of his initial victories, Joshua's reputation demoralized them. His troops crashed through towns and fortifications in the hills of Judah and Ephraim and took possession of Galilee in a decisive battle near Hazor, in which they defeated a powerful coalition of kings. Not that Canaan was occupied at one fell swoop. Ruins of Canaanite towns indicate that population centers in Judah, the coastal plain, and the land of Benjamin east and west of Jerusalem were razed in the thirteenth century B.C.E. at wide intervals of time—Jericho, at the beginning of the century; Beth El, in the middle; Lachish, in the final third; and Debir, at the end. The fortified cities of Megiddo, Beth Shean, Gezer, and Jaffa were not yet a part of Israelite territory. The Hebrews did not begin to penetrate the Canaanite enclaves in the coastal plain and the valleys until the period of the Judges.

In the year 1220 B.C.E., King Merneptah of Egypt sent a military expedition to crush rebellious towns in Canaan. After the return of his victorious troops, laden with plunder and dragging columns of slaves chained together, the Pharaoh had a monument erected to commemorate his triumph. On the stela Merneptah engraved the following inscription: "Plundered is Canaan with every evil; carried off is Ashkelon; seized upon is Gezer; Yanoam is made as that which does not exist; Israel is laid waste, his seed is not; Kharu (Canaan) is become a widow for Egypt. . . ."

This was the first time the name Israel was mentioned in a foreign source. Israel—according to the inscription, a people and not a geographical entity—was listed among the rebels in Canaan. Canaan had not yet become the land of Israel, but the Israelite tribes were powerful and confident enough to rise up against the Pharaoh of Egypt.

During the period of the Judges, not only were the Hebrews fighting stubbornly for the control of the country but also for their very existence there. From all sides, their enemies struck devastating blows at them. From Transjordania, the people of Ammon and Moab carried out swift raids against Israelite settlements. In the north, Canaanite tribes swooped down to kill, destroy, and plunder. And out of the desert the Midianites and Amalekites thrust into Hebrew territory to wipe out Israelite villages in the entire country from the Jezreel valley to the town of Gaza. But for the determined, courageous leaders known as Judges who emerged during this period of perennial insecurity, the Hebrew tribes would have been crushed by the jabbing onslaughts of their

(Opposite page) The Jordan meanders in a bed at the bottom of a rift and flows into the Dead Sea at the lowest point of the surface of the earth. The Bible describes the crossing of the Jordan by Joshua and the Israelites as a miracle similar to the passage of the Red Sea by Moses and the Hebrews fleeing before the Egyptians. The view is held by some scholars that the flow of the water was interrupted for several hours by an avalanche of soft limestone rock falling into the river

Jericho is the oldest walled city in the Near East. Archaeological evidence indicates that the site had continuous settlement for a period of 10,000 years. The Biblical narrative relates that it was taken by Joshua after its walls collapsed when the Israelites bearing the Ark of the Covenant completed seven circuits around the city

numerous foes. These men and women succeeded by dint of constant effort and personal inspiration in unifying a number of tribes and instilling in them an eagerness to go out and fight the enemy and put him to rout.

This was the time when the Hebrew tribes gradually gave up their nomadic existence and established permanent settlements in various parts of the country. Their social structure, however, remained patriarchal, based on families and clans organized in tribes. The various tribes preserved their individual identities and lived apart, united by common memories and traditions from the time of Moses and Joshua. Shiloh, in the middle of the country, was the religious center for most of the Hebrew tribes. There the Israelites went to pay homage to the Holy Ark, which contained the Tables of the Law, and to sacrifice to their ancestral God.

The permanent settlements of the Israelites were chiefly in the hill regions. Villages perched on the slopes and tops of hills afforded much better protection against the depredations of foreign raiders. Making use of the stones and other building materials from earlier, ruined Canaanite settlements, the Hebrews founded new villages. They plowed the fields on the slopes and even in the valleys below as

the danger of attack diminished. To gain more land on which to plant grain, the Israelites also cleared the forests on Mount Ephraim. The need for tools led to a rapid development of the uses of iron. The people began to employ various implements fashioned from this metal in their crafts, although bronze continued to predominate in the manufacture of agricultural tools and weapons until the early years of the Monarchy, during the reign of Saul.

But the Israelites were not allowed to turn their minds to the arts of peace for long. The Philistines — the "People of the Sea," brutal warriors of Greek extraction who had settled along the coast — marched against them out of the southwest and threatened the tribe of Dan. A popular hero, Samson, led the fight to beat back the invaders, but the Philistines succeeded in overrunning large areas in the coastal valley, Mount Ephraim, and the hills of Judah. It became increasingly clear that the loose confederation of Israelite tribes could no longer stem the advancing Philistine soldiers who were equipped with chariots and iron weapons. The time had come to weld the association of tribes into a single, powerful political unit capable of directing the will of a united people toward a common goal. The period of the Israelite Monarchy was at hand.

THE ISRAELITE MONARCHY: FROM SAUL TO THE BABYLONIAN CONQUEST

Proto-Aeolian capital (7th century B.C.E.) from palace citadel at Ramat Rachel, south of Jerusalem. Courtesy Dr. Yohanan Aharoni

No land stood up to them, according to an Egyptian inscription from the reign of Ramses III (1195-1164 B.C.E.). The so-called Peoples of the Sea swept across Asia Minor like a tidal wave, leaving corpses and rubble in their wake. Who were these invincible terrors who, the Egyptians said, were advancing against them "preceded by a raging flame"? These conquerors of the eastern Mediterranean came from the islands of the Aegean Sea, Greece, and Anatolia? They included the Siculi, who later settled in Siculia (modern Sicily), the Dananites, and the Philistines, who subsequently colonized the southwestern coast of Palestine.

The troops of Ramses III braced themselves for the attack of the invaders and succeeded in turning them back. But the Egyptian kingdom never recovered from the impact. The political structure of all the other countries in the Fertile Crescent also changed as a consequence of the repeated encroachments of the Peoples of the Sea. After they were beaten back from the gates of Egypt, the Philistines camped in the coastal plain between Jaffa and Gaza. They then rode roughshod over the towns of Gaza, Ashkelon, and Ashdod, established themselves firmly in the entire region, and spread terror throughout the valleys and hills.

The Philistines spoke Greek and followed Greek customs, although they are believed to have come from Crete. Like other "sea peoples," they were good seamen, merchants, and craftsmen, especially in metalwork. But, above all, they were excellent soldiers. Wearing plumed helmets of shining copper and chain mail, the Philistine warriors charged into battle brandishing weapons—swords, spears, and lances—of iron and copper and holding up thick shields for protection.

The use of iron had been known in Palestine before the arrival of the Philistines. An iron ring found at Megiddo and objects made of this metal discovered at Madeba in Jordan date from the fourteenth or thirteenth centuries B.C.E. An iron plowshare from the early days of the Hebrew Monarchy was unearthed at Givat Shaul (Tell el-Ful), north of Jerusalem. But during the period of the Judges and the early days of Saul's reign, and even in the time of David, copper and especially its alloy, bronze, were widely used by craftsmen and farmers.

The Philistines saw the advantages of this hard, fusible metal and, while people were still using it only for ornaments and jewelry, they were already fashioning it into weapons, and later into tools. It was not until the process of tempering iron to bring it to a high degree of hardness and tensile strength was developed that it began to supplant bronze. The Philistines realized both the economic and military advantages of controlling the entire metal industry in Palestine. For implements and weapons of iron or bronze, people had to go to the Philistines. The Hebrews paid good money for their new tools and exorbitant fees for sharpening or repairing their old ones. The roads from the hills of Judah to the Philistine cities were full of Israelites carrying dull plowshares, blunted axes, and chipped spades to be restored. And the Israelites were defenseless. There were times when not a man in Israel had a sword or a spear. Under the circumstances, whenever the Philistines clashed with the Hebrews, they made short work of them.

Even the inspiring leadership of the prophet Samuel was of no avail against the Philistines. The Israelites did succeed in putting up stiff resistance against attack but they could not destroy the powerful enemy strong-

(Opposite page) Winged sphinx and kneeling figure before Tree of Life. Box of carved ivory from 8th century B.C.E. found at Hazor excavations. Courtesy Archaeological Expedition to Hazor

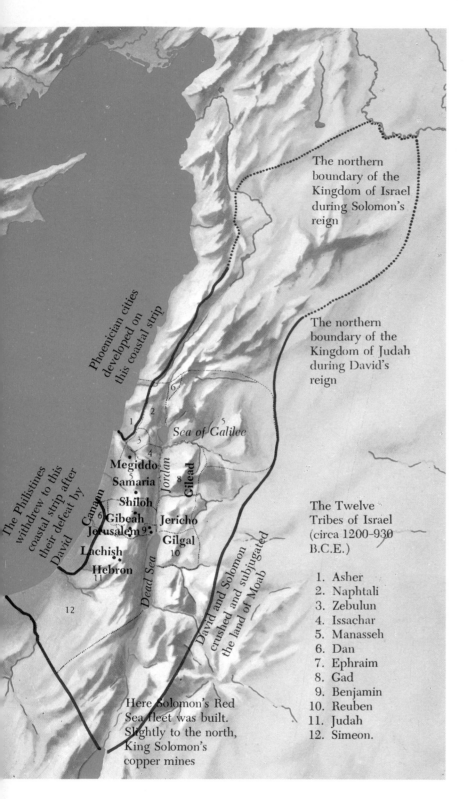

The northern boundary of the Kingdom of Israel during Solomon's reign

The northern boundary of the Kingdom of Judah during David's reign

Phoenician cities developed on this coastal strip

The Philistines withdrew to this coastal strip after their defeat by David

David and Solomon crushed and subjugated the land of Moab

Sea of Galilee

Megiddo
Samaria
Shiloh
Gibeah
Jerusalem
Lachish
Hebron

Jericho
Gilgal

Jordan

Gilead

Canaan

Dead Sea

The Twelve Tribes of Israel (circa 1200–930 B.C.E.)

1. Asher
2. Naphtali
3. Zebulun
4. Issachar
5. Manasseh
6. Dan
7. Ephraim
8. Gad
9. Benjamin
10. Reuben
11. Judah
12. Simeon.

Here Solomon's Red Sea fleet was built. Slightly to the north, King Solomon's copper mines

Map of Israelite settlement in Canaan from Joshua to Solomon (1200–930 B.C.E.)

ly entrenched in the southwestern plain. Their organization, both political and military, was far inferior to that of the Philistines, and they suffered a shattering defeat near the Canaanite city-state of Aphek, at the approaches to Mount Ephraim between Ono and Sokho. The ranks of the Israelite fighting men thinned, the survivors took to their heels, and the Ark of the Lord fell into the hands of the enemy. Israel lost its old leader, the priest Eli, and the Philistines made themselves masters of a large part of the country and destroyed the religious center at Shiloh.

There was obviously something wrong with the way the nation was organized. The state had to be refashioned according to the pattern followed by other countries in the Orient. But the prophet Samuel raised his arms in anger whenever the subject of the people's wish for a king was broached to him. The word "king" conjured up before him a vision of the Canaanite monarchs who transformed their people into their kingdom's slaves. But, in the end, he, too, yielded to the immediate necessity.

The Jews' first king, Saul, son of Kish, from the tribe of Benjamin, was known as a warrior, and it was he who launched the preparations for a showdown with the Philistines. The men who had volunteered to form an army were ready to face the powerful enemy. Accordingly, Saul established a select, professional fighting force. And, unlike the Judges, realizing that a single decisive battle was not enough, he directed the efforts of all the tribes to carrying on a prolonged war under his leadership.

However, although Saul inflicted a number of serious defeats on the Philistines, he did not destroy their war potential and their desire to conquer the Israelites. On one occasion, his troops succeeded in liberating Mount Ephraim, but the Philistines not only later regained the area together with large parts of the Jezreel valley but also badly mauled his forces on Mount Gilboa and killed the king and his sons.

It was King David who decisively crushed the Philistine power. Fierce battles broke out in the vicinity of Bethlehem and in the valley of Rephaim southwest of Jerusalem. David succeeded in trouncing the enemy and driving them back from the hills and foothills of Judah to the coastal plain, where they had originally lived in the period of the Judges. The Philistine threat to the Israelites' survival was gone forever. Much later, the Philistines did succeed in throwing off Israelite rule, but could no longer be considered a serious danger.

A number of factors determined the final triumph. The Israelites controlled the hill regions, the agricultural sources of sustenance were in their hands, and the establishment of the Monarchy had brought about the formation of an efficient army. The Philistines did not maintain their native culture and consequently adopted the language and religion of their neighbors and became assimilated among them. One reason for their failure to stress their own cultural values stemmed from their ties with foreign peoples such as the Aegeans, Egyptians, and Canaanites. The nation solidly united in one faith and shouting their God's name in battle simply overwhelmed them.

The far-reaching changes which transformed Israelite society after the establishment of the Monarchy oc-

curred gradually. The very formation of the kingdom involved a prolonged bitter struggle between the prophets and the priests. The pattern of Israelite family life based on clans still dominated the court of Saul. The king's officials were his closest relatives and exerted great influence over him.

Saul's capital, Gibeath Benjamin or Gibeat Shaul, was located at a spot three and one half miles north of modern Jerusalem at a site called Tell el-Ful. Burned and razed during the civil war between the tribe of Benjamin and the other tribes, the city was apparently

rebuilt in the second half of the eleventh century B.C.E. The city, built on a hilltop and fortified, had a rectangular citadel. A wall of undressed stones with square towers at each of the corners surrounded it. Archaeologists believe the Philistines built the citadel and maintained a garrison there.

The population of Gibeath Benjamin was not large. The people lived from farming. At the time, Israelite urban culture was still in its early stages. In the beginning of his reign, Israel's first king had time for agriculture in the midst of his military activities, and the

27

Assyria and Egypt. He overcame the Philistines and defeated the peoples of Transjordania and Syria, thus establishing a powerful buffer state in the Fertile Crescent between Mesopotamia and Egypt.

The country's eastern border was pushed to the edge of the Syrian-Arabian desert, and the frontiers of Israelite settlement expanded to include Edom, Moab, and Ammon in Transjordania. Syria of Damascus and Syria of Zobah became protectorates. David made himself master of the international communications arteries between the Mediterranean Sea and Mesopotamia and of the caravan routes between the lands of the Fertile Crescent.

Two major roads used by traders in times of peace and troops in times of war greatly influenced the contemporary civilizations. The first, *Via Maris* or the Maritime Road, extended southwest from Damascus across the Daughters of Jacob Bridge over the Jordan and divided in two. One branch cut through Beth She an, the other went by Mount Tabor. Both branches converged again near Megiddo. At the western entrance of Iron valley, this road joined a coastal highway which led southward along the Samarian hills as far as Rosh ha-Ayin and ran through Lod, Jabneh, Ashdod, Ashkelon, and Gaza as far as Egypt. The second was the King's Highway, which went from Elath to Rekem, Kir Moab, Madeba, Heshbon, Rabbath Ammon, Ramoth Gilead, and Ashataroth as far as Damascus.

David's image remained engraved on the hearts of the people as a great, just, and honest king. But, although he was considered a saintly person, the Bible also regarded him as a human being and, as such,

Ostracon (burnt pottery or fragment) bearing Hebrew inscription from 7th century B.C.E. *found in excavations at Metsad Hasha'yahu. Courtesy Israel Department of Antiquities and Museums*

Bible relates, "Saul came following the oxen out of the field" (I Samuel II:5).

David, son of Jesse (1010–970 B.C.E.), succeeded in establishing a great kingdom between the Euphrates and the stream of Egypt—Wadi el-Arish. From north to south, it extended from Levo Hamath to the Gulf of Elath. The new king, who ascended the throne after a long dispute with Saul, astutely knew how to take advantage of the rare opportunity when signs of weakness were revealed by the great powers of those times,

Ostracon (right) bearing engraved Hebrew inscription from 9th–8th centuries B.C.E. *from Tell Qasila. The inscription says: "Gold of Ophir from the house of Haran, thirty shekels." Courtesy Israel Department of Antiquities and Museums*

made no attempt to hide the darker sides of his personality. A poet as well as a man of action, David was known for his courage, grasp of military strategy, and generosity towards a defeated enemy—as evidenced by his treatment of Saul, Eshbaal, and Abner, son of Ner. Leading his people to battle, he shared all their discomforts and dangers and was a close comrade of each of his fighting men. But when it came to the foreign enemies of his people, he was merciless in grinding them out of existence in accordance with contemporary practice. And this he did to Ammon and Moab.

During critical moments of his reign, David also revealed his weaknesses. He was helplessly caught in the web of his court intrigues. His son Absalom was allowed to carry on as he wished, knowing that his royal father would ignore his evildoing. David treated his best friend Joab cruelly. And, in the case of Uriah the Hittite's wife, David allowed himself to be carried away by his heart. But when he was overcome by remorse the King of Israel would rise above petty personal considerations. In all humility, he would come before the prophet Nathan and whisper in deep sorrow, "I have sinned unto the Lord."

In the consciousness of the Jewish people, David remained the symbol of an ideal king who some day would once again appear to rule over them wisely and justly and protect them from all harm.

David's son Solomon (970-930 B.C.E.) inherited an economically sound, stable kingdom extending over a vast area bordering on the huge Syrian-Arabian desert. Israel now occupied an important position in the international commerce in horses and chariots. With the help of the kingdoms of Tyre and Sidon, Israel built up a merchant fleet. Based on Ezion Geber on the Red Sea's Gulf of Elath, Solomon's ships sailed to distant ports and brought back gold, silver, copper, precious stones, corals, and ivory.

Archaeological discoveries reveal that during David's reign Canaanite cities such as Megiddo and Beth She'an were destroyed and burned, and the foundation was laid for new Israelite building techniques which were developed still further under Solomon. The Israelites began to make use of dressed stone, and fortified cities were established near the main roads. During this period, walls were erected around such cities as Hazor, Megiddo, and Gezer. The gates at all these cities were identical, apparently having been

In the 8th century the typical containers made in Judah had government specifications. Royal seals were stamped on the handles. The word la-melekh *("Of the king") was engraved at the top, and below came the name of one of the cities: Hebron, Ziph, Socho, Mamshit, and others. In these cities there were government potteries. Here they used to fashion regular, uniform containers either for trade or the payment of taxes. The pictures on this page show two seals from the 7th century B.C.E. discovered at Ramat Rachel. The words* la-melekh socho *are engraved on the upper one and the lower one bears the inscription* la-melekh mamshit. *Courtesy Dr. Yohanan Aharoni*

Head of clay bull (?) belonging to a libation jug (kernos) found in a temple at Ashdod. Second Iron Age. Excavations of Israel Department of Antiquities and Museums, Pittsburgh Theological Seminary and Carnegie Museum, Pittsburgh

Head of clay figurine of Ashtoreth. Second Iron Age. Courtesy Department of Archaeology, Hebrew University

built to similar specifications, perhaps by the same architect. The traveler approaching such cities would find square towers on either side of the gate. Inside the arched area of the gate, there were three small chambers for the use of the guard. The passageway through the gate was wide enough to allow a horse-drawn chariot to enter. Many such cities in Solomon's kingdom were designed as headquarters for the royal cavalry.

But the principal construction works during the reigns of David and Solomon were carried out in Jerusalem. David had selected Jerusalem as his capital for geographic and political reasons. The only road in Judah linking the Jordan valley with the Mediterranean coast runs through the capital. The city lies on the central mountain range along which passes the watershed between Shechem and Beersheba. Furthermore, Jerusalem was not included in the territory of any one tribe and could thus serve as the supreme center of rival tribes.

The citadel on Mount Zion, called "City of David," was probably the king's private estate. It was situated on a hill southeast of the modern Old City, and most of it extended down the eastern slope descending to the Kidron stream. Jerusalem was three times as large at the time as any other city in the country. Solomon increased its fortifications and extended its walls considerably.

Jerusalem also became a religious center. On Mount Moriah, Solomon erected both the Temple to God and his own palace, thus giving concrete expression to the guiding principle of the House of David—government in the name of the Israelite God.

The Temple was built in the Canaanite-Phoenician style, but its form was determined by the ancient tribal tradition. It consisted of three parts, the hall, shrine, and inner sanctum or Holy of Holies. The hall *(ulam)* was a sort of vestibule designed to divide the sacred from the profane. Its entrance was flanked by two large copper columns called Jachin and Boaz. The main worship was performed in the shrine *(heikhal)*, the largest room in the temple, which measured 65 × $32\frac{1}{2}$ feet. The Holy of Holies *(kodesh kodashim)* was a windowless room with a raised floor, containing the Ark of the Covenant. At first, in the early years of Israelite settlement, the Ark was kept at Shiloh and was taken out in wartime. It was wheeled off to the fighting front while the Israelites chanted, "Rise up, O Lord, and let Thine enemies be scattered, and let them that hate Thee flee before Thee." After the destruction of Shiloh, the Ark had no permanent abode until David installed it in a tent which he had pitched in his city, and later Solomon set it up in the Temple.

A huge cauldron known as the Brazen Sea, supported by the figures of twelve bulls, stood in the southeast section of the Temple court. It is estimated as having had a capacity of twenty thousand gallons, and weighed thirty tons. Actually, it was a reservoir for the water used in the wheeled lavers in which the priests washed their hands and feet before going about their tasks.

Side of bronze pedestal from Cyprus. 12th century B.C.E. *British Museum, London*

The Temple was constructed of hewn stone and cedarwood which laced the internal coffering of the masonry. Reliefs of flowers either singly or in bunches decorated the structure in styles common throughout the Orient at the time. In fact, many of the objects in the Temple resembled those in various temples in the ancient East, in Mesopotamia, south Arabia, Canaan, Syria, and Cyprus.

The Scriptural narrative openly relates that Solomon had the help of foreigners in constructing the Temple. They supplied not only such materials as wood, stone, and copper but also workmen. Hiram of Tyre, a coppersmith, was the chief craftsman. The son of a man of Tyre and an Israelite woman of the tribe of Naphtali, he is said to have been endowed "with wisdom and understanding and skill, to work all works in brass."

From the outset, Solomon's Temple differed from all temples of the East. It was to be the symbolical abode of the Lord of the entire universe. The worship was not limited to sacrifices. From the beginning, it was used for public prayer, too, and individuals also came to entreat God for aid in time of distress when war, drought, or disease threatened them.

In time, the Temple assumed the universal function of being a house of prayer for all nations bearing a message of peace and brotherhood to the entire world. This is the significance of the prophecy of Isaiah for the "end of days" when "the mountain of the Lord's house shall be established as the top of the mountains, and shall be exalted above the hills; and all the nations shall flow unto it. And many peoples shall go and say 'Come ye, and let us go up to the mountain of the Lord, to the house of the God of Jacob; and He will teach us

of His ways, and we will walk in His paths.' For out of Zion shall go forth the law, and the word of the Lord from Jerusalem. And He shall judge between the nations, and shall decide for many peoples; and they shall beat their swords into plowshares, and their spears into pruning-hooks; nation shall not lift up sword against nation, neither shall they learn war any more."

But, although the country appeared to prosper, the growing economic needs of Israel and the numerous projects for developing the country were a heavy burden for the people to bear. The population was called on to furnish the needs of the lavish royal court and provide workers for the large-scale building projects. The Israelites began to grumble. Tribal loyalties aggravated the tension. Jeroboam, son of Nebat, an Ephraimite who was in charge of the workmen of the tribes

Ancient mines in Timna water course in which copper was mined in the Biblical period. They were apparently also exploited during the reign of King Solomon. The mines were discovered by the Arabah Expedition headed by Dr. Beno Rothenberg. The mines are located west of Timna valley, about five miles west of the new plant. The ore chiefly contains chalcocite and malachite with a copper content of about 40%. The mine extends over an area of 1–1/2 square miles. Mining hammers of basalt and numerous pounding implements of flint and Nubian sandstone were found there, as well as clay from the Ancient Iron Age. An inscription which has not yet been deciphered was discovered in the mines. Courtesy Dr. Beno Rothenberg

Holy of Holies of an Israelite temple (discovered at Arad 9th century B.C.E.). In the foreground are two stone altars on which there are the remains of sacrifices. In the rear—three monuments. Courtesy Dr. Yohanan Aharoni

of Joseph—Ephraim and Manasseh—took advantage of the Israelite tribes' grievances against the tribe of Judah, which apparently enjoyed a favored status, and openly came out against King Solomon. Fearful of the king's anger, Jeroboam then fled to Egypt.

The population also grew increasingly resentful at the pagan worship fostered in the royal court by the king's foreign wives. Economic difficulties, social differences, strong pressure, and tribal jealousies all combined to split the united kingdom. Insurrection was inevitable. A rebellion was plotted in secrecy, spurred on by the prophet Ahijah of Shiloh. Coming upon Jeroboam in a field, Ahijah tore his garment into twelve pieces and said, "Take thee ten pieces; for thus saith the Lord, the God of Israel: 'Behold, I will rend the kingdom out of the hand of Solomon, and will give ten tribes to thee.'"

The armed rebellion succeeded, and the ten northern tribes broke off from the Kingdom of Judah (including Benjamin) and set up an independent kingdom—the Kingdom of Israel: Relations between the two states ranged from open warfare to close alliances. Israel was the larger and richer of the two. Its agriculture flourished, its cities grew, and it established close ties with Syria of Damascus and with the Phoenician kingdom. However, its geographical location and foreign ties made its existence precarious for the two centuries it survived (930-721 B.C.E.). Situated astride the international Maritime Road, which ran through the Sharon plain and the Jezreel valley, Israel was on the invasion routes of a number of foreign conquerors from Egypt, Syria, and Assyria. Shishak (Sheshonk), King of Egypt, sent his troops battering through it in 926 B.C.E. and left a list of cities which he attacked and leveled to the ground. About eighty years later, Mesha, King of Moab, wrote an account of his wars against Israel and his victories in Transjordania. On a stone, the Moabite king inscribed the story of his fight against Omri, King of Israel, telling of the large numbers of Israelites his soldiers had killed and the destruction he had wrought. He concluded with the words, "Israel hath perished for ever."

Palace fortress, 7th century B.C.E., *discovered at Ramat Rachel. Center—gate of Jehoiakim's palace. Courtesy Dr. Yohanan Aharoni*

For a century, Israel had to withstand pressure from Aram (Syria) and the threat of the Assyrian army. Now and then, small states including Israel attempted to form an alliance against Assyria, and in one of these wars King Ahab fought alongside the king of Aram. Ahab's forces consisted of two thousand horse and ten thousand foot soldiers. However, the small states in Palestine and Syria were unable to form a strong, stable alliance against the victorious Assyrian army and, one after another, Aram, Israel, and the Philistine cities fell. In 721, the Kingdom of Israel was annihilated. Sargon II boasted that he exiled 27,290 people from Israel, transformed Samaria into an Assyrian satrapy, and exacted tribute from the survivors.

The Kingdom of Judah held out, thanks to its geographical location. It was remote from international communications routes and isolated in the mountains of Judah, with Israel serving as a buffer against the enemy to the far north. Unlike Israel, Judah was not involved in international affairs of state and, by exploiting the disputes between the great powers, succeeded in saving herself from Assyrian domination. But 135 years later, in 586 B.C.E., Judah was crushed by the armies of Nebuchadnezzar of Babylon, whose troops thrust as far as the Nile.

The Hebrew prophets were constantly warning the people and its leaders against becoming involved in international disputes. The greatest prophets, Isaiah and Jeremiah, raised their voices in protest against alliances with Egypt, "the staff of a bruised reed." These prophets considered the northern empires, Assyria and Babylonia, as God's staff of wrath for punishing nations and kingdoms for their ethical sins. The peoples on whom God vented His anger also included Israel and Judah, who had abandoned divine laws and were doomed to destruction and exile.

Sometimes the prophets would hold forth on other topics and preach rebellion against the rulers of the East. Assyria would fall and the world would rejoice at her destruction. But it was not long before another empire, the kingdom of the Chaldeans, would supplant her and also want to make herself mistress of the world.

The prophet Habakkuk, one of the great spiritual leaders of the ancient world, discoursed bitterly a-

(Above) Man playing a harp. Clay figure found in temple from Second Iron Age, Ashdod. Excavations of Israel Department of Antiquities and Museums, Pittsburgh Theological Seminary and Carnegie Museum, Pittsburgh

(Upper left) Clay mask from Ma'oz. First Iron Age. Courtesy Israel Department of Antiquities and Museums

(Lower left) Clay mask found in Phoenician cemetery at Achzib. 7th century B.C.E. Excavations of Israel Department of Antiquities and Museums

gainst this change of rulers. He demanded justice for subjugated peoples, protested against the use of force in relations between nations, and lamented the insignificance of man compared with those stronger than he: "How long, O Lord, shall I cry, and Thou wilt not hear? I cry out unto Thee of violence, and Thou wilt not save.... Thou that art of eyes too pure to behold evil, and that canst not look on mischief, wherefore lookest Thou, when they deal treacherously, and holdest Thy peace, when the wicked swalloweth up the man that is more righteous than he; and makest men as the fishes of the sea, as the creeping things, that have no ruler over them?"

The Israelite Monarchy granted the king considerable powers in matters pertaining to the army and the government. However, even the most tyrannical kings such as Ahab, Jehu, Ahaz, and Manasseh did not head dictatorships in the style of Oriental potentates. They flouted their splendor, their women, and their treasures and, particularly, their cruel deeds, but they did not possess unlimited authority in religious matters.

The nation was divided into classes and the position of the foreigner, the widow, and the orphan, and of people without land or property was especially bad. In periods of prosperity, the estates of the landowners grew while many people were driven off their lands and others became slaves. The Hebrew prophets demanded justice for the weak. They raised their voices to decry social injustice and were not deterred from

denouncing the upper classes, royal officials, and even the king himself. Isaiah's angry accusations rolled through the land like a thundercloud: "Thy princes are rebellious, and companions of thieves; every one loveth bribes, and followeth after rewards; they judge not the fatherless, neither doth the cause of the widow come unto them."

Israelite cities, like their Canaanite counterparts, were situated on hills near water sources. Typical Israelite architecture did not begin until the period of the Monarchy. The cities were surrounded by double, parallel walls—the inner one not as thick as the outer one. The space between the walls was filled with earth to strengthen them. The main gate was for chariots and wagons and a secondary gate was for pedestrians and people riding donkeys. Public meetings were held in a square in front of the gate, where business was also conducted.

The population in ordinary towns did not exceed seven thousand. As congestion increased, the inhabitants began building dwellings on the fortifications. The lower story served as a granary or storage space for containers of oil and wine. The household utensils were kept there and the ovens set up in the rooms. The second floor served for relaxation and rest. In the period of the Monarchy, many public buildings for the royal officials were erected. The furniture in such structures, like that of the king's palaces, resembled that of other countries in the ancient Orient and con-

sisted of chairs, tables, and beds. The ordinary Israelite house did not have such furnishings.

From Solomon's time onward, public granaries for keeping the grain were constructed. These may have been the storage cities mentioned in Scripture.

Palestine was chiefly an agricultural country. Wheat and barley occupied a central position in the farm economy. Since the second millennium B.C.E., the country was celebrated for its livestock and plantation crops. The Bible affectionately calls it "a land flowing with milk and honey." An Egyptian writer from the beginning of the second millennium B.C.E., Shenhat, sings the praises of Palestine in a style reminiscent of the Biblical language, "A good land with figs, and grapevines and wine as plentiful as water. Its honey is abundant and its oil ample. Its trees grow every kind of fruit, it has barley and wheat, and its cattle is without number."

The people living in towns were generally farmers who congregated there for the purpose of finding shelter from nomads and robbers. Even outlying suburbs were not far from a central city which afforded them protection in an emergency.

Several towns served as centers for various crafts. Families of weavers, potters, and scribes are mentioned in the Bible. The remains of dyeing establishments and weavers' implements have been found at Tell Beth Mirsim, which may have been the ancient Debir. Families of craftsmen lived in special quarters of the town

and their trades may have been transmitted from father to son. Spinning and weaving were apparently widespread in the country before the Israelite conquest. The ancient Israelites continued the tradition and supplied the needs of the entire region.

Israelite crafts, although not achieving the degree of artistic development of the great centers of culture in the ancient world, were famous for their unique qualities and original craftsmanship. Ancient Israel also produced metal ores. Crucibles, slag heaps, and mines from this period have been discovered in the hills of Edom in Jordan and on the slopes of the Arabah. Dwellings for the miners, cisterns, and fortifications near the mining installations indicate the presence of permanent operations carried out over extended periods. Signs of the production of copper in the period of the Israelite Monarchy, especially during the reign of Solomon, are scattered throughout the area south of the Dead Sea as far as Elath. In the Bible (I Kings 7: 46) there is a single verse which mentions the production and casting of metals, "In the plain of the Jordan did the king cast them, in the clay ground between Succoth and Zarethan." The mining was done by slaves housed in special camps established for the purpose. Advanced organizational techniques, a regular water supply, a food supply, and constant supervision were necessary in order to operate metal plants under the difficult conditions of life in the desert. Only strong kings with absolute power like Solomon could main-

tain an establishment for overcoming the difficulties connected with the mining activities. Not only slaves did the work but also craftsmen who knew how to smelt metal and purify and refine it.

It is not certain whether these craftsmen came from nearby Edom or from distant Tyre. These were the supervisors, planners, and executives. The same held true in Sinai where Semitic nomads showed the Egyptians how to produce copper. The Israelites learned the operations from their neighbors to the south and north. Although on a larger scale than copper production in Sinai, the work being done in the Arabah and in Edom still lagged behind the metal industries of Cyprus, which was the leading supplier of metals to the countries of the ancient East.

There is no explicit information about the production of iron in Israel during the Biblical period. There are numerous deposits of iron ore in the mountains of Gilead and in the vicinity of the Jabbok River, and there are indications that, during the period of the Israelite Monarchy, the ancients already produced iron from ore.

The land of Israel was poor. It was not a magnificent state like the great civilizations in Mesopotamia and Egypt. Its kings were neither gods nor their representatives. Its priests did not rule vast estates, and its of-

ficials and men of power did not accumulate untold wealth. Neither huge buildings, splendid tombs, nor enduring monuments were erected there. The Israelite religion preached simplicity and austerity. The Hebrew prophets scorned riches and luxury and did not bow their heads before rulers. They mocked royal palaces and placed an uncompromising morality above everything. They rose up against the social wealth which the men of power accumulated and spoke out to demand justice for the wretched as a primal religious duty.

The spirit of Israel was expressed not in artistic monuments, crafts, political power, or warfare, but in matters of the mind. The Hebrew prophets established ethical foundations for human civilization. It was Zechariah who said, "Not by might, nor by power, but by My spirit, saith the Lord of hosts."

Biblical Judaism's contribution to mankind consisted of the belief in a single God. It was expressed in the following ways: the moral ardor of the Hebrew prophets, the system of Biblical historiography, the guide to wise living in the Books of Proverbs and Ecclesiastes, and in the cry of man stricken by adversity in the Book of Job.

The ancient Jews made a major contribution to the narrative art which achieved supreme expression.

38

(Right) Clay figurine of pregnant woman found in the Phoenician cemetery at Achzib. 7th century B.C.E. *Excavations of Israel Department of Antiquities and Museums*

(Below) The god Baal, Lord of the city of Sidon, was described as a warrior wearing a helmet and smiting his enemies with a bolt of lightning in his hand. The Baal cult was widespread in all the lands of the East. The Louvre, Paris

Thousands of documents have survived from the ancient East—from Sumer, Assyria, Babylonia, the Hittite empire, Phoenicia, Canaan, and Egypt—but not one of them attains the artistic level of the Scriptural narrative as it finds expression in the Books of Genesis, Judges, and Samuel, and in the tales of the prophets and the story of Ruth. The Biblical narrative in all its nuances, shades of expression, wealth of tones, restrained language, and intrinsic harmony is unparalleled in the literature of the ancient East. It still speaks to the heart of modern man.

39

CHRONOLOGICAL TABLE OF THE KINGS OF JUDAH AND ISRAEL

(Prepared by Prof. B. Mazar and S. Yeivin for the Encyclopaedia Hebraica, Vol VI)

Length of Reign	Kings of Judah	Prophets of the Period	Date B.C.E.	Kings of Israel	Prophets of the Period	Length of Reign
17 years	Rehoboam	Shemaiah	930	Jeroboam son of Nebat	Ahijah, The Man of the Lord from Judah, the old prophet of Beth-El	22 years
3	Abijah	Iddo (Jedo)	914			
41	Asa	Azariah son of Oded, Hanani	912			
			909	Nadav		2
			908	Baasha	Jehu son of Hanani	24
			885	Elah		2
			884	Zimri		7 days
			881	Omri		12 years
			873	Ahab	Elijah (?)	22
25	Jehoshaphat	Jehu son of Hanani, Ezekiel son of Zechariah, Eliezer son of Dodavahu	872		Elijah, Micaiah son of Imla	
			853	Ahaziah	Elijah	2
			852	Elisha	Jehoram (Joram)	12
8	Jehoram		849			
1	Ahaziah		842			
6	Athaliah		841	Jehu	Elisha	28
40	Jehoash (Joash)	Zechariah son of Jehoiada	836			
			814	Jehoahaz	Elisha, Jonah	17
			798	Jehoash (Joash)	Jonah	16
29	Amaziah	Several prophets not mentioned by name	797			
			793	Jeroboam II	Hosea, Amos	41
52	Uzziah (Azariah)	Zechariah (II Chron. 26:5), Isaiah, Hosea, Amos	789			
			752	Zechariah	Amos	6 months
			751	Shallum	Amos	1 month
			751	Menahem		10 years
			740	Pekahiah		2
			739	Pekah	Oded	20
16	Jotham	Isaiah, Micah, Hosea	738			
16	Ahaz	Isaiah, Micah, Hosea, Oded	734			
			732	Hosea son of Elah		9
29	Hezekiah	Isaiah, Micah, Nahum, Hosea	728			
			721	Destruction of Samaria		
55	Manasseh		699			
2	Amon		643			
31	Josiah	Jeremiah	641			
3 months	Jehoahaz (Shallum)	Jeremiah, Zephaniah	609			
11 years	Jehoiakim (Eliakim)	Jeremiah, Zephaniah, Ezekiel	609			
3 months	Jehoiachin	Jeremiah, Zephaniah, Ezekiel	598			
11	Zedekiah (Mattaniah)	Jeremiah, Ezekiel, Obadiah	598			
			586	Destruction of Jerusalem		

FROM THE END OF THE BABYLONIAN CAPTIVITY TO THE DESTRUCTION OF THE SECOND TEMPLE

The destruction of the First Temple and the Babylonian Captivity were fateful turning points in the life of the Jewish people. The Hebrew prophets predicted not only the devastation which would befall the country, but also the subsequent return of the Jews from their exile in Babylonia. With the exception of Ezekiel, all these men repeatedly stressed the connection between penance and redemption. Ezekiel, whose prophecies date from the beginning of Judah's exile to Babylonia (although some of his first visions occurred while the First Temple was still standing), was the first to distinguish between the nation's history and the reward and punishment which is the lot of every man. He strongly emphasized the direct connection between sin and the punishment of the individual. He did not make the nation's redemption contingent on its doing penance: "Thus saith the Lord God, 'I do not do this for your sake, O house of Israel, but for My holy name, which ye have profaned among the nations.... For I will take you from among the nations, and gather you out of all the countries, and will bring you into your own land.... A new heart also will I give you, and a new spirit will I put within you'" (Ezekiel 36).

Liberation was not long in coming. About half a century after the destruction of Jerusalem, the Babylonian empire was supplanted by the kingdom of the Medes and Persians. On becoming the new ruler of the ancient world, Cyrus, King of Persia, gave permission to any of the Judaean exiles who so wished to return to Jerusalem and rebuild their Temple.

"Whosoever there is among you of all His people — his God be with him — let him go up to Jerusalem... and build the House of the Lord, the God of Israel..." (Ezra 1:3). Cyrus' proclamation sent a wave of jubilation throughout the villages of the exiles. More than forty thousand people answered the call of the Persian king and set out on the long harrowing journey to Jerusalem. This was apparently half of the exiles. Of those remaining behind, some had become assimilated among the local population and the rest had struck roots in their new homes. But, in any case, those who stayed in Babylonia helped the Jews leaving for Jerusalem, and many of them came to Judah later on.

Daily life in Judah was gray and bleak compared with the dreams of the prophets, and the first settlers in Judah encountered numerous obstacles and great difficulties. Their first problems were concerned with resettling a desolate land and restoring the Temple and its service. In their second year in Jerusalem, the Babylonian exiles began reorganizing their lives and rebuilding the Temple. However, they were soon confronted with problems which stemmed from the fact that their lands had been settled by foreigners. The area north of Jerusalem was inhabited by Samaritans, brought to Samaria by Sennacherib, King of Assyria, who wanted to join the Judaeans returning from exile and perhaps make themselves masters of the small Jewish community in the capital. The neighboring peoples, who were full of hate for the Jews, had extended the borders of their countries at the expense of ravaged Judah, and they did not like the idea of the Jewish return from Babylonia. Quickly, they began to cause trouble for the Jews.

The Samaritans offered to help in rebuilding the Temple, but this was refused by the heads of the returning exiles, Zerubbabel, son of Shealtiel, and Jeshua, son of Jehozadak, who were afraid of such participation for both spiritual and political reasons.

The Samaritans did not accept this decision and wrote libelous letters about the Jews of Jerusalem and Judah to the Persian king. Cyrus thereupon put a stop to the work of rebuilding the Temple, and construction was not resumed until fifteen years later, during the second year of the reign of Darius II, who commanded that Cyrus' initial order be implemented. During the sixth year of Darius' reign, the Temple was completed.

The problem of the people's spiritual individuality added to the political difficulties. The danger of assimilation had not disappeared on the exiles' return to their own country. Many of the newcomers, who were a small minority among their non-Jewish or semi-Jewish neighbors, were quickly assimilated into the rural population around them. Nehemiah relates that Jews "married women of Ashdod, of Ammon, and of Moab; and their children spoke half in the speech of Ashdod, and could not speak in the Jews' language...." If this trend of the Jews to assimilate with their neighbors had not been halted, the small community which had come to rebuild the ruins of Jerusalem would have been engulfed by the alien environment.

This state of affairs explains the zeal of Ezra, the Scribe, who with his own eyes saw the dangerous development when he arrived in Jerusalem together with the returning exiles, and of Nehemiah, the wine-bearer of the king of Persia, who dared ask the monarch, "Send me unto Judah, unto the city of my fathers' sepulchres, that I may build it."

Ezra's first act was to publish a complete text of the Pentateuch and appoint teachers and judges to give instruction in the Torah and judge the people in accordance with its precepts. Thus, he laid the groundwork for the charter which established the Pentateuch as the law of the land and the nation. His second major activity was his war against mixed marriages.

Ezra and Nehemiah saw no other way than to expel the alien peoples by force from the vicinity of Jerusalem. They made it clear to the Samaritans who wished to benefit from the prestige which the Jews enjoyed in the Persian court that they had no "portion, nor right, nor memorial in Jerusalem."

Nehemiah received extremely wide powers and even material and military assistance from the king. He overcame the opposition of the enemies all around — Samaritans, Ammonites, and Arabs — who attempted to interfere with the work of rebuilding the wall by force. He took steps to increase the Jewish population in Jerusalem and to cancel debts — a measure which strengthened the nation's unity. Nehemiah worked together with Ezra in drawing up the charter establishing the Torah as the basis of political and religious legislation.

THE JEWS OF THE DIASPORA

However, the proportion of the Jewish people which lived in Jerusalem and in Judah was very small. Most of the nation had struck roots in the Diaspora and had taken up permanent residence there. There were entire districts in Babylonia with a dense Jewish population which apparently sometimes even enjoyed autonomy. The Jews were actively engaged in all branches of the economy and occupied important positions in

An Israelite shekel — third year of the first war of liberation. The suppressive measures of the Roman procurators in Judaea ultimately led to an open revolt against Rome in 66 C.E. In the early phases of the war, the Jews succeeded in driving the Romans out of most of the country, and it was not until 67 that the Roman Senate sent Vespasian to put down the rebellion. One of the first acts of the rebels was to mint coins to bear witness to their independence. One side of the silver coin bears a leaf with three pomegranates and the inscription Yerushalayim ha-Kedosha ("Jerusalem the Holy"). On the other side there is a goblet surmounted by the ancient Hebrew letters sh. g., standing for shana gimel, i.e., "Year Three," to indicate the third year of the revolt. The inscription at the top says Shekel Yisroel ("Shekel of Israel"). These silver coins of the first war of liberation (66–70 C.E.) are the finest and most distinctive Jewish coins of the Hellenistic and Roman period. Ha-Arets Museum, Tel Aviv

The Wall of Jerusalem. Jerusalem has had a wall around it since Jebusite times. The picture shows a section of the eastern wall with a sealed gate ("The Gate of Mercy") built during the period of Ottoman rule. The lower part of the wall, hidden by Moslem tombstones, was constructed of stones from the time of Herod

the government. Such persons were Nehemiah, Mordecai, Esther, and Daniel.

In Egypt, too, Jews had been living since very ancient times. Throughout the period of the First Temple, many persons who were dissatisfied with the government left the country and settled in Egypt. These communities were enlarged by the arrival of Jews who fled from Judah in the period before and after the destruction of Jerusalem.

The Jewish community in Egypt maintained strong ties with the nation's spiritual center, in Jerusalem and even during the Babylonian Captivity. A letter has been found from the end of the fifth century B.C.E. in which Hananiah, an official of Darius II of Persia, sent instructions to the Jews of Yeb (Elephantine), a distant frontier village on Egypt's southern border, for observing the Passover festival on time and in accordance with Jewish law. At Yeb, near modern Assuan, many

papyri, most of them consisting of legal documents, have been discovered which shed light on this colony of Jewish soldiers dwelling among the local garrison. The names of the Jews appearing in these documents indicate that at least a part of them came from Persia or Babylonia, either along with the Persian conquering army or after it. And it is not by chance that part of the *Book of Ahikar,* a historical novel depicting the adventures of a courtier of the Assyrian king, was found in an Aramaic translation among the archives of the Jews of Yeb.

In his vision, Daniel tells of the changes which transformed the contemporary world. At the appearance of Alexander the Great in the East, the Persian Empire fell to the world conqueror like a ripe fruit.

The corruption in the court of the kingdom of the Medes and Persians is described in the Book of Esther, as well as the frivolity with which affairs of state were

43

The Sea of Galilee, which receives the water of the upper Jordan, lies in an extremely fertile valley in which there were numerous Jewish communities in the period of the Second Temple and after the destruction of Jerusalem. An ancient synagogue with a magnificent mosaic floor has been discovered at Hammath near modern Tiberias

conducted. The shaky cultural unity among the diverse peoples in the kingdom of Persia could not stand up to the unified, dynamic army of Alexander, and the Persian empire came to an end in a stormy battle.

Alexander the Great himself did not live long. The vacuum which was created by his death was filled by his successors, the Greek generals (*Diadochoi*). Thereafter, all the countries from the distant East to the lands to the west and south were ruled by Greek-speaking soldiers who considered themselves members of a superior people and their culture the only culture of man. And although Alexander's successors never ceased fighting one another, their world and its culture — the Hellenistic way of life — were one. The Greek language and culture were the identifying marks of the ruling class. The Hellenistic kings spared no effort to increase their influence, founding Greek cities everywhere, consolidating the mastery of the *Diadochoi* and paving the way for the language and culture of Greece.

The Jews of that period were distinguished for their spiritual and cultural level and their military prowess. Consequently, it is no wonder that the Hellenistic kings, and first of all Alexander, regarded the Jews, who settled in the cities they had built, with favor. And to be sure, there were Jews among the first inhabitants of many Hellenistic cities in Syria and in

Asia Minor, and even in the capital of Hellenistic culture,-Alexandria, Egypt. Jewish communities appeared in nearly every large city, and the Jews attempted to form a synthesis between the spirit of Judaism and Hellenism. It is interesting to note that, when Aristotle was in the middle of Asia Minor, he met a Jew who "was a Greek not only in language but also in his soul... [and he] associated with many of the learned men, but he gave them more than he received from them" (Josephus, *Against Apion,* A 181). However, notwithstanding this talent of the Jews to acquire the language and culture of Greece and become respected citizens, the Jewish communities in the Hellenistic Diaspora also succeeded in preserving their Jewish individuality and in time even in creating original works. Furthermore, these communities, scattered among non-Jews and dwelling far from Jewish centers, served to attract tens of thousands of strangers who adopted their faith.

PALESTINE IN THE PTOLEMAIC PERIOD

Palestine was at the time part of Syria and Phoenicia and accordingly was not without importance. Alexander's successors fought over her, and the country passed from hand to hand several times until finally, in the year 301 B.C.E., Ptolemy, king of Egypt, managed to wrest her from Seleucus and establish himself there. From then until 198 B.C.E., Palestine developed and flourished under the rule of the Egyptian Ptolemies. The Jews of Palestine were not organized in Greek cities resembling the *polis*, for, otherwise, there would have been no need for the Hellenizers a generation later, in the period of Judah the Maccabee, to demand the construction of a gymnasium in Jerusalem and change the city's name to Antiochia. Neither did the Jews have a tribal organization nor a local royal dynasty subservient to the Hellenistic king. In Judaea, the high priest was responsible to the central government in Egypt, and his principal duty was collecting taxes. He was also apparently granted authority in internal affairs and he was the supreme arbiter in all matters relating to observing the Torah, civil law, and penalties imposed on local Jews. This kind of administration had been handed down from the Persian period and existed in various parts of Asia Minor and Syria, where there were numerous regions governed by an authority based on a large temple.

The social structure of the times did not essentially differ from what it had been during the period of Ezra and Nehemiah. This structure consisted of three elements: the people as a whole, the council of elders, which was above the nation and comprised the representatives of the important families, and the head of the council of elders who was the leader of the people. Papyri discovered at ancient Fayum in Egypt, from the archives of a certain Zeno, an Egyptian official who served in Palestine during the reign of Ptolemy II, Philadelphos, reveal that the system of large

The Jordan flows into the Dead Sea. The Jewish purification sects of the 1st and 2nd centuries C.E. included the Baptists, whose leader was John the Baptist. The spot where John baptized his followers was near this region

estates from which the poor suffered so much during the days of Ezra and Nehemiah also existed in those days. The papyri provide information about the advances in commerce made in Palestine during the period. In addition to a traffic in slaves, there was an export trade of agricultural products which included wheat, wine, and oil. Palestine was at the time also a transit area for spices. The officials who supervised commerce as well as other functionaries were not natives of the country but persons sent by the Egyptian Ptolemies. The Zeno papyri make no mention of an autonomous administration in the country.

As in the period of the return from Babylonia, there were numerous non-Jews living in Palestine beside the Jewish communities. These peoples continued to occupy a large part of the country and play an important role in its government; they also put a foreign cultural stamp clearly Hellenistic in nature on the culture of the upper class of Jews. A member of this class was Joseph, son of Tobias, a tax farmer for the Ptolemies, a position he had received from his uncle, the high priest Onias II, who had refused to pay tribute to Ptolemy, apparently at the instigation of the Seleucids. Joseph succeeded in soothing the wrath of Ptolemy IV Philopater, and farming the taxes of Palestine and Syria. A detachment of soldiers was placed at his disposal and he began to squeeze the people. His rule brought about a heightening of the social differences in Judaea and established a wealthy propertied class. These social contrasts soon became identical with cultural distinctions, as Joseph and the members of his circle were close to the authorities and spread the spirit of Hellenistic culture in Jerusalem.

Relations between the leaders of the nation who had returned from Babylonia and the local non-Jewish aristocracy also constituted the continuation of a process which had begun in the period of Ezra and Nehemiah. At that time, numerous marriage ties were established among them. The vigorous steps taken to curb this phenomenon were evidently only partially effective and temporary. Marriages between the returning exiles and the local aristocracy did not cease.

This development, or the failure of Ezra's and Nehemiah's efforts, was one of the major factors leading to the eventual degeneration of the dynasty of high priests. The seed of spiritual deterioration which was sown during these times in the family of the high priests and in other distinguished families slowly sprouted and in subsequent generations produced all the phenomena which led to the Hasmonean revolt.

THE SEPTUAGINT

The Septuagint is the great treasure which the period of Ptolemaic rule in Palestine bequeathed to posterity. According to legend, the translation was made for the purpose of adding the Jewish Bible to the collection of books which Ptolemy Philadelphos had in

45

his museum at Alexandria. Aristeas, a Greek official at Ptolemy's court, wrote a letter to his monarch suggesting that learned Jewish elders be selected to implement the project. The Talmud also relates, "Ptolemy, the king, gathered seventy-two elders and installed them in seventy-two houses without telling them why he had brought them there. Then he came to each one and said, 'Write the law of Moses, your teacher, for me.' And God implanted wisdom in the heart of each one and they all were of one mind." The name Septuagint is the Greek word for "seventy."

In a letter to his friend Philokrates, Aristeas describes his mission and what he saw in Jerusalem, including the Temple and the service of Eleazer, the high priest, and his magnificent raiment. After the seventy-two elders came to Egypt, the king gave a banquet for them in accordance with Jewish law and asked them numerous questions about philosophical and religious matters. After a week of feasting, the king assembled the elders on the island of Pharos near Alexandria, and had each one translate a section. The men then met and compared their translations. Tradition has it that although they worked independently, the seventy or so translators all produced an identical text. Philo the Alexandrian, who lived during the first century C.E., tells that in his time both Jews and non-Jews celebrated a special holiday on the island of Pharos each year to commemorate the translation of the Bible into Greek.

The need for a translation of the Torah was felt among the Jews of the Diaspora who had already managed to forget the Hebrew language. On the other hand, the translation demonstrates to what extent Jews in the first generations of Greek rule had already achieved a cultural position in the Hellenistic world. The translation of the Bible into Greek exerted a powerful influence on the history of the human spirit, although it had been done only for the benefit of the people of its own generation.

SELEUCID RULE IN PALESTINE AND THE HASMONEAN REVOLT

Toward the end of the period of Ptolemaic rule in Palestine, grave events occurred in Jerusalem.

Hyrcanus, the son of Joseph, son of Tobias, succeeded in taking the tax farming away from his father. Joseph opposed his son, and Hyrcanus laid siege to Jerusalem. The people of Jerusalem, headed by Simeon II, the high priest, repulsed his attacks and forced him to withdraw to Transjordania. Joseph and his sons went over to the Seleucids who wrested Palestine from the Ptolemies in 198 B.C.E. The conquerors sought to base their rule on the Greek urban class, the same forces who served as a means of keeping the rural aristocracy under their thumb. Palestine was no exception to this practice.

It is consequently not surprising that Hellenistic circles among the Jews of the country asked the king's permission to transform Jerusalem into a *polis*, i.e., a Greek city. The king granted the request. This change in the city's constitution was favored by the Seleucids, not because they were anxious to establish government institutions based on the Greek pattern in Jerusalem, but because such a change had a practical value and a very tangible significance in the arena of internal politics: the change abolished the previous form of government.

Until then, Judaea had been a theocratic state headed by the high priest who governed it with the help of a council of elders chosen from all parts of the country. Now, the country became a state in which the city and its inhabitants ruled the rural population. All the aspirations of the Hellenizing urban class were assimilated into the Hellenistic cultural world while the agricultural class remained loyal to the heritage of its fathers.

The actions of the Seleucid monarch Antiochus IV Epiphanes, who was not satisfied with the natural process of Hellenization but tried to hasten it, brought on a crisis. Antiochus ordered the people to accept not only his own rule but that of his god, and the sons of Tobias helped him. These men joined the rival family of priests. The priesthood was sold to the highest bidder. However, the peaceful relations between the house of Tobias and that of Onias quickly came to an end, and a bitter struggle broke out between the two factions with one family siding with the Seleucids and

A Canaanite oil lamp with seven mouths. The Jewish candelabrum which stood in the Temple also had seven branches. The number was considered holy throughout the East. The Louvre, Paris

The synagogue at Capernaum, one of the most ancient synagogues in Galilee, remaining from the 2nd or 3rd century, was built in the form of a basilica, with two aisles of columns the length of the building and one crosswise. In contrast to later synagogues, the front of the building faced Jerusalem. (Upper left) Remnant of a Corinthian capital of acanthus leaves. (Upper right) Transverse aisle of columns at the rear of the building. (Lower right) Relief of ornamental columns

During the reign of his successor, his brother, Alexander Yannai, monarchistic features grew among the Hasmoneans, and the dynasty began more and more to resemble a Hellenistic royal family. Earlier, under Johanan Hyrcanus, foreign soldiers had been serving in the ranks of the army, and the king depended on them to maintain his power and fight his wars. In order to pay the salaries of these mercenaries, he had to rule the population harshly. Furthermore, in their desire to be more like the non-Jewish monarchs, these kings made the priesthood subservient to the crown. The people could not accept this development with equanimity.

PHARISEES, SADDUCEES, AND ESSENES

This period—which began with the liberation of the Jews from the yoke of one foreign ruler and their subjugation by another, Imperial Rome—was characterized by unceasing war to extend the country's borders. Most of these wars were successful and the country's territory grew during the reigns of Johanan Hyrcanus and Alexander Yannai. The latter made numerous conquests and in his time, the area of the Jewish state expanded. He conquered the country's southern coast after laying siege to Gaza for a full year, and extended his borders as far as the Zebulun plain, but without being able to take Acco. In Transjordania, too, he enlarged his frontiers and overran Moab, Gilead, and part of Bashan.

Freedom from foreign domination and the political upsurge were no doubt to the people's liking, but the price they had to pay for extending Hasmonean power was very high, and many were not prepared to bear the cost. The opponents to the Hasmonean house were the same circles which had been its chief supporters in the first generation. They consisted of those who regarded the commandments regulating the relationships between man and his fellows and between man and God as axioms not to be sacrificed on the altar of political expansion. These circles, apparently an outgrowth of the Pietists of the early period of the revolt, were called Pharisees, i.e., "those setting themselves apart," because of their approach either to Jewish law or to the political situation. Their first center of power was the supreme legislative and judicial body—the Sanhedrin. Josephus wrote that in time most of the people joined this faction, and the Pharisees became the leading current of Jewish life in Judaea. In opposition to them were the Sadducees. Because of their close association with the members of the high priesthood and governing circles, the Sadducees valued the sacerdotal office chiefly for its political implications and the great influence it bestowed on its incumbents, but did not appreciate its spiritual and religious importance.

On the contrary, on a number of occasions, they disparaged the religious sentiments of the masses of people. The profound feeling of respect which the masses felt for the high priesthood, their blind faith in the sanctity of the Temple and everything connected with it, and even fear of the government did not save the king-priests of the Hasmonean dynasty from the anger of the people when they acted in accordance with Sadducee practice.

There is a story that on the festival of Sukkot (Tabernacles), King Yannai was conducting the service in the Temple. When he reached the point where he had to pour water on the altar, he did not do so in accordance with the Pharisaic tradition which specified that it be done over the altar, but poured it out at the foot as the Sadducee practice required. In their anger, the people pelted him with citrons. The king did not forgive this offense to his honor and, furious at the Pharisees, he sent his foreign soldiers to attack them, and many were killed. The irate Pharisees called on Demetrius Eukairos, King of Syria, to help them against Yannai. They joined the Syrian soldiers and, in an engagement near Shechem, Yannai's army was defeated. Now the conscience of the Jews who had fought alongside the Syrians was stirred and they went over to the troops of the Hasmonean king and drove Demetrius' army out of the country. In revenge, Yannai had the rebel leaders executed.

During the reign of Salome Alexandra, Yannai's widow (76–67), an attempt was made to effect a reconciliation between the leaders of the Pharisees and the royal family. The queen appointed her son, Hyrcanus II, the Pharisees' candidate, high priest. The Pharisees now completely dominated the country. But the agitation and the dissension between the Sadducees and Pharisees continued, with the opposition to the Pharisees headed by Hyrcanus II's brother, Aristobolus II. At the death of Salome Alexandra, a struggle for power broke out between the two brothers, ended only by the intervention of Rome.

These two currents, the Pharisees and Sadducees, were the principal parties in the political arena and, in time, the differences between them became sharper, until they had no common language either on the political plane or the ideological level.

This sore which permeated the country's life, as well as the great suffering caused to the common people by the heavy taxes and the king's persecution, poisoned the atmosphere until many people were sick of living under the king's whip and, as in the period of Antiochus IV Epiphanes, numerous individuals now too fled into the desert.

In this way, various sects came into being in the deserts of Palestine. These sects were close to the Pharisees in their outlook and way of life, although they did not identify themselves with them. They differed from the Pharisees in that they were not prepared to participate in the life of the country as it was, in contrast to the Pharisees whose doctrine was based on the actual life of the population and was essentially predicated on peace.

Some groups among them set up closed societies. Entire communities, while engaging in work for their

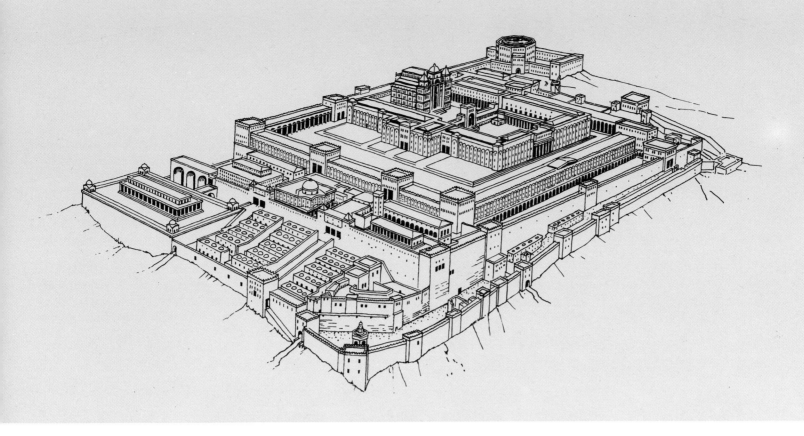

The First Temple, which was built during Solomon's reign (upper reconstruction) over a period of seven years, was destroyed by Nebuchadnezzar, king of Babylonia, in 586 B.C.E. Above it, on the horizon, Solomon's palace was visible. The Second Temple was erected about seventy years later in accordance with an unprepossessing plan, then rebuilt in the 1st century B.C.E. with unusual splendor by Herod (lower reconstruction). This Temple was destroyed by the soldiers of Titus in 70 C.E. Today, the Dome of the Rock occupies the site of the Temple.

The figures in the lower drawing identify: 1. Entrance to the Holy Place (heikhal). 2. Altar for burnt offerings and staircase and ramp for reaching it, in the Court of the Israelites. 3. Nicanor Gate, connecting the Women's Court and the Court of the Israelites by means of twelve steps. 4. Women's Court. 5. Eastern gate to the court, with a window on each side. 6. Compartment for storing oils for the seven-branched candelabrum and the ritual shovels. 7. The soreg, a wall encompassing the Temple Mount on four sides. This was a sort of low fence bearing signs in Greek and Latin warning non-Jews against entering the Temple area. Between the soreg and the Temple wall there was an open area called the bel, about fifteen feet wide, to which one descended by means of fourteen steps. 8. Temple court to which non-Jews were admitted. 9. Royal avenue of columns in the south, which was linked to the Upper City and Herod's palace in the west by a bridge. In the south it was possible to enter the area of the Temple Mount through the Hulda gates ("Triple Gate" and "Double Gate"), which were a sort of tunnels coming from the Lower City. 10. The area of the Temple Mount, which was surrounded by an additional wall. 11. The eastern gate, through which the priest went out to bury the ashes of the red heifer. It was called the "Shushan Gate" because of the picture of the Persian city of Shushan (Susa) engraved on it to commemorate the period of Persian occupation. 12. Tadi gate in the north, which was not used

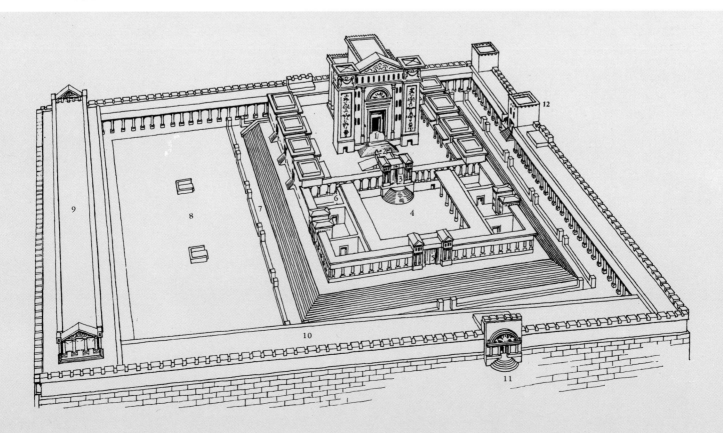

An Ark of the Law in the form of the Temple. Section of the balustrade frieze of the synagogue at Capernaum, which depicts the Ark of the Law mounted on wheels. The Ark, which has a monumental gate and a roof supported by columns, calls to mind the buildings of Hellenistic Temples and apparently represents the hall in the Temple

physical existence, concerned themselves principally with cleansing the body and purifying the soul to prepare for the coming of the Messiah in their lifetime. Other groups also withdrew from the authority of a man-made kingdom, but not from the political arena. They organized themselves along military lines and, in their burning zeal for freedom and liberation from a foreign power, attempted to bring redemption closer by the sword.

In recent years, scrolls have come to light in caves in the Wilderness of Judah, apparently the writings of one of these retiring sects. This sect, which seems to have consisted of Essenes, lived in a closed commune under a military regimen, and whoever wished to join it had to undergo a long, difficult trial period. They regarded commerce as a source of corruption, and most of them engaged in farming, with a few working as craftsmen. They eschewed all luxury and ate sparingly. Their clothing was of the simplest kind. They opposed slavery and, in order not to be disturbed in serving God, they generally did not marry, but adopted orphans whom they raised in the spirit of their faith. The Essenes were careful not to offer blood sacrifices and, in the Temple, they made offerings only of meal, consisting of fine flour mingled with oil.

The fratricidal hatred fanned by this sectarianism finally caused the complete destruction of the nation; but the positive aspects of the various sects should not be ignored. The Sadducees were concerned with making it possible for the people to share in the world's culture, and they brought the achievements of the contemporary outside world to Judaea. The Essenes,

on the other hand, aspired to establish God's rule on earth in the guise of a people of Israel purified of all dross, and they were wholly intent on bringing on the Messianic Age. Early Christianity apparently originated with these groups, and other factions may have produced the men who later conducted the Great Revolt against Rome in 66 C.E. The Pharisees developed the tools by means of which the Jewish people were saved from annihilation after the destruction of the Temple and Jerusalem. The Pharisees were also concerned with the "good life" but, in contrast with the Sadducees, they did not worry only about the body and, unlike the Essenes, not about the soul alone. Pharisaic ideology was political and social. They favored a regime to provide for the material and spiritual needs of Jewish society. Apparently this goal did not remain a mere wish. Although the whole structure of society was not run by the Pharisees, they did succeed in securing a firm foothold within the juridical and legislative system—in the Sanhedrin.

THE HOUSE OF HEROD

Indications of Rome's interest and her intervention in the affairs of Syria and Palestine were apparent many years before the tragic events which terminated in the destruction of the Temple. It is no wonder then that Judah the Maccabee and his brothers who succeeded him sent emissaries to the Roman Senate for the purpose of concluding a treaty and renewing the friendship with this mighty empire which could intervene at will in the affairs of the region.

But, where the early Hasmoneans considered Rome a prop in their political struggle against foreign powers, the later members of the dynasty called in this giant to ride roughshod over the people's liberty and everything it held sacred. The Roman legions first trod on the soil of Palestine in 63 B.C.E., during the struggle of the Hasmonean brothers for the throne. Hyrcanus and Aristobolus, the sons of Alexander Yannai and Salome Alexandra, asked Pompey, who happened to be in Syria at the time, to settle their dispute. They were accompanied by a delegation of Pharisees. Pompey decided in favor of Hyrcanus, the older man. Aristobolus was forced to defend himself against Pompey's troops, who suspended their campaign against the Nabateans and marched on Jerusalem. After a short struggle, lasting three months, Aristobolus was taken prisoner and he and his family were taken to Rome. In accordance with Pompey's decision, Hyrcanus was deprived of the title of king and named *nassi* (prince and high priest). Actually, he was under the domination of his adviser, Antipater the Idumaean, a Roman slave; and henceforth the authority of the Hasmonean leader derived entirely from the great foreign power.

A foreign dynasty now clambered up on the wreckage of the Hasmonean family. Antipater the Idumaean successfully exploited the internal dissension in order to establish his power over the throne from the inside.

He secured Roman citizenship and was confirmed in the position of Judaea's administrator.

In 47 B.C.E., Antipater's son, Herod, was appointed governor of Galilee. One of his first acts was to put down a rebellion which had broken out under the leadership of Hezekiah the Galilean. The suppression of the rebellion was accompanied by the slaying of the insurgents. Because of the executions, Herod was summoned to come before the Sanhedrin to give an account of his actions. He appeared with an armed escort and, because of the irresolution of the judges, managed to escape. In Syria, Herod was appointed *strategos* (general) in Samaria. He then hastened to Jerusalem, intending to take revenge upon the judges, but his father succeeded in dissuading him from carrying out his plan.

Six years later, in 41, Herod bribed the Roman ruler, Mark Antony, who had just arrived in the East. On the advice of Antony and Augustus, the Senate proclaimed Herod King of Judaea. At first, Herod had to fight one of the survivors of the Hasmonean house, Mattathias Antigonus, after which he attacked Jerusalem, which he captured with the aid of the Syrian governor, Gaius Sosius. Herod decided to consolidate his power by getting rid of his opponents, and murdered the Jewish dignitaries in the capital. He abolished the Sanhedrin as a government institution and appointed and discharged high priests for the purpose of taking the office out of the hands of the Hasmoneans.

Herod was an enterprising, courageous, tyrannical man. However, where the Hasmonean kings had not met with the people's approval in their efforts to imitate other Hellenistic rulers, this usurper was now thoroughly hated by most classes.

Herod tried to win over the people by marrying Mariamne the Hasmonean, granddaughter of Hyrcanus and Aristobolus. He also thought he could curry favor with the population by adding magnificent structures to the Temple which were more splendid than anything which had existed previously. He constructed beautiful edifices in the Greek cities of Palestine as well as in Asia and Europe. By spending large sums of money on public buildings, which was a wise domestic policy, and establishing marriage ties with the ruling dynasties of the region, Herod succeeded in transforming Judaea into an important international power. He extended the country's frontiers, and annexed Trachonitis and Hauran in the northeast and reached the borders of Egypt.

But whatever he did was for himself. The glory and prestige in which he mantled Judaea brought no benefit whatsoever to the local population, for Herod was essentially a Hellenistic monarch and not a Jewish king. To be sure, he ruled the people, but he was not accepted by them; he greatly feared the Hasmoneans and consequently had his wife Mariamne and her mother, Alexandra, executed. Ten years after Herod's death, when the government was taken away from his son Archelaus and handed over to the Roman procurators, the change was received quietly and even with a trace of satisfaction.

Balustrade frieze of the second story of the synagogue at Capernaum, depicting a fig tree

AN IDOL IN THE SANCTUARY

Before his death, Herod appointed his sons as rulers of various parts of his kingdom. Archelaus became King of Judaea, Idumaea, and Samaria; Antipas ruled Galilee and western Transjordania; and Philip was tetrarch of northern Transjordania. Because of Archelaus' cruel behavior, the Jews and Samaritans sent a delegation to Augustus, who listened to their requests and removed him. Judaea then became a part of a Roman province under the administration of procurators.

The rule of the procurators led to a clash between the Roman authorities and the Jews. The procurators did not regard their appointment as a mandate to establish a just administration; on the contrary, they considered themselves the officials of an empire which believed itself to be the mistress of the world and looked upon all people as its thralls. They viewed the province to which they were sent as a legitimate field for violence and robbery in which no one would interfere. Accordingly, an all-pervasive hatred of Rome burgeoned in the country.

The tension reached its climax at the end of the reign of Emperor Gaius Caligula. Since the time of Emperor Augustus, all the inhabitants of the Roman Empire, except the Jews, had been worshiping the emperors as divinities. The Jews, however, instead of offering sacrifices and praying to the god-emperor, had been allowed to make offerings and pray to God for the emperor's well-being. Caligula, in his madness, abolished this special dispensation and ordered his statue put up in all the synagogues in the Diaspora and his image set up in the hall of the Temple.

This stirred up a powerful ferment among Jews in all parts of the Empire. Agrippa, the grandson of Herod the Idumaean and Mariamne the Hasmonean, who was a boyhood friend of Caligula and who happened to be in Rome at the time, attempted in vain to dissuade the emperor from carrying out this idea. The Jews of Alexandria, Egypt, also sent a delegation to the capital of the Empire, headed by the celebrated philosopher Philo, which tried without any success to persuade Caligula to change his mind about implementing the harsh decree. However, the Roman governor of Syria, Petronius, who was responsible for carrying out the emperor's order, delayed its execution, despite the great personal risk involved in disobeying Caligula. And the emperor actually condemned Petronius to death for his failure to erect his statue in the Temple. Luck was with Petronius, however, and the ship bearing the sentence arrived several weeks late because of storms at sea, so that the vessel bringing the news of Caligula's death reached port before it.

AGRIPPA I, KING OF JUDAEA

The population had a short breathing spell in the period 41–44 C.E. During this time, Claudius, Caligula's successor, added Judaea to the territories which Caligula had given to Agrippa as part of his kingdom. Agrippa, despite the tradition he absorbed in his home and his Roman education, was seriously concerned for his people. The nation, which longed so much for the restoration of the country's ancient glory, was ready to consider him a scion of the Hasmonean dynasty, and they joyfully accepted him.

The Mishna (*Sota* V 45), in the course of a discussion dealing with the laws for reading the portion of Deuteronomy concerning the king, describes to what extent Agrippa displayed respect for the sacred institutions of the Jews and how much the people loved him. It says, "The [Biblical] portion concerning the king, how is it be [read]?... The high priest gives it [the scroll of the law] to the king, and the king stands and takes it and reads it and sits down. King Agrippa stood up and received [the scroll] and read and remained standing—and the sages praised him. And when he came to 'Thou mayest not put a foreigner over thee,' he wept. They [the people] said to him, 'Do not fear, Agrippa, you are our brother, you are our brother, you are our brother!'"

Agrippa made an effort to fortify Jerusalem and began erecting a third wall. However, he was compelled to suspend the work at the order of the governor of Syria. The governor also forbade the convening of a meeting of the kings of the East, which was supposed to have taken place in Tiberias at the initiative of Agrippa. This brightening of the political climate was simply a brief interval. After Agrippa was suddenly taken ill and died in the year 44, the Romans did not renew this experiment. They again placed Judaea under the rule of Roman procurators.

The rebelliousness which smoldered in the people's breasts and flared up periodically had its origins in the period preceding Agrippa's reign. In the hills of Galilee, Judah, son of Hezekiah the Galilean, was captured and put to death when he rose up in revolt at the death of Herod, just as his father had been killed at the beginning of the king's career. A certain Simon also raised the standard of revolt at the head of a group of men in the district of Perisa. And Josephus tells about a man called Ethronges who with his brothers led armed attacks against the Romans.

Despite the fact that not every Messianic stirring originated in political ferment and not every preacher advocated armed rebellion, the Roman authorities made no distinction between them. They regarded every Messianic movement as a threat to stable government, and not entirely without justification. Little wonder, then, that when one of these Messianic preachers by the name of Jesus of Nazareth began attracting gatherings, the authorities considered him a danger, since large masses of people listened to him. He was the son of a simple family of craftsmen which traced its origins back to the House of David. The authorities could not but look upon this scion of the Davidic dynasty preaching imminent redemption as a potential pretender to the throne. Consequently, he met the same fate as the other pseudo-Messiahs and he was put to death at the age of 33, in 29 C.E., at the order of the Roman procurator, Pontius Pilate—a governor known for being more malevolent than others who had held this office.

However, the hatred of Rome which had burned in the hearts of the people before Agrippa's reign blazed up sevenfold after they had tasted the crumbs of freedom and independence and were once more forced to bow their heads before the Roman tyrants. And pseudo-Messiahs continued to appear. Josephus tells about such a man called Theudas, who led a mass of people down to the Jordan, where he promised to perform miracles. Roman soldiers swept down upon them, scattering the people in all directions, and killed him.

THE GREAT REVOLT

Clashes also broke out between the non-Jewish population in the cities and their Jewish neighbors. The Gentiles regarded the Romans and Roman rule as a means for building up their power in relation to the Jews, and bloody fighting between Jews and non-Jews became commonplace. During the term of office of Gessius Florus (64–68), in the wake of a clash over a synagogue in the mixed city of Caesarea, the patience of moderate Jewish circles gave out when they realized that Florus had no intention of seeing justice done, and they too joined the rebels. And, to be sure, this evil, unscrupulous, heartless procurator, of whom Josephus wrote, "he devoted himself to fanning the flames of war," went too far.

While the disturbances were still continuing in Caesarea, "He sent men to the Temple and had 17 talents removed.... The nation was immediately in a turmoil

and many hurried to the Temple from all directions...
and a few... poured imprecations and insults on Florus
and brought a basket [for collecting alms] and asked
for pennies for him, for he is a pauper" (*The Jewish
War*, II, pp. 293–295 [Hebrew edition]).

This joke and Florus' brutal behavior which followed upon it led to the outbreak of a general revolt.
Henceforth, all attempts to make peace were fruitless.
Leading personalities in Judaea did not really believe
in the possibility of defeating Rome, but no one listened to them any longer, even among the masses,
which were generally moderate in their views.

On hearing of the revolt, Agrippa II left Alexandria
and hurried to Jerusalem to try to calm the populace.
He attempted to prove to the people that they were
extremely weak by comparison with Roman might,
and urged them to yield to Florus. When he voiced
this demand, Agrippa II was driven out of Jerusalem,
subsequently joining the Roman forces marching on
Judaea.

The rebels succeeded in making themselves masters
of all places in Jerusalem which had been controlled by
a Roman garrison or had been in the hands of the peace
party. In other cities, Jews and Gentiles clashed, with
many killed on both sides.

The governor of Syria, Cestius Gallus, left Antioch
to restore peace in Judaea and suppress the revolt. He
came to within nine and one-half miles of Jerusalem
and succeeded in capturing one of its suburbs. However, when he attempted to attack the Temple Mount,
he was repulsed and forced to retreat. Jewish forces
swooped down on the Roman legions as they were
withdrawing near Beth-horon, killed many of the soldiers, and captured large quantities of equipment and
supplies which they subsequently put to good use in
their war against the powerful empire.

Now the Jews began preparing themselves for a

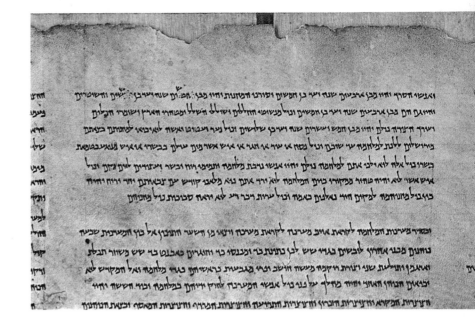

*The War of the Sons of Light against the Sons of Darkness: One
of the first of the Dead Sea Scrolls, acquired by Prof. E. L. Sukenik as early as 1948, it contains the description of a symbolic future
war which would end in the destruction of the evil government and
the restoration of the monarchy to Israel as an "eternal kingdom."
The picture shows a section of the War Scroll depicting the army's
deployment to prepare for decisive battle. Shrine of the Book,
Jerusalem*

great struggle. Commanders were chosen for the defense of Jerusalem and other parts of the country.
Galilee, the region exposed to the first onslaught of the
Roman legions, was placed under the command of Josephus. He began fortifying the area for which he was
responsible, but the Galileans apparently sensed that
he had reservations about his mission and the entire
revolt. However, before the Sanhedrin in Jerusalem,
Josephus rejected the views of the distrustful Galileans
headed by Johanan of Gush Halav. In Jerusalem, too,
preparations were made for the bitter fight.

In the spring of 67, Vespasian, one of Nero's experienced generals, invaded Galilee at the head of an
army of sixty thousand men. Josephus' troops fled to
the fortress of Yodphath, where they succeeded in

*(Left) One of the Dead Sea Scrolls. Since the discovery of the
parchment scrolls in the caves of Khirbet Qumran on the west bank
of the Dead Sea in 1947, scholars have been disagreeing as to their
period and significance. They have been variously attributed to the
2nd century B.C.E., the 2nd century C.E., and even the 7th century
C.E. The most reliable view ascribes them to a monastic sect like the
Essenes which was active during the 1st century C.E. Many of the
scrolls contain Biblical books. Some of them are homiletical works
which contain sections from the Bible and haggadic interpretations
of the texts, and one describes the sect's organization and way of
life. The picture shows part of an apocryphal work on the Book of
Genesis. The excerpt glorifies the beauty of Abraham's wife, Sarah.
Shrine of the Book, Jerusalem*

holding out against the Roman assaults for forty days. Josephus and forty of his men escaped to a cave, and, when their refuge was discovered, they decided to take their own lives. Josephus managed to slip away from his comrades, and fell into the hands of the Romans. Vespasian spared his life when Josephus predicted that he would become emperor.

After Yodphath, Tiberias, Gush Halav, Mount Tabor, and the town of Gamla in Transjordania were taken by the Romans. The setbacks in Galilee led to civil strife in Jerusalem, and the Zealots got rid of the leaders whom they accused of inefficiency. Johanan of Gush Halav, who had fled to Jerusalem, became the leader of the Zealots, and their first act was to oust the high priest, a member of the moderate faction, and appoint an ordinary priest in his place. The moderates then surrounded the Temple Mount, where the Zealots had fortified themselves. In order to lift the siege, the latter called in Idumaeans, who burst into the city and massacred moderate leaders and distinguished members of the community. Now, the Zealots were in control and Johanan of Gush Halav was complete master of Jerusalem.

Vespasian refused to listen to his advisers who sug-

gested that he take advantage of the internal struggles in Jerusalem and capture the city. He preferred to bide his time until the civil war should weaken the Jews; then it would be possible to vanquish them without any difficulty. In the course of several months he succeeded in overrunning territory which had been under Jewish control, while engaging in warfare with Simon bar-Giora, who time and again struck at the Roman legions from ambush. Bar-Giora had been summoned to Jerusalem to oppose Johanan of Gush Halav, who was hated by most of the inhabitants of the capital. The struggle between the two men had not yet been decided. In addition to the factions backing each of these leaders, there was a third group in Jerusalem headed by Eleazar, son of Simon, which also fought the party of Johanan of Gush Halav.

In the year 70 C.E., the Roman army led by Titus marched on Jerusalem. The Roman commander was the son of Vespasian, who had hurried back to Rome to ascend the imperial throne after the death of Nero. However, the fratricidal struggle in Jerusalem did not cease. That Passover, Johanan's troops defeated Eleazar's men and killed them. Now two contenders for power remained—Johanan of Gush Halav and Simon bar-Giora. They did not cease fighting each other until the Romans carried out their first assault.

The Jews nearly succeeded in capturing the Romans' heavy weapons and delivered unsettling blows against the enemy. However, after fifteen days of fierce fighting, the Romans breached the city's third wall. Five days later, they broke through the second and, in four days, they succeeded in taking possession of it. Titus then ordered his men to construct ramps opposite the upper city. The Jews dug tunnels under the ramps and they collapsed. The Romans erected an embankment around Jerusalem and set up patrols on it to prevent anyone from leaving the beleaguered city. Starvation wrought havoc among the population, and Josephus gives horrifying accounts of the suffering of the inhabitants.

The Romans erected new ramps. Their battering rams crashed through the wall and, after a furious fight, Titus' troops reached the Temple court. However, the new wall which the Jews had constructed

Stone ossuaries for collecting the bones of the dead, found in Jewish cave tombs of the Second Temple period and later; they were ornamented chiefly with geometric designs. The two six-leaved or many-leaved roses on either side of a branch or a stylized column were the commonest designs

(Opposite page) The caves of Khirbet Qumran, northwest of the Dead Sea, in which the first scrolls of the "Judaean Desert Sect" were found in 1947

The vessels of the Jerusalem Temple. In Titus' triumphal procession after his victory over the Jews and the burning of the Temple in 70 C.E., all the vessels and magnificent furnishings of the Temple were taken to Rome as war booty. The relief on the Arch of Titus in Rome depicting this procession shows the seven-branched candelabrum and its shovels, as well as the golden altar with its accessories

during the siege withstood the Roman assaults. Titus ordered the gates set on fire, and a Roman soldier, in pursuit of the Jews doggedly fighting with their remaining strength as they withdrew step by step, hurled a blazing torch into the Temple. The flames enveloped the structure, with the Romans constantly flinging incendiary material into it. Josephus relates, "And, when the flame flared up, the Jews raised a terrible cry in their realization of the magnitude of the disaster, and they rushed in from all sides to stop the fire, and they were not concerned for their lives nor did they spare their strength when they beheld the loss of their Temple and their House of Life, for which they had kept their spirits." Further, Josephus goes on to say, "And, when the fire continued to consume whatever was around it, Titus came inside the building with his officers and looked at the Holy of Holies and the hall and whatever else was there and saw that the Temple's splendor was greater than the Gentiles had said it was, and the Jews are justly proud of it and praise it highly. And when he saw that the flames had not yet touched the interior hall . . . . a fitting thought occurred to him that he could still save the building, and he hurried outside and attempted himself to persuade the soldiers to extinguish the fire . . . but the ire of the soldiers and their hatred of the Jews exceeded their respect for the emperor and their fear of being punished by him . . . And after the emperor had departed . . . one man hastened to place fire . . . between the hinges of the gate . . . and so the Temple was consumed by fire despite the emperor and his wrath."

The upper city was still in Jewish hands. Titus rejected the request of Johanan and Simon to be allowed to leave freely, but they escaped and managed to hold out there an extremely short time.

Jerusalem was conquered after a five-months' siege. The Jews who fell into Roman hands were killed, sent to mines or circuses, or brought to Rome for Titus' triumphal procession.

The Jews continued their resistance in the fortresses of Herodium, Machaerus, and Masada. The defense of Masada was conducted by Eleazer, son of Yair, who had not fought in Jerusalem. He had fortified himself on the bare hilltop of Masada with part of his men at the beginning of the war. For three years after the destruction of Jerusalem, Eleazer and his handful of Sicarii desperately continued fighting the Romans with great courage. But, when the wooden wall which the Jews on Masada had constructed inside the outer wall was breached and there was no longer any hope, Eleazer in an eloquent, moving speech persuaded his people to take their own lives and not fall into the hands of their enemies. "For we rebelled against the Romans with courage and a spirit of sacrifice. . . . Our hands are not yet bound and still hold a weapon; let them give us salvation this time! Let us die before becoming slaves of our enemies and let us remain free as we leave the land of the living; we, our wives, and our children. . . ." And when the Romans besieging the mountain fortress "donned their weapons at dawn and erected bridges across the passages between the ramps and the breaches in the wall and broke through [into

After the fall of Jerusalem, a small group of Zealots commanded by Eleazar, son of Yair, withstood for over two years a siege by the Roman general Flavius Silva against Mount Masada. The end of the beleaguered Jews, who took their own lives in order not to fall into the hands of the Romans, is told in detail in Josephus' work on the wars of the Jews against the Romans. Mount Masada apparently also served as a refuge for monastic sects before and after the destruction of Jerusalem. The picture (overlooking the Dead Sea) shows the isolated rock with its perpendicular cliffs, as well as the ramp which the Romans constructed for the purpose of reaching the top

the fortress, they saw] there was no one of their enemies there, but only a terrible desolation inside the palace and stillness all around, [and they] tried in vain to understand what had happened . . . and, when they discovered the mass of dead bodies, they did not rejoice this time at what they saw of their enemies but were amazed at their spirit of sacrifice and their exalted counsel which laughed at death and did not shrink from this great deed."

This was the final act in the war which destroyed Jerusalem.

The nation continued living on its soil. To a large extent, the leadership remained in the hands of the same circles which had held it before the war, and Messianic ferment and political and religious creativity which draw their inspiration from this faith in the God of Israel and imminent redemption still produced fruits for many generations to come.

JEWISH ART IN THE SECOND TEMPLE PERIOD

The style of Jewish art in the period of the Second Temple was basically Hellenistic. But, in the years after the return from the Babylonian Captivity, Persian influence left its mark on Jewish art, just as, at the end of the period, Roman influence was apparent. Not much has remained of the period prior to the destruc-

tion of the Temple. There are more written details than concrete evidences of the two buildings of the Temple — the one erected in the days of Zerubbabel and the structure put up during Herod's reign. Ezekiel's description of the Temple's ornamentation, which consisted of "cherubim and palm-trees; and a palm-tree was between cherub and cherub, and every cherub had two faces; so that there was the face of a man toward the palm-tree on the one side, and the face of a young lion toward the palm-tree on the other side; thus was it made through all the house round about" (Ezekiel 41:18-19), would indicate the influence of Persian art. The relief which encompassed Darius' palace at Persepolis also included winged griffins facing each other, with a palm-tree between them and the trees on either side. The wreaths of inverted leaves decorating the lower ring of the seven-branched candelabrum on the Arch of Titus in Rome most resemble the capitals of Persian columns. In compliance with orders of Judah the Maccabee, the seven-branched candelabrum had been fashioned according to the oldest model of the Persian period which had been brought to Syria by Antiochus Epiphanes.

Josephus describes the doors to the hall in the Temple as follows: "And before them there was a Babylonian screen, the work of a skillful workman of blue, fine linen, scarlet, and purple. And the workmanship of the screen was wonderful, for the mixture of colors had not been made haphazardly but had been designed

61

to describe the form of the world" (*Jewish War* V, 5–4). The Babylonian screen was apparently a woven Persian rug of huge dimensions hung at a height of more than twenty-seven feet. The influences of Persian culture were taken for granted in a period in which the Judaean exiles benefited from the liberal attitude of the Persian rulers. The fact that many Jews attained important positions in the courts of the kings of Persia must have furthered this acclimatization. The exiles who returned to Judah and built their Temple in Jerusalem were imbued with Persian culture and it is not surprising that this influence left its mark on the style of their art.

From the Hasmonean period, too, only a very small number of artistic finds have survived, and whatever remained of tombs, sarcophagi, and coins testified to a basic Hellenistic influence which was preserved in just a single feature, i.e., the absolute disappearance of human faces and figures and excessive stress on symbolic elements and pure ornamentation. The Hasmoneans, like the first Pietists before them, regarded pagan worship as the most serious threat to the people's survival. In order absolutely to avoid any identification with the picture of a Greek god or his statue, they were extremely strict about observing the Second Commandment and took it literally. In the coins which represented their political independence, the Hasmoneans refrained from portraying the figures and heads of human beings and concentrated chiefly on depicting ornamental plants and fruits and symbols of the Temple worship. The seven-branched candelabrum, the *shofar* (ram's horn), the *lulav* (palm branch), and the *ethrog* (citron) were at that time the most important national symbols, together with the representations of the plants for which Palestine was famous — the grapevine, pomegranate, dates, and wheat, The dragon on the octagonal base of the candelabrum on Titus' triumphal arch is an ornamentation added at the beginning of the Hasmonean period under the influence of contemporary Hellenistic art. The bases of the octagonal columns at the temple of Apollo in Didyma were, for example, also ornamented with dragons, but these had human heads while the dragon at the base of the candelabrum of Judah the Maccabee is depicted as having the head of an animal. Josephus relates that the table with the shewbread in the Temple resembled the one at Delphi and had animal's legs "resembling the legs which the Dorians fashioned for their beds."

Eastern Hellenistic art chiefly influenced the principles of Jewish monumental construction. It may be assumed that this influence was reflected not only in the structures which remained from a relatively later period but also in those which preceded them, e.g. the palaces and tombs of the Hasmonean kings which were built in the Eastern Hellenistic style. The descriptions of the Hasmonean tombs in the works of Josephus and the Books of the Maccabees provided information concerning the structure which Simon built on the tombs themselves. It was probably a tall building of dressed stone surmounted by seven towers (for the parents and their five sons) with pyramidal or cone-shaped roofs. "And he embellished them very skillfully and erected large columns around them, and on the columns were formed series of various kinds of weapons in eternal memory, and he engraved ships near them for all those who go down to the sea to behold" (I Maccabees).

Although the tombs of the Hasmoneans were destroyed, examples of large family tombs have survived which were constructed in the Hellenistic style with pyramidal or cone-shaped roofs. These monuments, which were erected in the Kidron valley on either side of the road leading up to Jerusalem from the north, were built at the end of the Second Temple period during the first century C.E. This was a huge cemetery extending for miles on both sides of the road; the family tombs were carved out of rock on the slope and *batei nefesh* or *yadayim* constituted the entrance halls to the cave tombs and occasionally the burial places of heads of families. The structures in the Kidron valley known as the "Tomb of Zechariah," with a pyramidal roof, and "Yad Abshalom," with a conical one, are only two examples of the numerous buildings erected along the road leading to Jerusalem exactly like the monuments constructed on either side of the Via Appia leading to Rome. The architectural style of both monuments is Hellenistic; both are square structures, the front beams of which stand on columns with Doric capitals, and the ornamentation of the beam also resembles that of the Doric temples. The pyramid at the top of the "Tomb of Zechariah" may indicate greater Egyptian influence.

During Herod's reign, there was an upsurge of monumental architecture and there are signs of a certain revolution in style chiefly influenced by Roman building. For the first time, the Roman arch was introduced in construction, and much use was made of it not only in public buildings, including the Temple, but also in palaces and private dwellings. Characteristic of Herod's building style is dressed stone on the surface of which a smooth frame enclosed the central rough, prominent area. This was the style in which the walls of Jerusalem, the Temple, the king's palaces in Jerusalem, Masada, and Caesarea, and other public buildings, such as the structure of the Tombs of the Patriarchs (Cave of Machpelah) at Hebron, were constructed. The latter building and the remains of other structures give some conception of the monumental nature of the Herodian style of architecture. The clash between the various contrasting influences of the East and West, writes Maximilian Kohn in his article on Jewish art in the Second Temple period, "became the decisive factor which left a characteristic stamp on the individuality of Jewish art in the Herodian Period." From Josephus' writings Jerusalem in the Herodian period is revealed as a magnificent city of which the Temple was the crowning glory. Jerusalem extended over four hills. The upper city (or "Upper Market") was linked to the Temple square by two bridges across the central valley. One of these bridges (the remains of which, forty-five feet wide and seventy feet high, are preserved to

The sarcophagi at Beth She'arim are ornamented with reliefs containing numerous Jewish symbols such as the seven-branched menorah, the *shofar,* and the *ethrog (citron), as well as Biblical figures like Noah and Daniel and the representations of birds and wild and domestic animals. This one has two lions*

and the length of thy days." If we neglect it, how much greater the danger!' They said, not many days passed before the Romans seized Rabbi Akiva and put him in prison; they also seized Pappus ben Judah and put him with Rabbi Akiva. Rabbi Akiva said to him, 'Pappus, who brought you here?' He replied, 'You are fortunate, Rabbi Akiva, that you were caught for

studying the Torah; woe to Pappus for having been caught for foolishness.'

"When they took out Rabbi Akiva to execute him, it was the time to recite the *Shema.* They rent his flesh with iron combs while he was acknowledging the power of Heaven....[Akiva] prolonged his utterance of the verse, 'Hear O Israel, the Lord is our God, the

Beth She'arim became famous as one of the seats of the Sanhedrin in the 2nd century C.E. after the Jewish center had moved to Galilee. Here Rabbi Judah ha-Nassi lived and worked and the Mishna was collected and redacted around the year 200. When Rabbi Judah died about 220 at the age of eighty-five, he was buried here. The city, built on a hill during the Hasmonean period in the 2nd century B.C.E., was destroyed in 352 C.E. when Gallus was suppressing a Jewish rebellion. The height of its flowering was in the 2nd century C.E.

Lord is One,' and his soul departed at the word 'One.' A divine voice was heard to say, 'Happy are you, Rabbi Akiva, that your soul departed at the word 'One'.... The ministering angels said to the Holy one, Blessed be He, 'This is the Torah and this is its reward?'....A divine voice said, 'Happy are you, Rabbi Akiva, that you have been designated for life in the hereafter''' (*Berakoth* 61, 2).

Judah ben Bava, Rabbi Akiva's friend, also paid with his life for ordaining five of Rabbi Akiva's pupils in order to keep the chain of ordination from being severed. He assembled them between the cities of Usha and Shefar'am in Galilee and ordained them. When the Romans approached, the old sage ordered the young men to flee for their lives. The Roman soldiers found him and jabbed him with their lances until he was covered with wounds.

The firm stand the Jews took against their enemies brought the latter to the point of admiring the objects of their persecution. According to legend, Hadrian was supposed to have expressed his admiration to Rabbi Joshua ben Hananiah in the following words, "How great is the ewe among seventy wolves."

The almost uninterrupted rebellions during the seventy years between the Great Revolt (66–70 C.E.), which led to the destruction of Jerusalem, and the end of the Bar-Kokheva uprising, leading to the destruction of the Jewish population in Judaea, are indisputable testimony to the power of the faith which beat in the hearts of the people, both in its own land and in the various countries of the Diaspora, that Israel's redemption was near.

But the flame of the belief in a Messiah did not impel only Jews to rise up against the government. It also drew large numbers of non-Jews to its glow—some of them to complete conversion, others to fear of the Jewish God, and certain individuals to Christianity.

The period after the destruction of Jerusalem was one in which Jewish life in the Diaspora struck roots, while the non-Jewish population in Judaea succeeded to an increasing degree in obliterating the Jewish nature of the country and putting an alien stamp on it. The Hellenistic historian and geographer Strabo, as quoted by Josephus, asserted that the Jewish people have "already entered each and every town and it is not easy to find a place in the settled world which has not received this race and is not under its domination" (*Jewish Antiquities*, XIV, 115). In an apocryphal work—the *Sibylline Oracles*—written in the Diaspora, apparently during the early Hasmonean period, there is a reference to the Jews: "The whole world is full of you, and the whole sea" (III, 271).

Jews were already living in Egypt in the period of the Temple. During the reign of the Seleucid King Antiochus IV Epiphanes, Onias, the son of the Jerusalem high priest, traveled to Egypt in connection with the struggle for the high priesthood, to which Alcimus had been appointed. Onias founded a colony of soldiers in Yeb and even built a temple there for them.

His sons continued in their father's footsteps, and

The fact that Rabbi Judah ha-Nassi was buried at Beth She'arim and the Roman edict forbidding Jews to bury their dead on the Mount of Olives near Jerusalem led to the transformation of Beth She'arim into a burial place for Jews from all over the world. The cave tombs were cut in the rocks on the slopes of the hill on which the city stood, and the bones of the dead were put into sarcophagi. The most magnificent cave tomb contained the facade of three arched gates. In it inscriptions were found which mention Rabbis Gamaliel and Simon, evidently the sons of Rabbi Judah ha-Nassi

the House of Onias played an important role in Egyptian politics for a number of generations. There were several more colonies of Jewish soldiers in the land of the Ptolemies, including one for guarding the frontier near Pelusium on the road to Palestine and Syria; these men extended considerable aid to Julius Caesar at one time. However, although it may be assumed that there were sizable Jewish communities in various parts of Egypt, the center of that country's Jewry was most assuredly in Alexandria. Two of the five quarters of the city were populated by Jews, and they enjoyed a respected position both as individuals and as a community with institutions of its own.

This community flourished for hundreds of years and served as one of the focal points of Jewish life in the Diaspora. Here, the Bible was translated into Greek (Septuagint), as mentioned above, and it was in this city that Philo, the great spiritual light of Hellenistic Judaism in the Roman period, lived and worked. He wrote many books in the Judaeo-Greek spirit of commentary, and, since he was permeated with the spirit of Greek philosophy on the one hand and nur-

tured on the Torah and homiletic works on the other, it is difficult to decide whether Philo dressed the heritage of his fathers in a Greek mantle or imparted a Jewish aspect to Greek philosophy. But Alexandrian Jewry was creative not only in the field of philosophy. Here, a number of apocryphal works were apparently written. Of the literary works, mention should be made of the fragments by Ezekiel the Tragedian which have been discovered. These utilized the events of the Exodus from Egypt as the basis of their plot.

The size of the community becomes clear from the story in the Talmudic tractate of *Sukkah*, "Rabbi Judah says, whoever has not seen the synagogue of Alexandria, Egypt, has not seen Israel's glory. They said: it was a sort of large basilica. . . . which took in twice the number of people who went out of Egypt, and it had seventy-one golden chairs corresponding to the seventy-one members of the Great Sanhedrin. . . . and it had a wooden platform in the center of which the cantor of the assemblage stood with scarves in his hand; and when the time came for the congregation to say Amen, he would wave a scarf and the whole congregation would respond 'Amen'.... and the [various crafts-men] would not sit together but the goldsmiths by themselves, and the silversmiths by themselves, and the ironsmiths by themselves, and the weavers of gold threads by themselves, and the simple weavers by themselves; and when a poor man entered, he would recognize the members of his own craft and go there and from them he would be able to support himself and his family."

In Cyrenaica, too, the Jews constituted a special class. Strabo writes that "There were four [categories of inhabitants] in the city of the people of Cyrene: one of citizens, one of farmers, a third of Gentiles who were not pagans, and a fourth of Jews."

In effect, throughout the Mediterranean region, in Rome itself, in the islands of Greece, in cities on the mainland, and especially in Asia Minor and Syria, there was not a Greek city which did not have a Jewish community with synagogues and various kinds of public institutions. Particularly noteworthy were the huge communities in Antioch, Syria, and in Ephesus, Sardis, Smyrna and elsewhere in Asia Minor. Many Jews even dwelt on the northern shore of the Black Sea and in distant Hyrcania on the shore of the Caspian Sea and, of course, in central Asia. In the region designated as Babylonia—i.e., under Parthian rule and beyond—the Jews constituted an important, outstanding element among the many peoples of the area.

The picture of the Jews living under Roman domination is one of settled Hellenized communities to which numerous non-Jews were attracted. Part of these Gentiles adopted Judaism completely, while others were satisfied with the status of "God-fearing."

This astonishing phenomenon of numerous non-Jews who wanted to adopt the spiritual heritage of a weak minority in their midst stems from the social and cultural background of the second and third centuries C.E. The population of the Roman Empire became more and more concentrated in the towns, and this separation from the soil undermined the personal ties between individuals and the fertility gods, who had been the divinities of their ancestors, and gave rise to social rootlessness. The trend from the rural areas to the towns also brought about the emergence of serious social differences. There was a gap between the sated individuals, those with enough to eat and steeped in pleasure and licentiousness, and the hungry, those starved for bread and faith.

But both classes were hungry for a meaning to life. The literature of the period is full of ethical and philosophical works on the nature of the world and the right path the individual should elect to follow.

In addition to being cut off from traditional values and a sincere interest in a good way of life, the population of the Empire shared the arbitrary rule of Rome, which was an inescapable harsh fact – a fact very difficult for the world to countenance. This situation gave rise to hopes for better days, not only among Jews but among all the inhabitants of the Empire — both Jews and Gentiles.

Thus, the following combination of circumstances occurred: the Jewish people, with their religion based on a faultless divinity and a high-minded moral philosophy imbued with national pride and a belief that the predominance of its truths was imminent, were living in scattered communities among the general population; and Jews and Gentiles alike were under the Roman eagle. Consequently, many people in the Empire, tired of both their sufferings and their pleasures, sought out Judaism with its long spiritual tradition, its sublime values, and its faith that the day was near when a scion of the House of David would appear to crush the evil kingdom out of existence. The Roman Empire witnessed numerous cases of proselytizing and semi-proselytizing to Judaism in all classes of society— even among members of the imperial family. The spread of Judaism was not limited to the confines of the Roman Empire. In the East, too, there were numerous instances of proselytism. An example of this is the dynasty of Queen Helena of Adiabene, who was completely converted to Judaism together with her sons. From that time on, they identified themselves with the fate of the Jewish people and the tomb they built for themselves in Jerusalem remains to this day a monument to these early converts.

PALESTINE AT THE END OF THE PERIOD OF PERSECUTION

From the beginning of the Roman occupation of Palestine, the nation was divided into four factions in its attitude toward the authorities: the assimilationists, the Hellenizers, the indifferent, and the diehard antagonists. The assimilationists were always a small minority, and after the Bar-Kokheva revolt, no trace of them remained. There is a short, apt description of the position of the various parties during the end of the period of the anti-Jewish religious persecution in the Mishna (tractate *Shabbat* 31, 2): "Rabbi Judah [ben Gerim] said, 'How fine are the deeds of this nation [i.e., the Romans], they have built markets, they have built bridges, they have built baths.' Rabbi Yose kept quiet. Rabbi Simeon bar Yonai retorted, 'Whatever they built, they built only for themselves. They built markets for putting whores into, baths for pampering themselves, bridges for collecting tolls.' Judah ben Gerim then repeated their words, which came to the attention of the authorities. They decided: Judah who praised shall be elevated to high office, Yose who kept quiet shall be exiled to Sepphoris, Simeon who condemned shall be put to death."

Thus, no tangible change occurred in the attitude of the parties to the government, but their relative strength underwent a transformation. During the war, most of the Zealots were killed and, from the time of the abolition of Hadrian's tyrannical edicts, the majority of people once more put their faith in the moderate leaders.

70

RISE OF THE NASSI AND REDACTION OF THE MISHNA

On the accession of Antoninus Pius to the throne (138), a number of Hadrian's edicts were abolished. Now the sages looked for another site for a spiritual center, since Yabneh had been destroyed in the Bar-Kokheva war. The *tannaim* chose Usha and met there at the initiative of Rabbi ben Ilai. Here, the sages could proclaim, after the abolition of the prohibitions against circumcision, keeping the Sabbath, and studying the Torah, "Everyone who studies should come and study, and everyone who does not study should come and study."

A Sanhedrin was again chosen, headed by Rabbi Simeon ben Gamaliel of Yabneh. Like his father, he, too, took steps to increase the powers of the *nassi's* office and now and then clashed with the sages. But he ultimately prevailed and his opinion became the deciding factor in the discussions of the religious court, with respect to laws dealing with the relations between both man and God and man and his fellows. The half shekel which had previously been paid to the Temple was henceforth collected for the *nassi's* fund in all the lands of the Diaspora. The emissaries whom he sent to collect money also served as an important link between the Jews abroad and the center in Palestine. The money was used for various public purposes, including support for poor deserving students and the needy in times of shortages and famine.

When the country was still in ruins during Hadrian's reign, friction had arisen between him and the Sanhedrin which had been established in Babylonia. This Sanhedrin had assumed the functions of the Jewish center in Judaea and begun handing down decisions concerning the dates of festivals and leap years. The establishment of this institution outside the country was enough to threaten the unity of the nation, since Jews in other parts of the Diaspora were liable to act in a similar fashion. Rabbi Simeon sent his representatives to Babylonia to dissolve the Sanhedrin and, after a series of wearisome negotiations, exclusive authority was restored to the Sanhedrin in Palestine.

After the death of Rabbi Simeon ben Gamaliel (165), his son, Rabbi Judah ha-Nassi, who was said to combine both learning and greatness, succeeded to the office. His powers, according to a contemporary historian, were no less than those of a king; he had juridical authority and even the right to sentence a person to death. There are no allusions to this in the Talmudic sources; however, they indicate that he had a sort of police power by means of which he could enforce verdicts of the religious courts.

The Romans acknowledged Rabbi Judah's rights as the head of the Jewish people. In this capacity he had the authority to appoint the members of the central religious court, and he was also in charge of communal affairs in Palestine and abroad. In establishing laws, Rabbi Judah made an effort to be as lenient as possible, and he accordingly exempted a number of Jewish enclaves in Gentile areas from observing those com-

Vespasian regarded the conquest of Jerusalem and the destruction of the Temple (70 C.E.) as his greatest achievement and made a great effort to immortalize it. In addition to the triumphal procession conducted in Titus' honor in Rome which was immortalized on his triumphal arch, a series of gold, silver, and bronze coins was minted. The coins bear the inscription Iudaea capta *("Judaea has been taken") and depict a Roman soldier in a victorious pose behind a woman mourning under a palm tree above the letters S C (Senatus Consulto). A likeness of Vespasian crowned with a laurel wreath appears on the other side, surrounded by an inscription containing all his titles:* IMP(erator) CAES(ar) VESPASIAN(us) AVG(ustus) P(ontifex) M(aximus) TR(ibunicia) P(otestate) P(ater) P(atrice) CO(n)S(ul). *Ha-Arets Museum, Tel Aviv*

The second Jewish war against Rome (132–135) was properly planned, unlike the war of 66–70. The revolt was headed by Rabbi Akiva and the general Simon ben Kosiva, called Bar-Kokheva, whom many regarded as the Messiah. This was the last period in which Jewish coins were minted and, although they were issued during the war, Bar-Kokheva's silver coins were of a high quality. One side of the coin depicts the facade of a building with four columns flanking an arched structure: apparently the former Temple with the Ark of the Covenant inside. The inscription Simon *appears on both sides of the Temple, which has a star (or kokhav) above it. The other side bears a bound lulav and an ethrog, with the inscription* le-herut Yerushalayim *("For the liberation of Jerusalem"). Many of the coins of the second Roman war were minted on defaced Roman money. Ha-Arets Museum, Tel Aviv*

The most complete synagogue mosaic floor in Israel was discovered by chance in 1928 between Beth Alpha and Hefzibah in the Jezreel valley and unearthed by I. L. Sukenik. In the middle of the floor is the zodiac, in the center of which is Helios, the chariot of the sun. On the southern side facing Jerusalem is the Ark of the Covenant flanked by two lions and two seven-branched candelabra. There is a portrayal of the sacrifice of Isaac on the northern side at the entrance. Inscriptions in Hebrew and Greek indicate that the synagogue and its floor were constructed during the reign of Justin between 518 and 527 C.E.

mandments predicated upon living in the land of Israel. He apparently also wished to abolish the fasts to commemorate the destruction of the Temple. While he was in office, the Sanhedrin was transferred from Usha, which had declined, to Sepphoris.

Rabbi Judah ha-Nassi's principal achievement was the completion of the work of Rabbi Akiva and Rabbi Meir; he prepared the final form of the Mishna, collecting and arranging the oral traditions which supplemented the written law of the Torah, and formed the legal system for both theoretical and practical applications of the law. This collection is divided into six Orders: *Zera'im* ("seeds"), *Mo'ed* ("season"), *Nashim* ("women"), *Nezikin* ("damages"), *Kodashim* ("holy things"), and *Toharoth* ("purities"). Each Order is divided into tractates which are further subdivided into chapters. The chapters contain smaller divisions called *mishnayot*. The language of the Mishna, which does not contain legal sections only, differs from the Hebrew of the Bible and is characterized by its compactness, precision, and specialized terminology.

After the death of Rabbi Judah ha-Nassi, his son, Gamaliel III, assumed the office. He was not so great as his father, and only a few traces of his activities remain. However, the office once more gained in prestige during the incumbency of his son, Rabbi Judah II Nessia, who transferred its seat from Sepphoris to Tiberias, which became the country's cultural center for the next two centuries. Rabbi Judah II continued his grandfather's policies, designed to free the Jewish community of a number of restrictions connected with prohibitions against ties with non-Jews. The rulings he introduced include one permitting the use of oils produced by pagans, which had been forbidden by the Jerusalem Sanhedrin. Judah II also established a large number of schools for the study of the Torah.

CRISIS IN THE EMPIRE

In the generation of Rabbi Judah II, the period of progress and prosperity in Palestine came to an end, and a crisis appeared there as the result of general crisis in the Roman Empire.

Changes of emperors led to the imposition of unbearable taxes, oppressive not only because of their very high rates but also due to the disorderly fashion in which they were collected. A decline in the value of the currency and the subsequent galloping inflation also caused a great deal of suffering. Poverty was so great that when Rabbi Shammai told the people of Tiberias to change their clothes for the Sabbath, his listeners replied, "Rabbi, our garb on the Sabbath is as our garb during the week" (Palestine Talmud, *Pe'a* 6, 8). The distress reached the stage of starvation. In the midrashic *Avoth de-Rabbi Nathan* there is a complaint, "At first they used to say, grain in Judah, straw in Galilee, and chaff in Transjordania. Then they said, there's no grain in Judah but straw, and there is no straw in Galilee but chaff, and in Transjordania there was neither one nor the other." And the following is attributed to Rabbi Johanan of the second generation of *amoraim* (Talmudic scholars), "I remember that women would not accept employment in the eastern part of the city [the quarter of the wealthy] for they would die from smelling bread" (*Baba Metsi'a* 81b). His brother-in-law, Resh Lakish, related as a customary incident, "He entered his house and found his sons and daughters in the grip of starvation" (*Sanhedrin* 98b).

The economic decline in the country naturally affected the standard of halakhic studies on which the interest of the generation was centered. The *Pesiktha de-Rab Kahana* (a collection of midrashic homilies for the holidays and special Sabbaths) has the following to say in describing these times, "At first, when people had money, a man would have a desire to hear some Mishna or Talmud; and now, when there is no money, and we suffer most of all from the government, a man has a desire to hear some Bible or *haggadah* [i.e., simple narrative texts]."

During this period, the authorities were more op-

אברהם

והשתחוה

וה[ם] אלי

יצחק

The sacrifice of Isaac, part of the mosaic floor in the Beth Alpha synagogue from the beginning of the 6th century C.E.

pressive as a result of the general bad conditions than out of any deliberate plan—economic or religious—and, accordingly, the relations between the Jewish community and the Romans did not as a rule deteriorate. Under conditions of general insecurity, the Romans were not interested in making new enemies by persecuting religious groups, and few of the emperors ruled long enough consistently to follow a single political policy. Together with the other peoples in the Empire, the Jews suffered from Rome's military weakness and her failure to defend the borders adequately, and the depredations of nomadic tribes became a common occurrence.

Generally, the Jews continued their tradition of reconciling themselves to the powers-that-be. During the Persian invasion of the Empire, the Jews living

73

The zodiacal sign Aquarius, representing the Hebrew month of Shevat (February), depicts a man carrying a pail of water. Mosaic floor of the Beth Alpha synagogue

The family of the *nassi* and the Sanhedrin ruled the nation for five consecutive generations, from the end of the period of persecution after the Bar-Kokheva revolt until the third generation of *amoraim* — approximately from 140 to 320. In the third century, a change in mood occurred, under the pressure of difficult conditions. In the wake of the prolonged economic and political crisis, the powers of the Sanhedrin and the *nassi* were somewhat undermined, and the nation again began to ponder its attitude to Rome. The third generation of *amoraim* was distinguished for its great haggadic scholars, whose blazing enmity for Rome was boundless. Thus, the ancient Messianic hope flared up anew. At first, it assumed the form of a longing, soon to become a powerful desire for immediate redemption. The feeling of confidence that salvation was imminent struck roots in the Jewish community and became an aspiration for liberation from the Roman yoke through action — man's doing in this world. And so the Messianic vision again became transformed from a religious belief into a political force. For the time being, this change in mood carried no practical consequences.

While, during the first century, the Jews were entirely devoted to active attempts to bring redemption and, in the third century, economic distress gnawed at the country's vitals, in the fourth, Christianity took possession of the land. A single basic fact determined Christianity's attitude toward Judaism — the absolute refusal of most Jews to accept the new religion. After their failure in Judaea, Jesus' followers, headed by Paul, directed their principal efforts toward scattered Jewish communities abroad. The fact that Jesus' own people refused to accept him led not only to Paul's abandonment of Judaism but to his attempt to rob Judaism of its image and prestige. By proclaiming that Christians alone were the "true Jews," Paul acquired a rich past, a sacred literature, and assurances of redemption for his new faith. However, as long as the Jewish people existed, they served as indisputable evidence of the artificial nature of this Christian doctrine.

The spread of the new religion to various other peoples was to determine the mutual relations between the two faiths. The attitude of Jews to Christians was clear in Palestine itself — that of a majority to a minority. On the other hand, the attitudes of Christians to Jews in the West, where Jewish communities were confronted by growing Christian congregations, were conditioned by a constant struggle and effort by the Christians to suppress the Jewish communities.

The condition of the Jews deteriorated steadily and, during the reign of Constantine, the emperor formed an alliance with the Church, from considerations of both faith and policy. Termination of the tolerant attitude toward the Jews was part of the price the government paid for the Church's support. Jewry was now compelled to go over from attack to defense, and the statements of the sages of that generation reflect an extremely bitter tone. Rabbi Hillel said, "The Jews have no Messiah, for he has already been destroyed in

abroad participated in the war on the side of Rome, and Shappur, King of Persia, killed twelve thousand Jews in Cappadocia in revenge. The invasion did not reach Palestine, so the loyalty of the local Jews was not put to the test,

The position of the sages, that the Jews must remain loyal to Rome, is also reflected in their attitude to the kingdom of Palmyra. Despite the fact that Palmyra was a Semitic state, the sages remained loyal to Rome. Nevertheless, the appearance of the Palmyrenes in Palestine and their struggle with the Persians once more stirred up Messianic hopes among the Jews, and they were already seeing visions of "kings of the East meeting in Palmyra." But these hopes were soon dashed and, in the wake of the persecution inflicted on Jewish leaders, hatred of the Palmyrenes mounted. The following observation appears in the Talmud: "The day on which Palmyra is destroyed will be a holiday for the Jews" (*Yebamoth* 17a).

the reign of Hezekiah" (*Sanhedrin* 99a), i.e., Hezekiah was the Messiah. These words angered the other sages, for, although they contradict the contention of Christianity, they strike at the very existence of the Jewish people. The Christian claim to being the "true Jews" was derisively rejected by the sages, who contrasted the Written Law (the Bible) which the Christians appropriated almost entirely for themselves, with the Oral Law (the Talmud) in which the Christians had no part. Rabbi Judah ben Shalom told the following anecdote: "Moses also wanted the Mishna to be written down [the Mishna was at first entirely an oral tradition], and the Holy One, Blessed be He, foresaw that the peoples of the world would eventually translate the Torah and read it in Greek and say, 'We, too, are Jews.' The Holy One, Blessed be He, said to him, 'I shall write down most of my Torah for you...,' but the Mishna is His secret, and the Holy One, Blessed be He, reveals his secret only to the righteous."

THE AMORAIM—SUCCESSORS TO THE TANNAIM

After the redaction of the Mishna, the Jewish sages continued to collect the traditions which were not included in Rabbi Judah ha-Nassi's Mishna, as well as to interpret various Mishnaic laws. The new collections were arranged to correspond to the order of the six books in the Mishna. The largest were called *Baraitha* and *Tosephta*. The exegetes, called *amoraim*, continued the activity of the *tannaim*, exploring their statements as they appear in the Mishna, in a terse form which often leaves room for differing interpretations, not always producing final, binding decisions. They elucidated vague expressions in the Mishna, sought Scriptural authority for various laws, and made an effort to reconcile the Mishnaic text with diverse texts of the *Baraitha,* and sometimes even with contradictions in the Mishna itself.

The first *amoraim* were Rabbi Judah ha-Nassi's pupils. After his death, they founded schools in Galilee, Judah, and Babylonia. In accordance with a provision in Rabbi Judah ha-Nassi's will, Rabbi Hanina bar-Hanna headed the *yeshiva* (Talmudic academy) at Sepphoris. He followed his teacher's system in interpreting the law and the latter's views were for him immutable truths. His well-known aphorism concerning free choice, "Everything is in the hands of Heaven, with the exception of fear of Heaven," played an important role in medieval philosophic thought. In Lod, which was apparently rebuilt at the time, a *yeshiva* directed by Rabbi Joshua ben Levi was established. He was very active in public affairs, and he may also have gone to Rome to conduct negotiations on matters pertaining to the country. In the southern part of the country, he was a sort of substitute for the *nassi,* and appointed and ordained teachers, a right granted only to the *nassi.*

One of the greatest scholars of the second generation

(Above) Zodiacal sign of Sagittarius representing Hebrew month of Kislev (December), depicted on the mosaic floor of the Beth Alpha synagogue as an archer

(Below) Lion in the marginal ornamentation of the floor. Beth Alpha synagogue

of *amoraim* was Rabbi Johanan bar-Nappaha, the head of the Tiberias *yeshiva,* who had been Rabbi Judah II's assistant. He was one of the authors of the Palestinian Talmud. His decisions on halakhic law had the backing of the *nassi's* authority. His brother-in-law, Simeon ben (Resh) Lakish, who had been the leader of a group of gladiators in his youth, achieved fame as one of the greatest *amoraim*, and was noted for his incisive cleverness. He often disagreed with his brother-in-law, and thus helped him formalize and clarify the Mishna.

Rabbi Abbahu had also been a student in the school of Rabbi Johanan of Tiberias. He lived and worked in Caesarea, the seat of government and headquarters of the Roman governor as well as of the Christian bishops. The authorities had a high opinion of him and received him with respect. Occasionally, he even succeeded in convincing them to cancel their harsh decrees against the Jewish community.

RENEWAL OF MESSIANIC FERMENT

The bitterness and suppression aroused hopes among the Jews for the imminent advent of the Messiah. Before his death, Rabbi Jeremiah issued instructions that he be clothed in white raiment, his feet shod in sandals, his stick put into his hand, and that he be laid on his side so that be would be ready as soon as the Messiah came. This hope again assumed a local, political guise. Rabbi Eliezer ben Abbina made the statement, "When you see kingdoms fighting one another, look for the advent of the King-Messiah."

There were, of course, more cautious voices. Many of the people's leaders wanted to continue a moderate policy and warned against attempts to calculate the advent of the Messianic era. For instance, when Rabbi Ze'ira found scholars engaged in such calculations, he would ask them to stop, saying, "Three things come unexpectedly, the Messiah, a found object, and a scorpion" (*Sanhedrin* 97a). But, nevertheless, during the disorders in the Empire, in the reign of Gallus, when the Persians once more burst across the borders, many Jews helped the invaders. The leaders, *nessi'im* (plural of *nassi*) and sages, were particularly careful, however, not to offend the authorities. They were so anxious to preserve the peace that they permitted numerous special dispensations to facilitate the delivery of regular supplies to the army. The sages of Sepphoris permitted baking on the Sabbath and even went so far as to permit the baking of prohibited leavened bread on Passover. The sages justified their decision in two ways: "The public might need him [the Roman general]" and "Ursicinus [the Roman general] did not have forcible apostasy in mind but only wished to eat hot bread."

Gallus' rule and the unrestrained excesses of his soldiers led to an uprising. The first to rebel were the people of Sepphoris, who had suffered most; they attacked a company of soldiers encamped in their town and wiped them out. From there, the revolt spread to Tiberias, Lod, and other cities. The initial successes of the rebels aroused Messianic hopes, but the size and the economic conditions of the Jewish population at the time militated against the conduct of a real war. The rebellion was soon crushed, with the Romans demolishing many Jewish communities.

As a consequence of the disorders, numerous spiritual leaders left for Babylonia. The prestige of the Tiberias *yeshiva* declined. Under the political circumstances of the period it was impossible to maintain regular discussions with the Diaspora on vital religious questions, such as the date of the new moon (for determining the beginning of a new month) and the incidence of leap year. The Palestinian sages therefore apparently relinquished one of their great major prerogatives and transferred the determination of leap year to scholars in the Diaspora.

After Gallus' execution, Constantius elevated his cousin Julian, Gallus' brother, to the imperial throne, and sent him to conduct the affairs of the West, which had become disorganized in the wake of internal rebellions and German invasions from the outside. Julian defeated the enemies of the State on the field of battle and his personal foes in the emperor's court, and in 360, the army proclaimed him Augustus, i.e., as having the same rights as Constantius. The latter, refusing to recognize this rise in Julian's status, marched out against him at the head of his army. On his way westward, however, Constantius died, and Julian became the sole ruler of the Empire.

The policy of Julian, known as "The Apostate," was based on his realization that the alliance between the government and the Christian Church which had been concluded in the reign of Constantine was a disaster for the country. This conviction came from his belief in the Hellenic religion in its Neo-Platonic form, which he wished to revive by erecting temples, renewing the worship, and restoring the priesthood.

His first step was to proclaim the absolute freedom of religion, and he adhered to this principle. It was his intention to convince the citizens of the Empire that the old religion was the best and the most powerful. For this reason, he was extremely anxious to win the war against the Persians in order to prove the power of the ancient gods.

As a thinker and anti-Christian propagandist, he frowned upon the Jewish people as the source of Christianity, and did not regard them as chosen people; but, in his religious policy, he supported Judaism as a counterweight to Christianity. In addition, Julian had other practical reasons for a positive attitude toward the Jews. The invasion route which he chose against Persia ran through Mesopotamia, where there was a large, dense Jewish population, and Julian wanted to win it over to his side, or, at least, weaken its hatred of Rome. However, although the political considerations were no doubt paramount, his writings to the Jews do show some personal sympathy for the Jewish people of his time. In the spring of 362, Julian left Constantinople for the East. During his stay in Antioch, he met with Jewish representatives. The following conversation is believed to have taken place between him and the leaders of nearby Jewish communities: "Why don't you offer sacrifices to God as the Torah of Moses requires?" the emperor asked. The Jews answered, "According to our Torah, we have no right to make sacrifices outside our Holy City. How then can we offer sacrifices? Return our city to us, rebuild the Temple and the altar, and we shall offer sacrifices as in the past." "I will rebuild the Temple of the Supreme God," Julian replied.

Julian obviously had no intention of rebuilding the Temple and only wanted to win over the Jews. Nevertheless, his proclamation aroused great enthusiasm throughout the Diaspora. Ephraim the Syrian, an inhabitant of Nisibis, wrote, "A mad enthusiasm seized the Jews; they blew the *shofar* [ram's horn] and rejoiced." Another Christian, Rupinus, who lived in Italy, wrote, "The Jews became so impudent that many of them imagined the days of prophecy had returned; they began insulting our people [i.e., the Christians] as if the period of their kingdom had returned." Other writers mention the collection of large sums in money and jewelry, the gifts of noble Jewish women throughout the known world.

However, in the circles of the *nassi* and the sages, the nation's leaders, the news was received with mixed feelings and reservations. Although the incident itself made them happy, they were full of anxiety at the possible consequences to the unity of the national leadership and the purity of the religion under a priesthood restored by the foreign, pagan king and supervised by him. They were also afraid of depending too much on a plan which was entirely based on the life of a single man — an emperor liable to lose his throne. And the facts demonstrated the correctness of their cautious assessment. Julian was killed before a year ran out and, on the accession to the throne of his successor, the Christian Jovian, all hopes foundered.

CHRISTIANITY REIGNS SUPREME

At Julian's death, Hellenism disappeared as a historical factor. This also marked the end of the authorities' tolerance towards the Jews. Henceforth, all legislation concerning the Jews was designed to limit their rights in the spirit of the needs of the Christian Church. The purpose of the legislation enacted at the beginning of the fifth century was to isolate the Jews in society and completely suppress Judaism by eliminating its central and local organizations.

The authorities did succeed to a certain extent in isolating the Jews, although the Jews did not accept the government's edict to cease proselytizing, which continued as long as there were Gentiles ready to adopt Judaism; and there were certain Christians still willing to become Jews at the beginning of the fifth century. The authorities harassed the central institutions — the office of *nassi* and the Sanhedrin — more

One of the most widespread Jewish symbols after the destruction of Jerusalem was the seven-branched candelabrum, which became an identifying mark as well as a means of disseminating Judaism from the beginning of the 2nd century C.E. onward. The numerous household articles bearing this national symbol included pottery and bronze lamps and bottles of glass or clay. This is a small glass bottle. Ha-Arets Museum, Tel Aviv

Of the numerous synagogues discovered in Galilee, the 3rd-century one at Chorazin is outstanding for its special ornamentation, which includes human faces and even agricultural scenes. Here are the remains of a frieze and capitals.

Christian basilica from the 5th century at Avdat; view from the apse. Avdat was a major center of the short-lived, brilliant Nabatean kingdom for nearly a hundred years between the middle of the 1st century B.C.E. and the middle of the 1st century C.E. The Nabatean Arabs transformed the southern desert regions into fertile valleys by means of cisterns and a ramified network of irrigation canals. On land which the Nabateans reclaimed, agricultural and urban communities succeeded in existing for about another seven hundred years. The Byzantine community and its church were only one of the phases of the glorious history of Avdat in the Negev

and more. To be sure, for several generations there had been no *nessi'im* of the stature of their predecessors, but the mere fact that they were scions of the House of David was enough to make them a unifying factor for all Jews everywhere. In the middle of the fourth century, as a result of the edicts which rendered any contact between Palestine and the Jews of the East beyond the borders of the Empire difficult, Hillel II published a permanent calendar, thus freeing the

Jews of the Diaspora of their dependence on the Sanhedrin and the *nassi* in matters pertaining to the dates of festivals. The office of the *nassi* deteriorated still more when in 399 the Western Empire prohibited the transfer of funds to the house of the *nassi* from the areas under its jurisdiction. Actually, this decree was abolished in a short time, but it served as an indication of the mounting intervention of the government in the affairs of the *nassi's* office.

The sages felt that the time had come to collect the works of the Palestinian scholars. Accordingly, they set down the results of the discussions which had taken place since the redaction of the Mishna, and the fruit of their work is the Palestine Talmud, which contains material on the first four Orders of the Mishna, *Zera'im, Mo'ed, Nashim,* and *Nezikin,* but not on the last two Orders, *Kodashim* and *Toharoth,* because they were unable to complete the project before the waves of the great storm put an end to the center of learning in Palestine.

The end did not come all at once. In 415, a stringent order was published, accusing the *nassi* of violating the Empire's laws. The prohibition against proselytizing and the construction of synagogues, and the abolition of the autonomous judiciary, were diametrically opposed to the principles of the *nassi* as leader of the Jews. Consequently, matters reached an open break between the *nassi* and the authorities. However, the *nassi* still had power, and the emperor contented himself with a warning to the *nassi* Gamaliel VI that he would punish him severely if he violated the laws of the Empire once more. However, at his death in 426, the authorities were granted the opportunity for which they had been waiting. Gamaliel had no sons, and the dynasty of Hillel apparently refused to appoint another relative, thus bringing the dynasty of Hillel and the office of *nassi* in Palestine to an end.

THE BABYLONIAN CENTER

The Diaspora in the East was the oldest, most deeply rooted, and largest of the Jewish communities outside Palestine. Its Jews enjoyed a large measure of autonomy. The Jewish community was headed by the *Rosh Gola* (or Exilarch), who traced his ancestry back to the House of David through Jehoiachin and enjoyed the same status as the *nassi* in Palestine. He was considered as governing in the name of the king and being close to the authorities. In the Persian hierarchy, his position was fourth after the king. He lived in a special quarter of Nehardea and conducted himself as a member of Persian royalty. His income was derived from gifts and property. An entire judicial system was subject to his jurisdiction and he had the power to sit in civil cases and sometimes even in capital cases. The principal religious court was headed by judges representing him, who were called *Dayanei Gola* ("Judges of the Community in Exile").

Every community was directed by seven "town dignitaries." The community employed inspectors for

The Roman amphitheater at Beth She'an is one of the largest and most magnificent in Israel. The theater was one of the basic cultural institutions of the Roman town

measures, supervised the education of children, took care of charitable matters, and was responsible for securing the release of captives, providing dowries for impecunious brides, and supplying food for the children of the poor. The taxes which were collected served among other things for building walls and gates, as well as for hiring an official to ride through the town and "see to its needs."

The Parthian government was generally lenient and did not interfere with the internal life of the Jews. When the Sassanids assumed power (in the first quarter of the third century), the condition of all other religions changed for the worse, including that of the Jews. However, about twenty years later, the authorities acknowledged the power of the large Jewish minority living in their country and made use of it in their wars against the Romans.

The principal occupation of the Jews of Babylonia was agriculture. The farmers concentrated on growing wheat and barley for beverages—a sort of beer which was the national drink of Babylonia. They also produced poppy seeds for the manufacture of oil and palms from whose fruit honey was gotten and wine made. In addition, the Jews engaged in the manufacture of linen goods, pottery, and woven baskets, and worked as tailors and surveyors. Piercing holes in pearls was also one of their occupations.

Economic prosperity paved the way for a cultural flowering. Literary creativity had already begun at the end of the First Temple period. A number of Books of the Bible had been compiled there, e.g., Ezekiel, Daniel, and Esther. After the destruction of the Second Temple, there was a religious court at Nisibis headed by Judah ben Bathyra which conducted disputations

"The boar out of the wood doth ravage it." *The Roman mosaic floors laid in Palestine during the period of occupation contain scenes which appear to have been taken from nature. Here is a wild boar on a mosaic floor. Hanita, Upper Galilee*

with the Palestinian sages. The famous *yeshiva* at Nehardea, at first headed by Rabbi Nathan, who later went to Palestine and settled in Usha, may have been founded at that time.

After the destruction of Betar, when the number of Jews emigrating to Babylonia increased, Hananiah, Rabbi Joshua's nephew, established a religious court there and tried to give it the prerogatives of the Sanhedrin. However, on the intervention of Rabbi Simeon ben Gamaliel, Hananiah dropped the plan.

The most outstanding scholars in Babylonia, who were chiefly responsible for the flowering of Jewish learning there, were Abba Arika, also known as Rav, and his colleague and halakhic opponent, Samuel Yarhina'a, both of whom were pupils of Rabbi Judah ha-Nassi. Samuel headed the *yeshiva* at Nehardea and Rav founded a *yeshiva* at Sura, which until then had not

been a center of learning. Many pupils flocked to this *yeshiva;* according to Talmudic sources they numbered as many as twelve hundred. It is quite possible that special months devoted to study courses *(kalla)* were instituted at this time. In the months of Adar and Elul, large numbers of people would gather from all parts of the country, and the assemblies were conducted with great splendor. According to tradition, more than twelve thousand persons participated in these *kalla* months at the beginning of the fourth century.

After Samuel's death (254), Rabbi Nahman bar Yaakov was appointed head of the Nehardea *yeshiva.* Like Samuel, he too was an expert in civil law. About five years later, in 259, the ruler of Palmyra, whom the Talmud calls Pappa bar Netser, attacked the city and destroyed it, and Rabbi Nahman was forced to leave, subsequently founding a *yeshiva* at Mahoza. In Pumbedita, too, a new center arose under the leadership of Rabbi Judah bar Ezekiel, one of the inventors of the Talmudic style of argumentation in matters of halakhic law. Many *amoraim* were against this method and would mock the sages of Pumbedita for trying to "draw an elephant through the eye of a needle."

At the Sura *yeshiva,* Rabbi Huna succeeded Rav. Rabbi Huna was one of the major authors of the Babylonian Talmud and exercised much influence and authority. He had very many pupils, tradition numbering them at eight hundred. He was admired even in Palestine, and the heads of the school in Tiberias were under his jurisdiction. After him, Rabbi Hisda, one of the greatest of the third- and fourth-generation *amoraim,* headed the *yeshiva* at Sura. He was known for his keen mind in matters of halakhic law and was also well-versed in *haggadah*—the non-legal part of the Talmud.

Simultaneously, with the study of the Talmud, scholars began to devote themselves to the study of the *Masorah*—the body of traditions regarding the correct spelling, writing, and reading of the Hebrew Bible. However, the *haggadah* did not develop here to the same extent that it did in Palestine. But the development in the compilation of the prayer book paralleled that of Palestine.

The activity of the third generation of *amoraim* centered around the two great *yeshivot* (plural of *yeshiva*) of Pumbedita and Mahoza. The Pumbedita *yeshiva* was headed by Rabbi Rabbah bar Nahmani, whose sharp mind attracted many students to the academy; the *kalla* sessions during his incumbency drew large masses of people, which led to a report that he was responsible for a decline in the state revenues. The authorities were told that the people who came for the courses did not work during those months and consequently did not pay taxes. Rabbah had to flee, and died in the course of his wanderings. He was succeeded by Joseph bar Hiya, who fell ill after his appointment and could not remember what he had learned previously.

Rabbah had two illustrious pupils, who are considered the backbone of the Talmud, Abaye and Raba. Abaye directed the *yeshiva* at Pumbedita, and Raba,

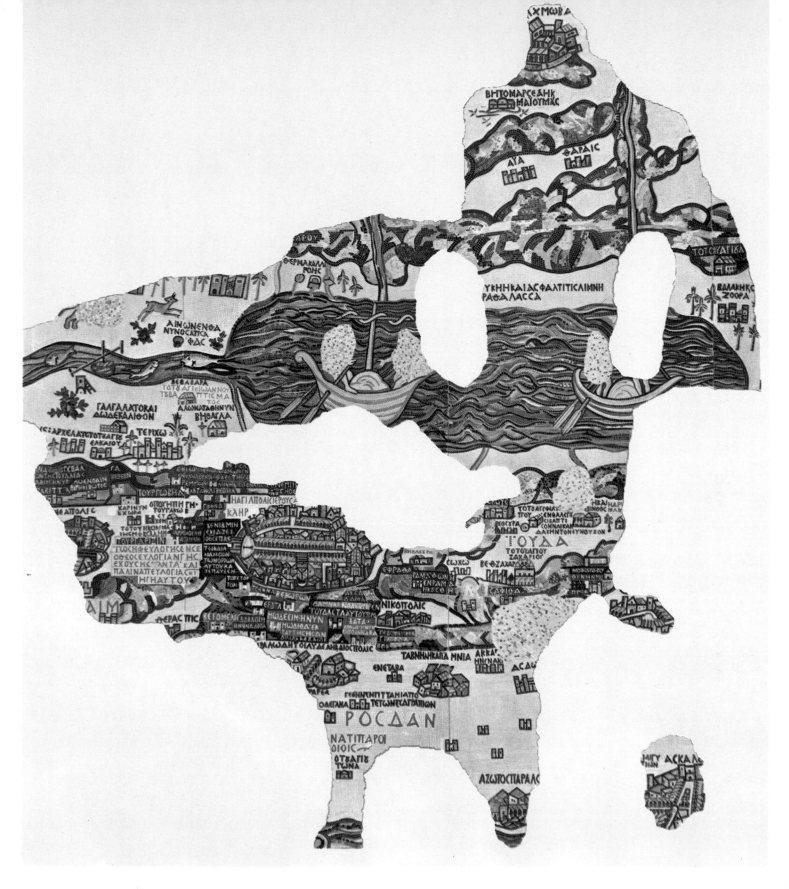

The Madeba Map *is a fragment of a mosaic floor from the second half of the 6th century. It was discovered in the last century during the building of a new church in the town of Madeba in Transjordania. This remaining portion of the map depicts the southeastern part of Palestine. The map was a sort of briefing to Christian holy places, designed for the use of pilgrims. Its background is white, with the drawings outlined in black mosaic and the inscriptions in red. The picture shows just a piece of the floor. The body of water is the "Sea of salt and asphalt and also the Dead Sea." A number of fish are visible in the Jordan which flows into it; the last has its tail toward the Dead Sea. The figures of the people in the boat on the Dead Sea and of the lion pursuing the gazelle on the bank of the Jordan were deliberately defaced by the Iconoclasts—Byzantine destroyers of icons in the 8th century. Jerusalem appears below the Dead Sea, looking like a beleaguered city "in the inheritance of Benjamin." To its right is the "inheritance of Judah," and to the left, the "inheritance of Ephraim." Under it is the "inheritance of Dan, why doth he sojourn by the ships" (from* Mappat Madeba*—"The Madeba Map," by Michael Avi-Yonah)*

81

the one at Mahoza. In their time, the Talmudic method of disputation reached a new stage of development, and the halakhic discussions between them were a sort of generic term for the entire system of Talmudic argumentation. After Abaye's death, many of his pupils left Pumbedita for Mahoza to study at Rav's *yeshiva.* In halakhic disputes, the law was always in accordance with the decision laid down by Raba, except for six specific instances. Raba died about twelve years before Julian the Apostate's army destroyed Mahoza.

At the end of the fourth century, a process resembling that which had occurred in Palestine about two centuries earlier took place. The need arose to collect all the laws which had been formulated in the Babylonian *yeshivot.* This project was headed by Rabbi Ashi, who is credited with the restoration of Sura as a center of learning, following its decline on the death of Rabbi Hisda. With the help of his pupils, led by their most outstanding scholar, Rabina, he embarked on the huge task of collecting the vast quantity of material which had accumulated. The work was not completed until after his death. The year of his passing (499 or 500 C.E.) is considered the date of the redaction of the Talmud.

The Talmud (or Gemara, as this specific part of it is called) is divided to correspond to the six Orders of the Mishna. Its language is a mixture of Hebrew and Aramaic. It embraces all aspects of law, civil cases, capital cases, matters of personal status, and regulations pertaining to what is and is not permitted—a compendium of the beliefs and opinions produced by the Jewish intellect in Babylonia over a period of centuries. Much information concerning law, medicine, and agriculture appears together with religious practices and ethical principles.

The Talmud consists of two basic elements: (1) the *halakha,* or law, which embraces all aspects of the life of both the individual and the group, the relationships between man and his fellows and man and God, between the individual and the community and between communities, between the Jews and other peoples, and even between nations; (2) the *haggadah,* or non-legal part, which consists of stories and ethical anecdotes to illustrate the value of wisdom and moral values—to the extent that it cites laws and commandments, it only discusses their reasons and motives.

UNDER BYZANTINE RULE

At the end of the fourth century, Palestine was divided into three parts, in two of which consuls were appointed. Another part, in Transjordania, was incorporated into the province of Arabia. The country was divided as follows: Palestina Prima (the First) included Judaea, the coastal plain, Samaria, the Negev, and part of Transjordania; the major city in this division was Caesarea and its most important district was Eleutheropolis (Beth Guvrin). Palestina Secunda (the Second)

consisted of the Jezreel valley, Galilee, the cities of the Golan, and the Decapolis ("League of Ten Towns") in Transjordania; the leading city was Scythopolis (Beth She'an), and other important towns were Diocaesarea (Sepphoris), Tiberias, Hippos, and Pella. Most of the Jews of that period lived in this part of Palestine. The Third Palestina comprised parts of the Negev and the Sinai Peninsula. Its principal city was at first Halousa and later Petra (Rekem); its major towns included Mampsis, Zoar, and Elath. The major town in the province of Arabia was Basra; Philadelphia (Rabbath Ammon, Amman) was another important center.

When the news arrived of the death of Julian the Apostate, on whom the Jews had pinned many hopes for their political rehabilitation, Christians living in the country began to kill Jews and destroyed many communities in the south. Christianity continued spreading, and the Christians became the most important element in the population. The special laws benefiting the Jews, which Julian had enacted, were abolished. Christian communities increased. While in the third century eight such communities had been founded, and eighteen in the fourth century, fifty-eight were established in the fifth century. The Christian inhabitants were mostly refugees fleeing from the Germans and Huns invading Italy. These refugees brought a great deal of money with them and Palestine grew rich.

The growth of the Christian population in the country increased its importance to Christians. Palestine became one of the major sources for supplying "relics of saints." Christian monks "discovered" the bones of the prophet Elisha and John the Baptist. In 395, the bones of "our father Joseph" were transported from Shechem (Nablus) to Constantinople; twenty years later, the remains of the prophet Samuel were brought there. In 412, a church was built over the tomb of the prophets Zechariah and Habakkuk. These and other discoveries, such as the remains of the clothes of Mary, Jesus' mother, stimulated mass pilgrimages and brought prosperity to the country. Together with all the other inhabitants, the Jews also benefited materially, especially because of their large store of knowledge concerning the places and persons mentioned in the Bible.

The economic progress of the Jews gave rise to the publication of laws designed to restrict their commercial and agricultural activity. Robbing Jews of their money and property was not punished by the local authorities. Furthermore, the desecration of synagogues, encouraged by Christian monks, was always accompanied by robbery and looting.

JEWISH ART IN THE PERIOD OF THE MISHNA AND THE TALMUD

The synagogue as a meeting place in Jewish communities outside Palestine apparently existed before the destruction of the Temple in 70 C.E. There may also have been synagogues in Palestine and even in Jerusalem itself for Diaspora Jews making a pilgrimage to the Holy City. After the destruction of Jerusalem, the synagogue became the center of the Jewish community throughout the Roman Empire and beyond its borders. Architecturally, the choice fell on the form of the basilica, which in the Roman cities became a meeting place and a court for dispensing municipal law. For the Jews it now became an assembly hall and house of prayer. The earliest synagogue of which remains exist dates from the beginning of the third century. Synagogue remains are found in Galilee, the buildings usually being square, with their facades facing Jerusalem. Unlike Christian basilicas, these synagogues lack a round apse in the rear section, which in a number of them contains a transverse colonnade in addition to the two colonnades running the length of the structure. An example of such an ancient synagogue is the one at Capernaum, at the northern tip of the Sea of Galilee, in which part of the transverse colonnade still stands. A number of synagogues also had a second story, which served as a women's gallery and was separated from the main hall by an ornamented balustrade. The ornamentation of the early synagogue consisted chiefly of stone reliefs of floral and geometrical designs, especially acanthus leaves, but also the figures of human beings and objects. In the Capernaum synagogue, the frieze of the carved balustrade contains the figure of an Ark of the Law resembling a miniature temple mounted on wheels. The synagogue frieze at Chorazin contains the figures of grape harvesters, soldiers, and even Hercules and other images from Greek mythology. Other reliefs contain some of the characteristic symbols of Judaism expressing longing for the restoration of the service in the former Temple, such as the seven-branched candelabrum, the shovel, the *shofar,* the palm branch *(lulav),* and the citron *(ethrog).* In architecture as well as in ornamentation, Jewish art is influenced by Hellenistic and Roman art.

The principal architectural difficulty of the ancient synagogue stemmed from the fact that the worshipers entered the building from the side facing Jerusalem, exactly the same side which they faced in prayer. But, if it is assumed that the worshipers were to enter the building through the two side doors in the wings of the nave, the major problem was in the location of the Ark of the Law with the Torah scrolls. In a number of synagogues, the Ark and the scrolls were kept in a side room and during the service were apparently brought into the main hall to a raised platform facing Jerusalem opposite the main entrance. The problems of the Jewish architects of the third century ultimately produced a uniform solution and a revolution in the construction and ornamentation of synagogues in Palestine and abroad. The main entrance was transferred to the opposite end and the Ark set up in a special niche, and sometimes even in the apse, to face Jerusalem. This revolution in synagogue structure also brought about a change in the method of ornamentation and instead of heavy stone reliefs, the walls were now covered with colorful sketches, decorations, and even narrative

Ascalon was one of the major Roman centers in the southern part of the country which were built during the reign of the great builder of the Second Temple period, Herod. The picture shows the remains of a column and entrance to the ornamented gate of a Herodian building at Ascalon (Ashkelon), 1st century C.E.

material. A reference in the Palestinian Talmud testifies to this revolution with a vague statement: ''In the time of Rabbi Johanan (third century C.E.), they began drawing on the walls, and he did not protest'' (*Aboda Zara* 2, 3). From the rest of the quotations it appears

One of the most beautiful, delicate mosaic floors of the 6th century discovered in Israel was laid bare at Shikmona on the beach south of Haifa. The pictures show sections of its ornamentation. Museum of Ancient Art, Haifa

that in the fourth century they began to decorate synagogues with mosaics and Rabbi Avin did not attempt to prevent it.

There are no drawings from ancient Palestinian synagogues, but in a synagogue at Dura-Europos on the Euphrates River, which was discovered after World War I, walls were found covered with drawings on Biblical subjects. The drawings were apparently executed in 245, the year in which, according to an inscription in Greek and Aramaic found there, the building was renovated by Samuel ben Idi, "Elder of the Jews." The synagogue was partially destroyed about eleven years later, in the wake of a siege by the Persians on Dura-Europos, which was a Roman border fort at the time. The western wall of the synagogue facing Jerusalem and several parts of the other walls survived, since they were covered with earth during the siege for the purpose of strengthening the western wall of the fort which bordered on the synagogue. The seven-branched candelabrum, a palm branch, a citron, and a *shofar* were drawn above the niche for the Ark in the west wall, beside a scene of the binding of Isaac on the altar by his father. Other walls depict events of Jewish national and personal importance, such as Pharaoh's daughter finding Moses in the bulrushes, the Jewish exodus from Egypt, the anointment of David as king, Solomon on a throne, Ezekiel's vision of the dried bones coming back to life, the Hasmonean revolt, and the victory of the Jewish God over Dagon, the Philistine god, and the false prophets on Mount Carmel.

The mosaic floors discovered in synagogues in Palestine and elsewhere are even more famous than the frescoes of Dura-Europos. A relatively large number of such mosaics have survived. Outside Israel, the most famous mosaic floor is located at Naro (Hammam Lif) in Tunisia. The most magnificent mosaic floors in Israel are at Maon, at Hammat-Gader near Tiberias, and at Beth Alpha. In addition to the signs of the zodiac representing the agricultural seasons, these floors also contain national symbols of redemption, such as representations of the doors of the Temple, an Ark of the Law flanked by two lions, the seven-branched candelabrum and a shovel, a palm branch and a citron, and even scenes from the Bible. The most celebrated floor is the one in a synagogue near Beth Alpha, dating from the beginning of the sixth century, in which the sacrifice of Isaac is portrayed with great simplicity and in a design with numerous details.

In Jewish burial caves and on sarcophagi from the second century on, there are Jewish symbols resembling those on murals and mosaics. At the large burial center at Beth She'arim, in which the great rabbis of the Diaspora were interred, ornaments and reliefs depicting the symbols of national renaissance are most numerous. Such symbols are even found on objects with miniature art work, such as oil lamps, ink bottles, and glasses with bottoms having painted leaves on them. This miniature art may even have served as a means of spreading religious propaganda and inducing people to adopt Judaism, which became widespread at the decline of the Empire.

84

DATES IN JEWISH HISTORY FROM THE RETURN TO ZION

UNTIL THE REDACTION OF THE BABYLONIAN TALMUD

B.C.E.

538	Cyrus' proclamation and return of the first group from Babylonia
522–15	Rebuilding of the Second Temple
457	Ezra leads the second group of returning exiles back to Judah
445	Nehemiah comes to Jerusalem
444	Completion of rebuilding of the wall of Jerusalem; conclusion of the Covenant
332	Alexander the Great conquers Palestine
301	The Ptolemies conquer Palestine
198	The Seleucids become masters of Palestine
187	Death of Simeon II, the high priest, succeeded by Onias III
175	Joshua (Jason) is appointed high priest
172	Menelaus is appointed high priest
170	Joshua the high priest appears in Jerusalem and expels Menelaus to Acra; the Tobiads persuade Antiochus IV Epiphanes to march on Jerusalem and expel Joshua (Jason)
169	Antiochus IV plunders the Temple
168	Publication of decrees against the Jews; Mattathias ben Johanan sparks off a revolt at Modin
167	Death of Mattathias; Judah the Maccabee assumes command
166	Battle with Apollonius; Seleucid forces are sent to Judaea under the command of Siron, whom the Jews fight near Beth-horon; Siron's death; battle near Emmaus
165	Lysias marches on Judaea; battle near Beth Zur; purification of the Temple and rededication of the altar; Judah the Maccabee's punitive expedition against Idumaea, Rabbat Anon, and Gilead; reprisals against the forces of Gorgias
163	Conclusion of peace between Judaea and Syria
161	Alcimus is appointed high priest; Bacchides marches on Jerusalem and is defeated; Nicanor attacks Jerusalem; alliance is concluded between Judaea and Rome; Judah the Maccabee dies and Jonathan is appointed to succeed him
142	Jonathan dies and is succeeded by Simon
141	Simon's appointment as high priest, general, and ethnarch
139	Simon sends a delegation to Rome to renew the alliance
135	Simon is murdered by his son-in-law; his son Johanan Hyrcanus assumes power
133	Antiochus Sidetes invades Judaea; restrictions on the Jews' political freedom
107	Johanan Hyrcanus conquers Samaria
104	Death of Johanan Hyrcanus and assumption of power by Aristobolus I; conquest of Galilee and southern Lebanon
103	Death of Aristobolus; Alexander Yannai accedes to power
97	Alexander Yannai conquers Gaza
76	Death of Alexander Yannai and accession to power of his wife Salome Alexandra
67	Death of Salome Alexandra; struggle for power between Hyrcanus II and Aristobolus II
63	Pompey fights Aristobolus II and takes him prisoner; Hyrcanus II assumes power
57	Alexander, the son of Aristobolus II, arrives in Judaea and rebels against Hyrcanus II
40	Parthians invade the country; Antigonus seizes power in Judaea; Roman Senate proclaims Herod King of Judaea
37	Herod rules Judaea
4	Death of Herod and division of the country among his heirs

C.E.

6	Beginning of Roman procurators in Judaea
26–36	Pontius Pilate is procurator of Judaea
29	Crucifixion of Jesus
40	Agrippa I King of Galilee and Transjordania,
41	Agrippa I King of Judaea
52–60	Felix procurator of Judaea
64–66	Gessius Florus procurator of Judaea
66	War with Rome breaks out; Agrippa II comes to Jerusalem to calm the population; rebels conquer Masada
67	Vespasian's army takes Yodphath
68	Civil war in Jerusalem
70	Destruction of the Second Temple
73	Fall of Masada
80	Rabbi Gamaliel of Yabneh succeeds Rabbi Johanan ben Zakkai
115–18	Quietus' disorders
132–35	Bar-Kokheva revolt
140	Rabbi Simeon ben Gamaliel, *nassi* of the Jews
165	Judah ha-Nassi, *nassi* of the Jews
200	Redaction of the Mishna
210	Rabbi Gamaliel III, *nassi* at Tiberias
219	Rav founds *yeshiva* in Sura
230	Rabbi Judah II, Nessia, becomes *nassi*; Rabbi Johanan bar Nappaha establishes *yeshiva* in Tiberias
259	Pappa bar Netser destroys Nehardea
260	Rabbi Judah bar Ezekiel founds *yeshiva* in Pumbedita
338	Babylonian center shifts to Mahoza
365	Gamaliel V becomes *nassi*
371	Rabbi Ashi becomes head of Sura *yeshiva*
385	Judah IV, *nassi* of the Jews
400	Gamaliel VI becomes *nassi*; redaction of the Palestine Talmud
500	Redaction of the Babylonian Talmud

THE JEWS IN THE EASTERN ROMAN EMPIRE

The signs of the Ram and the Fishes. Detail from the zodiac in the mosaic floor in the ancient 4th century synagogue of Hamat

The first emperor of the Eastern Roman Empire, Flavius Arcadius (395-408), confirmed the privileges which the Jews had been granted in the Roman Empire before its division. The purpose of these privileges had been to assure the religious freedom of the Jews. Of special importance was the law published in 396, one year after the emperor ascended the throne, which determined the penalty for officials of the Empire interfering in fixing prices for merchandise Jews brought to the market. Only Jewish merchants were permitted to fix these prices. In other decrees, Arcadius proclaimed as an accepted fact that Roman law in no way limited the Jews and he also ordered the governor of the eastern regions to make sure nothing was done to offend the *nassi* (prince) of the Jews. Arcadius also required the authorities of Illyria to protect synagogues from all harm and confirmed the privileges of the officials conducting synagogue services, making them equal to the officials of similar rank serving in churches. Juridically, the Jews were permitted to be judged in their own courts, although the execution of sentences was taken out of their hands and made the responsibility of the Roman authorities. One of Arcadius' laws was calculated to serve warning on Jews who wished to adopt Christianity for material reasons. The officials of Jewish communities were exempted from a number of duties which were incumbent on persons holding public office if the performance of such duties involved offense against the Jewish faith.

The government's attitude toward the Jews changed for the worse under the influence of the patriarch John Chrysostomos. In 404, a law was published forbidding Jews to be appointed to office in the army, the courts, or subordinate positions in the service of the state. On the other hand, they were forbidden to avoid taking positions which called for heavy tax payments to the state. The execution of this law encountered numerous difficulties and was consequently changed in 418.

At the beginning of the reign of Theodosius II (408–450), Arcadius' son, Jews living in northern Syria were forbidden their customary amusements of the Purim holiday, including the presentation of a play in which Haman was hanged on a tree and burned. This prohibition, which was issued at the instigation of the Church, was imposed by the emperor since he was firmly opposed to any disruption of public order; the law was actually designed to protect the Jews.

By virtue of this approach to administering the affairs of state, the Empire outlawed attacks against the Jews in 412 after Jewish houses and synagogues had been burned in various acts of violence that year. That year, too, Emperor Theodosius II ordered that Jews not be served on the Sabbath and Jewish holidays with summonses to appear before government officials, in order not to disturb their religious observance. Three years later, the emperor laid down a law which required all disputes between Jews and Christians to be brought before state courts. However, that year, a law was enacted by the emperor forbidding the Jews to purchase slaves; but, two years later, this ruling was rendered less harsh when he permitted Jews to acquire slaves by inheritance or by making them the permanent possession of the family. The slave law was a hard blow for Jewish workshops. In those days, the enterprises of Jewish artisans and manufacturers were based on slave labor, as were those of their non-Jewish competitors. This serious harm to the Jewish economy gave rise to considerable resentment which even stirred up rebellions against the anti-Jewish authorities.

However, despite all attempts to mitigate the laws against them, the condition of the Jews steadily deteriorated due to the influence of the Church. For instance, out of seventeen laws, only four were enacted to alleviate their condition, and all the rest were designed to apply stricter measures against them. In 414, a blood libel was leveled against the Jews of Imnestar in northern Syria; that same year or a year later, the Alexandria synagogue was demolished and the

(Opposite page) Symbolic representation of Autumn. Detail from the mosaic floor of the synagogue of Hamat

86

Jews expelled from the city. In 419, the synagogue in Magina was destroyed and, in 442, the authorities expropriated the synagogue in the coppersmiths' market at Constantinople and converted it into a church on the pretext that it had been built by permission of the city governor and not with the explicit permission of the emperor.

JUSTINIAN HARASSES THE JEWS

The recognition of Christianity as the source of imperial law, which received official sanction during the reign of Justinian, was accompanied by the abolition of the special legal attitude toward Judaism which had previously existed in Roman law. The restrictions and harsh decrees which had been imposed on the Jews and which had been repeated time and again now took the form of statutes. The emperor forbade the appointment of Jews to civil and military positions and they were allowed to be named only to the most minor posts, which were more of a burden than an honor. In a law published about 530, the emperor confirmed a law of 423 which, although requiring the authorities to protect Jewish property against Christian rioters, determined that compensation for such acts of violence should be double, and not triple as the previous law had provided.

The emperor also tightened the laws concerning the Christian slaves of Jews—an economic problem which was a source of perennial conflict between the authorities and the Jews. Justinian also revived the ancient regulations, and he decreed a more stringent ruling governing Jewish owners of Christian slaves, increasing the fine to which they were liable. Jews had to manumit every Christian slave they owned as well as every slave who wished to adopt Christianity. Justinian also added a strict proviso that if a slave was baptized and consequently released and his master became a Christian, the former slave would not be restored to him. Like his predecessors, Justinian encountered the opposition of the Jews in this matter and was compelled to revise his law to make it applicable to slaves of Christians as well.

Jews were granted the right to serve as witnesses for certifying documents, but they were not allowed to testify in court trials unless the litigants were Jews. The testimony of Jews was rejected if it was directed against Christians, whereas evidence on behalf of Christians was valid. Another paragraph in the law provided that the testimony of a Jew against a Christian would be acceptable only in the case of a member of a municipal council accused of failing in his duty.

The Jews were deprived of the right of ownership of land on which a church had been built and they were also forbidden to acquire such land, hold it, or receive it in the form of a mortgage. This law also applied to slaves of the Church. In this way, the Church acquired much property, especially in Palestine.

In 553, the emperor published a law in which he granted himself the authority to interfere in the reading of the Torah scroll in the synagogue service. This desire of the emperor to mix in the affairs of his Jewish subjects came to him on the occasion of a dispute in the Constantinople synagogues; the controversy was between those who demanded that the Pentateuchal reading be only in the original Hebrew and those who insisted that it should be rendered in Greek translation. The emperor favored the party which wanted the Greek, and published a law applying to all synagogues throughout the Byzantine Empire and not just those involved in the quarrel. The formulation of the law clearly indicates the desire to persuade the Jews to adopt certain principles of Christian theology. The Emperor rejected the Jewish belief in the simple text of Scripture contrasting with the "vague prophecies" in which the Christians sought the announcement of Jesus' coming.

In order to bring the Jews closer to the Christian interpretation of the Bible, Justinian accorded equal rights to the Hebrew original and to translations. To those who required a Greek translation, he recommended the distorted Septuagint, since this rendition was approved by the Church. The emperor also agreed to the other translations and did not prohibit the use of the Greek translation of Aquila (end of the first century or beginning of the second), but he did not refrain from commenting that Aquila had not been a Jew by birth, in order to influence the Jews to give precedence to the Septuagint. At the same time, it was forbidden to interpret the Bible in accordance with the haggadic and halakhic Midrashim (homiletic works on the Bible which the emperor designated by the common Christian term of "Deuteronomy"). Persons failing to obey the emperor's order to the letter were liable to penalties of flogging, exile, and the confiscation of their property. The same penalties were imposed on those who did not believe in resurrection, the Day of Judgment, and the existence of angels.

Another, more serious, incident of interference with the religious life of the Jews was the emperor's prohibition against celebrating the Passover festival if it came before the Christian Easter. In this way Justinian forced the Jews, as the historian Procopius put it, "to desecrate the honor of God and violate their laws."

The emperor also issued decrees concerning a Jewish family in which several members had adopted Christianity. He confirmed previous laws concerning the rights of the son of an apostate and added a ruling that, in the case where one of the parents wanted to baptize a child and the other was against this step, the wishes of the former would prevail whether it were the father or the mother, even though generally in Roman law, the wishes of the father took precedence over those of the mother.

Another subject which had occupied an important position in previous Roman legislation regarding the Jews was not mentioned at all in the Justinian Code. None of the laws deals in any way with attacks on

Justinian I, Emperor of the Eastern Roman Empire (527–565). Detail from mosaic in the church of San Vitale, Ravenna, Italy

synagogues. This was probably due to the fact that in this period the monks were already curbed by the authorities and there was no longer any need for a law to forbid attacks by mobs against synagogues. In 545, Justinian reinstated the old law forbidding the construction of new synagogues. He also forbade the maintenance of synagogues in Africa.

However, as far as the Jews were concerned, the emperor's acts were more important than the laws themselves. Archaeological remains provide ample proof of the destruction of numerous synagogues in that period. For instance, at Geres, a church was built on the ruins of a synagogue. During the reign of this emperor, the first occasion of forced apostasy by the authorities occurred. It is mentioned in the history of the Eastern Roman Empire. In the city of Borion in Cyrenaica there was a magnificent synagogue which local tradition ascribed to King Solomon. Justinian ordered this synagogue transformed into a church and forced all the Jews of the city to adopt Christianity. This was not an isolated occurrence. The great Byzantine poet Romanos, who himself was a Christian of

Jewish extraction, mentions in his works instances of many Jews who abandoned the faith of their fathers and were baptized out of fear of existing laws.

THE INSTRUCTION BOOK OF JACOB THE APOSTATE

Instances of forced conversion also took place during the reign of Mauricius (582–602). Domitinos, the emperor's nephew, who was serving as bishop of Melitene, compelled the local Jews to accept Christianity. But the Christian historian who tells of this incident adds, "They were hypocritical Christians." During the reign of the Emperor Phocas (602–610), attempts were also made to enforce a general conversion of the Jews. According to a source of that period, *The Instruction Book of Jacob the Apostate of Karub,* the conversion decree was issued by Sergios, the governor of Africa, and the act took place in Carthage. Jacob writes that the governor summoned the Jews and asked them:

"Are you the servants of the Emperor?" The Jews' reply was, "Yes, my lord, we are the servants of the Emperor."

"The benevolent Emperor orders you to accept baptism," Sergios told them.

The Jews were thunderstruck and seized with fear. No one dared open his mouth.

"Have you no answer?" the governor wanted to know.

One of the Jews by the name of Nonos replied, "We shall not do anything of this sort, for the time of sacred baptism has not yet arrived."

Irately leaping to his feet, the governor struck him on the face with both hands and shouted, "If you are servants why don't you obey your master's wishes?"

The Jews were petrified with fear. The governor ordered them baptized whether they agreed or not. Baptism became a state affair, a symbol of loyalty to the emperor, and the Jews could not oppose it unless they wished to appear as traitors to the country. Generally, however, the Jews accepted the conversion decrees as one of the signs of the Messiah and were certain that redemption was imminent. The Persian invasion of the Empire was considered a sign from heaven by them. Accordingly, this invasion moved the fanatical Christians of Antioch to attack the city's Jews. The Jews attempted to defend themselves and the dispute developed into a virtual war. At first the Jews stood firm at the gate of the Byzantine city of Bonosos, but when outside reinforcements reached their enemies they were defeated. Numerous Jews were executed, and many were exiled and their possessions confiscated. The Jewish community of Antioch came to an end.

The Jews of Constantinople played a large part in the rebellion which broke out after Emperor Heraclius' death in 641. Forty years later, after the Empire had lost its eastern regions, Christian hostility toward the Jews grew to such an extent that the Sixth Ecumenical Council (680–681) forbade any kindness to Jews and proscribed going to a Jewish doctor or receiving medicines from him.

The renewed siege of Constantinople in 717 at the assumption of power by the father of the Isaurian dynasty, Leo III (717–741), once more kindled hope in the breasts of the local Jews, who were unable to conceal their joy. The emperor then (721) ordered the Jews forcibly baptized. Many Jews began leaving the city and headed for Syria, where a Messianic movement was gathering. Many others went to Khazaria, where Bulan, the king, had adopted Judaism. A more moderate attitude toward the Jews became apparent when Constantine V, the son of Leo III, married Bulan's daughter (732). Seven years later, on the publication of Leo's code condemning to death various unbelievers in Christianity, the Jews were not on the list. The Council of Nicaea, which convened in 780, permitted Jews who had adopted Christianity superficially to return to Judaism openly, providing all anti-Jewish laws of the state applied to them, too. The Council also decided that Jews would not be accepted for baptism until a careful investigation proved that their loyalty to Christianity was unimpeachable.

During the reign of the Amoric dynasty (first half of the ninth century), the pressure on the Jews was further alleviated. A historian wrote the following about Michael II (820–829), founder of the dynasty: "He exempted the Jews from all taxes and made them free, because he liked them and did them favors, and honored them more than other people." During the reign of his son, the Emperor Theophilus (829–842), the Jews occupied a major position in the commercial relations between the Byzantines and the Khazars as well as with distant kingdoms in eastern Asia — India and China.

On the accession to power of the Macedonian dynasty during the reign of Basil I (867–886), decrees compelling the Jews to accept baptism were once more issued, and only a few communities managed to escape them. The emperor also published a collection of all the anti-Jewish decisions which had been adopted by the various Church Councils. During the reign of Basil's successor, Leo VI, the Wise (886–912), the Jews were again permitted to return to the religion of their ancestors; but during the reign of Romanus I Lekapenus (919–944), decrees ordering the Jews to adopt Christianity were again issued.

However, it would appear that, during the second half of the tenth and into the eleventh century, the condition of the Jews improved considerably, although they were still subject to special decrees which limited their activities. At any rate, an eleventh-century writer describes the condition of the Jews at the time as follows: "The Byzantines permit many Jews in their kingdom and allow them public worship and the construction of synagogues. The Jew in Byzantine lands can unhesitatingly admit 'I am a Jew.' He can act in accordance with the precepts of his religion and pray in public without being called to account for it. No one harasses him with prohibitions."

90

AN INDEPENDENT
JEWISH KINGDOM
IN CENTRAL ASIA

THE JEWS OF ARABIA

The Jews of Arabia have a tradition that they have been living in the peninsula since the destruction of the First Temple. Even though this may be excessive, it is clear that, in the period of persecution at the end of the Second Temple period, many Jews did flee to Arabia to become the ancestors of a number of independent tribes in the vicinity of Yathrib—a fertile district with numerous springs. These tribes erected fortresses and successfully defended themselves against the savage Bedouins around them. To the north, an independent Jewish kingdom, whose people considered themselves the descendants of the Children of Israel, was founded in the region of Khaibar at the beginning of the sixth century. In rich Yemen, in the southern part of the peninsula, there was also a large Jewish community. Here, however, in contrast to the Jews in the north, they lived among the pagan population without constituting a separate political entity. Nevertheless, their power was so great that they were successful in excluding Christianity from Yemen, despite the efforts of the Byzantine emperor to extend Christian spheres of influence. On the island of Yotvata, commanding the entrance to the Red Sea and situated on the trade route between Arabia and India, there was an ancient independent Jewish community.

The customs of the Jews of Arabia resembled those of their neighbors. Like their neighbors, the Jews of southern Arabia made a living from the trade between India and the Byzantine Empire and Persia. The Jews in the northern part of the peninsula were semi-nomads and, like the rest of the population, made a living from meager farming, grazing livestock, transporting merchandise on camel caravans, and arms traffic. They were organized in tribes headed by sheikhs who led them in war as well as in peace.

However, with all their resemblance to their neighbors—to the extent that tribes of Jewish nomads sometimes fought one another—the Jewish tribes were aware of their joint responsibility to fellow Jews and, according to the Koran, regarded the redemption of captives, even of a hostile Jewish tribe, as having the force of a Biblical commandment. The Jews of

Arabia established strong ties with the centers in Palestine and Babylonia; their religious way of life was based on practices universally observed by Jewish communities. They strictly kept the dietary laws, celebrated the Jewish holidays, and rigorously observed the Sabbath, even refraining from going out to fight their enemies on the Day of Rest.

These customs and the high level of culture of the Jews made a strong impression on their neighbors, who called them *Ahl el-Kitab*, i.e., the People of the Book. The center of learning of the Arabian Jews in Yathrib, the Medina of the Moslem period, was famous for its observance of tradition.

YUSSUF DHU-NUWAS

The tradition originating in the Book of Genesis that the Arabs are the descendants of Joktan and Ishmael was accepted by the Arabian tribes and, accordingly, they regarded themselves as being blood relatives of their distinguished, intelligent Jewish neighbors. Bible stories strongly influenced the Arabs, who had no tradition of their own, and many of them wanted to adopt Judaism as had their leaders, the sheikhs. In Yemen, too, one of the major royal houses adopted the Jewish religion.

In this connection, the Arab writer Tabari tells the following story: When the king returned to his capital of San'a after having become a Jew, the townspeople shut the gates and would not let him in and prepared to rebel against him for having abandoned the faith of his fathers. However, he proved to them that the religion of the Jews was the true faith. In San'a there was a cave in which a person who did not speak the

91

truth would die immediately on entering, as his body burst into flames and was consumed. Idols and their priests, as well as two Jewish sages with scrolls of the Torah hanging around their necks, were brought into this cave; the fire destroyed the idols and their priests, but did not touch the Jews at all.

The sons of this king, Yussuf dhu-Nuwas, abused Christian merchants from the Byzantine Empire who happened to be staying in his kingdom, in reprisal for the suffering caused to his fellow Jews in lands under the domination of the emperor of Constantinople. These acts stirred up a rebellion against the Jewish king, actively supported by the Byzantine ruler. Attacks were also carried out against the Jews of Tiberias, who were tortured until they agreed to ask Dhu-Nuwas to stop harassing the Byzantine Christians.

Hard times also came to the Jews of Yathrib as a result of the wars in which they were defeated by rival tribes. However, at the beginning of the seventh century, they recovered and became the equals in military prowess of other Arab tribes in Yathrib. The birth of the Islamic religion, as well as its rapid spread in the peninsula among tribes which had just become acquainted with the monotheism of their Jewish neighbors, should be understood against this background.

MOHAMMED, FOUNDER OF ISLAM

Mohammed's first principle, which proclaimed "Allah is Lord of the Universe and there is no other," is essentially a Jewish doctrine. The phrase "and Mohammed is His prophet" was added only later.

The saying, "No one is a prophet in his own town," held particularly true for Mohammed. In Mecca, his birthplace, he was not received well; Mecca was the center of the paganism of the Arabian tribes. Mohammed was forced to flee, and to make his hegira to Yathrib (Medina) in 622. There, he initiated efforts to win converts to his faith among the city's Arab population. He became very close to the Jews and adopted various Jewish practices, such as fasting on the Day of Atonement and facing Jerusalem in prayer; even his scribe was a Jew. All these facts led the Jews to consider him one of the "God-fearing" and "a light to the Gentiles," and they even helped him. But they did not regard him as a prophet of God. His demand that the Jewish tribe of Bani Qanuqa' adopt his doctrines, the religion of Islam, was contemptuously rejected. It was this rebuff which accounted for Mohammed's eventual great hatred of the Jews. He abandoned the observances he had borrowed from Judaism, and as soon as his position among the Arab tribes grew stronger he began attacking the Jews and their customs and even waged open warfare against them. The armies of the Arab tribes surrounded the Jewish communities in the vicinity of Medina and in northern Arabia and completely destroyed them. Only a few survivors succeeded in escaping the sword of the Faithful, fleeing to southern Palestine and Mesopotamia. After Mohammed's death in 632, his followers in the Arabian peninsula increased in numbers and power. Their religious fanaticism was combined with a lust for battle, a passion for conquest and plunder.

IN THE SHADOW OF ISLAM

Ten years after the death of Mohammed, the Moslems had overrun Arabia, Persia, and part of North Africa. In 638, Caliph Omar conquered Jerusalem and built a mosque, named for him, on the site of the Temple Mount. This rapid conquest of the lands of the Middle East was possible not only because of the power of the invading tribes but chiefly because of the weakness of the regimes of the region. The corruption, tyranny, and perfidiousness of the governments in Persia, and particularly in the Byzantine Empire, discouraged the peoples of the East from making a stand against the invaders; the latter, despite their fanaticism, were regarded as liberators by the suppressed populations.

The attitude of the Moslem conquerors to the populations of the areas they occupied and their religions was more liberal than that of the previous rulers, although there was discrimination by the followers of Mohammed against the adherents of other faiths. Caliph Omar established a code of laws which limited civil rights, discriminating against atheists and infidels and harassing them.

Non-Moslems were forbidden to pray aloud, even in eulogizing a deceased person. They could not try to dissuade relatives from adopting Islam. A non-believer encountering a Moslem had to accord him special respect. Unbelievers could not serve in government positions, nor could they sit in judgment on Moslems. Infidels were not permitted to ride horses nor wear elegant clothing, but had to don special attire as a sign of shame that would warn the Faithful away. Non-Moslems could not wear signet rings and had to pay special taxes—a poll tax and a land tax.

However, in Palestine these laws were not observed even in his day. The conquerors quickly realized that

(Opposite) "Every man with his own standard, according to the ensigns; a good way off shall they pitch round about the tent of meeting. Now those that pitch on the east side toward the sun rising shall be they of the standard of the camp of Judah... the standard of the camp of Reuben according to their hosts.... On the west side shall be the standard of the camp of Ephraim according to their hosts.... On the north side shall be the standard of the camp of Dan according to their hosts...." The 13th-century Jewish artist from southern Germany pictured the leaders of the hosts of Israelite tribes in the desert as armed soldiers carrying banners. The flags show the emblems of the tribes—a lion for Judah, an eagle for Reuben, an ox for Ephraim, and a snake on the flag of the prince of the tribe of Dan. Opening page of Book of Numbers from the manuscript of a Bible, the Five Scrolls, and weekly reading from the Prophets, which belonged to the Duke of Sussex. British Museum, London

they could not retain their conquests and could not by themselves maintain the administration in the advanced countries which they had overcome. They needed the local population to help them carry out administrative, juridical, and financial functions. The only right retained by the early conquerors was the abolition of the payment of taxes. The local inhabitants soon realized that if they adopted Islam, they would be exempted from paying taxes, and some officials in close contact with the authorities became Islamic converts. The Jews, however, kept the principles of their religion without adopting Islam and secretly continued to spin their dreams of redemption and national rebirth.

In the book *Nistarot de-rabbi Simeon bar Yohai* (The Secrets of Rabbi Simon ben Johai), written in Palestine in the eighth century, there is a beautiful legend which expresses the feelings of the Jews of that generation and their hopes for their people: "And when he saw that the kingdom of the sons of Ishmael would eventually spread throughout the world, Simeon bar Yohai wept and said, 'Lord of the Universe, is it not enough for Your sons what the evil kingdom of Edom [Rome] did to them, that You must also send the kingdom of Ishmael against us?' The Holy One blessed be He answered, 'Do not fear, son of man, for the Holy One blessed be He brings the kingdom of Ishmael only to save you from this evil one, and He sets a prophet of His choice over them who will conquer the land [of Israel] for them, and they will come and restore it [to the Jews], and there will be a great hatred between them and the children of Esau [Rome].'"

BABYLONIAN JEWRY

During the generations in which the Romans succeeded in dimming the glow of the Jewish center in Palestine, Babylonian Jewry was well off. "There were neither conversions nor plunder there, and neither Greece-Byzantium nor Edom-Rome ruled them, and the Lord did the Jews a favor...and they lived in Babylonia with their Torah from the exile of king Jehoiachin until these last generations...." (Midrash *Tanhuma*).

The Jews who had been living in Babylonia since the exile of Jechoiachin became very numerous, outnumbering any other Jewish center in the Diaspora. There were large areas and big cities in which the Jewish population constituted a majority. This Jewry with its state and religious institutions was the pride of the Jewish people, and difficult inquiries from all the lands of the Diaspora were directed to it. This was the case during the periods of the *sevoraim* (the Babylonian Jewish scholars in the period 500–700 C.E.) and the *geonim* (scholars in Babylonia from the sixth to the eleventh centuries) until the end of the eleventh century.

The Jews as well as the other inhabitants of Babylonia regarded the Arab conquerors as liberators from the yoke of the Persian Sassanids. To show his appreciation for the help of the Jews during the conquest, Caliph Omar granted Bustanai ben Haninai (618–670) the powers which the exilarch had had, and also gave him the daughter of the Persian king as wife. The caliph authorized the head of the *yeshiva* at Sura, Mar Isaac Gaon, to serve together with him in a post of equal importance in the capacity of *Resh metivta geon Ya'akov*, i.e., "Head of the Academy which is the Pride of Jacob." At this time, the position of *gaon* (head of a *yeshiva*) became an office with temporal powers in addition to that of the exilarch and, properly speaking, the period of the *geonim* (plural of *gaon*) began. The office of the exilarch, the head of the political leadership, since the days of Jehoiachin's exile by the Babylonians, had been hereditary in the Davidic dynasty. The exilarch collected the taxes and assessments from all the Jews of Babylonia. He wore special robes of office, runners preceded his chariot, and a detachment of special troops served as his bodyguard at all times. According to Natan ha-Bavli in his work *Yuhasin*, "He comported himself as one of the king's high officers."

GEONIM OF SURA AND PUMBEDITA

The religious and judicial leadership was for the most part in the hands of the *geonim*—the heads of the *yeshivot* at Sura and Pumbedita. The *geonim* and the students of their academies assiduously studied the Talmud in order to deduce laws from it. They enacted laws and introduced regulations for specific instances as well as to serve as permanent statutes, and made sure the people observed their rulings, punishing offenders. The exilarch appointed the heads of the *yeshivot* in both Sura and Pumbedita with the consent of the members of the *yeshivot* themselves; but the importance of the head of the *yeshiva* at Sura, which was close to Kufa, the country's capital, was greater than that of the *gaon* of Pumbedita. Similarly, the exilarch was appointed only with the approval of the members of the *yeshivot*, despite the fact that the position was hereditary in the Bustanai family. The appointment ceremony was quite elaborate. Rabbi Natan ha-Bavli describes the installation of the exilarch as follows: "The heads of all the *yeshivot* and the leaders of the people would assemble.... They would select a large hall decorated in fine cloth and embroidery, and they would set up chairs for the heads of the *yeshivot*—the elders and the sages—and a magnificent chair for the exilarch, and to his right and left two chairs for the heads of the *yeshivot* of Sura and Pumbedita. Then the head of the Sura *yeshiva* would rise and admonish the *nassi* not to regard himself better than his fellows, for he was being given servitude and not power, as it is written, 'If thou wilt be a servant unto this people this day' (I Kings 12:7). And then on Thursday they would all go to the synagogue and the heads of the *yeshivot* would lay their hands on him and bless him, and then they would blow trumpets and ram's horns and proclaim to the people for young and old to hear, 'Long live our master the *nassi*, son of ——— the exilarch! He is our *nassi*! He is the Head of the Exile, Israel's exile!'"

Second to the exilarch in rank was the head of the Sura *yeshiva*, followed by the head of the *yeshiva* at Pumbedita. The presiding officer of the religious court served as the deputy to the head of the *yeshiva*. Under them in the hierarchy were the seven heads of the *kalla* sessions and directors of the *yeshiva*. These seven offices were hereditary, providing the sons were worthy, unlike the position of head of the *yeshiva*, which was not always transmitted from father to son.

The members of the *yeshivot* met twice a year, in Adar and Elul, for *kalla* months. During these sessions, they discussed the Talmudic treatise which had been selected at the previous *kalla* as the topic for the ensuing five months, between one *kalla* and another. Mostly, however, they introduced regulations to supplement the laws in the Torah and answered inquiries sent to them from Jewish communities throughout the world, from Spain in the West to India in the East. The replies were given in accordance with decisions reached by the members of the *yeshiva*. Rabbi Natan ha-Bavli goes on to say, "And at the end of the month, they would read the inquiries and responsa in the presence of the entire assemblage and the head of the yeshiva would sign the letters with his seal."

The appointment of judges for every town in Babylonia was made in accordance with the decision of the head of the *yeshiva*, with the approval of his deputy, the head of the religious court, and the seven heads of the *kalla* sessions. These judges sat in civil cases and handed down judgments establishing what was forbidden and what was allowed. Official papers —promissory notes, titles, marriage contracts, divorces, etc.—were drawn up in the court office. Each community was headed by a "Community Committee" of seven members called the *parnassei ha-knesset* ("administrators of the congregation"), whose actions were apparently supervised by a representative of the exilarch.

After God told Moses to deliver the Israelites from Egyptian bondage, speaking to him from a burning bush, Moses met his brother Aaron and the two went before the elders, showed them the signs God had told them to display, and convinced them of their mission. In this miniature from the manuscript of a 14th-century Spanish haggadah, the page is divided into four sections, each depicting a different scene. British Museum, London

THE KHAZARS

In this period of glory for the autonomous Jewish community in Babylonia, the religion of the Jews and their way of life attracted many persons. Numerous tribes in the Arabian peninsula and in the various lands of the Near and Middle East adopted Judaism. The most famous of these were the Khazars.

The land of the Khazars in southern Russia extended from the Caspian Sea to the Black Sea, as far as Crimea. The Khazars were a seminomadic pagan tribe whose chief was the kagan. At the beginning of the eighth century, the Khazars became very strong by virtue of their domination of the trade route between the Byzantine Empire and the Far East. For this reason both the Byzantine emperors and the Baghdad caliphs were interested in cultivating the Khazars and in bringing them under their influence, by winning them over to their religion.

Paganism was on its last legs. Kagan Bulan of the Khazars, who reigned over his people in the middle of the eighth century, decided to abandon his pagan faith, but could not make up his mind what new faith to adopt.

There are stories of the efforts of the Moslem caliph and the Christian emperor of Byzantium to win over the kagan to their belief. They sent delegations to him with letters and expensive gifts, accompanied by men learned in their religion, to influence Bulan. The confused kagan ordered a Christian and a Moslem to conduct a debate to establish whose faith was better. The debates lasted for a long time without concrete results.

The kagan noticed that both the Christian and the Moslem debaters referred to the Jewish Torah to support their arguments. The Christian priest admitted that the Jewish religion was superior to that of Mohammed, and the Moslem imam asserted that Judaism was better than Christianity. This being the case, the kagan decided to adopt the faith of the Jews. He summoned a Jewish scholar to teach him the Torah. Bulan then had himself and his officers and soldiers circumcised.

There are reliable documents which prove that the Khazar rulers retained their Jewish faith for about a hundred and fifty years, although the people had the right to observe whatever religion they preferred. The favored position of Judaism in the land of the Khazars remained until the Khazars themselves fell on evil days when they were defeated by the Russian Sviato-slav. This disaster marked the beginning of the Kha-zars' political decline.

THE MASORETES

In Babylonia, meanwhile, a traditional Jewish culture based on the Talmud developed. But Judaism also provided other channels of creative activity, in the form of literature, both sacred and profane. Babylonian Jewry produced outstanding poets. Interest in liter-ature stimulated renewed attention to the Hebrew language and to all the various aspects of the Biblical text. Scholars began devoting their time to the study of Hebrew grammar. In this period, two systems of vocalization were invented to indicate the vowel read-ings in Hebrew (the Hebrew alphabet consists only of consonants). The Tiberian system, with the marks writ-ten below the consonants, is the one generally in use to-day; the Babylonian system, which uses marks above the letters, has survived only in the tradition of the Jews of Yemen. Constant occupation with the Scrip-tures led to the fixing of the final text of the Books of the Bible with regard to their verses, words, and letters as well as the vocalization and cantillation. The Masoretes—the men who preserved the Masorah, the correct tradition regarding the spelling, writing, and reading of the Hebrew Bible—were well-versed in all the variations of the sacred text. The tendency to study the sources of Judaism—the Bible—at the ap-pearance of new religions gave rise to the first great schism in Babylonian Jewry.

THE KARAITES

The political and religious organization of Babylonian Jewry was based on the Talmud. Whatever threatened the supremacy of the Talmud also constituted a menace to the public institutions and the precepts of the Jewish religion. But in the eighth century, some people objected to the authority of the Talmud. They wished to found Judaism only on the Bible (the so-called "Written Law") and rejected the rabbinical inter-

pretations embodied in the Talmud, the so-called "Oral Law." These men made a strong impression on society but, until the sixties of the eighth century, they and their opponents did not come to an open clash.

Although the position of the exilarch was heredi-tary, his appointment required the approval of the heads of the *yeshivot* of Sura and Pumbedita. In 761, the exilarch died without leaving any sons. In ac-cordance with the order of appointments, his nephew Anan ben David should have been named to succeed him, but the latter's anti-Talmudic views displeased the heads of the *yeshivot,* and they chose Hananiah, his younger brother instead. The events which ensued are not entirely clear. In any case, Anan had to leave Babylonia and together with his followers he settled in Palestine, where he continued his dispute with the authorities in Babylonia. His adherents regarded him as the true exilarch and even appointed another man as head of the Sura *yeshiva.*

Anan ben David's disagreement with the heads of the Babylonian *yeshivot* became more intense. Anan assailed them and the Talmud, which he considered the source of these men's power. He argued not only that the Talmudic tradition is not binding but that it distorts the plain text of the Bible by not intepreting it literally, thus leading to sin. The controversy grew and, as their views diverged more and more, each side became more extreme, and fanaticism turned to hatred.

The dispute was concerned with the authority to interpret the Bible, and had nothing to do with reforms to abolish or modify the commandments so as to make everyday life easier. The abolition of the Oral Law demanded by Anan ben David was enough to undermine the authority of the rabbis, but it would have made life harder for the Jews rather than easier. Anan did not acknowledge the calendar which had been in use for generations, but determined each month's beginning separately, in accordance with the testimony of witnesses who followed the phases of the moon as had been the custom in the period of a *nassi* in Palestine. For the members of this sect in Palestine, observing the phases of the moon in the country was no problem, but the practical difficulties for the com-munities in the Diaspora involved in an arrangement of this sort are obvious.

Following the interpretation of the Sadducees, Anan established *Shavu'ot*—the Feast of Weeks (Pentecost) —fifty days after the Sabbath of Passover, differing from the Pharisaic practice which all Jews observe of keeping the festival fifty days after the first day of Passover. A ruling which the people found very dif-ficult to observe was Anan's interpretation of the Scriptural verse, "Ye shall kindle no fire throughout your habitations upon the Sabbath day," to mean that it is forbidden to use a fire for the purpose of il-lumination and heating even if it is started before the Sabbath. Accordingly, the members of his sect were required to extinguish even their Sabbath candles before ushering in the Day of Rest at sundown on

Not only Bibles, but also books of festival prayers which appeared in Germany in the 13th and 14th centuries contained pictures depicting Biblical events. Illustrations for the story in the Book of Esther were added to the prayers and liturgical poems for the Sabbath of Purim in the manuscript of the Leipzig Mahzor. They should be read from left to right—the reverse order of the Hebrew text. Ahasuerus extending his scepter to Esther appears first; then Haman is seen leading the king's horse to Mordecai, who, according to legend, was a teacher of small children. The second page shows Haman's daughter pouring the contents of a chamberpot on her father in the belief that he was Mordecai leading the horse bearing Haman. According to the legend, on realizing that she had brought additional disgrace to her father, she threw herself out of a window and was killed; she is depicted lying dead under the tree on which Haman and his ten sons are hanging. University Library, Leipzig

Friday, and then sit in darkness all evening, and eat cold food the next day. (Orthodox Jews leave a fire or light burning for the entire Sabbath after lighting it before sundown on Friday.)

Anan forbade his adherents to leave their houses on the Sabbath, giving a literal interpretation to the Biblical prohibition, "Let no man go out of his place on the seventh day." He also made the dietary laws more stringent, adding restrictions not found in the Talmud. In the end, the restrictions which Anan added outweighed the few items which he abolished. His interpretations of the Bible were incorporated in his Aramaic work, *Sefer ha-Mitsvot* (The Book of Commandments), of which only a few fragments are extant.

The Babylonian *yeshivot* excommunicated the head of this new sect, who called themselves Karaites (from the word *kara*, "to read", i.e., to read the Biblical text literally). The schism was so great that the excommunication applied not only to Anan himself but to all of his followers; they were completely severed from all contact with Jews and the ban stated that the "breach would never be healed."

The Karaites on their part left no stone unturned absolutely to sever all ties with the orthodox adherents of the Talmud, the Rabbanite Jews. They refrained from intermarrying with the Rabbanites, eating with them, and even coming to their homes on the Sabbath. Strong Karaite communities subsequently developed in Palestine, Babylonia, Egypt, and Spain, and later in the Crimean peninsula.

ECLIPSE OF THE EXILARCH

The Karaite schism brought about a fundamental change in the structure of the Babylonian community's leadership. The exilarch's prestige declined, and his dependence on the heads of the *yeshivot* mounted. A change also occurred in the relations between the *yeshivot*. In the ninth century, the influence of the head of the Pumbedita *yeshiva* exceeded that of the head of the *yeshiva* at Sura, because of Pumbedita's geographical proximity to Baghdad, the new capital of the caliphate. As a consequence, numerous controversies, both for legitimate reasons and for motives not so praiseworthy, broke out. Nevertheless, the eyes of Jews in all the lands of the Diaspora, from Spain on the West to the remote reaches of the East, were still turned to the heads of the *yeshivot* in Sura and Pumbedita. The heads of the *yeshivot* continued their struggle against the seceding Karaites and kept on sending replies to inquiries directed to them. During this period, Rabbi Amram (850–880), the pupil and successor of Gaon Rabbi Natronai, established the form of the prayer book for European Jewry *(The Prayer Book of Gaon Rabbi Amram)* in compliance with a request by the Jews of Spain.

This period is known for its major historical and Talmudic works. In addition to halakhic works and collections of responsa, a number of "word books," dictionaries and commentaries on the Mishna and Talmud, were compiled. The work called *Halakhot Gedolot* (Great Halakhot), a large codification of laws and customs, was apparently the first to fix the number of commandments at 613—365 negative precepts and 248 affirmative ones, to correspond to the number of organs in the human body. This work and similar ones (e.g., *Halakhot Pesukot* or Decided Laws and *Halakhot Kevutsot* or Collected Laws) laid the foundation for Maimonides' monumental compendium of Jewish law, the *Yad ha-Hazakah*. A number of contemporary scholars did not regard these works favorably, "because most of the people heed fragmentary laws and say 'the question and discussion of the Talmud do not interest us.'" The most noteworthy historical works of the time are the early work, *Toledot Tannaim va-Amoraim* (The History of the Tannaim and Amoraim), and the Epistle of Gaon Rabbi Sherira (about the year 1000), which is the most important source for the gaonic period and especially for the history of the Pumbedita *yeshiva*.

SAADYA GAON

The decline of the Gaonate in the tenth century was a dangerous period for Judaism, especially in the centers of Arabic culture. The secular disciplines—mathematics, astronomy, philosophy, etc.—flourished and attracted Jewish scholars who applied themselves to their study with great energy. Many even abandoned their religion or adopted an outlook of philosophical skepticism, and the Karaite movement continued to spread, especially in Egypt.

There was additional danger in the attempt made by Aaron ben Meir of Palestine to put an end to the authority of the Babylonian *yeshivot* in Jewish life and re-establish that of the Palestinian *yeshivot*. In 921, he claimed that the calendar which had been established in Babylonia had been based on a false premise and that the festivals should be observed two days earlier. This statement nearly split Jewry, and for two years the holidays were celebrated on different days in Babylonia and Palestine.

The Babylonian Jews decided to call in a strong man from the outside to stand in the breach. Rabbi Saadya Gaon of Fayum, in upper Egypt, was summoned to head the *yeshiva* at Sura.

This fact was a clear indication of the decline of learning and authority in Babylonia and a sign of the impending end of the hegemony of this country over the Diaspora and the emergence of other centers.

Saadya ben Joseph was born in Egypt in 882 and died in Sura in 942. He was well-versed in the Bible, the Talmud, and contemporary knowledge. He began writing when he was still a young man. His early works include the *Agron*, the first dictionary of the Hebrew language, designed to be of use to poets. At the very start of his career, he began writing strong attacks against the Karaites, and the Karaite leaders regarded him as their most powerful adversary. Thanks to him, traditional Judaism succeeded in overcoming this dangerous schism.

Rabbi Saadya also took up the cudgels against Aaron ben Meir and succeeded with his broad knowledge of astronomy and chronology in proving that he had erred. Saadya thus saved the nation from a further division which could have been no less dangerous than the Karaite schism.

Saadya's appointment as the *gaon* of Sura had been made against the counsel of the advisers of the exilarch David ben Zakkai. He soon quarreled with the exilarch and had to leave Sura for Baghdad, where he lived for four years until a reconciliation was effected and he returned to head the *yeshiva*.

This period was rich in creative activity. Rabbi Saadya did not have to bother with being a leader of the community and was able to devote his time to writing. He wrote commentaries to the Mishna, liturgical poems *(piyyutim)*, and prayers, also compiling a prayer book for the entire year, not unlike the work of Rabbi Amram.

Rabbi Saadya compiled a new reckoning for determining leap year, and wrote a book attacking the tenth-century Masoretic scholar, Aaron ben Asher of Tiberias, who prepared the vocalization and accentuation of the accepted Biblical text. It was at this time that he wrote his two greatest philosophical works, *Emunot ve-De'ot* (Beliefs and Opinions) and a commentary to the *Sefer Yetsira* (Book of Creation), the earliest surviving Jewish cabalistic work.

Emunot ve-De'ot, which was written in Arabic and completed in 934, was designed for the intelligent Jew of the period. Saadya's purpose in writing this work was to refute the disreputable views which had gained currency among the Jews. On the one hand, the number of skeptics denying or close to negating the fundamentals of Judaism had increased and, on the other, there was a large mass of ignorant people steeped in faith. An Arab contemporary of Saadya, Abul-Ilan, wrote, "The Moslem, Jew, Christian, and the Zoroastrian are sunk in madness and folly. There are now two kinds of people in the world, learned persons without belief and believers without learning." Rabbi Saadya was the first to attempt to lay a safe path between these two kinds of people in his endeavors to create a synthesis between Arab-Greek philosophy and Judaism, by constructing a complete philosophic system. Among other subjects, he discussed the nature of faith, the meaning of God, the nature of man and the universe, and the basic doctrines of Judaism. He succeeded by his method of bringing religious precepts and logic closer to one another. Saadya's very free discussion of religious precepts in his *Emunot ve-De'ot* was of tremendous importance for the future development of Judaism.

THE DECLINE OF THE BABYLONIAN CENTER

In the middle of the tenth century, difficult times came to the Jewry of Babylonia. The religious and national fanaticism of the Moslems mounted steadily; fanatics made an attempt on the exilarch's life, and the Jews refrained from appointing a successor for fear of their enemies. This was the end of an ancient office, of which Diaspora Jewry had been proud for many generations.

The prestige of the *yeshivot* also declined. On the death of Rabbi Saadya in 942, the importance of Sura diminished and, in 948, the *yeshiva* was closed, although there was still a considerable number of persons who continued to affect the exalted title of head of the Sura *yeshiva*.

The Pumbedita *yeshiva* continued to exist, but, with the exception of the gaonates of Rabbi Sherira and his son, Rabbi Hai, at the beginning of the eleventh century, Babylonia no longer served as a center, and the torch of learning passed to the West. Rabbi Hai's successor, Rabbi Hezekiah ben David, did not stay in office long, and the Gaonate of Pumbedita also came to an end. The *yeshiva*, which moved to Baghdad, only existed until the Mongol invasion at the end of the thirteenth century. The centers of Judaism were now in North Africa and Moorish Spain.

"It is not good that man should be alone." Illuminations were added not only to sacred works but also to books on Jewish law during the Middle Ages. Evenha-Ezer, *the third of the four works on Jewish law* (Arba'a Turim) *by Jacob ben Asher, which deals with personal and family matters, is represented by a wedding scene. The picture shows a page from the manuscript of* Arba'a Turim *written and illuminated in Mantua in 1436; it depicts a Jewish wedding in Italy in the middle of the 15th century. De Rossi Manuscript, Vatican Library, Rome*

"COURT SLAVES" OF THE EUROPEAN KINGS

"And what shall we eat at this feast?" — "The wild ox and the whale!" According to a Jewish tradition, the meal of the righteous in the hereafter will include the flesh of the female whale (leviathan) and of the wild ox, which God salted for their feast; for, had He not done so, these gigantic beasts would have destroyed the world in their quest for food. In addition to these animals, a huge mythical bird called the ziz or bar-yokhani, which lives forever and symbolizes rebirth, is shown. The righteous themselves, wearing crowns, have the heads of animals both because of the prohibition against picturing the human form and because that is how the righteous men of God, and even the Apostles of Jesus, were generally portrayed in the early Middle Ages. Last page of a Bible manuscript written by Joseph ben Moshe of Ulm, southern Germany, between the years 1236 and 1238. Ambrosian Library, Milan

The early development of the Jewish spiritual center in the West is described by the chronicler Abraham ibn Daud in his work *Sefer ha-Kabbala* (Book of Tradition). There is a story that, after the death of Saadya Gaon, the people of Sura sent four important rabbis to the West to solicit money from wealthy Jews for the Babylonian *yeshiva*. The ship bearing the four men was wrecked in a storm and was apparently flung ashore on the coast of Bari in southern Italy, where the passengers were taken prisoner by the admiral of the fleet of Abd ur-Rahman III, the Caliph of Cordoba. Together with everyone else, the four Jews were sold as slaves. One of them, Rabbi Shemariah bar Elhanan, was sold in Alexandria, Egypt, which he subsequently left for Cairo, where he became the head of a *yeshiva*. Another, Rabbi Hushiel, was redeemed by the Jews of Kairouan in North Africa. The third emissary, Rabbi Moshe, was brought to Cordoba with his son Rabbi Enoch, where they were redeemed by the Jewish community. The fourth, whose name Abraham ibn Daud did not remember, was apparently Rabbi Natan ha-Bavli; he seems to have been brought to Narbonne, in southern France, where Rabbi Judah, the teacher of the eminent Rabbi Gershom ben Judah, was giving instruction. In this way, the four Jewish scholars were scattered to various places where each founded a *yeshiva* and taught the customs of Babylonian Jewry which left a mark on the Jews of the West.

The Jews of Cordoba, headed by Rabbi Hasdai ibn Shaprut, constituted the richest, most powerful Jewish community in Europe, and its prestige was enhanced still more when Rabbi Moshe settled in it. The reason which the Jews of Cordoba gave to the Caliph Abd ur-Rahman for allowing Rabbi Moshe to remain with them is characteristic: they agreed that henceforth they would not be dependent on Babylonia and would stop sending large sums of money to the Eastern Moslem caliphate, the rival of the Spanish caliph.

Three of the communities in which the captives from Babylonia settled — Egypt, North Africa, and Spain — had for centuries been under the rule of the Arabs, who in religious matters were more moderate than the Christian Church in their attitude toward the Jews. The fourth community, in southern France, was also located in a part of Europe in which the oppressive hand of the Pope was not felt. In prosperity and growth, the French communities lagged somewhat behind those in Spain, but in time they became an important center, which even superseded the Spanish one. The Ashkenazic communities of Germany, which had developed much more quickly than the older Italian congregations, furnished teachers to the Jewish populations of Christian Spain.

SPANISH JEWRY

Jews had been living in the Iberian peninsula since Roman times and, in the period after the destruction of Jerusalem, their number reached tens of thousands. Proof of this is the fact that, before the Arab conquest, Granada was called the "City of the Jews." The Jews had been citizens of the country even before the barbaric Visigothic and Germanic tribes had overrun it. Most of the Jewish families were of aristocratic origin and traced their ancestry back to the House of David, proving their claims by means of genealogical documents and seals in their possession.

In the first period after the fall of the Roman Empire, both pagans and Christians regarded the Jews with respect. Under the rule of the Arian Visigoths, the Jews enjoyed an honored social and political status, for the Visigoths had been helped by the Jews in their struggle against the hated Catholics. However, after the Visigoth King Reccared surrendered to Rome and accepted the authority of the Catholic Church at the end of the sixth century, the condition of the Jews deteriorated. From that time until the conquest of Spain by the Moslems in the eighth century, the history of the Jews in that country becomes a series of persecutions calculated to force the Jews to change their religion by means of religious, political, and economic pressure.

In view of this situation, Jews obviously regarded the Arab conquerors as saviors and redeemers. The Arabs, unable to leave large garrisons in the towns they had conquered, relied on the Jews and appointed them to top administrative posts. This happened in Cordoba, Granada, Malaga, Toledo, and other major cities.

At one fell swoop, the Jews of Spain were liberated at the beginning of the eighth century from the dark tyranny of the Catholic Church, and began enjoying the same comfortable circumstances as Jews in other Moslem countries. These conditions made it possible for the Jews of Spain to maintain a dynamic Jewish life, rich in spiritual and material resources and enjoying a respected social status. The period known in Jewish history as the "Golden Age in Spain" had begun.

The Arabs entrusted a considerable part of the country's administration to their loyal allies, the Jews. Under the rule of the conquerors, the Jews enjoyed religious freedom and even internal autonomy. They were also influenced by the relatively advanced cultural atmosphere of the Arab countries, which resulted from the enlightened policies of the Arab rulers.

THE GOLDEN AGE

A number of people, each in his own way, contributed to the creation of this "golden age" in Jewish Spain. All are associated with the name of Hasdai ibn Shaprut. The first, already mentioned, was Rabbi Moshe ben Enoch, the captive from Babylonia, who arrived in Cordoba after numerous adventures. On arriving in the city, he entered a school where the Talmud was being taught and sat down on one of the rear benches. When Rabbi Natan, the local teacher, had some difficulty in explaining an obscure passage, Rabbi Moshe rose and elucidated it simply. Out of respect to the Torah, Rabbi Natan at once addressed the assembled students, "I am no longer your judge in matters of Jewish law. This poor man wearing a sack, this man who was taken prisoner, is my teacher and I am his pupil from today on. You men appoint him religious judge and rabbi in the Cordoba community." And, that very day, Rabbi Moshe became the rabbi of the Cordoban Jews. "The congregation fixed a high salary for him, honored him with expensive clothes, and gave him a magnificent chariot to ride in." That is how a great *yeshiva* came into being in Cordoba.

Another field in which the members of the first generation of the Spanish Golden Age were active was that of the Hebrew language and literature. Menahem ben Saruk (910–970), who was born in Tortosa, Spain, succeeded in advancing the study of Hebrew grammar. He made use of ancient studies in Hebrew and Arabic to compile the first dictionary (*Mahberet*) in which the words were arranged by their roots. Ben Saruk's system was opposed by Dunash ben Labrat, a grammarian who had studied in Baghdad during the time of Saadya Gaon. He published a sarcastic work entitled *Sefer ha-Teshuvot* in which he attempted to prove Menahem's ignorance. A bitter controversy ensued and finally Menahem was put under arrest by Abd ur-Rahman's chamberlain, Hasdai ibn Shaprut. Dunash ben Labrat is credited with having been the first to write Hebrew poetry in Arabic meter.

The shining light of Spanish Jewry of the period was Hasdai ibn Shaprut, who brought it glory by his varied activities. He supported learned men and was famous for his extensive knowledge of the languages and literatures of Moslem and Christian peoples. Well-versed in medicine, he was appointed Abd ur-Rahman's physician and later became the caliphate's finance minister and minister for foreign affairs. Hasdai ibn Shaprut, like many other Jews who followed him in the service of Spain's rulers until the expulsion in 1492, made an important, decisive contribution to the country's rise as a leading international power.

His correspondence with Joseph, King of the Khazars, is very interesting, for it provides numerous details about the history of the kingdom. Hasdai was so excited by the existence of an actual independent Jewish kingdom that he wrote the following letter to Joseph: "If there is a place where there is glory and a kingdom for Israel's exiles and no one lords it over them and rules them... and if I knew that this is true, I would scorn my honor, leave my greatness, abandon my family, and I would go from mountain to hill, across seas and dry land, until I should reach the place where your majesty dwells, in order to gaze upon your power and splendor and the array of your slaves,

The form of the seven-branched candelabrum with its ornamental flowers, almonds, base, and arms was fixed in the Jewish tradition of Spain, Germany, and Italy. In addition to representing rebirth, the candelabrum was also a mystical symbol in Jewish cabala. Illustration shows the candelabrum in the manuscript of an Italian prayer book written and illuminated in Pisa in 1397 for a member of the Danieli family. Sassoon Collection, Letchworth, England

the position of your servants, and the peace of the remnant of Israel.''

Later on Hasdai asks, ''Give an order to inform your servant what tribe you are from and how the kingdom is conducted, how the kings succeed to the royal throne, whether or not from a well-known tribe or a family worthy of ruling, and whether the son of a king rules as was the custom of our ancestors when they lived in their own land. And I would also like to hear the wonder from you, if your people have any knowledge of reckoning the time of the Messianic age, for which we have been waiting for many years, when we shall leave our lands of captivity and exile. And how can I remain silent about the destruction of our magnificent Temple and the fact that we have remained few out of many and we have lost our honor, for they say to us all the time, 'Each and every people has a kingdom, and you do not have the trace of one on the earth.'''

Joseph, the Kagan of the Khazars, wrote Hasdai the following reply: ''You mentioned in your letter that you wish to see me; I, too, am very anxious to look upon your pleasing countenance and the splendor of your wisdom and greatness—I wish I could be in your presence and behold your honored, pleasant, and fine face. You will be a father to me and I shall be your son, and all my people shall be ruled according to your word, and in your ways I shall go and come according to your reliable counsel. . . .''

However, the Khazar kingdom was doomed and, in a few years, it declined and its area was reduced considerably after the defeat by the Russians which forced the Khazars to flee southward to the region of the Caspian Sea and the Crimean peninsula. Hasdai ibn Shaprut remained in Cordoba, serving as an officer and adviser of the caliph. He continued to act as the teacher and leader of his people until the day of his death in 975.

In accordance with medieval tradition, the city of Jerusalem is pictured as a magnificent Gothic structure for which the Jews yearn and to which they raise their arms in adoration. Illustration shows the final page of the Birdhead Haggadah. *Israel Museum, Jerusalem*

JEWISH COURT CULTURE

Hasdai ibn Shaprut was one of the first Jewish leaders who maintained a sort of royal court, with poets, scholars, and writers. But he was not alone in this. He represented an entire social class—the Spanish-Jewish aristocracy. Many Spanish Jews were part of the country's upper social class. They lived among their aristocratic Arab colleagues, sharing their spiritual qualities; for, in contrast to the contemporary Christian aristocrat, who was all too often a vulgar ignoramus, the Arab aristocrat of the period was not only brave but usually also a man of culture devoted to poetry and literature. Thus, Cordoba, Lucena, and Granada became the centers of prosperous Jewish communities with a flourishing material and spiritual life.

SAMUEL HA-NAGID

Another outstanding personality was Samuel ibn Naghdela known as Samuel ha-Nagid ("The Prince"— a title applied in Moslem lands in the Middle Ages to the head of the Jewish community). He was born in Cordoba in 993 and died at Granada in 1056. He was a pupil of Rabbi Moshe ben Enoch, the son and spiritual heir of Enoch the Babylonian, the son of Moshe, the captive who reached Spain from Babylonia in the time of Hasdai ibn Shaprut. He excelled in his knowledge of the Talmud and was well-informed on secular matters. He knew Arabic, Latin, and Berber thoroughly, and mastered philosophy and mathematics. After the conquest of Cordoba by Berber tribes, his family was compelled to move to Granada, where he rose high in the royal court, finally achieving the position of viceroy, in which he served for twenty-eight consecutive years.

Despite his high position at court, Samuel ha-Nagid remained rooted in the Jewish community. He was the head of the Granada community and the Rabbi of the local *yeshiva*. His major works include an introduction to the Talmud, in which he explains the Talmudic method of presentation in simple language and lists the bearers of tradition from the Men of the Great Assembly (*Anshe Knesset ha-Gedola*) in the early period of the Second Temple down through the *tannaim, amoraim, sevoraim,* and *geonim,* to the days of his teacher Moshe ben Enoch. Samuel ha-Nagid wrote a book on Hebrew grammar and a dictionary of the Hebrew language and compiled numerous secular poems and prayers. As viceroy, he was also commander-in-chief of Granada's army. In the midst of wars, Samuel found time to fortify his heart by writing poems and prayers. He was generous to scholars and distinguished people, not only in Spain but also in North Africa, Sicily, Jerusalem, and Baghdad. He also spent huge sums on copying manuscripts of the Bible, Mishna, and Gemara, which he presented to talented scholars and poets. One of the most gifted of these men was the great poet, Solomon ibn Gabirol.

SOLOMON IBN GABIROL

Solomon ibn Gabirol was a contemporary of Samuel ha-Nagid. He was born in Malaga in 1020 and became orphaned in childhood. His youth was spent in loneliness and illness. In his poems, he complains of being feeble, short, skinny, and ugly. His large poetic legacy includes poems of love, laments on his bitter fate, and praises for various patrons. His secular poems are distinguished by a Hebrew language purified of all dross, combined with the diversity of Arabic prosody.

His sacred poems are marvelous expressions of the poet's profound religious fervor. His liturgical poems for the Sabbath and festivals, the High Holy Days, and the fasts were adopted by numerous communities and are preserved not only in the festival prayer books of the Ashkenazic (Western) and Sephardic (Eastern) Jews, but also in the litanies of the Karaites.

Ibn Gabirol also achieved greatness in the field of philosophy. His system served as a guidepost for Christian scholasticism. The work *Fons Vitae* (Source of Life), in which he presents his system, survives only in the Latin translation, which was made a century after his death by a Dominican monk and a converted Jew. It was originally written in Arabic. In the Latin, the author's name was distorted to Avicebron, which for centuries was regarded as that of a Moslem or Christian, until Hebrew selections of the work were discovered about a hundred and fifty years ago.

The eleventh-century writers of ethical works include Bahya ibn Pakuda, author of *Hovot ha-Levovot* (Duties of the Hearts) which stresses the importance of inner devotion in carrying out the commandments.

Of contemporary Hebrew philologists, mention should be made of the grammarian Jonah ibn Janah, the greatest medieval authority on Hebrew philology. His work *Sefer ha-Rikma* (Book of Structure) was translated from Arabic into Hebrew no less than four times. Rabbi David Kimhi, the famous commentator, made use of it to compile his grammar and Biblical dictionary, *Sefer ha-Shorashim* (Book of Roots), and even Gesenius, the father of modern Hebrew grammar, relied on it considerably.

ISAAC BEN JACOB ALFASI

A great luminary in the spiritual life of the Jewry of Spain and North Africa in those days was Rabbi Isaac ben Jacob Alfasi. He was born the year the last of the *geonim* was serving in Babylonia—in 1013—in the city of Fez in North Africa. Celebrated Talmudic scholars in Kairouan were his teachers. At the age of seventy-five, he was forced to flee from his native city after having served there as rabbi for many years. He reached Spain and, after a short stay in Cordoba and Granada, settled in the city of Lucena, where he founded a large, important *yeshiva* and, toward the end of his life, again instituted the method of intensive study then current in Kairouan. He died in 1103 at the age of ninety.

The Jewish cemetery at Worms. In the foreground are the tombs of Rabbi Meir ben Baruch of Rothenburg and Alexander Süsskind Wimpfen. After Rabbi Meir's death in the prison at Ensisheim, Alsace, in 1293, where he had been incarcerated at the order of Emperor Rudolf of Habsburg, the emperor refused to deliver his body to the Jewish community. The body was not released for burial in Worms until 1307, when the wealthy Alexander Wimpfen paid the authorities a large sum of money in ransom for it. At Wimpfen's request, his body was buried beside the grave of his teacher, Meir ben Baruch

Haman and his ten sons hanging from a gallows prepared by Mordecai, as a Jewish artist pictured the scene in accordance with popular tradition in northern Germany in the mid-14th century. Page from the De Castro Bible, *a manuscript of the Bible, the Five Scrolls, and the weekly portion from the Prophets, written by the scribe Nathaniel and vocalized by Levi ben David in January, 1344. Sassoon Collection, Letchworth, England*

Alfasi—named thus for his native city—achieved fame for the work *Sefer ha-Halakhot* (Book of Legal Decisions), which in popular speech is referred to as *Alfas*, after its author. It is one of the first systematic works on the legal discussions of the Talmud. The book follows the order of the Talmudic tractates, but the Talmudic argumentation is arranged in logical order. All the codifiers who came after him, from

Maimonides to Rabbi Joseph Caro, the compiler of the compact legal code known as the *Shulhan Arukh,* based their writings on this immense work, which is today studied in all *yeshivot,* although in the first generations after Alfasi's death there was severe opposition to it.

ITALY

There were Jews in Italy even before the fall of Jerusalem to Pompey in 63 B.C.E., when Aristobolus, King of Judaea, and countless Jewish captives were brought to Rome and forced to march behind Pompey's chariot in his triumphal procession. Four years later, in 59, the greatest of Roman orators, Cicero, delivered an irate address on the power of Roman Jewry, whose quarter was situated near the Aurelian steps, when he spoke in defense of the governor of Asia, Flaccus. The latter was being tried for misappropriating the contributions which the Jews of the district had sent to the Temple in Jerusalem.

The power and numbers of the Jews of Italy gradually increased during the period of Roman rule in Palestine. After the destruction of Jerusalem in 70 C.E., many Jews reached Rome and were sold into slavery. According to one account, there were ninety-seven thousand Jews in the city of Rome itself. Some of the captives were freed and part of them were ransomed by their fellow Jews.

A tenth-century legend tells of five thousand captives whom Titus brought to the district of Otranto in southern Italy. In the port city of Bari, there were Jewish families in the Middle Ages which traced their origin back to the Jerusalem exiles. There is evidence of the uninterrupted existence of Jewish communities in various Italian towns from letters of the Roman classicists, tombstones, Jewish catacombs, and even a number of synagogues with mosaic floors and murals.

After the conquest of Rome by barbarian tribes, the Jews, like the members of all other religious sects, were permitted to maintain their own autonomy, although nominally the ancient laws established by Constantine the Great with reference to the Jews and confirmed by both parts of the Empire were still in force. Theodoric the Ostrogoth, who ruled Italy during the years 487–526, decided that the Jews should continue enjoying the rights they had and maintain their own judges, although he insisted on enforcing the prohibition against the construction of new synagogues and the repair of old ones. However, Theodoric was an Arian, while most of the Christian clergy was Catholic, and for them Judaism was their primary enemy.

Very little is known about the Jews of Italy during the sixth and seventh centuries. In the letters of Pope Gregory the Great (590–604), there are indications that there was a large Jewish population in all of Italy, especially in the southern part of the peninsula, and even in Sicily. Gregory energetically fought against Jewish customs which had taken root in Christianity, but, on the other hand, he also insisted on respecting the Jews' rights.

In the four hundred years between the fifth and ninth centuries, the Jewish centers continued to increase in southern Italy, which was under the rule of the Byzantines. The attitude of the Byzantines toward the Jews in the sixth century was defined by the Justinian Code, which deprived them of their autonomous rights and saddled them with additional obligations. This state of affairs continued until the beginning of the ninth century, when Moslem pressure on Sicily and southern Italy grew. The Jewish center in southern Italy about which most is known is the community of Oria, because of the work of Ahimaz ben Paltiel, *Megillat Yuhasin* (Scroll of Descent), a genealogical study in verse describing in great detail the history of the author's family for ten generations, a period of two hundred years, from the time Amittai ben Shephataiah settled there.

This genealogical scroll reveals an astonishing picture of personalities—statesmen, writers and poets, scholars, magicians and cabalists, mischief makers, miracle workers, and believers in superstitions. The pride of the family was the poet Shephataiah ben Amittai who died in 886. In addition to being a talented poet, Shephataiah also engaged in practical cabala and performed miracles; he was said to have changed the paths of the heavenly bodies. Shephataiah learned practical cabala from Aaron the Babylonian, who was apparently the son of the exilarch Samuel. Arriving in southern Italy about 850, the exilarch's son brought the splendor of Babylonian learning to Europe.

The cultural renaissance in southern Italy from the seventh to the tenth centuries also bore a Hebraic stamp as in Moslem Spain, and this linguistic flowering in the south of Italy may also have resulted from the brief Moslem occupation. The Jews produced an advanced school of religious poetry, and even Hebrew prose works appeared.

One of the most celebrated works among European Jews during the Middle Ages was the popular chronicle of Jewish history called *Josippon*, an imitation of the books on Jewish history by Flavius Josephus. In this work, the author carries forward the history of the Jews to the tenth century. During the same period, a number of important homiletic and halakhic works were also written in Italy. One of the most outstanding Jewish personalities of the time was Sabbatai ben Abraham, known as ''Donnolo the Physician.'' Also a native of Oria in southern Italy, he was the first medical writer in post-classical Europe and a student of the cabala. His writings include a commentary on the mystical work *Sefer Yetsira*.

The principal importance of the Jewish center in southern Italy was the fact that it served to link the Jewish community in Babylonia to that of Europe. Through the communities in Oria, Bari, and Otranto, knowledge of the Talmud and mystical cabala reached Western Europe. The twelfth-century saying (parodying the verse in Isaiah 2), ''For out of Bari shall go forth the law, and the word of the Lord from Otranto,'' may have accurately expressed the importance of the Jewish communities in southern Italy.

Crossing of the Red Sea, from a prayer book which belonged to the pious Rabbi of Riesen, Germany, about 1470. Moses is depicted as a rabbi, with the angel guiding him hovering above a mountainous landscape. The miniature is shown here in triple enlargement. Israel Museum, Jerusalem

The Jewish community on the upper Rhine in southern Germany maintained close ties with the Jews of southern Italy. One of the pupils of the cabalist Aaron of Baghdad was Moshe ben Calonymus (whose Greek-sounding name points to his origin from Byzantine Italy), who first settled in Lucca in northern Italy. Either he or one of his descendants bearing the same name was the emperor's physician and took up his abode at Mainz-on-the-Rhine in the second half of the tenth century. From that time there were members of

וְלֹא עָשָׂה בָּהֶם
שְׁפָטִים בֵּאלֹהֵיהֶם
אִלּוּ עָשָׂה בָהֶם
שְׁפָטִים
וְלֹא עָשָׂה
בֵאלֹהֵיהֶם בֵּאלֹהֵיהֶם
אִלּוּ עָשָׂה
בֵאלֹהֵיהֶם
וְלֹא הָרַג
בְּכוֹרֵיהֶם בֵּאלֹהֵיהֶם
אִלּוּ הָרַג
בְּכוֹרֵיהֶם
קְרִיעַת יָם

"And Moses stretched out his hand over the sea....But the children of Israel walked upon dry land in the midst of the sea." (Exodus 14.) Page from the Birdhead Haggadah *depicts Moses and the children of Israel during their flight from the Egyptians. Israel Museum, Jerusalem*

the Calonymus family in the Rhineland. Moshe ben Calonymus wrote liturgical poetry, besides being a Talmudic scholar and cabalist who spread Jewish learning in southern Germany.

FRANCE

The Jews first reached Gaul long before the destruction of the Roman Empire. The Jews of Gaul, like those of Spain and Italy, enjoyed full civil rights, and their condition did not become worse during the early period of conquest. The Jews engaged in trade, crafts, and medicine. There were even landowners among them. They bore arms, had non-Jewish names in addition to their Jewish ones, and lived in peace and unity with their Gentile neighbors.

The condition of the Jews did not worsen when Clovis, King of the Franks, was converted from Arianism to Catholicism. The king knew how to curb the Church in his kingdom, and his sons who succeeded him were not dependent on foreign elements as were the Visigoth rulers in Spain.

In time, however, hatred of the Jews also spread through the Frankish kingdom, and laws were published forbidding social contact between Jews and Christians. The Jews were harassed in various ways, but the persecution was generally of a local nature, and most of the laws against them were not enforced.

After Charlemagne seized power, he encouraged the Jews in his kingdom and helped them, as a means of enhancing the prestige of his domains culturally and economically. Since the Jews were the principal merchants of the Middle Ages, he believed they would be very useful in this respect. Thanks to this attitude, the number of Jews increased in the areas later to become France and Germany. From the tenth century on, there is ample evidence of Jewish communities in Magdeburg, Merseburg, and Ratisbon (Regensburg).

THE REIGN OF LOUIS THE PIOUS

Charlemagne's son Louis the Pious followed in his father's footsteps. He took the Jews under his protection and defended them against both the plundering barons and the fanatical clergy. The Jews were permitted to dwell throughout his kingdom, hire non-Jewish laborers, and even keep non-Jewish slaves, despite the fact that Church Councils had repeatedly prohibited such practices. The regular market day was even transferred from Saturday to Sunday to make it easier for the Jews. Jews were exempted from the lash and from the barbaric methods of proving innocence by ordeal. They were even granted autonomy in judicial matters. The Jews were permitted to engage in commerce and the crafts without hindrance, and they became tax farmers despite the fact that this explicitly contradicted the laws of the Church. The emperor also appointed a special official to protect Jewish rights from the nobility and clergy.

Louis the Pious' attitude can be explained by the fact that he was interested in developing commerce. But he helped not only merchants but Jews in general, because of a personal reason — his second wife, whom

(Upper right) "Every son that is born ye shall cast into the river," says this page from the Prayer book of the Rabbi of Riesin, *compiled in Germany in the late 15th century. The illuminations show strong Italian influence*
(Lower left) Opening page of Passover liturgical poems from the same prayer book. Israel Museum, Jerusalem
The other two pictures are from prayer books written in northern Italy at the end of the 15th century. (Upper left) A page devoted to the Sukkot *(Tabernacles) festival; (lower right) one that deals with marriage. Respectively, Sassoon Collection, Letchworth, England, and Jews' College, London*

Jews kneeling in prayer and Isaac on the sacrifical altar. Drawing birds' beaks and animals' ears on the human figures was one of the ways to avoid portraying human beings which was widespread in medieval Germany. Because of the prominent beaks, the name Bird-head Haggadah *was given to the* Jerusalem Haggadah *written by a scribe called Menahem and illuminated in southern Germany in about 1300. Israel Museum, Jerusalem*

services and greatly enjoyed the rabbis' sermons — evidence of the fact that the rabbis preached in the vernacular.

As the admirers of the Jews increased so did their enemies, headed by Agobard, bishop of Lyons, who wished to reduce them to their previous inferior status.

At the death of Louis the Pious, his successor, Charles the Bald, continued his father's tradition and protected the Jews. However, his weakness and the anarchy which prevailed at the time instilled a hope among the enemies of the Jews in the Church, headed by the bishop Amulo, that they could increase their influence over the king and persuade him to persecute the Jews. But both Charles and his successors managed to withstand the pressure of the Church and took the Jews under their protection.

"COURT SERFS"

As the power of the kings declined, that of the Church grew, and the condition of the Jews deteriorated in countries dominated by the Catholic Church. Now the fate of the Jews was dependent on the wishes of each individual prince. While in one district in southern France the Jews were entitled to be landowners and even officials of the king, their status somewhere else was inferior to that of the serfs. The only function which the advanced feudal system left to the Jews was that of merchants and usurers, and, even as such, they could only exist under the king's protection — or, as they were called for years, *servi camerae regis* (serfs of the royal chamber). The "court serfs" financed the struggles of the emperors against their various rivals. The history of this institution was, more than that of any other group, a function of the jockeying for power among the diverse elements in general Christian society.

As a rule, the king protected the Jews — in exchange for certain benefits of course. However, when the monarch came under the influence or authority of Church leaders, he would occasionally issue anti-Jewish edicts and even orders for their expulsion. Sometimes it appeared that these orders were issued as a direct means of squeezing money out of the Jews without any consideration for the long-range consequences of such actions.

Accordingly, the fate of European Jewry in general, and of the Jews of Germany in particular, was dependent on shifts in the political patterns as a whole. Jewish history was henceforth a long concatenation of repeated expulsions alternating with the granting of privileges and their violation and annulment, accompanied by attacks against life and property, massacres, and migration. Jewish fellow-feeling developed apace in those days, so that, when a community was expelled from one principality, it could find refuge nearby. However, as a consequence of such conditions, Jews were hated not only for having a different religion but also for being strangers. In addition, the Jew was

he loved very much, was an admirer of Judaism. She brought a love of Judaism and all things Jewish to the court. In her time, Christian intellectuals read the writings of the Jews Josephus and Philo more than they did the works of the Church Fathers. Some of them even asked rabbis to bless them and pray for them. Jews frequented the royal court and associated with the king and his intimates.

Thus, in practice, the various ecclesiastical decisions against Jews were not enforced, although they had not been abolished. The Jews were again permitted to build new synagogues, for the first time since the last Roman emperors. Many Christians attended synagogue hated for his occupations—for being a tax collector, a collector of customs, or a usurer.

Despite all these limitations and difficulties, European Jewry succeeded in establishing an organized communal life with permanent institutions and even in creating enduring spiritual achievements.

RABBI GERSHOM BEN JUDAH, "LIGHT OF THE EXILE"

The center of Jewish learning in southern France was at Narbonne, where a *yeshiva* had been in existence since before Charlemagne's reign, when Rabbi Machir had come there from Babylonia. Prominent scholars who studied at the Narbonne *yeshiva* included Rabbi Natan ha-Bavli and his pupil Judah ben Meir Leontin. The latter's most celebrated pupil was Rabbi Gershom ben Judah, called *Me'or ha-Gola* ("Light of the Exile").

Rabbi Gershom (960–1028) was born in Metz, near the French border, but moved to Mainz, Germany, where he served as rabbi and founded a *yeshiva* which attracted many students from Germany, France, Italy, and even the Slavic lands. The teacher of the celebrated scholar Rashi was one of his pupils.

Rabbi Gershom compiled commentaries on the Talmud and studies on the Masora and Biblical exegesis, but his chief claim to greatness was his leadership. His regulations, which the communities of Speyer, Worms, and Mainz adopted, to be followed by all the Jewish communities in Europe, determined the form of Jewish society in the towns of the Continent throughout the Middle Ages and even afterwards.

These regulations include a ban on polygamy, and the obligation to secure the wife's consent for a divorce. In the domain of social relations, Rabbi Gershom established that a Jew might interrupt the synagogue service if he had a grievance. He also forbade a Jew to rent from a Gentile a house from which another Jew had previously been illegally evicted. An extremely publicized regulation was the one forbidding a person carrying a sealed letter for delivery to open and read it. Anyone violating these regulations would be excommunicated. Rabbi Gershom also protected the dignity of the Jews who had adopted Christianity during the expulsion edict of 1012 and had penitently returned to Judaism when conditions improved. The rabbi forbade all offensive remarks against the penitents and even threatened those making them with excommunication.

RASHI (RABBI SOLOMON YITZHAKI)

French Jews enjoyed a quieter and happier life than their fellows across the Rhine. The year the last *gaon* in Sura died, a great Western Jewish luminary came into the world at Troyes in Champagne—Solomon ben Isaac (Yitzhak) (1040–1105)—known by the name of Rashi (acronym for Rabbi Solomon Yitzhaki). In his

Abraham, Isaac, and Jacob at the gates of paradise. Medieval Jewish tradition pictured paradise as a real place in which the nation's righteous and holy men lived happily and well, wearing crowns and praising the Lord's deeds along with the angels. The artist of the Birdhead Haggadah shows paradise as being the home of angels, coming and going by the light of the sun and the moon, to which the righteous are being led by a special angel. Israel Museum, Jerusalem

youth Rashi studied at the *yeshiva* in Worms. After his marriage, he returned to his native city, where he founded a *yeshiva*. Like other French Jews in his time, he apparently lived from farming and owned an estate on which he grew grain, as well as vineyards. This fact reflects the relatively favorable position of the Jewish community.

Rashi was the Jewish commentator of all time. His commentary on the Bible was accepted with such fervor that, to this day, it is the most popular one. Rashi's commentary is a concise explanation of the plain text with an admixture of homiletic ideas. His presentation is both clear and profound. The importance of his commentary is shown by the fact that this

The bravery of Samson, who was as courageous as a lion, apparently symbolizes the strength of the worshiper here. Miniature from Leipzig Mahzor

was the first Hebrew work to be printed (1475). Although the homiletics undoubtedly add to the pleasure of the person using the commentary, Rashi's grandson, Rabbi Samuel ben Meir, testifies how much his grandfather valued a simple interpretation of the text above any other. "And our teacher, Rabbi Solomon, my mother's father, the illuminator of the eyes of the exiles, who interpreted the Torah, Prophets, and Hagiographa, paid heed to explain the simple text of the Bible; and I, too, Samuel ben Meir, his grandson, may the soul of a righteous man be blessed, disputed with him, and he admitted to me that, if he had had time, he would have had to make additional commentaries as other interpretations of the text daily became clear."

Rashi's commentary on the Talmud is a wonderful, tremendous work, as is his commentary on the Bible. First, he examined the reliability of the text before him, comparing it with various manuscripts and commentaries. His commentary on the Talmud is distinguished for its succinctness and clarity. His greatness lies in his perception of the difficulties and his ability to clarify them very briefly. A single line in his commentary is sometimes enough to shed light on the most abstruse matter. His commentary is printed beside the text in all editions of the Talmud.

Rashi transformed France into the center of Talmudic study in Europe in his time and for generations to come.

END OF A PERIOD

At the end of the tenth century, two giants in the field of Jewish thought had thus appeared — Rashi in France and Rabbi Alfasi in North Africa and Spain. These two outstanding scholars were active and created their great works before the waves of disaster, which were to come to Europe at the end of Rashi's lifetime, broke.

The Jews were a foreign element in medieval Europe — an object of envy and animosity on the part of all the population and of unceasing attempts to compel them to abandon their faith. The kings made use of the Jews as a means of overcoming their rivals and as a permanent source of money. The Jews also supplied knowledge to the kings, which even leaders of the Church did not have, since they knew how to read and write in many languages and also how to conduct transactions with non-European nations.

Consequently, the Jews served as a scapegoat during periods of rapid social and economic changes; and the kings, just like the Church, were ready to sacrifice them on the altar of the mob's wrath. The political and religious changes which gave rise to the Crusades transformed the lives of the peaceful Jews into a hell from which there was no escape.

JEWISH ART IN THE MIDDLE AGES

Jewish art in the Middle Ages was outstanding in only two spheres — the illumination of manuscripts and the ornamentation of synagogues. In these two fields, the Jews generally conformed to local styles. If there happened to be a specific Jewish element in the painting or decoration of Jewish artistic works, it was chiefly in the domain of the subject matter, the method of its presentation, or in special Jewish motifs and symbols. The illumination of Jewish manuscripts, like the construction of synagogues, became most traditional as Jewish communities in Europe crystallized. At the end of the thirteenth century, this tradition became a permanent formula, from which hardly anyone ever deviated during the Middle Ages.

The special Jewish symbols, such as the seven-branched candelabrum and its appurtenances, the Ark of the Covenant, or the entrance to the Temple hall which had developed and crystallized in ancient times, and the application of which had continued in synagogue art throughout the Byzantine period as well, were transferred in a somewhat different form to the Jewish world under Arab domination. The Rabbanite and Karaite Bibles, which were copied in Moslem Palestine and Egypt in the ninth to the eleventh centuries, added various parts of the Sanctuary or the Temple to the basic symbol of the candelabrum, and sometimes even transformed the entire structure into an actual design of the Temple. The style of painting in these Bibles is extremely ornamental and bears the influence of local Moslem art, which forbade painting images. Even the pictures of the candelabrum and other items of the Sanctuary appear very much stylized and almost abstract, sometimes making exact identification difficult.

There is no exact information about how these Bibles reached Europe from the East, but, from the beginning of the thirteenth century, parts of the Sanctuary and the Temple appear as opening pages to Spanish Bibles, sometimes as a collection of articles, and occasionally in the general plan of the Temple. Another element shared by tenth-century Egyptian Bibles and Spanish Bibles is the ornamental page with carpet-like decoration which at first constituted a kind of binding page, and passed in this form to medieval Christian art as well.

In the thirteenth century, illustrations of Biblical events also began appearing in Hebrew Bibles in manuscript, at first in southern Germany and in the upper and central Rhine region and, later, in France, Spain, and Italy as well. In Bibles from Germany, isolated pictures appear at the beginning and at the end of the book; it was not until later, during the thirteenth century, that illustrations of events were inserted in the margins beside the text. In addition, pictures of Biblical subjects also appear in manuscripts of *mahzorim* (festival prayer books) and in Passover *haggadot* (text of the *seder* service for the home ceremony) from Germany.

From the end of the thirteenth century, paintings of holiday customs and ceremonies begin to appear in *mahzorim* and in *haggadot*. The *Leipzig Mahzor*, for example, contains the picture of a Jew holding a *lulav* (palm branch), an *arava* (willow branch), and an *ethrog* (citron), next to the prayer for Sukkot (Tabernacles), and women cleansing dishes before Passover to make them ritually pure. In the South German *Birdhead Haggadah*, which dates from about 1300, there are pictures of a family sitting down to the ritual Passover meal and the perforating of *matsot* (unleavened bread), beside a representation of the Jews departing from Egypt and crossing the Red Sea which had opened to let them pass.

The question of the origin of these Biblical pictures, which has been claiming the attention of art historians, has not yet been solved. One view holds that the Jewish artists borrowed the series of pictures from the surrounding Christian world in which they lived and added to them elements and motifs from Jewish legends and customs. Other historians believe that the existence of illustrations of Jewish legends in Biblical paintings of the thirteenth and fourteenth centuries proves that a tradition of Jewish art dating back to antiquity existed throughout the Middle Ages. Obviously, until illuminated Hebrew manuscripts from ancient times and the early Middle Ages are found, this question will not be settled.

FOUR

HUNDRED

YEARS

OF HORROR

Barcelona synagogue. The cantor wearing a tallith *(prayer shawl) and standing on a raised, roofed platform* (bima) *is seen lifting a Torah scroll in its case. Four Jews with their children (one of them a girl) are standing in prayer. Glass Moslem-style lamps preserved in the Jewish tradition of Christian Spain are suspended from the ceiling. Opening plate from manuscript of Spanish Passover* haggadah *illustrated in Barcelona in the 14th century. British Museum, London*

Europe at the end of the eleventh century was seething with horrifying rumors of the desecration of the Holy Sepulcher by Moslems who had taken Jerusalem in 1071. Fanciful tales were spread of the torture of Christians in the Holy Land, in which Jews were also said to have participated. It is difficult to determine the source of these rumors. Someone may have been interested in disseminating these tales, with their venomous overtones, for the purpose of stirring up the feelings of European Christians and fanning a desire for vengeance. The call of Pope Urban II to redeem the Holy Sepulcher, which he issued at the Council of Piacenza and later at Clermont, aroused a great deal of enthusiasm. One year later, in 1096, large masses of men gathered under the flag of the cross. A minority of these people believed that this was a way to secure the remission of their sins, but most of the assembled Christians regarded the Crusade as an escape from economic servitude, heavy taxes, and degrading poverty. The knights among those who responded to the summons considered the Crusade an opportunity for finding adventure, glory, and personal wealth.

THE FIRST CRUSADE

The throngs who had abandoned their homes and families were seized with a wild enthusiasm, which the mobs accompanying them fanned to a white heat. Ignorant commanders undermined the organization, which was defective anyway, and a lack of discipline permeated the entire movement. Excitement bordering

on ecstasy drove the unruly hordes to attack peaceful citizens they happened to encounter in the villages and towns, and they robbed and plundered whomever and whatever they could.

However, whereas the Christian population suffered only from the violence of greedy men and bullies, fanatical priests stirred up the wild mobs to kill Jews. Describing the Crusader hosts as being "as numerous as locusts," a Jewish chronicler writes, "And when they passed through towns in which Jews were dwelling they said to one another, 'Behold we are going to avenge ourselves against the Ishmaelites, and here there are Jews dwelling in our midst whose fathers killed and crucified Jesus. Let us settle accounts with them first and utterly destroy them and obliterate the name of Israel, or let them be like us and acknowledge Jesus as the Messiah.'"

Jewish communities in the Rhine region were stricken with panic. The Jewish leaders issued a call for fasting and prayer. Rabbi Calonymus ben Meshullam, head of the Mainz community, sent an urgent letter to

114

Henry IV to call his attention to the danger threatening the Jews. However, the hopes which the Jews had pinned on his letter to Henry failed to materialize. Christian mobs attacked the Jews of Metz and killed twenty-two of them. In Speyer, Bishop Johannes succeeded in quieting the rioters after they had slain eleven Jews. At Worms, the Jews believed the assurances of their Christian neighbors that they would protect them, and locked themselves in their houses. However, the local Christians did not lift a finger when the bearers of the cross broke into the town and brutally massacred all the Jewish inhabitants. "They smashed steps, demolished houses, plundered and robbed and took the Torah scroll and trampled it in mud and tore it and burnt it," says a chronicle.

Many Jews were killed proclaiming the unity of God and refusing to abandon their faith, and the rest found refuge in the bishop's palace. However, the wild mobs broke into this building, too. While they were attempting to overrun the palace, the representatives of the Jews decided to take their own lives and not meet their deaths by Christian swords. "And a man slew his brother and his relatives and his wife and children, and men killed their affianced, and compassionate women their only children. And all devotedly accepted the fate decreed by Heaven and, reconciling themselves to the wishes of their Maker, they shouted, 'Hear O Israel, the Lord is our God, the Lord is One.'"

The same horror was repeated at Mainz. The Jews huddled together in the palace of the bishop, who had promised to protect them after receiving a large sum of money. However, he did not keep his promise. The surrounded Jews headed by Rabbi Calonymus went out to defend themselves and, when the mob got the upper hand, a suicidal impulse seized them and men and women slaughtered one another, shouting, "Look down and see, our God, what we are doing to sanctify Your great Name."

The Jewish victims in the Rhineland during the First Crusade numbered about twelve thousand. After the Crusaders had left for the Holy Land, Henry IV permitted the Jews who had forcibly been baptized to return to Judaism (1097). The Jews went back to their daily affairs, despite the impressions which the terrible disaster that had befallen them had carved deep in their souls.

Under the influence of the Crusades, a slow revolution in the economic life became apparent and the demand for credit mounted. The Jews who had been driven out of the different branches of commerce and the economic structure had no alternative but to turn to moneylending. Usury, which had been forbidden to Christians by the Church, afforded Jews an opportunity to accumulate much capital. Everyone needed them, from the farmers who had to pay the landlords higher rental fees to the members of the nobility, the ruling classes, and the clergy. The word "Jew" now became a synonym for usurer. In Spanish, the word *judaizar* ("to Judaize") came to mean to lend money at usurious rates of interest. Hatred of the Jew "sucking the blood of the believers" grew.

BLOOD LIBEL AT BLOIS

Pope Eugenius III knew exactly how to take advantage of the hate of the Jews to secure his ends. In a special bull, he announced that those who joined the Second Crusade to save the Kingdom of Jerusalem would not have to pay back any debts they owed to Jews. The monk Peter the Venerable, one of the leading advocates of the new Crusade, went even further. He tried to persuade Louis VII of France, who headed the Second Crusade, to confiscate Jewish property acquired from Christians. On the other hand, Bernard of Clairvaux adopted a sympathetic attitude to Jews and issued a call to refrain from persecuting them or confiscating their possessions. Conrad III of Germany promised the Jews to take them under his protection. But none of these measures helped. Fanatical monks, headed by a certain Rudolf, traveled from one town to another stirring up hatred and encouraging the people to "avenge the crucifixion of Jesus" by killing those "who had crucified Him"—the Jews. Attempts by Church leaders to stop Rudolf's agitation did not avail. The mob began rioting, and the Crusade started with the murdering of Jews. On the discovery of the body of a dead Christian at Nürzburg, the Jews were accused of killing him and many were killed. At Carentan, France, the Jews made an effort to defend themselves, but their Christian enemies overcame them and killed them. At Ramerupt, the rabbinical authority Jacob ben Meir Tam was nearly killed, but was saved at the intervention of a government official.

Almost twenty years later, in 1171, a ritual-murder charge was raised in the French city of Blois. A servant of the mayor told his master of having seen a Jew throwing a little boy into the river. On hearing this, the district governor ordered the arrest of every Jew in town. After conducting a thorough investigation, the governor convinced himself that the Jews were blameless, and was inclined to release them for a sum of money. However, one of the local priests dissuaded him. The prison was set on fire after the Jews had refused to accept baptism. This event had a shocking effect on the Jews of France, and Jacob ben Meir Tam established the twentieth day of the Hebrew month of Sivan as a fast day to commemorate the martyrs of this blood libel. King Louis VII, to whom the Jewish community of Paris presented a complaint concerning the blood libel at Blois, promised a Jewish delegation to protect the lives and property of their people.

Philip Augustus was not as tolerant toward the Jews as his father, Louis VII. From childhood he had been under the influence of teachers and friends who were steeped in a deep hatred of Jews. They incited the king to confiscate the property of the Jews, and the monarch, who needed much money to rehabilitate the kingdom, was not averse to such a plan, which he carried out with acts of violence. Several days after ascending the throne, he arrested the wealthy Jews of Paris and confiscated their property and clothing. They were not released until they paid vast sums into the royal treasury. Several months later, Philip Augus-

The exact form of the Temple candelabrum with its tubes, cups, and floral designs was traditionally painted in the opening pages of the manuscripts of Bibles from Spain. The tongs and the snuffers of the candelabrum hang from it. To the right there is a traditional jug of wine, and at left two trees representing the Mount of Olives, an additional symbol of national, Messianic hope alluding to the resurrection of the dead. Manuscript from northern Spain, end of 13th century. National Library, Paris

tus canceled all debts which Christians owed Jews, and three months afterward the king issued an order expelling all Jews from their homes in the Île-de-France region, thus enabling the royal treasury to take over all the real estate left behind by the Jews banished from the area of Paris. Sixteen years later, he permitted them to return, because the royal treasury missed the taxes paid by the Jews.

The condition of the Jews in southern France in the twelfth century was better than that of Jews in the northern part of the country. These Jews engaged in farming and did not have to make a living from moneylending. They were appointed to responsible positions in the municipal governments, even becoming judges and notaries. Here, the Jews could concentrate on their religious life, and they established large *yeshivot*, headed by the leading French Jews of the period.

The Crusades drove the Jewish communities deep within themselves and impelled them as much as possible to avoid contact with the Christian world. The Jewish world began to regard the cross as a symbol of horror and cruelty in the name of which attempts were made to force the Jew to abandon his religion by abominable means never before resorted to. Now the Jews began to congregate in separate quarters far from areas inhabited by Christians, and Jewish communities began developing internal self-government—either new institutions were established or existing ones were given new administrative functions. The communities of northern France and the Rhineland took the initiative in unifying the self-governments of Jewish communities scattered across Europe. The rabbis, who assembled for this purpose in Troyes under the leadership of Jacob ben Meir Tam, discussed introducing the general regulations of various communities and defined the rights and obligations of religious ministrants and the judges of religious courts. They also considered establishing their authority to introduce temporary regulations in times of trouble. It was decided that Jews should not go to non-Jewish courts, but must appear before a Jewish tribunal. Jews were also forbidden to solicit the assistance of the Gentile authorities in efforts to secure posts in the Jewish community.

THE TOSAPHISTS

Study of the Talmud occupied the center of the community's spiritual life. Rashi's illustrious achievements determined Jewish thought for generations to come. The men who continued his work came from his household; they were the Tosaphists Samuel ben Meir and his brother Jacob ben Meir, known as Tam. Samuel completed Rashi's commentary on the Talmud, especially on the tractates *Baba Bathra* and *Pesahim*. He also wrote a simple commentary on the text of the Pentateuch, in contrast to his grandfather's commentary, which was homiletic. Jacob ben Meir was one of the greatest of the Tosaphists, the French and German scholars of the twelfth to fourteenth centuries who supplemented Rashi's Talmud commentary. He was a wealthy man with influence at the royal court, versed in worldly affairs as well as in Jewish learning. Rabbi Isaac ben Sheshet, one of the great Spanish codifiers who lived about one hundred and fifty years after him, said of Jacob ben Meir that "in Talmudic argumentation there has been no one like him since the redaction of the Talmud." Scholars from many countries addressed their inquiries to him. In his responsa he tended to leniency because of the economic situation. He was lenient in matters pertaining to forbidden foods, permitting the consumption of cheese made by Gentiles, as well as the trade in wine purchased from the vineyards of non-Jews. His novellae and responsa were collected in his work *Sefer ha-Yashar*, which was designed to settle textual discrepancies in the Talmud and determine the original version, which had been distorted by various proofreaders. The book was not preserved in its original form, but in a version adapted by his pupils, who added various parts.

Jacob ben Meir was the first Jewish scholar in France to display interest in the scholarly and literary achievements of Spanish Jewry. In his *Sefer ha-Hakhra'a* (Book of Decision), he endeavored to prove that, in the dispute between Menahem ben Saruk and Dunash ben Labrat, the former was generally right. He also compiled commentaries on the Bible, liturgical poems, and *selihot* (penitential prayers); he was firm in matters of Jewish law. In the matter concerning the order of the verses in the phylacteries, he opposed Rashi's judgment; however, his view was generally not accepted.

Rabbi Isaac ben Samuel of Dampierre, also known as Isaac *ha-Zaken* (i.e., the Elder), was a nephew of Samuel and Jacob ben Meir. On the death of the latter, he assumed leadership of the Tosaphists. There is a story that he had sixty pupils, each of whom knew a tractate of the Talmud by heart. His addenda were not preserved in the original; his pupils inserted them into their own works. His responsa also show consideration for contemporary conditions.

Study of the Talmud was at the time based on subtle analysis and developed into argumentation for its own sake. It lacked the power of generalization until the appearance of Maimonides, a native of Cordoba, in Spain, who sought a way out of the spiritual confusion of generations. Dry study might be enough to satisfy the mind of a person with sharp wits, but it could not encourage the individual to hold out against sufferings. For this, fervent faith was necessary. Jewish sages of the twelfth century attempted to inspire this faith by compiling an ethical literature designed for the masses and reflecting their way of life. One of the most popular books of this sort for the moral uplift of the reader was *Sefer Hasidim* (Book of the Pious).

SEFER HASIDIM

Sefer Hasidim is the result of the efforts of three generations, from the middle of the twelfth century to the middle of the thirteenth. Two of its authors were members of the same family, Rabbi Samuel Hasid and his son Judah. Rabbi Samuel was in his childhood taken from Mainz to Speyer, where he founded a *yeshiva* devoted chiefly to the study of homiletics. "There are in my generation men learned in the Torah and in all kinds of wisdom and deeds, and more God-fearing than I," Rabbi Samuel said, "but in their abundant wisdom, they endlessly dispute over the Talmud." Fifteen years after his death, his son, Rabbi Judah Hasid, left for Regensburg, where he founded a large *yeshiva*. Like his father, he placed not learning but faith, prayer, deeds of piety, and moral integrity at the center of Judaism, and, like his father, he too aspired to achieve such integrity in his personal life. Rabbi Judah compiled the principal part of the work,

A baker baking matsot *(plural of* matsa, *unleavened bread) for Passover is a traditional figure in most* haggadot *of both Spanish and German origin. Picture also shows women carrying trays of matsot to be slid into the oven. Miniature from Spanish Passover* haggadah *from the beginning of 14th century. British Museum, London*

and his pupil, Rabbi Eleazer ben Judah of Worms, the author of *Sefer ha-Rokeah* (Book of the Spice-Dealer), completed the work begun by father and son.

Sefer Hasidim is a strange conglomeration of moral aphorisms, superstitions, common sense, and stories about demons and magicians. The work is permeated by a general atmosphere of ardent Judaism based on a love of the Creator and the Torah and painfully concerned with the fate of the people. It demands a moral attitude toward Gentiles but also enjoins Jews to isolate themselves completely from the non-Jewish world.

The writer advocates fear of God but not asceticism, and fights pride. Humbleness and prayer are of supreme importance, and inner devotion is a great achievement.

The following is one of the stories in the book: "A cowherd did not know how to pray. The only prayer he knew was to say to God every day, 'Lord of the universe, you must know that if you had livestock and would give them to me to watch, I would tend them for you for nothing, even though I watch everyone's herd for payment.' One day a learned man passed the cowherd and, hearing his prayer, said to him, 'This is sacrilege.' The cowherd told him, 'I don't know any other prayer.' The scholar thereupon taught him the order of prayer. After he left, the cowherd forgot the prayers. At night, the scholar was told in a dream, 'You have made me lose a man in the hereafter.' The scholar returned to the cowherd and asked him, 'What happened?' The man replied, 'I do not pray at all. You told me that I must not say to God, "I'll tend your cows for nothing," and whatever you taught me, I have forgotten.' The scholar then said to him, 'From now on say whatever you said before.'" From this anecdote, *Sefer Hasidim* concludes that inner devotion is the most important element of religion.

The poetry of the Jews of France and Germany during the twelfth century consists of *kinot* (lamentations) and *selihot* (penitential prayers). The poets wrote about the destruction of Jerusalem and the communities of Speyer, Worms, and Metz, the massacres in Mainz, and the blood libel at Blois. One of the greatest liturgical poets of the period was Ephraim ben Jacob of Bonn. In his work *Sefer Zekhira* (Book of Remembrance) and in his *kinot*, he lamented the bitter fate of the Jews during the Second Crusade. He also compiled liturgical poems for the holidays and festivals. His commentaries on liturgical poems survived in manuscript and discuss various traditions concerning ancient liturgical poets, poems, and prayer customs. The story about Amnon of Mainz, author of the prayer *U-Netanneh Tokef*... ("And we shall proclaim the greatness of the day's sanctity"—recited on the New Year and the Day of Atonement), is attributed to him. According to tradition, Rabbi Amnon was one of the great men of his generation; he was of a good family, wealthy, of fine physique, and handsome. The bishop of Mainz and his officials tried to persuade him to adopt Christianity, but he refused. To put them off, he asked for three days to think the matter over, but then was very sorry that he had not given them a negative reply immediately. When the bishop sent for him on the third day, he refused to come and had to be taken by force. Asked why he had not kept his promise and come on time, he replied, "I shall decide my own fate; the tongue which spoke and lied should be cut out" (he made this request for not having said no at once).

The bishop replied, "Not that. I shall not cut the tongue out, for it spoke well, but the feet, which did not appear on the time you had designated; and I shall scourge the rest of the body." Rabbi Amnon was sent home in horrible agony, with his legs cut off. On the New Year, which came several days later, he was carried to the synagogue. When the time came for the cantor to chant the prayer of sanctification (*kedusha*), Rabbi Amnon requested permission to sanctify God's name, and recited the *U-Netanneh Tokef* prayer on the personal fate of the individual in the year to come. Rabbi Calonymus ben Meshullam later introduced this prayer throughout the Jewish communities of the Diaspora.

ENGLISH JEWRY IN THE TWELFTH CENTURY

In the final years of the twelfth century, even before the First Crusade, Jewish communities appeared in England. The beginning of mass Jewish settlement occurred at the time of the Norman conquest (1066). Social and economic conditions in England attracted merchants and moneylenders. The country badly needed credit and cash after William the Conqueror had ordered that taxes be paid in money and not in grain. The transition from a natural economy to a money economy could not have succeeded without the Jews. Many Jews continued immigrating to England after the shocks which had struck the Jewish communities on the Continent during the First Crusade. Jews settled in London, Norwich, Lincoln, York, Lynn, and Southampton. The communities were headed by great rabbis who had come from France. In a letter, Henry I (1100–1135) established that the Jews of England should enjoy complete freedom to travel wherever they wished and could take their possessions with them; they were granted permission to settle throughout the realm and trade in every kind of merchandise, including land, with the exception of Christian holy articles. The internal administration of the communities was free of all outside interference, and they had their own courts in which Jews took an oath on the Torah. For all these benefits, the king collected vast sums from the Jews both in regular taxes and special imposts. The king took a certain percentage of all commercial transactions and, in the case of loans, he received a share both from the lender and borrower.

Here, too, the Jews accumulated riches, since money-lending was forbidden to Christians. Many estates were mortgaged to Jews by landlords, bishops, and others to raise money for the Crusades. Everywhere, Jewish wealth aroused resentment. However, the king always protected them, so that he could have access to Jewish property as if it were his own. Jews were required to pay special taxes, numerous fines were imposed on them, and the debts owed to Jews who died were confiscated by the authorities. This happened during the reign of Henry II at the death in 1185 of one of the great English financiers, Aaron of Lincoln. The latter's property was confiscated by the Crown and a special branch of the Exchequer called *Scacarium Aaronis* was set up to exact the debts due to his estate and transfer them to the Crown.

dered all copies of the Talmud burned. For two years the Jews persistently and at the risk of their lives fought to have the verdict rescinded. It was no use. On June 17, 1242, twenty-four cartloads of Talmud manuscripts were publicly burned in the center of Paris.

News of the burning plunged Jews everywhere into deep mourning. *Kinot* (lamentations) were compiled, including a famous one by Rabbi Meir of Rothenburg, "O, thou who art burned in fire, ask how fare those who mourn for you," which has been incorporated in the *Tisha B'av* (fast day commemorating the destruction of the First and Second Temples) service. In Rome, a special fast was decreed in memory of the event.

In 1247, Innocent IV met Jewish leaders at Lyons and later informed Saint Louis that Jews should be allowed to live according to their religion. At this meeting, the Jews also complained of the blood-libel charges which had been leveled at the Jews in Pulda, Germany, in 1235. The Jews of the town had been accused of burning down the house of a certain miller in order to kill his five sons and make use of their blood for medicinal purposes. Fanatics in the Church could not reconcile themselves to the Pope's decision on this point. A papal bull on the ritual-murder charge at Pulda also infuriated them. In this bull, the Pope asserted that the charge made against the Jews must be a lie, since the Commandment "Thou shalt not kill" is shared by both Judaism and Christianity, and the accusation but a pretext for persecuting them. Christians were advised to be patient until the Jews should return to the right path and accept the true religion. Extremists urged the Pope to set up a new committee to re-examine the Talmud and its views. The committee met and, in the middle of 1248, published its findings, that the Talmud was full of superstitions and blasphemy. As a consequence, a new hunt for manuscripts of the Talmud and other sacred works was inaugurated. Study of the Talmud was discontinued for a time after a number of rabbis, including Rabbi Jehiel of Paris, left for Palestine.

In the years that followed the burning of the Talmud, Jews were also thrown into the flames. This occurred in Troyes, Rashi's native town, in 1288. The Christians accused the Jews of murdering a Christian, and the Inquisition sentenced a local wealthy Jew and his family — thirteen persons in all — to death by burning. Two years later, Paris was shocked (just as the people of Belitz, Germany, had been forty-three years earlier) by a rumor that a local Jew had stabbed the Host in order to kill Jesus again, as it were; on this occasion, too, the Jew and his wife were condemned to the stake.

RITUAL-MURDER CHARGES IN ENGLAND

The life of Jews in the thirteenth century in England was essentially no different from that of Jews on the Continent in the same period. When John Lackland,

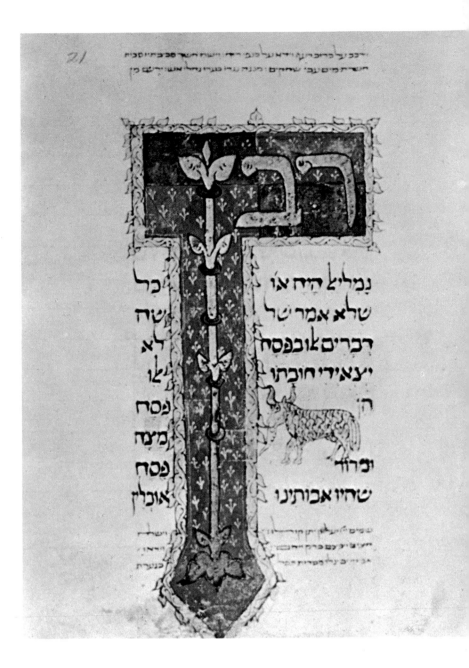

Rabbi Gamaliel required everyone to recall three aspects of the Passover event at the ceremony on the eve of the festival: the paschal lamb, the matsot, and the bitter herbs. There are illustrations of these three features in a number of Spanish haggadot, *and their representation has become traditional. The picture of a lamb—the paschal lamb—from the manuscript of a 14th-century* haggadah *is shown here. The vertical and transverse geometric figure in color, dividing the page and representing the Hebrew letter* nun *(the final letter in the word* Rabban, *i.e., "rabbi"), is also traditional in Spanish illuminated manuscripts. British Museum, London*

the son of Henry II, ascended the throne in 1199, he made an effort to preserve the existing charter of liberties of the Jews. In 1201, he confirmed this in a letter permitting Jews to dwell wherever they wished, freely engage in trade, and be judged in their own courts on matters pertaining to their community; the king also reiterated the order that anyone violating

Jewish rights would be punished. However, as the kingdom's needs increased, he began cruelly and mercilessly to exploit the Jews. He imposed huge taxes on them and caused the complete impoverishment of their communities. As a consequence, local rabbis joined the French Tosaphists and went to Palestine with them. In the period of internal struggle in England during the final years of the king's life, from which the British Parliament emerged, the Jews suffered severely from the barons who opposed the regime and considered the Jews the property of the hated monarch.

In 1222—six years after the death of John Lackland—during the reign of Henry III, Stephen Langton, archbishop of Canterbury, convoked a Council at Oxford which confirmed the decisions of the Fourth Lateran Council and added a number of additional restrictions. Jews were compelled to wear the badge of shame, and were forbidden to build new synagogues. The king also increased the Jews' burden and in the six years between 1226 and 1232 taxes on the Jews were raised fivefold. During this period, a ritual-murder charge was made in Norwich (1230). About fourteen years later, a ritual-murder charge was made against the Jews of London, and in 1255 there was rioting against the Jews of Lincoln, in central England, after the discovery of the body of a Christian child in a cesspool near a Jewish house. The Christians, convinced by the confession of the occupant of the house, exacted under torture, that "each year the Jews crucify a child to mock Jesus," attacked the Jews of the town. A number of Jewish dignitaries were taken to London, where they were hanged, and the rest were allowed to go free in exchange for extremely large sums of money.

The Jews now wanted to leave England, as the persecution and torment mounted, but the departure of the "king's serfs" was absolutely forbidden. The special request which they presented to the brother of Henry III, Richard of Cornwall, to permit them to leave the country, was answered with a great deal of hypocrisy. The king could not allow them to leave for France, for example, since Saint Louis had just announced a new law against the Jews; and, furthermore, no other Christian state would agree to take in Jews. However, the king was prepared to do his servants a favor and content himself with a not inconsiderable sum of money. The Jews, of course, received nothing out of this transaction, with the exception of perhaps selling themselves to Richard, the king's brother, for five thousand English pounds. And, to be sure, Richard did not treat them as brutally as Henry III. However, not many days passed before the Jews were once more delivered into the hands of the king, and responsibility for them was assigned to his son, the future Edward I.

Three years after the accession of Edward I to the throne (1275), he enacted a law forbidding the Jews of England to lend money at interest to Christians, and all such transactions were declared null and void.

Their right of domicile was limited to certain towns, and all of them had to wear the Jewish badge and pay a special head tax. However, the king, who had forbidden the Jews to engage in commerce, was not prepared to relinquish his previous profits. Furthermore, in 1287, the heads of the Jewish communities were arrested and kept in prison until the members of their communities paid the huge sum of twelve thousand pounds. Three years later (1290), when the money was delivered to the Treasury, the king issued an order expelling the Jews from England, as he had done shortly before to the Jews of a French district under English rule. Most of the Jews headed for France. Philip IV the Fair, King of France, permitted them to settle only in certain sections at the onset and imposed numerous severe restrictions on them. From the time of his ascension to the throne in 1285 he fought all heretics, especially Jews, and persecuted the Jews with dogged fury. Treating them as if they were merchandise, he sold them to the highest bidder and haggled with barons who wanted to sell him their Jews.

In 1306, when the treasury of France was empty and the king urgently needed large sums of money, he decided to expel the Jews and confiscate their property. The expulsion affected not only French Jews, but also those who had come there from England sixteen years before. Part of them went to Spain and some of them moved to the regions bordering on France, in the hope of some day returning to their native land. And, to be sure, nine years later (1315), when the country had become impoverished, Louis X asked them to come back.

THE PERIOD OF FLOURISHING IN SPAIN

The twelfth century was a distressing period for the Arabs who had taken possession of Spain four centuries earlier. The Christian reconquest drove the Arabs southward, until their kingdom was limited to Granada and its environs. However, despite these inauspicious external conditions, Jewish creativity blossomed as it had not for centuries. Ibn Gabirol was followed by Moses ibn Ezra, a pupil of Isaac ibn Giat. He was well-versed in both Hebrew and Arabic culture and held a high official post. At first he wrote secular poetry, but, after having experienced a crisis as a result of an unhappy love, he turned his mind to religious poetry and compiled a work of *selihot* (penitential prayers). In addition to his poetic writings in Hebrew, he wrote Arabic works of philosophy and literature.

The poetry of Judah ha-Levi, Ibn Ezra's friend and pupil, is celebrated for its strict meter, artistic polish, symbolism, and imagination, It deals with a large variety of topics and is ingenious and rich in Biblical and Talmudic references. His early poems were on the ordinary subjects of Hebrew poetry in Spain; however, after the destruction of a number of Jewish communities during the war between the Christians and Moslems and the mental shock accompanying it, he began to write nationalistic, religious poems, sacred poems amazing in their profound feeling and completeness of expression interlaced with philosophical motifs—the terrible contrast between the nation's mission and its miserable fate. Judah ha-Levi fully expressed his religious and philosophical views in an Arabic work, *The Cuzari* (i.e., Khazars). The book deals with the problem of Jewish exile and redemption, and of the Jews' mission and their wretched state. As he formulated it at the beginning of the work, it was "the book of argument and proof in the defense of the degraded faith." He explains this contradiction by the statement that the Jews are the heart of mankind, which feels the agony of the whole human race. In his opinion, the Jews' dispersion purifies them of sin, and when the people is suitably cleansed and returns to its own land, it will serve as a physician to heal the world's nations. The book emphasizes the duty to settle in Palestine, thus bringing redemption closer, And, true to his beliefs, Judah ha-Levi left Cordoba for Palestine in the 1130s. He was last known to have been in Cairo; after leaving the Egyptian city, all trace of him was lost. There is a legend that he reached Jerusalem and was killed by an Arab horseman while praying before the Western Wall—the surviving wall of the Temple.

At the same time that Judah ha-Levi was on his way to Palestine, Abraham ibn Ezra, the poet, grammarian, commentator, philosopher, astronomer, and physician from Toledo, was also on his way there. All his known writings were written during the period of his travels. He compiled numerous poems, both profane and religious. Many of his penitential prayers and exhortations have been incorporated in the book of daily prayers and in the festival services. His poems reveal that he experienced a great deal and had a profound knowledge of all the vicissitudes of life. His riddles and epigrams are noted for their pungency and fine humor. He was one of the greatest Biblical commentators of all time and his exegetical writings are known for their depth and perspicacity; his style is rich and compact. Abraham ibn Ezra's commentary is based on a direct, linguistic examination of the plain meaning of the text. There are many instances where he alludes to unconventional opinions. He also distinguished himself in grammar, science, and philosophy. By translating into the Hebrew the works of grammarians who wrote in Arabic, Ibn Ezra acquainted the Jews of Christian Europe with new developments in Hebrew language study. His own works cite the achievements of previous philologists. His scientific activities centered chiefly on mathematics and astronomy, and a number of his works in these fields, which were translated into Latin, influenced medieval Christian scholars. His Biblical commentary interprets religious belief in the spirit of Platonic philosophy.

The last great poet of the Jewish flowering in

The building of a house is shown, depicting Jewish slavery in Egypt, to illustrate the text of a 14th-century Barcelona haggadah. *The bottom of the picture shows a man mixing mortar with his feet and a brickmaker whose assistant is carrying the finished product to the basket used for raising the bricks to the top of the building by means of a pulley. In the center of the page there is a stonecutter, with a helper walking up a ladder, carrying a stone on his back. The foreman is standing at the top of the building. The architect on horseback is issuing instructions to the taskmaster. At the top, a dog is handing a drink to a hare. British Museum, London*

Spain was Judah al-Harizi. He was born about 1170, either in Barcelona or Toledo, and died in 1235. Al-Harizi traveled extensively in western and southern Europe and the Near and Middle East, as far as the Persian Gulf. These travels, reflected in most of his writing, had great value, for he brought the spirit of Spanish-Jewish culture wherever he came. His principal work is the book *Tahkemoni* (Apothecary), written in the form of *maqamat* (narratives in rhymed prose popular in Arab writings), a literary form which Al-Harizi was among the first to introduce into Hebrew literature. In the book's fifty chapters, the author wrote amusingly of his journeys and adventures in several countries, weaving in fables, descriptions of

Miniatures from the Golden Haggadah. *In the 13th and 14th centuries, series of paintings on Biblical subjects were added to many manuscripts of Spanish haggadot as full-page miniatures. One of the earliest and most magnificent of these is the* Golden Haggadah – *so named because of the gold leaf serving as background for the miniatures. The* Golden Haggadah *was apparently painted in Barcelona at the beginning of the 14th century by at least two artists. Four of the fifteen pages of miniatures are shown here. Each page is divided into four parts and should be read from right to left. The first panel of the first page shows Noah in the nude after having become inebriated with wine; his sons are covering him. In the second panel there is a view of the Tower of Babel after the Lord "confounded the language of all the earth." In the third panel (bottom), Nimrod is ordering Abraham thrown into a fiery furnace in which (according to a Midrashic tradition) an angel who will save Abraham is visible. In the fourth panel, the three angels inform Abraham that his wife, Sarah, will give birth to a son. The second page is devoted to the life of Joseph. The upper panels show Joseph being taken out of the pit and sold to the Ishmaelites after his coat of many colors was smeared with goat's blood. In the lower right panel, Joseph's coat is brought to Jacob, who tears his garments in grief. The fourth panel is divided into two parts: in the upper one, Potiphar's wife is seen "catching Joseph by his garment" while her husband is hurrying home; in the lower, Joseph is interpreting the dreams of the butler and baker in prison*

personalities, and literary criticism. One of his other works is the collection of poems entitled *Sefer ha-Anak* (The Giant's Book), which contains more than two hundred and fifty short verses dealing with fear of God and moral topics. Al-Harizi wrote on a wide variety of subjects in an original, light, amusing style. His outstanding importance lies in the fact that he wrote in Hebrew, while other great Jewish figures of the period wrote in Arabic. He also translated numerous works, including the *maqamat* of the celebrated Arab poet Al-Hariri. His translation of Maimonides' *Guide for the Perplexed* acquainted the Christian world with the philosophy of the Spanish-Jewish thinker.

About 1165, a certain Benjamin, from the town of Tudela in northern Spain, set out on an extensive series of travels. He visited southern France, Italy, Greece, Constantinople, Palestine, and the Arab lands. His book, *The Travels of Benjamin*, written in the third person, details the impressions of journeys which

lasted about thirteen years. In a clear and concise Hebrew, he wrote of remote Jewish communities in the Byzantine Empire, Asia, and Africa, of the organization of communities in Babylonia, Syria, and Egypt, and of the condition of Palestine under Crusader rule. He listed the names of the leaders of the various communities and their outstanding scholars. The book provides population figures for the Jewish communities and describes the economic activities of their members. Benjamin's book discusses at length the various sects in Judaism or associated with it—the Samarians in Palestine, the Karaites in Constantinople, and a sect in Cyprus which observed the Sabbath from dawn until dawn. In a lively style, the traveler also described the life of non-Jews. He wrote of battles between Genoa and Pisa, the Crusaders' ports of embarkation in southern Italy, palaces in Constantinople, the wealth of the Byzantine Empire, and the Assassins in the Lebanese mountains, the movement of religious

126

The third page shows four of the ten plagues, boils, hail, locusts, and darkness. The lower part of the panel, depicting the plague of darkness, shows the Israelites borrowing various household articles from Egyptian houses, for that is how the Midrash interprets the Biblical verse, "And they despoiled the Egyptians." The fourth page is the last in the haggadah. *The upper right panel, showing Miriam and the Israelite women going out to celebrate after the crossing of the Red Sea, concludes the series of Biblical pictures. The remaining three panels depict preparations for Passover. In the first, the head of the household orders the distribution of* matsot *and* haroset *(dish of fruits, nuts, and wine to resemble mortar) to the children. In the second, the women are cleaning the house for Passover while the husband and son seek out any leavened bread. The third shows the Paschal lamb being slaughtered and dishes being cleansed. British Museum, London*

and political fanatics which disparaged the practical commandments of Islam. *The Travels of Benjamin* was translated into most European languages and, because of its importance as a direct source, is indispensable to all historians of the Middle Ages.

MOSES BEN MAIMON (MAIMONIDES)

Rabbi Moses ben Maimon (known by the acronym *Rambam*) was the greatest Jewish personality of the twelfth century. It is said of him, "From Moses to Moses, there was no one like Moses." He was born in Cordoba, Spain, in 1135. His father was the religious-court judge of the Jewish community. When Moses was thirteen, Cordoba was captured by the Almohade Arabs, and Moses and his family fled, eventually reaching Fez, Morocco. In the course of his travels, Moses continued his studies of Arabic philosophy,

geometry, natural sciences, astronomy, and medicine. At the age of thirty, he was forced to take to the road again. Moses headed eastward and reached Palestine, where he found no possibility of settling, and subsequently moved to Egypt. In Egypt, he went into the business of precious stones, in partnership with his brother; however, after his brother drowned and the business collapsed, Moses made a living as a physician, finally receiving appointment as doctor in the court of the Sultan, Saladin. During this period, he also became the leader of the Egyptian Jewish community with the official title of "Head of the [Jewish] Nation."

While on his travels, he had already begun to write a commentary on the Mishna, called *The Book of Light*. Written in Arabic, this work interprets the Mishna on the basis of the Gemara and its conclusions, and determines which rabbinic opinion has the force of law.

In Cairo, Maimonides began a systematic compilation of the entire body of Jewish law, which he called *Mishne Torah* (Repetition of the Torah). *Mishne Torah* consists of fourteen volumes and is accordingly also called the *Yad Hazaka* (Strong Hand), since *Yad* has the numerical value of fourteen. It covers every halakhic subject discussed in the Talmud, meticulously arranged. As an introduction to this monumental work of codification, Maimonides wrote *Sefer ha-Mitsvot* (The Book of Commandments), in which he established an accurate system for counting the commandments in the Torah. He thus reached the figure 613 mentioned in the Talmud—248 mandatory commandments and 365 prohibitive ones.

Not everyone was satisfied with *Mishne Torah*. Some leading scholars regarded it as a new, advanced Talmud, which lays down laws in instances where the Talmud itself reaches no decision. Certain authorities considered it dangerous, since those having recourse to *Mishne Torah* would refrain from studying the Babylonian Talmud itself. They argued that Maimonides tended to heresy and took too many liberties in deciding controversial matters.

So, while some were astonished at the greatness of "The Illuminator of Israel's Eyes," who "knew how to shake the entire Talmud as flour in a sieve and remove the waste from it," others regarded an abridgment of the Talmud as being detrimental to scholarship. However, Maimonides stated categorically, "If it were possible to put the entire Talmud into one chapter, I would not put it into two."

The controversy mounted, especially after the publication of his philosophical work, *Moreh Nevukhim* (Guide for the Perplexed), written for the individual who had learned a great many disciplines and had also studied philosophy but was confused when it came to reconciling Judaism with a rational approach. Maimonides considered ethics and obedience to the commandments of the Torah the necessary means for the improvement of the human mind, the "only way to achieve eternity."

Moreh Nevukhim, which attained fame in several countries, also sparked off controversies among Christian and Moslem scholars. Both the adherents and opponents of Maimonides carried on correspondence with him to elucidate obscure points in his work. His correspondents included the translator Samuel ibn Tibbon, who requested information about difficult parts for purposes of translation. Maimonides also wrote books on medicine and logic.

The arduous work in which the great philosopher engaged impaired his health and he died in Egypt at the age of seventy.

lished regulations imposing heavy taxes and requiring Jews to wear a distinctive badge, and interfered with Jewish activity in the country's economic life. Nevertheless, the Jews lived in relative peace under the cross, conducting their internal life as they saw fit. They were even grateful to the monarchs, and fought beside them against the Moslems.

At this time, Spain was divided into several kingdoms, which had come into being after the expulsion of the Arabs. The attitude toward the Jews differed from one country to another. In Castile, where Jews had been living since the tenth century, their position was relatively good until the end of the fourteenth century. Ferdinand III el Santo (1217–1252) gave the Jews a large measure of freedom, and ignored the Church's demands to treat them severely by requiring the Jewish badge and prohibiting the construction of synagogues.

During the reign of his son Alfonso el Sabio (1252–1284), the Jews enjoyed wide autonomy. Under the influence of the Church, the king published a number of anti-Jewish decrees which included the prohibition to go outside on Easter, a prohibition against building new synagogues, a law forbidding Jews to give medicines to Christians, and the obligation to wear a special badge on the hat. Many of these offenses were punishable by death. However, Alfonso did not implement his own laws strictly. He appointed Jews to government posts and ignored the law requiring Jews to wear special garb. His physician was a Jew, and new synagogues were erected. Pope Nicholas sent the king a letter in which, at the urging of Spanish priests and monks, he reproved him for allowing Jews to dominate Christians. However, Alfonso ignored the letter, and the condition of the Jews remained as good as it had been previously. During the struggle between Alfonso and his son Sancho IV el Bravo (1284–1296), the condition of the Jews deteriorated, and they were compelled to pay very heavy taxes. However, even during the reign of this king, the requests of the Cortes—the assembly of notables—to make difficulties for the Jews, because it considered their economic progress a danger to the state, were refused.

In Aragon, Jaime I el Conquistador (1213–1276) wanted to emulate his friend Saint Louis of France. At first, he wanted to make life difficult for the Jews and even lent his support to monks who were trying to convert them. However, ultimately the king was unable to give up the Jews' money, and they were allowed to hold any position they wanted. The king granted them numerous rights, including the privilege

SPAIN IN THE THIRTEENTH CENTURY

Thirteenth-century Christian Spain experienced a flowering in which Jews played an important part. The Jews did not suffer under Christian rule, despite the fact that the kings, for the sake of appearances, pub-

(Opposite page) Drinking the first cup of sanctified wine and washing the hands are depicted on a page of this Barcelona haggadah of the second half of the 14th century. The position of reclining while drinking wine is shown as resting the head on one hand. A servant boy is pouring water over the hands of the head of the family. Under the table, a dog is gnawing a bone. British Museum, London

העולם שרחינו וקימנו
והגיענו לזמן הזה ״

כהסבת שמאל ו
ונוטלין ידיהם ומברכין

"The perfection of beauty: Pentateuch, Prophets, Hagiographa."
This inscription in the Bible of Bishop Bedell shows in what
veneration the Holy Writ was held throughout the Middle Ages.
This Bible, with ornamental opening pages for each of the Books,
was written and illuminated in Rome in 1284. Emmanuel College,
Cambridge

of having capital cases judged in Jewish courts. In litigation between a Christian and a Jew conducted in a state court, the judges also included a Jew. It was forbidden to summon a Jew to court in a civil case on the Sabbath or a Jewish holiday, and any Jew who happened to be in prison on such a count would be permitted to go home for the duration of the Sabbath or festival. The king also invited Jews from North Africa to settle in Spain, and reduced Jewish taxes. He, like other Spanish monarchs, also passed laws against the Jews, but he never enforced them. Jews fulfilled important diplomatic functions in his court and occupied high administrative and financial positions. Nevertheless, now and then harsh edicts were issued against the Jews, especially under pressure from the Dominican Inquisition, which exerted great influence in the country.

Toward the end of his life, Jaime I decided to do penance for his sins to the Church and made concessions to the priests and monks. He gave them a free hand to attempt to convert Jews. The priests rallied apostates to their aid to support them in their disputations with the Jews on the harmfulness of the Talmud and, on the other hand, to prove the greatness of Christianity publicly. In the second half of 1263, many of the king's officers and knights assembled in the royal palace. Present also were numerous monks and bishops, headed by the apostate Pablo Christiani. They were there to debate with a small group of Jewish scholars, which included Moses ben Nahman (Nahmanides), a leading rabbi of the time and a great authority on Jewish law, who combined the qualities of depth and perspicacity of the medieval Jewish scholars of France with the orderliness and decisiveness of contemporary learned Jews in Spain. This leader of Spanish Jewry worked as a physician in his home town of Gerona. He also devoted himself to cabala, secular studies, and foreign languages. Nahmanides wrote many works, of which the most noteworthy are his commentary on the Pentateuch and the Book of Job, his glosses upon most of the tractates of the Talmud, critical observations on Maimonides' *Sefer ha-Mitsvot*, and a commentary on the mystical *Sefer Yetsira*. He left numerous responsa in halakhic matters in reply to inquiries from many Jewish communities.

Details of the debate which he conducted in the king's presence are described in his work *Vikkuah ha-Ramban* (Nahmanides' Disputation). It was a brilliant debate, with Nahmanides confuting Christian arguments with devastating logic. The debate ended with each of the two sides persisting in its own interpretations and, a month later, Nahmanides was forced to leave Spain, and copies of his work on the disputation were burned at the king's order. The Jewish scholar went to Palestine.

Another of the great Jewish personalities of the period lived in Barcelona. He was Solomon ben Adret (known as the *Rashba*, from the acronym of his name), who exerted a great deal of influence on the development of Jewish law. In Toledo, Asher ben Jehiel, a pupil of Rabbi Meir of Rothenburg, was appointed rabbi. He was noted for his sharp mind, logic, and method. His son, Jacob ben Asher, was one of the greatest Jewish codifiers and the author of the *Arab'a Turim*—four volumes of Jewish law which became a guidepost for most of the scholars of the period.

In Jerusalem, in which he found only two Jews—dyers by trade—Nahmanides completed his commentary on the Bible. He was the first to introduce the spirit of the cabala and mystical elements to Biblical exegesis, just as Todros Abulafia did to his Talmudic commentaries. Mysticism found fertile soil; rationalism, and the war between science and religion which accompanied it at the time and continued until the expulsion from France in 1306, were not enough to solace people suffering torments and persecution. The leading cabalist was Abraham ben Samuel Abulafia,

The table set for the Passover ceremony. Its Sephardic basket of matsot *corresponds to the Ashkenazic plate, carafes of wine, and goblets, and there are decorated circular* matsot. *The participants in the ceremony are all raising their goblets and one is pointing at a passage in the* haggadah. *Page from the manuscript of a Spanish Passover* haggadah, *beginning of the 14th century. British Museum, London*

a native of Saragossa. He proclaimed himself a prophet and went to see Pope Nicholas III with the intention of converting him to Judaism. The Pope's sudden death saved the great cabalist from the stake. His numerous works greatly influenced the cabalistic literature of the sixteenth century.

Mysticism's greatest accomplishment of the period is the book of the *Zohar*, which is generally attributed to Rabbi Simeon bar Yohai, but according to one theory was written by Moses de Leon, the famous Spanish cabalist. The language of the book is Aramaic with an admixture of medieval Hebrew. The central theme of the work is that only by closely studying the stories and commandments in the Bible is it possible to find an answer to the profound secrets of Creation. According to the *Zohar*, the principal mission of the Torah is man's elevation to the upper worlds.

GERMAN JEWRY IN THE THIRTEENTH AND FOURTEENTH CENTURIES

The ritual-murder charge in Fulda was the first of a series of libels against the Jews of Germany. It was followed by the accusation of the desecration of the Host which was accompanied by degradation and large numbers of victims. Religious fanaticism mounted together with a social ferment among the common people. Mobs attacked Jews at every opportunity. Six years after the Fulda incident, a "battle with the Jews" occurred in Frankfurt, because of the activities of a local apostate, and all the Jews were savagely murdered. In 1259, the Jews in the Mainz district were ordered to wear a badge of shame, and in 1285, the priests of Munich burned one hundred and eighty Jews at the stake. During this period, one of the greatest Tosaphists, Meir ben Baruch of Rothenburg, endeavored to lend the Jews courage to bear their suffering. When he attempted to flee from the violence and torment of Germany, with other Jews, he was apprehended and thrown into prison, where he died in 1293.

Changes in the government brought no relief to the Jews. At the end of the thirteenth century and the beginning of the fourteenth, the persecutions grew more intense. In the years 1298–99, mobs headed by a certain Bavarian noble, Rindfleisch, ravaged more than 150 communities. In the period from 1336 to 1338, vicious gangs called *Armleder* devastated 114 communities. Ten years later, when the rumor was circulated that the Jews were responsible for the spreading of the Black Death, the Jews of three hundred communities were tortured and massacred.

But German Jewry, despite the horrors which befell it, still had a great deal of vitality left. The Jews reappeared in various towns to eke out a meager living under difficult conditions and numerous restrictions.

In addition to the disasters they shared with their coreligionists in Germany, the Jews of France also suffered from expulsion. After they were expelled by Philip the Fair in 1306, they were recalled in 1315, during the reign of Louis X. In 1317, during the reign of Philip V, the younger brother of Louis X, who also tried to treat the Jews fairly, a ritual-murder charge was made against the Jews at Chinon. Three years later, 120 communities were ravaged by mob violence in the wake of the "Shepherd's Edict."

One year after that, the Jews were accused of having incited lepers to poison wells. They were savagely tortured and put on trial and 160 were burned at the stake. The king wanted his share of this, too, and imposed heavy taxes on the Jewish communities. The brutality employed in collecting these taxes during the reign of Charles IV, the successor of Philip V, forced the Jews to leave the country. Thirty-seven years passed before the Jews were permitted to return to France for twenty years in 1360. On its termination, this period of grace was extended by Charles VI, in order to enable the king to fill the country's empty treasury by both exacting heavy taxes from the Jews and exploiting them in the collection of the taxes. However, after fourteen harrowing years of Christian persecution, Charles VI published an order expelling the Jews for "their serious crimes against the holy faith."

In contemporary Germany, persecution also continued. The kings of the House of Luxemburg and the first monarchs of the Habsburg dynasty occasionally showed kindness to the Jews because of their money, but the royal families could do nothing against the deep-seated German hate. The priests did not miss an opportunity to incite the mob, and even during the reign of Frederick III (1440–1493), who "because of his affection for them was considered by the people to be King of the Jews," there were ritual-murder charges and violent attacks. In 1453, the blood-libel charge was made against the Jews of Breslau, just as it had been made thirty-two years earlier against the Jews of Vienna. The reign of Frederick III is full of numerous instances of cruelty and violence, despite the king's efforts to prevent such manifestations. In 1450, the Jews were expelled from Bavaria. Two years later, the king succeeded in preventing the expulsion of the Jews from Regensburg, but they had to wear the Jewish badge. In 1474, the Jews of the town were accused of the murder of a seven-year-old Christian child and, four years later, the Jews of Trent in the southern part of the country were charged with a similar crime.

THE INQUISITION AND EXPULSION FROM SPAIN

In fourteenth-century Spain, the condition of the Jews was relatively good. Throughout the entire century, Jews in Castile and Aragon were part of Christian society and succeeded in securing positions at court and political influence. However, Christian hatred of the Jews emerged at the end of the century. In 1391, the Christian fanatics of Castile loudly clamored, "Baptism or death!" The cry was soon also taken up in Aragon. Unlike the Jews of Germany and France, many in Spain chose the first alternative and adopted Christianity, at least outwardly.

The Jews who remained loyal to their faith were in 1412 ostracized by a royal decree. They were forced to live in special quarters, shave their heads and beards, and wear distinctive clothing. They were forbidden to do business in bread, meat, and wine, the autonomous rights of their internal court were restricted, and they were deprived of the right of imposing communal taxes. In addition, acts of violence became commonplace. The financial structure was soon affected adversely and, in 1414, the king was compelled to rescind the economic edicts against the Jews, especially since the principal aims of the anti-Jewish campaign had already been achieved—tens of thousands of Jews had become converts to Christianity. However, this was not enough for the fanatical priests. At the order of Pope Benedict XIII, and with the consent of the king of Aragon, the rabbis of the Jewish communities were forced to participate in a public debate on the principles of their religion.

The disputation, presided over by the Pope, was held in the city of Tortosa. At the first of the sixty-nine sessions which took place in 1413, the Jews were forced to defend themselves against the calumnies of Geronimo de Santa Fe. The rabbis did not have the courage to answer the Christians resolutely and criticize their religion as Nahmanides had done. At the beginning of the debate, the Pope announced clearly, "I did not come and have not sent for you for the purpose of proving which of the two is the true religion, for I know that my religion and my faith are true, and that your Torah was once true, but it has been abolished." At the end of the disputation, the Pope ordered the manuscripts of the Talmud burnt, but the edict was not carried out.

The forty years (1415–54) which followed were a period of relative peace for the Jews of Spain. Pope Martin I forbade the forcible conversion of Jews and rescinded many of the decrees issued by Benedict XIII. The Spanish-Jewish communities which had been rehabilitated by the *Rab de la Corte* (Rabbi of the Court) Abraham Benveniste once more became a decisive factor in the country's economy. However, this activity of the Jews stirred up considerable resentment among the Spanish clergy, who influenced Pope Eugenius IV to rescind the ameliorations which Martin V had granted the Jews twenty-one years earlier.

The various restrictions imposed on the Jews of Spain also applied to the Marranos—Jews who had only adopted Christianity outwardly. Slander and violence came to them, too, and, in 1451, Pope Nicholas V even issued a bull to appoint special inquisitors to ferret out "persons who are Christians outwardly but actually observe Jewish customs."

The "new Christians" fought for their right to be regarded like other members of the Church. However, in the rioting which occurred in 1467, many Marranos

"This is the bread of affliction." According to a Barcelona custom, the head of the household would place the basket of matsot on the head of the youngest son while reciting this prayer. Another old man is seated at the other end of the table in an armchair like the father's, and the women and girls sit behind the table. There are copies of the haggadah, a carafe, and a glass of wine on the table, and candelabra are suspended from the ceiling. Opening page of a Spanish Passover haggadah, apparently painted in Barcelona in the second half of the 14th century. British Museum, London

in Toledo were killed when Christians wished to expel them from public positions. Four years later, numerous Jews and Marranos were murdered by a wild mob in a town near Segovia. And, two years after that, Marranos were butchered in Cordoba to prevent them from participating in Christian religious festivals.

Severe persecution also came to the Jews of Portugal, who had sought refuge there from the religious fanaticism of Spain. With the exception of a period of relative peace during the reign of Alfonso V (1447–1481), the Jews in the country, together with the Marranos, suffered harassment and harsh decrees. To be sure, even during Alfonso's reign, fanatical priests found excuses for arousing violence against the Jews, but the king knew how to quell the rioting firmly;

because of this, much resentment was directed against the king and his troops were forced to intervene.

During the last fifteen years of Alfonso's reign, Don Isaac Abravanel served as his finance minister. Describing the condition of the Jews of Portugal, Don Isaac wrote that he was living a life of abundance in Lisbon and that his home was a meeting place of scholars; the king was a just man and the Jews had nothing to fear.

The merging of the kingdoms of Castile and Aragon by the marriage of Ferdinand of Aragon and Isabella of Castile (1474) did not immediately affect the condition of the Jews in Spain. Furthermore, many Jews and Christians served in high posts in the united kingdom. But the fanatical priests were active, and six years after the union of the kingdoms a special court of the Inquisition was established, headed by Thomas de Torquemada, with the approval of Pope Sixtus IV. The purpose of this tribunal was to find Marranos secretly observing Judaism. Hundreds of Marranos were thrown into prison, where horrible torture was inflicted on them to force them to confess their sins and inform on the sinning of their relatives and friends. At the beginning of 1481, a Christian throng in Seville celebrated the first *auto-da-fé* ("act of the faith"—public ceremony at which verdicts of the Inquisition were announced to the victims) and witnessed the burning of six Marranos in the public square. By the end of the year, more than three hundred Marranos had been sent to the stake. Ferdinand, whose coffers were filling with the money of the victims, rejected the protest of Sixtus IV that the condemned be permitted to defend themselves in a fair trial. The officers of the Inquisition invented outlandish instruments of torture and their diabolical imagination knew no bounds. Besides physical tortures, they employed various methods of degrading Marranos who had "repented"; the "penitents" were compelled to walk naked and barefoot through the streets so that the crowds gathered on either side could "forgive" them.

However, despite all the horrors of the Inquisition, there were still many Marranos who did not "confess." The Church authorities believed that in order to make good Catholics out of them, they must be separated from the Jews. Since attempts to keep them apart inside Spain had not succeeded, the Jews had to be expelled. Torquemada supplied the monarchs with a pretext for expulsion: under torture a Marrano was forced to "confess" that the rabbis of the Jewish communities in Spain had sent him, together with a number of other Marranos and Jews, to crucify a Christian child in a cave for the purpose of harming the officials of the Inquisition and delivering the Catholic faith to the devil.

Now there was nothing to delay publication of the decree expelling the Jews from Aragon and Castile in order to put a stop to the dangerous association of Christians and Jews. Actually, the king intended to withdraw from this plan after Jewish leaders had offered him thirty thousand gold dineros for canceling the edict; however, Torquemada cleverly dissuaded the king from agreeing. Appearing before the king with a picture of Jesus on the cross, he announced, "Judas Iscariot sold Jesus Christ for thirty pieces of silver, and you wish to sell Him for thirty thousand of gold. Here He is." The words strongly moved the queen, and the order was confirmed. In the second half of 1492, about two hundred thousand Jews left Spain. The exiles scattered to all points of the compass, with about half of them going to Portugal.

Eight months after the Spanish exiles had found a refuge in Portugal, they again had to resume their troubled wandering; few of the exiles survived their travels. However, the fate of the Jews remaining in Portugal was no better than those who left. In the six years which elapsed since the expulsion from Spain, the rulers of Portugal could not decide whether or not to follow the example of the neighboring country. Like the rulers of many other countries in Europe, they wanted to make use of the Jews' money. However, in 1498, the religious fanatics gained the upper hand, and the Jews were forced to leave Portugal.

The Portuguese exiles, like those from Spain before them, who settled wherever they were allowed to come in, brought with them their cultural treasures. Wherever they established their new homes, they exerted a strong influence on the cultural progress of the country.

THE SPANISH HAGGADAH

The amalgamation of Biblical pictures and festival customs into a single continuous unit was made in Spain. In Spanish Passover *haggadot* (plural of *haggadah*) from the end of the thirteenth and the fourteenth centuries, the illustrations of Biblical scenes and local customs were combined in the form of complete miniature pages, placed either at the beginning or at the end of the text of the *haggadah,* until it sometimes appeared as if they had been made in a different workshop and added to the text only by the purchaser. These pages of miniatures are occasionally divided into two and sometimes into four parts, with each part picturing a number of episodes. These paintings in the Spanish *haggadot* constitute a consecutive series of Biblical events—in some manuscripts, from the Creation to the death of Moses; in others, only events connected with the Exodus. It is worthwhile noting that, in subject matter and even in their method of portrayal, there are occasionally amazing parallels between the Sephardic and Ashkenazic Biblical illuminations; this fact supports the assumption that an uninterrupted Jewish tradition of Jewish paintings based on the Bible existed from antiquity down to the later Middle Ages. Miniatures illustrating customs and ceremonies generally follow Biblical miniatures in the Spanish *haggadot.* They depict the preparations for Passover, the removal of leavened bread, the baking of *matsot* (unleavened bread), the making of *haroset* (mixture of fruit, nuts, and wine to resemble mortar), and the slaughtering of the Paschal lamb. Paintings illustrating the text are usually limited to ornamental *matsot*, bitter herbs, and sometimes to scenes of Rabbi Gamaliel and his pupils, an angel pouring God's wrath on the pagans, the four sons (the wise, the wicked, the simple, and the one who does not even know how to ask) and their interest in the Passover ceremony.

Just as in the world of the Ashkenazic Jews, so also in the world of the Sephardis, Jewish artists were influenced by the style of the non-Jewish environment and, essentially, Jewish painting does not differ from non-Jewish painting of the same period. The cultural atmosphere in Spain gave considerable support and encouragement to plastic arts, although Germany, too, was not lacking in artists and their patrons. The problem of drawing the human figure was more acute in southern Germany in the thirteenth century. It was revived with greater force chiefly because of the Puritanical movements which developed in the Christian environment. The asceticism and the hatred of beauty and pomp which accompanied the monastic movement of Francis of Assisi exerted a strong influence on the customs pertaining to morality and everyday living of the Ashkenazic Pietists headed by Rabbi Samuel and his son Rabbi Judah he-Hasid. The Jewish artists found a suitable way of circumventing the prohibition against drawing the human figure by concealing the people's faces, painting their backs, or drawing the heads of animals or birds instead of human heads. Numerous examples of such manuscripts from the beginning of the thirteenth century to the middle of the fourteenth are extant.

A very small number of thirteenth-century illuminated manuscripts from Italy have survived. They increase in number from the end of the fourteenth century and during the fifteenth. Generally the Italian manuscripts derive their elements from Jewish art in Germany and Spain; but they soon adopted a native tradition in marginal illuminations, especially in the style of local Italian art. A large number of prayer books, Passover *haggadot,* halakhic works, and even secular books from fifteenth-century Italy—some of them extremely magnificent specimens of this kind of art—still exist.

THE SYNAGOGUES

In synagogues, too, as in the illumination of manuscripts, the local art style was copied. This was the case with respect to the eleventh-century synagogue in Cairo, in which the wooden doors were decorated with the same kind of carved panels which adorned the palace of the Fatimid caliph. The capitals of the pillars in the Worms synagogue or in the Altneuschul house of worship in Prague are almost absolutely identical with the capitals of local church columns. Decorative tradition remained essentially Moslem in Christian Spain, and the arabesques or ornamental

Illuminated page from the manuscript of a Spanish Passover haggadah *from the end of the 13th century. The dragon at the bottom is purely ornamental. Mocatta Library, University College, London*

inscriptions are an indication of the brilliant period of Jewish culture in Moslem Spain in the tenth and eleventh centuries.

The number of medieval synagogues which survived is smaller and the structures afford only an idea of the general design of the interior and the outside appearance. The special women's gallery was probably a permanent element in synagogues in Germany, Spain, and Italy in the Middle Ages, just as was the position of the Holy Ark containing the Torah scrolls in a niche in the eastern wall. However, the location of the cantor's desk differed in Ashkenazic and Sephardic synagogues.

The only information about murals in synagogues is from literary sources. Rabbi Eliakim opposed stained-glass windows at Mainz. Rabbi Isaac of Vienna, the famous codifier who compiled the work *Or Zarua,* recalled from his youth that there had been murals in the synagogue at Meissen, in southern Germany. His pupil, Rabbi Meir ben Baruch of Rothenburg, believed that paintings on synagogue walls, like those in prayer books, distracted persons in prayer.

ADAPTATION

TO A

NEW WORLD

OF VALUES

Silver niello chest, late 15th century, Italy, designed for a woman to keep her house keys in on the Sabbath. On the front is a scene depicting the three commandments obligatory for Jewish women: hallah *(in Temple times, setting aside a portion of dough for the priest; later, burning a quantity from each loaf baked);* niddah *(observing the laws connected with menstrual uncleanliness); and* Hadlakat Nerot, *lighting of candles in honor of the Sabbath. The knobs on the top are eight counters for keeping track of the linen sent for washing. Israel Museum, Jerusalem*

The Renaissance is a rather imprecise term to designate the period in European history when the Middle Ages ended and modern times began. It extended roughly between the thirteenth and sixteenth centuries, when modern art, thought, literature, science, and criticism had their beginnings.

Renaissance means "new birth," for it was a period in European history filled with hope and promise. In Jewish history, however, it was, in many respects, a period of gloom, punctuated by expulsions in England, France, and Spain, and massacres in Germany. Conditions in Italy were somewhat better, but the Jews were expelled from southern Italy by the Spaniards in 1492–1541, while in the northern part of the peninsula the religious reaction among the Catholics after the Reformation led to the introduction of the ghetto and of all the oppressive institutions which that term evokes.

As will be seen later, there were only two havens of refuge open to the Jews. One was the Moslem world, especially the great and tolerant Ottoman Empire. Turkey generously opened its gates to the Jewish exiles from Spain and allowed them to attain the highest degree of influence and distinction in its territories. The second asylum was Poland, then a great empire, which desperately needed to develop its trade and economic life, and therefore avidly welcomed the Jews who were finding conditions in Germany intolerable and were frantically seeking a land of refuge. This now became the great center of Jewish life for the Ashkenazi world, as the Turkish empire to the south was to the world of the Sefardis.

Worst of all now were conditions in Spain and Portugal, where the Inquisition with its *autos-da-fé* reigned supreme and took its deadly toll of Jews and Marranos. Marranos fleeing from the brutal hands of the Inquisition founded new Jewish communities in Amsterdam, Hamburg, and London, and from the end of the sixteenth century onward in the New World now being opened up by the explorations of the great age of discovery.

DISPERSION OF THE JEWS OF SPAIN

"In the same month in which Their Majesties issued the order to expel the Jews from the kingdom and the lands belonging to it, in that same month, they gave me the order to board a properly outfitted vessel on an expedition of discovery to India." With these words Christopher Columbus began the diary in which he describes his search for a route to India. Despite the apparent implications of this opening sentence, most of the aid extended to Columbus in preparing his voyage came from Jews. The expedition to discover the New World was made possible chiefly thanks to the large loan to Their Catholic Majesties advanced by Luis de Santangel, the chancellor and comptroller of the royal household of Aragon, from his own pocket. Santangel was of Jewish extraction, as was Gabriel Sanchez, the Finance Minister of Aragon. He and a number of other Marranos were the most loyal supporters of Columbus.

Accompanying Columbus on his expedition were the following men of Jewish origin: Alonzo de la Calle, Rodrigo Sanchez, the physician Bernal, the surgeon Marco, as well as Luis de Torres, who was baptized before sailing and was the official interpreter for the Semitic languages which, according to a common belief, were the tongues spoken in India and the Orient. Consequently, there were Jews among the first white men to tread on the soil of the New World. The money earmarked for Columbus' second voyage was mostly derived from Jewish property which had been confiscated in Spain.

The expulsion was set for the end of July, 1492, and was postponed for two days — to August 2 — at the last minute. Several groups left before the designated date, but most of the Jews remained in the country until the very last. Among those who left before the time was up was the the dean of Spanish rabbis, Isaac Aboab of Toledo, who came to Portugal at the head of a delegation of thirty leaders of Castilian Jewry to request permission to reside in that country. His efforts were successful, and the Portuguese monarch granted the Spanish exiles the right to sojourn in his country for a period of eight months and collected an exorbitant head tax from them.

Half of the Spanish exiles reached Portugal, where they were doomed to destruction by hunger and disease (1493) and finally by expulsion (December 25, 1496). King Manoel of Portugal hoped that, by his marriage to the young Isabella, the daughter of Their Catholic Majesties, either he or his son would become the legal heir to the Spanish throne. That is why he presented the Jews with the alternative of expulsion or baptism, although he was no fanatical Jew-hater.

The peaceful existence of the Jews of Portugal in the last years preceding the expulsion is quite interesting. During this period, one of the first Jewish printing presses after the invention of movable-type printing by Gutenberg was established in Lisbon. In the years between 1489 and 1492, a number of important works, including books illustrated with woodcuts, were printed in Lisbon. This feeling of security must have been based on the position of Abraham Zacuto (author of *Sefer Yuhasin*, on the history of rabbinic scholarship), who was the king's astrologer and also helped plan Vasco da Gama's journey to India.

Shortly afterward, when Ferdinand of Spain annexed the kingdom of Navarre to his country (1498), the exiles from Aragon, who had found a haven in this small kingdom, were again forced to begin wandering.

In the short space of a few years, the large Jewish community in Spain, rich both spiritually and materially, became extinct. In agony, with death a constant companion, and with indescribable suffering, hun-

dreds of thousands of Jews were forced to find themselves a new home, a new place to live, new sources of livelihood, and a new corner where they could live by themselves and practice their own religion. The Spanish exiles scattered to the four ends of the earth. Those who did not find a temporary refuge in Portugal and Navarre settled in North Africa, Italy, Turkey, and Poland. One of the major communities, under the leadership of Don Isaac Abravanel, settled in Naples, in southern Italy.

THE DIASPORA IN THE MODERN WORLD

The dispersion of the Jews of Spain and Portugal occurred in a period of profound economic and social crisis in all of Europe. The discovery of new communication routes in the Atlantic Ocean completely changed the limited outlook of the Mediterranean merchants. It transferred the commercial hegemony from Venice and Genoa first to the ports of Spain and Portugal, then, after the latter's decline, to the Netherlands and England in the west and Turkey in the east. The exiles from Spain and Portugal who came in large numbers to Italy and Turkey at the beginning of the

Wedding rings from Italy of the 16th and 17th centuries. Jewish wedding rings, especially those from Italy, were already known for their beauty in the 15th century, but not many remain. The oldest, most typical are wide bands of gold with filigree ornamentation, decorated with greenish-blue stones, such as the one at left in the lower illustration. Beside it there is another kind of gold filigree ring surmounted by a miniature gable representing the home established by a marriage. The gable can be opened to reveal a compartment containing either a seal or a miniature picture. The commonest rings are silver filigree bands decorated with colored enamel surfaces, such as those in the upper illustration. Generally, the Hebrew words mazel tov ("good luck"), either in full or abbreviated to their initials m. t., are engraved inside the band in this variety as well as in other kinds of wedding rings. Jewish Museum, New York, and Israel Museum, Jerusalem

fifteenth century contributed toward the commercial development of these countries, particularly in the trade between Europe and Asia and that of the Mediterranean region. The Marranos who fled from the persecution of the Spanish Inquisition played an important part in the development of commerce in the Netherlands, England, and America, to which masses of them had come to seek refuge.

The destruction of the Jewish community in Spain also brought about the shifting of the national leadership from the Iberian peninsula to other centers. Because of their dynamism, the Jews of Spain became bearers of the national culture wherever they settled, and it is no wonder that large numbers of Italian Jews, who had been living in the country for many years, were assimilated among the Spanish Jews and became part "Sephardi." The largest number of Spanish exiles went to Turkey, where the Jews found a haven because of the tolerance of the young Moslem Ottoman state. The fact that in 1517 Palestine became a part of the Turkish empire must also have been an important factor in attracting Jews fleeing from Spain. Within a very short time, the Jewish community in the Holy Land grew, chiefly in Jerusalem and Galilee, and developed firm social and cultural foundations. During the second half of the fifteenth century, Don Joseph Nasi, the Duke of Naxos, attempted to establish a Jewish autonomous center in Tiberias, an event he regarded as marking the beginning of redemption.

DOÑA GRACIA

After the expulsion of the Jews from Spain and Portugal at the end of the fifteenth century, hundreds of wealthy Jewish families, Christians outwardly but clandestinely observing Jewish traditions at the risk of their lives, still remained there. These Marranos hoped for the day when they could leave the lands of Christian fanaticism and openly return to the faith of their fathers.

One of the most important aristocratic families of Spanish Marranos was the Mendes family. This family, the scions of one of the most famous Spanish-Jewish families, the Benvenistes, was forced to adopt the name of Mendes on outwardly accepting Christianity.

A member of the family, Francisco, directed large banks in Lisbon with branches in the Netherlands and France. His wife, Beatrice de Luna, was known by the name of Doña Gracia. After her husband's death, she left Portugal for Antwerp in Flanders, a district in the Low Countries which was then under Spanish rule.

Antwerp was at the time (1537) one of Europe's major commercial centers. Here, Diego Mendes, Doña Gracia's brother-in-law, did considerable business. He achieved an important position in the commercial world and had a great deal of influence on the economic life in the Low Countries and neighboring lands. The House of Mendes became a byword in the business world and maintained ties with European kings and princes.

However, wealth and honor were not enough for Doña Gracia, who was anxious to return to Judaism openly. In Flanders, too, it was difficult for Marranos to live as Jews, because of the Spanish authorities. Doña Gracia accordingly determined to liquidate her bank business in Antwerp and go to Turkey, where she could openly return to the religion of her fathers without incurring any danger.

The son of one of the brothers of the House of Mendes was João Miguez, better known by the name of Don Joseph Nasi. He was a man with energy and initiative and an associate of kings and nobles. He helped Doña Gracia to conduct her large business in Europe, and his efforts made it possible for the family to move to Venice and subsequently to Turkey. When the Mendes family reached Venice, the Senate was informed that Doña Gracia was planning to transfer all her capital to Turkey and return to Judaism there. At the Senate's order, her property was confiscated and later the French king also announced that he would not repay the large debt he owed to the House of Mendes, since it belonged to Jews. Then, by means

"This bitter herb which we eat, what reason has it?" Like the ornamental matsa, a giant bitter herb supported by two men became a traditional illumination in Spanish haggadot. Beneath the plant, a man and his wife are seated at the Passover table. From the manuscript of a 14th-century haggadah. British Museum, London

of friends of the House of Mendes in Turkey, Don Joseph Nasi appealed to the sultan to intercede in its behalf, because the family wished to settle in Turkey and transfer its entire fortune there.

The sultan knew that Turkey would benefit greatly from the immigration of the House of Mendes and other wealthy Marrano families and from the transfer of their business and wealth to the country, and decided to intercede on its behalf with the Venetian authorities. A special envoy of the sultan asked the Venetian Senate to release the property of the House of Mendes and enable the family to leave the country. In their desire to avoid a dispute with the Ottoman sultan, the rulers of Venice freed all the property of the Mendes family. Doña Gracia and her household and other Marrano families thereupon left for Turkey.

THE HOUSE OF MENDES IN TURKEY

In 1553, Doña Gracia arrived in Constantinople. She made a magnificent entry into the Ottoman capital. Four splendid carriages, escorted by mounted men, agents, servants, and a large entourage, passed through the streets of the city, and the Jews of Constantinople received Doña Gracia in great excitement. The members of the Mendes family were now able to breathe freely and return to Judaism openly. Doña Beatrice de Luna officially changed her name to Doña Gracia. Her nephew João joined her in Constantinople and also openly returned to the ancestral faith, under the name of Joseph Nasi. He married Doña Gracia's daughter, Reyna.

The sultan received Doña Gracia courteously and welcomed the transfer of the center of activities of the House of Mendes to his country. The House of Mendes had a network of enterprises in many countries, and the Turkish authorities granted special privileges to the company and its operations, for its wealth and the scope of its commercial activities brought considerable benefit to the economic life of the Ottoman Empire. The House of Mendes conducted commercial agencies in the Balkans, the Aegean Islands, Italy, and France. Special ships transported raw materials from Turkey to other countries and brought back cloth.

Doña Gracia's magnificent palace on the shores of the Bosphorus was open to scholars and learned men whom she cultivated and generously supported. Her name was celebrated throughout the Jewish world for her generosity and extensive activities to save persecuted Marranos in Spain and Portugal and reestablish them in countries to which they succeeded in fleeing. She even helped Marranos save themselves from the claws of the Inquisition and find a safe haven of refuge. Her beneficence was boundless and embraced many countries. Her philanthropic activities were numerous and varied; she helped the poor, contributed large sums for the release of captives, and maintained *yeshivot*, schools, and charitable institutions.

Doña Gracia Mendes. Bronze medallion cast at Ferrara by Pastorino about 1552. Among the Marrano families in Portugal, the House of Mendes was one of the richest in the 16th century.

After the introduction of the Inquisition in Portugal, the members of the Mendes family realized the immediate danger they were in, and after the death of the head of the family, Francisco Mendes (1536), his widow, Gracia (née de Luna), moved from Lisbon to Antwerp. She was followed by many of her relatives, including her daughter, Reyna, and her nephew, João Miguez, who later married Reyna and achieved fame under his Jewish name, Don Joseph Nasi. With great difficulty, the Mendes family succeeded in transferring its huge fortune to Venice, where Gracia set up her household. However, it was Gracia's intention to move with her fortune to free Turkey, where she could openly profess Judaism. The ruler of Venice attempted to prevent the removal of the money. At this point, João Miguez stepped to the fore. He had already established diplomatic ties with the Jews of Turkey, who were enjoying economic and social freedom under Sultan Suleiman the Magnificent (1520–1566). One of Suleiman's Jewish advisers was the court physician Moses Hamon, whose intercession made it possible for the Mendes family to reach Constantinople.

After settling in Constantinople, Gracia was very active in the rescue of Spanish and Portuguese Marranos. She spent a great deal of her fortune in developing the Jewish community of Tiberias, which she and her son-in-law Don Joseph Nasi wished to transform into the nucleus of a Jewish state. Gracia died at Constantinople in 1569. National Library, Paris

עוד וחולצות שעוצטמעד יום והלך לבו חמא ולי התפל ...
וחים הגמין יובי וסבי עיטי מטפייה מנטול תוטא ; ול וחיוןומספר ...
גחיל דבי יחין מגעעל וכבי יוטר ; לימה וזברכי על ההם יותר ...
"
והש בציוע מובי עליהם שו
שטוה שלם ; ויש לי וטובת

אהה יי אליהינצאמילד העי
העריוה ; ראסר לבו אהר
ידי חופה וקהגוטיך ; בי
חופה וקידוש
ווינ בחח
הרי אב בקירבה
ונייחדין שני ערים
נמחכ חורן הכר
הכתוב

ויכיתפקטעה של מטמוחד־
ועליהוביטוזמך ; ווינבריך
קלהביזרוטומין המוחב י
ימך עייתום ; נמיך לבהי ה
תווות המחטר יבלה חומם וסויך
יה כליכוטור כטמנבוחלמ י מ
נמטן ויחפר מיך '
הרי ייוותוי /חוקה הגנוספר־
קטוימ ; עיהדיזלי ; וות ה
חטוין כיות וטך רט ווין ; יל
ביזלמית י

Marginal illumination to the text of the marriage ceremony. The officiating rabbi is shown standing between the bride and groom and reciting the benedictions. The groom extends his right hand, holding the ring toward the bride's hand. Fragment of a page from a manuscript written and illuminated in northern Italy at the end of the 15th century, containing various texts, among them an arrangement of daily prayers. Israel Museum, Jerusalem

DON JOSEPH NASI

Doña Gracia's nephew and son-in-law, Don Joseph Nasi, attained much renown in Turkey. His extensive knowledge, political acumen, charming personality, and wide experience in dealing with the courts of Europe helped make him an intimate of the sultan's court in a short time. Sultan Suleiman the Magnificent had a special affection for Don Joseph Nasi and made him his adviser in political affairs pertaining to the relations between Turkey and Christian Europe. Don Joseph Nasi was conversant with everything that went on in the courts of the European kings, for the agents of the House of Mendes supplied him with information not only on commercial matters, but also on political affairs. His close relationship with the sultan enhanced his prestige in the estimation of all the foreign ambassadors at Constantinople.

Don Joseph Nasi also knew how to use his influence on behalf of his fellow Jews. When, in 1556, Pope Paul IV ordered the arrest of the Marranos in the Italian city of Ancona for handing over to the Inquisition, Don Joseph requested the intercession of the sultan. The latter demanded the release of Jews who were Turkish subjects and threatened to take retaliatory measures against Christians living in the Ottoman Empire if the Pope refused. The sultan's determined stand was effective and the Jews in Ancona who were Ottoman subjects were set free.

THE REVIVAL OF TIBERIAS

At the peak of his influence at the sultan's court, Don Joseph Nasi conceived the idea of redeeming the Jewish people and their land. He wanted to establish a national refuge in Palestine, where Jews from all parts of the world could come to live free of the yoke of tyrannical rulers. At his request, Sultan Suleiman the Magnificent granted him a lease for the city of Tiberias and seven adjacent villages and appointed him governor of the area. Don Joseph regarded the establishment of a Jewish autonomous district in Tiberias and its environs as the beginning of the redemption of the land of Israel.

Why did Don Joseph select Tiberias? His choice of the site was conditioned by a popular belief that the first place to be redeemed would be Tiberias, in accordance with a Talmudic statement, "From there [Tiberias] they would be redeemed" (tractate *Rosh Hashana*).

The city of Tiberias was in ruins and had to be rebuilt. Don Joseph Nasi and Doña Gracia had visions of Jews returning to their own country, cultivating the soil, planting vineyards and fruit trees, developing a silk industry, and transforming the region into a major Jewish center to serve as the nucleus of a Jewish state.

Don Joseph initiated preparatory work for the rehabilitation of the city of Tiberias. He sent his reliable agent Joseph ben Ardot to supervise the construction

140

Illuminated marriage contract from Krems, Austria, 1391–92. One of the earliest European marriage contracts, of which only fragments are extant. Four of its parts later served as the binding of a book, which accounts for the fact that the center section is missing. According to the surviving fragments, Shalom ben Menahem took a wife on "Friday, the fifth day" of an unnamed month in the year "5152 since the creation of the world." The marginal illumination shows the groom at right in a Jewish hat, holding up a large ring with a superimposed miniature building like those most common in Italy and the Netherlands during the Renaissance period. The bride, wearing a crown, is extending her hand to the groom on the other side of the page. The marriage contract is Gothic in its style of ornamentation and portrayal of the human figure. The tradition of ornamenting marriage contracts on parchment is very old; fragments of Egyptian Jewish marriage contracts from the 10th and 11th centuries are still extant. National Library, Vienna

work and erect a wall around the city for the security of the inhabitants. By order of the sultan, building workers from Safad and Damascus were sent to construct the city wall. Despite the efforts of the Arabs, incited by Moslem religious leaders to hamper the building of the wall, the work was accomplished.

Joseph Nasi sent a summons to Jewish communities abroad to come and settle in Tiberias, "in order to restore the land and its population." He dispatched ships to Venice, Ancona, and other ports in Italy to transport Jews to Palestine. However, only a few Jews answered Don Joseph Nasi's call, and only small groups of Jews from Italy, who were suffering from papal persecutions, went to Palestine and settled in Tiberias.

Don Joseph also helped the newcomers earn a livelihood. He had mulberry trees planted for the purpose of developing a silk industry, and arranged for the import of wool from Spain for weaving cloth, in order to further a clothing industry resembling that of Venice. However, his great dream of establishing a Jewish state in Tiberias and the adjacent area, which with the island of Naxos and twelve other small Greek not materialize.

During this period, Suleiman died, to be succeeded by his son Selim, Joseph's friend. Selim presented him with the island of Naxos and twelve other small Greek islands and conferred the title of Duke of Naxos on him.

Joseph's influence increased greatly during Selim's reign and he became the sultan's chief counselor. At Joseph's advice, the sultan declared war on Venice and conquered its island of Cyprus. After being crowned King of Cyprus, Don Joseph had another idea—to settle Jews persecuted in Christian lands there.

But on the accession of Sultan Murad III to the throne, Joseph Nasi's influence began to wane. He died in 1579. Jews everywhere mourned the death of the Jewish prince and statesman.

An Ark of the Law from Mantua, dating from the 16th century. Large iron lamps decorated in the style of the Ark in contemporary North Italian art stand on either side of it. Roman Synagogue Collection, Jerusalem

THE JEWISH CENTER IN THE NETHERLANDS

At this time, living and working in Palestine were Rabbi Joseph Caro (1488–1575), author of the codification of Jewish law embodied in the *Shulhan Arukh*, and Rabbi Isaac Luria, the founder of practical cabala in Safad. The development of practical cabala in Safad eventually led to the emergence of Messianic hopes, which attained their peak in the middle of the seventeenth century with the appearance of the movement of the pseudo-Messiah Sabbatai Zevi. The falseness of Sabbatai Zevi's claims and his subsequent adoption of Islam occasioned a serious crisis among the Jewish

communities of the Orient, more so than among the Jews of Europe. The social and cultural development of Oriental Jewry was stopped short by the collapse of the Sabbatian movement.

Italy was the principal center in which the Jews were influenced by the spirit of the Renaissance. Political conditions were better there. However, the Jews were expelled from southern Italy by the Spaniards in 1492 and were not permitted to return until 1541. During the second half of the sixteenth century, Catholic reaction, combating the Lutheran Reformation with the aid of the Inquisition and the Jesuits, dominated the life of most of Christian Europe. To a certain extent, this reaction restored the Middle Ages and is responsible for introducing the ghetto and all the other suppressive institutions associated with that concept. The Jewish Renaissance which developed in Italy and will be described below did not go far, chiefly because of the Catholic reaction. However, internally, too, the rigorous spirit of the rabbinate and Messianic cabala did not allow the liberal current of humanism to develop. They denounced the critical views of scholars such as Azariah dei Rossi and Judah Leone Modena.

The Jewish center in the Netherlands developed slowly and was not to reach its full flowering until the first half of the seventeenth century. It had been founded by Marranos who fled from the Spanish and Portugese Inquisitions and the flames of the *auto-da-fé*. Marranos who escaped the horrors of publicly confessing their sins before being burned alive established the Jewish communities of Amsterdam and Hamburg and, later, of England and America. After their liberation from the power of the Spanish crown, the Low Countries became the world's leading commercial center. The Jewish community which flourished there produced such unusual personalities as Baruch (Benedict) Spinoza, Manasseh ben Israel, and Uriel da Costa.

THE JEWS IN RENAISSANCE CULTURE

One of the great events which made the period of the Renaissance a major dividing line in human history was the series of important maritime discoveries culminating in the discovery of America by Christopher

(Opposite page) The magnificent Ark of the Law of the Sermide community was originally built for the Jews of Mantua in 1543, as is indicated on one of the chairs placed at either side of it. When another Ark was later set up at Mantua, this was sent to Sermide, where it remained for about three hundred years, until brought to Israel in 1936. The Ark stands in the exhibition hall of the Roman Synagogue in Jerusalem. It is made of wood carved in relief in the typical North Italian style and was painted entirely in gold color. On the outside of the doors, on which Italian Jews customarily write the Ten Commandments, the embossed letters of a poem dealing with the number of the Commandments were engraved, each line of the poem ending with the word el, *meaning God. The Torah scrolls, in embroidered mantles with silver and gold crowns on top, are visible inside the Ark. The finial ornaments on the staves and the plate suspended on one of them are Italian art work of various periods*

142

Interior of the Portuguese Synagogue at Amsterdam, by the Dutch painter Emanuel de Witte (1618–1692). The apparel of the Jewish men and women in the picture corresponds to the general fashion then current in the Netherlands. The painting is somewhat dramatic and to a certain extent resembles a fashion show. Israel Museum, Jerusalem

piece, in *terza rima*. A number of Jews also wrote prose compositions in Italian. In fact, Italian-Jewish society of the Renaissance period combined what was best in secular and Jewish culture—thus anticipating the phenomenon which was to become general in Europe in the nineteenth century—but without surrendering or endangering its Jewish cultural, or even less its religious, identity. An unbroken tradition of Hebrew poetry and *belles-lettres* existed in Italy long before the days of Moses Mendelssohn and the beginnings of the so-called "enlightenment" in Germany. Moses Hayyim Lussatto, who is generally considered the earliest modern Hebrew poet and playwright, was only continuing the tradition of Jewish *belles-lettres* which had been known in Italy without interruption from the Middle Ages on. Although his genius was exceptional, from the point of view of Italian Jewry, he was not a great originator.

The typical Jewish Renaissance figure, although he belongs to the seventeenth century rather than the sixteenth, was Rabbi Leone (Judah Arye) Modena of Venice, who wrote and published plentifully in Italian as well as in Hebrew, composed poems and plays, and also wrote responsa to inquiries on points of halakhic law. He preached so eloquently in Italian that princes of the royal blood and high members of the clergy came to hear him. Rabbi Modena was a mainstay of the Jewish theater in Venice, as well as of the Jewish musical society which once flourished there, and wrote in Italian a treatise on Jewish customs for King James I of England. But, at the same time, he was unstable and of poor personal character, and frequented low company. Because of his addiction to gambling, he lost most of the money he earned, with the result that he had to follow twenty-six vocations in his lifetime in order to earn a living. For the Italian Jews of the Renaissance were influenced by the surrounding atmosphere not only in their intellectual life—and the loose living and vices characteristic of the age were by no means unknown in the Jewish quarter.

147

Majolica Passover dish apparently made by "Isaac Cohen, the First" of Pesaro, Italy, 1616. The center of the plate contains the benediction for the wine and the catchwords listing the order of the ceremony; the flange border is decorated with a floral design in which there are cartouches with figures of Moses and Aaron, and David and Solomon. The upper cartouche shows Joseph revealing his identity to his brothers; the lower one consists of a scene of Passover in Egypt—the Israelites carrying their packs and weapons are seen eating of the paschal lamb as they walk around a table. Special ceramic Passover plates were common in Spain in the 14th century, and from there their use spread to Italy and other countries. Jewish Museum, New York

JEWISH ART

The artistic spirit of the Renaissance penetrated into every aspect of Jewish life. The synagogues built in the period by the Jews, not only of Italy but of other lands as well, were designed by the finest architects, and in their graceful proportions and elaborate decorations—especially of the reading desk and the Ark—reflected the artistic spirit of the environment. Some of these synagogues have been transported to Israel. The embroideries and silver appurtenances for the Torah scroll were lovely and sometimes made by master craftsmen.

The *ketubba*—marriage contract—was gracefully illuminated to express the joy of the occasion, and sometimes even human figures were painted on it. Betrothal rings were masterpieces of the goldsmith's craft. Sometimes documents such as the *semikha*—ordination document of a rabbi—or the *kabbala* (written license) for a *shohet* (ritual slaughterer) were similarly illuminated.

The favorite subject for illumination after the *ketub-*

ba was the scroll of Esther—not the copy used by the cantor for the public reading, which had to be plain, but the scrolls in which the ordinary worshipers followed. Of these there are very many copies still extant, some of which contain most remarkable examples of Jewish art of the period.

At an earlier date, Jews refused to have their portraits painted; the earliest surviving portraits of Jews were made by malevolent Christians, such as one in Mantua located in a church, the site of which had been confiscated from a Jew. But from the Renaissance period on they began to make their appearance not only in the form of paintings and engravings but also, in rare cases, in the form of medals, such as one which shows the great Marrano lady, Doña Gracia, after her return to Judaism, and therefore bears a Hebrew inscription.

JEWS IN THE CHRISTIAN WORLD

The characteristic function of the Jew throughout history has been to interpret people to people and civilization to civilization. This was the case for the Renaissance period as well. In fact, it is possible to say that the Renaissance in Europe owed its origin to the series of translations carried out largely by Jews or with Jewish collaboration, often by way of the Hebrew language, of the great classics of ancient science and philosophy preserved by the Arabs. Increasing knowledge of these classics in the West started the revival of learning. This process was at its height in the twelfth and thirteenth centuries, but continued into the sixteenth. Thus, Christian scholars became aware of the importance of Hebrew for scholarship in general, and at the end of the fifteenth century a revival of Hebrew study got under way in Christian circles. The most significant figures in this trend were Pico della Mirandola in Italy and Johann von Reuchlin in Germany. When, at this period, an apostate named Pfefferkorn tried to have Hebrew literature condemned to be burned, it was Reuchlin who defended it in a series of famous books. In part, this Christian revival of the study of Hebrew was what rendered the original Hebrew Bible accessible to them, thus resulting in the criticism of Catholic traditions and institutions which culminated in the Reformation.

(Opposite page) Montefiore Ark Curtain, embroidered at Pesaro in 1620 by "Rachel, wife of Judah" of the "House of Monte Fiore," an ancestor of Sir Moses Montefiore. The floral decorations on the curtain are similar in conception to the designs on the Passover dish shown above at left, and date from the same period. The curtain is now hanging on the Ark of Conegliano Veneto (early 18th century) which serves as the Ark of the Law in the Roman Synagogue, Jerusalem. The Ark and the curtain were brought to Israel along with the numerous other ritual objects by Dr. S. A. Nahon of Jerusalem

The first printed Passover haggadot *were made from engraved wooden blocks. The first printed illustrated* haggadah *was executed by Gershon Cohen in 1526—27 in Prague. This page from the Prague* haggadah *is the beginning of the second part of the Passover home ceremony, after grace has been said. Within the text is a picture of Elijah, the announcer of the Messiah's advent, mounted on his donkey. In the border around the text are representations of Samson carrying the gates of Gaza and Judith holding the head of Holofernes. Above them are Adam and Eve eating of the apple. It is believed that the letter* shin *at the bottom of the page (to the left of the shield with the lion rampant) is the initial of the artist's name,* Shahor

Although Martin Luther himself was a ferocious anti-Semite, the Jews thus came to be suspected by the Catholic Church of supporting and even instigating the movement which threatened its existence. Accordingly, when the Counter-Reformation or Catholic Reaction began in the mid-sixteenth century, the Jews were among the principal sufferers.

An effort was now made to thrust them out of cultural life, which formerly they had adorned, and to cut them off from the contact with non-Jews which had hitherto had such fruitful results. In theory, this was not new. It had begun in the Middle Ages. The Fourth Lateran Council of 1215 had formulated regulations to bring this about. But, in the Middle Ages, laws laid down an ideal rather than a rule of conduct, and these elaborate regulations were enforced only locally, sporadically, and leniently—and least of all in the dominions subject to the rule of the popes themselves. Henceforth, however, conditions were changed, and the new savage code became the general rule in Catholic countries, where it was implicitly obeyed.

The general lines were laid down by the bull *Cum Nimis Absurdum* of Pope Paul IV in 1555. According to this papal edict, Jews were henceforth to be rigorously shut off in a special quarter known as the Ghetto, from which they were not allowed to be absent at night and into which no Christian was to be allowed after nightfall, when the gates were to be closed and barred. Jews were no longer to practice medicine or any other honorable way of earning a livelihood. They were not allowed to have Christians in their employ. At all times, they had to wear a disfiguring hat, or a badge of a special color, to mark them off for contumely from Christians (this, too, had been enacted by the Lateran Councils, but had hitherto been honored more in the breach than in the observance). A rigorous censorship of Hebrew books was instituted. The Talmud was burned, and other Hebrew works were permitted only if they were certified to have nothing in them which Christians might consider objectionable. Conversionist sermons, generally given by apostates, which Jews were compelled to attend, were instituted, and Jewish children were frequently seized and baptized.

Thus, the entire nature of Jewish life deteriorated, and the environment of the Renaissance became tragically changed. Now, the ghetto spread in Italy and adjacent lands, lasting in fact until the nineteenth century. On the other hand, although the spirit changed, it is important to realize that toleration still continued. Conditions in the seventeenth century in Italy were far worse than they had been in the fifteenth, but, on the other hand, they were immeasurably better than in Spain and Portugal, where the pyres of the Inquisition were still being kindled. It was only later that the new Jewish communities founded by the Marranos in northern Europe began to flourish. Although, in certain periods, the popes treated the Jews worse than at other times, Jews were at least permitted to stay alive in the countries of Europe under papal domination.

Fragment of a page of a Passover haggadah *printed at Venice in 1609. The Venice* haggadah *was set up in fine type and printed with translations into Spanish, Italian, or German, in Hebrew characters. The illustrations, made from wooden blocks, were accompanied by a rhymed explanation in the language into which the* haggadah *was translated. A fragment from a copy translated into Ladino (Judaeo-Spanish) is shown here. According to the explanation, the picture shows "husband and wife sleeping apart, so as not to witness the throwing of the newborn infants into the river." The word* separtidos *(apart), used simply to find a rhyme for* nacidos *(newborn infant), apparently determined the scene in the picture*

In the seventeenth century, when the so-called Period of Enlightenment began in the Western world, a large part of European Jewry dwelt in Poland. The beginnings of Polish Jewry are obscure. Remnants of the Khazars' kingdom arriving by way of the Ukraine may have constituted its first communities. Jewish merchants from the Byzantine Empire came to Poland on business, and a number of them may have settled there.

There is an account of special privileges accorded to Jewish settlers in 905. The Jewish community increased in size and power, particularly at the end of the eleventh century and during the twelfth, after the arrival of many refugees from Germany fleeing from the violence engendered by the Crusades. Economically, the country was retarded and, besides physical security, the Jews found ample opportunity for business and financial activities there. The first Polish coins were minted by Jews in the twelfth century and bear Hebrew inscriptions. The Polish rulers approved of the Jews' activities, which contributed to the country's development, and saw to it that they were granted a legal status. In 1264, Boleslaw the Chaste, Duke of Kalisz, granted them a charter of protection. At first it applied only to the region of Great Poland, but after the country's unification the charter was con-

firmed in 1334 by Casimir the Great. Following the annexation of Lithuania by Poland, Grand Duke Witold gave the charter force in that country, too, in 1389.

The charter laid down the rights and obligations of the Jews, and legal procedures between Jews and Christians and among Jews themselves. It granted the Jews assurances that their lives and property, including religious institutions such as synagogues and cemeteries, would be safe, by imposing severe penalties on anyone harming them. Jews were allowed to engage in business and financial transactions and granted complete freedom of movement. According to legend, King Casimir expanded the privileges granted by Boleslaw at the urging of his Jewish mistress, Esther.

The growth of the Jewish community thanks to the privileges it received aroused the resentment of the Catholic clergy, which was powerful and exerted considerable influence on the masses. Various Church Councils strongly demanded the implementation of the Church's decisions regarding Jews, especially those concerning the limiting of contact between Jews and Christians, concentration of Jews in special quarters, and the introduction of distinctive marks on their clothing. However, the demands went unheeded. The Church's regulations were not enforced in Poland, and the badge of shame was never introduced there.

EUROPE AT THE END OF THE RENAISSANCE

POLAND IN THE FIFTEENTH AND SIXTEENTH CENTURIES

A change for the worse in the condition of the Jews in Poland occurred at the end of the fourteenth century and the beginning of the fifteenth, during the reign of Ladislas Jagello (1386–1434), the first king who refused to confirm the Jewish constitution. Under the influence of accounts reaching Poland of anti-Jewish persecution in Germany, the burghers began to harass their Jewish competitors with the active help of the clergy.

Prayer Part from an illuminated manuscript of Jacob Ben Asher. Mantua, Italy, 1436. Private collection

During the reign of Ladislas, the Jews were for the first time accused of desecrating the Host (Poznan, 1399). In 1407, priests in Cracow charged the Jews with the murder of a Christian child, and an incited mob attacked the local Jewish population, killing many of them and robbing their houses and stores. A Church Council held in Kalisz in 1420 succeeded in making trouble for the Jews, especially with regard to financial transactions.

King Casimir IV (1447–1492) was by nature an enlightened and liberal man, but Cardinal Olesnicki, an avowed Jew-hater, had a great deal of influence over him. The Cardinal even brought the Dominican monk John of Capistrano, infamous for his anti-Jewish activities in Italy and Germany, to Poland to help him in his war against the Jews. It took the Jews six years to persuade the king to renew their privileges in 1453. But it was a transitory victory. At the insistence of Cardinal Olesnicki, the king abolished the Jews' privileges in 1454, and thereafter the situation of the Jews went from bad to worse. A crusade against the Turks proclaimed by Pope Pius II in 1463 set off serious attacks against the Jews at Lwow, Cracow, and Poznan.

The poisoning of the atmosphere by the agitation of the clergy on the one hand, and the hate of the burghers stemming from economic reasons on the other, brought about considerable changes in the living conditions of the Jews of Poland. Prior to this, they had enjoyed complete freedom in their choice of a place to live or in traveling for business reasons. Now, a number of towns were anxious to secure a special privilege to forbid Jews within their limits. In cities in which they were permitted to dwell, Jews were forced to crowd into their own quarters. A number of cities expelled their Jews, and others imposed restrictions on their commercial activity. An extremely serious turn for the worse came toward the end of the fifteenth century when Alexander Jagello, Archduke of Lithuania, decided in 1495 to expel the Jews from his country. Some of the Jews forced to leave made their way to Turkey, and others went to Poland. In 1503, the Jews were permitted to return to Lithuania, with the promise that their property would be restored, but in the meantime German and Swedish settlers had established themselves there and forced the Jews out of commerce and the crafts.

Despite all the difficulties with which they had to contend, the Jews succeeded in developing the coun-

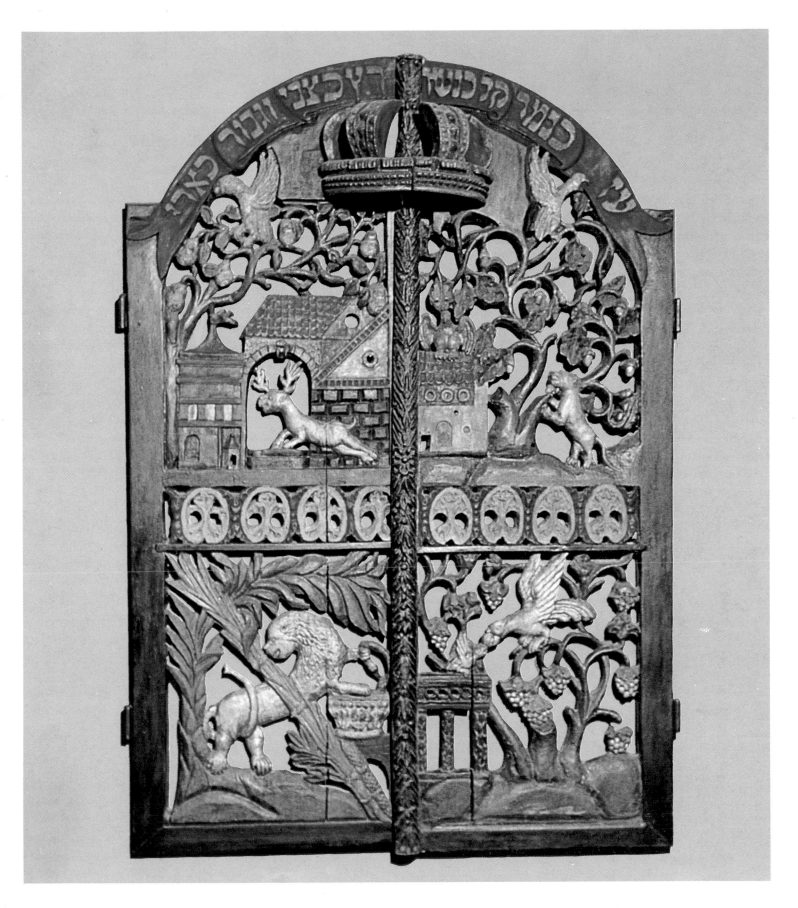

"Be bold as a leopard, light as an eagle, swift as a deer, and strong as a lion, to the will of your Father Who is in heaven."
These words in the Ethics of the Fathers *by Judah ben Tema served as an important source for the decorations of the synagogue and the Ark of the Law in many Jewish communities in Europe. The illustration shows the carved and painted 18th-century wooden Ark doors of the Cracow synagogue. Dor Va-Dor Museum of the Chief Rabbinate, Hekhal Shelomo, Jerusalem*

153

try's commerce for the benefit of the Polish economy and, of course, for their own good, too. Jewish commercial houses maintained close business ties with the markets of Central Europe, Italy, and Turkey. They also played a conspicuous role in financial affairs, and in various cities there were Jewish banks. The number of Jews engaged in the crafts mounted steadily.

Most Polish Jews lived in towns and were organized in communities possessing a certain measure of autonomy in conducting their internal affairs and religious

life. They had rabbis, of course, and it is quite certain that study of their spiritual treasures was central to the existence of Polish Jewry. Nevertheless, it is noteworthy that until the end of the fourteenth century, no names of outstanding scholars appear in the sources. Only in the fifteenth century did rabbis come from Western Europe to lay the foundation for the spiritual activity which was later to develop and transform Poland into the center of Jewish lore in Europe. On the other hand, Jews in Poland early turned their attentions to the study of medicine, which promised a good income and also a respected position in Christian society. In the fifteenth century, young Jews from Poland were already studying medicine at the university of Padua, Italy. Polish kings and nobles mostly employed Jewish physicians.

The sixteenth century was a glorious period in Polish history, and the Jews, too, had it a little easier. King Sigismund I (1506–1548) was an enlightened ruler who advocated liberal views. He had a Jewish physician who exercised considerable influence at court. In addition, Jewish commerce was an important source of revenue for the state treasury. Consequently, the king protected the Jews and supported them against the agitation of the clergy. He also approved of the immigration of more Jews into the country. With a view to making the collection of taxes imposed on the Jews more efficient, the king attempted to introduce centralization. He appointed Jewish tax collectors and also named rabbis to work together with them and help them by virtue of their spiritual authority. However, the communities opposed the arrangement, which interfered with their autonomy, and it was abolished during the reign of Sigismund Augustus (1548–1572), who restored the privilege of the communities to appoint their own rabbis.

Despite the king's desire to protect the Jews, he did not always have the power to resist the combined pressure of the clergy and the burghers, which grew as the Jews' economic condition improved. Here and there, their freedom of commercial activity was restricted, and certain towns, including Warsaw, insisted on their right to forbid Jews to reside within their borders.

The spread of the Reformation from Germany to Poland in the sixteenth century stimulated the Catholic clergy to redouble their efforts against the Jews. The priests called the members of the reformistic sects "Judaizers" and accused the Jews of seeking converts among Christians. At this time, the blood libel and charges of desecrating the Host were revived.

(Above left) This Dutch Hanukkah lamp of beaten brass, with its back plate and two side plates, is typical of the 18th century. The ornamentation containing figures is not unusual for Dutch Hanukkah lamps. Gift of Werner Vadubinsky, Amsterdam, to Israel Museum, Jerusalem
(Below left) Delftware for Passover bearing Yiddish inscriptions. From left to right: "festive," "Passover," "happy holiday"

TAX COLLECTORS AND THE KING'S "SERVANTS OF THE TREASURY"

The power of the Jew-haters became greater, especially during the reign of Sigismund III (1587–1632), who was under the influence of the Jesuits. He, too, confirmed the privileges of the Jews on acceding to the throne, and on certain occasions defended them against attempts to deprive them of their rights, but, in the face of the intensified activity of the clergy and the stubbornness of the burghers, he could not do much.

As a consequence of the restrictions on their commercial activity in the second half of the fifteenth century, many Jews sought other ways of making a living. Even previously, a considerable number found employment as the agents and stewards of the nobility. Now the importance of this kind of work increased. It was very convenient for the Polish aristocrats to entrust the management of their estates and other enterprises to Jews who collected the taxes and customs, thus allowing them to remain free to engage in politics or devote themselves to idleness and amusements. Accordingly, the nobility generally did not participate in the war which the clergy and the burghers waged against the Jews. However, for the Jews, the rental transactions were disastrous. They stood between the renting nobles who were interested in as high an income as possible, meaning a maximum exploitation of the farmers, and the farmers who did whatever they could to avoid fulfilling their obligations. All pressure on the peasants was exerted by means of the Jewish agents, and, of course, this state of affairs stirred up a strong hatred of the Jews among the farmers who regarded them as being responsible for their wretched position.

By law, the Jews were directly subservient to the king as "servants of the treasury." They paid the monarch an annual money tax (from 1549 on, this head tax consisted of one zloty per person). In addition, the Jews were also required to pay taxes in goods and services, which varied from one town to another and from region to region. Only in the middle of the sixteenth century did the king, under pressure from the nobility, relinquish income from Jews living on private lands, which was thereafter paid to the landowners, i.e., the nobles.

The large communities enjoyed considerable autonomy in their internal affairs; only litigation with Christians had to be conducted in the court of the voivode, who would appoint a special representative to act as "judge of the Jews." Jurisdiction in litigation between Jews resided with Jewish religious courts, which functioned according to Jewish law. Rabbis and community leaders had wide powers and conducted the affairs of the community firmly. They managed every aspect of life in the Jewish quarter, regulating business, supervising the crafts, keeping an eye on the moral conduct of the members of the community, maintaining synagogues and charitable institutions,

Delftware for the holidays. In every country, Jews customarily made use of conventional means of artistic expression for ornamenting ritual objects connected with Jewish observances. In the Netherlands of the 18th century, they used delftware for special occasions. The Jews had plates made for their holidays, bearing decorations and inscriptions appropriate to each festival. On Passover, special dishes were required not only for ornamentation but also for everyday use. However, Dutch Jews introduced the use of special plates for other holidays as well. Upper picture shows a Passover plate with the word Pesach *(Passover) in the center. The bottom picture contains a special plate for the Day of Atonement, with the inscription, "May a good verdict be sealed for you." Israel Museum, Jerusalem*

155

(Above) Torah crown and finials. Silver finials were placed on the ends of the staves of the Torah scroll and a silver crown set around them. The crown is from San Daniele del Friuli. Presented by the poet Isaac Luzzatto. Roman Synagogue Collection, Jerusalem

(Below) A silver basin and jug for ritual washing of the hands by the Cohanim (priests) before the blessing of the congregation, on a wooden carved capital. Roman Synagogue Collection, Jerusalem

etc. To defray their expenses, they imposed taxes on the members of the community which were stringently collected.

"THE COUNCIL OF FOUR LANDS"

The communities were responsible to the state treasury for collecting taxes from the Jews. The treasury official preferred to reach an agreement with the communities on an overall sum and leave the internal distribution among the members up to the communal leaders. At first, the treasury negotiated with each community individually. In time, closer ties were established among the communities in each district, and they began paying their taxes in a single lump sum through the principal community. Collaboration in the fiscal sphere also led to consultations and joint religious, spiritual, and social activities. District committees thus established ties which constantly grew closer.

This development brought about the unification of Polish Jewry in an unusual form. In 1580, the *Vaad Arba Aratsot* (Council of Four Lands) came into being as the body centralizing the payment of Jewish head taxes to the treasury. The organization took its name from the four provinces comprising the Polish kingdom which were represented on the Council: Great Poland, Little Poland, Red or Polish Russia, and Lithuania. The name was not changed when the Jews of Lithuania seceded in 1623, nor when the three remaining provinces were divided into twelve fiscal districts. A "parliament" consisting of the leaders in the various provinces met twice a year—at Jaroslaw in the summer and at Lublin in the winter—for the purpose of arranging current matters. The Council of Four Lands, which played a major role in preserving Jewish rights, annulling severe anti-Jewish laws, shaping the spiritual life of Polish Jewry, and adapting Jewish society to changing conditions, lasted until 1764, when it was abolished by the Polish Diet.

THE TALMUD AS THE BASIS OF LIFE

The Jewish community's principal concern was education. Each boy had to attend *heder* (elementary religious school) from the age of six until his confirmation at the age of thirteen. For boys whose parents could not afford tuition, the community maintained a free school, called a Talmud Torah. In the *heder*, the children learned to read and write Hebrew, the prayers, the Pentateuch with Rashi's commentary, and a little Mishna and Gemara. The language of instruction was Yiddish, the medieval German which refugees from Germany had brought to Eastern Europe and enriched with numerous Hebrew words and expressions. This tongue, written in Hebrew characters, was the vernacular of the Jewish home and street—a national language in the full sense of the word, precious to those speaking it.

Ark of the Law with sliding doors ornamented in silver, on which are two tablets bearing the Ten Commandments. Inside are four Torah scrolls wrapped in embroidered mantles, bearing crowns and finials. The breastplate hanging on the scroll second from the left has the words Sefer Shelishi *(Third Torah Scroll) engraved on it, indicating that this is the third scroll to be read on* Shabbat; *this is an unusual practice. The Ark is from the Mantua community*

After completing their course of study in the *heder,* the boys could continue their education in *yeshivot* which existed in many towns. There they studied the Talmud and its commentaries and received the training required to enable them to serve as rabbis. However, many boys attended *yeshivot* to acquire an education for its own sake, with no intention of entering the rabbinate. The educational standards in Jewish lore were quite high even among businessmen and craftsmen, and Talmudic scholars were held in high esteem.

157

The synagogue of Conegliano Veneto near Venice was established between 1701 and 1719 in a small but flourishing Jewish community. Its design is typical of Italian bipolar (i.e., with the Ark and reader's platform placed opposite each other) synagogues of the Baroque period. The Ark of the Law of gilded carved wood stands at the eastern wall and the platform bearing the reading desk is against the western wall. The interior was narrow and long, with benches and compartments placed along the northern and southern walls. The women's gallery was in the upper story and was separated from the synagogue interior by a latticework

Talmudic studies began to flower in Poland during the sixteenth century, especially on the arrival there of Rabbi Jacob Pollak, a native of Prague who in 1503 was appointed Rabbi in Cracow. Several years later, he became involved in a controversy with the leaders of the community and left the rabbinate; nevertheless, he remained head of the *yeshiva* and developed a system of dialectic which struck deep roots in the Polish *yeshivot*. His pupils included Rabbi Shalom Shakhna, who founded the *yeshiva* at Lublin, which

of carved wood. The synagogue was transferred to Jerusalem in 1952 at the initiative of Federico Luziano with the active participation of Dr. S. A. Nahon and under the professional supervision of the late Mordecai Narkiss, then director of the Bezalel National Museum. To fit the interior hall in which the synagogue was installed, the women's gallery was set up on a higher level behind the reading platform. These two pages show the splendid Ark of the Law from Conegliano Veneto with the Torah scrolls inside. Roman Synagogue, Jerusalem

he built into a major spiritual center. His pupil and son-in-law, Rabbi Moses Isserles, acquired worldwide fame as one of the last great codifiers. His emendations to the popular abridgment of Jewish law, Joseph Caro's *Shulhan Arukh* (Prepared Table), which he called *Mappa* (Tablecloth), became an integral part of this work for Ashkenazic communities everywhere and helped establish its authority among Jews of European origin.

Whereas Rabbi Isserles acknowledged the authority

159

of the *Shulhan Arukh* and was concerned only with adapting it to the rulings of the scholars of France and Germany and to the practices of the communities in Germany and Poland, Rabbi Solomon Luria, the sixteenth-century East European codifier, opposed the *Shulhan Arukh*. He doubted the authority of the codifiers and in his response to inquiries on halakhic questions preferred to rely on Talmudic sources. He was also against the system of dialectics. He revealed an unusual critical sense in his partial commentary to the Talmud, *Yam shel Shelomo* (Solomon's Sea), in which he made an important contribution to correcting the Talmudic text.

A number of famous scholars who served as rabbis and the heads of *yeshivot*, and became renowned as codifiers, appeared in Poland in the second half of the sixteenth century also. They included Rabbi Mordecai Jaffe, author of *Levush Malkhut* (Royal Garb), a partial commentary on Jacob ben Asher's code *(Tur)*; Rabbi Joshua Falk, author of *Me'irat Einayim* (Light for the Eyes), a commentary on the section on civil law and administration in the *Shulhan Arukh*; Rabbi Eliezer Edels, one of the most celebrated Talmudic commentators, who wrote *Hiddushei Halakhot* (Halakhic Novellae) and *Hiddushei Haggadot* (Homiletic Novellae); and Rabbi Joel Serkes, author of *Bayit Hadash*

(A New House), on Jacob ben Asher's comprehensive code, *Arab'a Turim*. These and many others spread knowledge of Jewish lore and glorified learning in the *yeshivot* of Poland, profoundly influencing the development of Judaism.

In the sixteenth century, knowledge of printing also reached Poland, and in 1530 the Hebrew Pentateuch was first printed at Cracow. Printing shops were also opened in other towns and in time they became serious competitors of the veteran printers in Venice and Prague.

In addition to the Talmud, many Jewish scholars in Poland also devoted themselves to the cabala. These included the above-mentioned Rabbis Moses Isserles and Mordecai Jaffe. One of the greatest cabalists in Poland was Rabbi Isaiah Hurwitz, author of *Sh'nei Luhot ha-Berit* (Two Tablets of the Covenant), who went to Palestine in 1621 and died in Safad.

THE HORRORS OF 1648–49

The beginning of the seventeenth century found Polish Jewry well organized, after having successfully withstood numerous trials. It knew how to stand up

Torah cloth from the Castilian synagogue in Rome, 1790. Embroidered cloth for the table on which the Torah scroll was placed for reading was common in Italy. The cloths were made of expensive brocade which was interwoven with gold threads and splendid Baroque ornamentation. In the 18th century, it was customary to embroider the cloth with the names of the donor and the recipient synagogue. Roman Synagogue Collection, Jerusalem

Women's gallery in the Conegliano Veneto synagogue, as arranged in the Roman Synagogue in Jerusalem. Instead of two doors, one on either side of the reading platform located at the western end of the synagogue, only one door was installed in the reconstructed interior. The latticework of the women's gallery, which was on the second story of the original building, is visible on either side of the doorway. On the reading desk on the platform (called teva in Italy) are silver candlesticks set on cornucopias as they were in the original synagogue

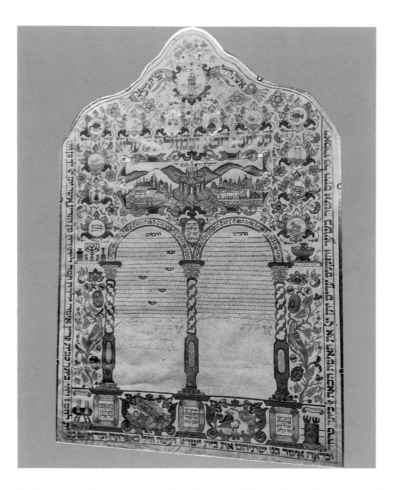

Italian marriage contract illuminated with traditional scenes of rebuilt Jerusalem at the top and signs of the zodiac at the sides. Private collection

Silver binding of festival prayer book made in Venice in 1750. Israel Museum, Jerusalem

for its rights, defend itself against its enemies, and adapt itself to changing circumstances. It took pride in its *yeshivot* and learned men who served as a beacon to all of Jewry. Suddenly this Jewish community was beset by a wave of destruction, when the Ukrainian peasants rose up against their Polish oppressors and against the Jews who served them.

The Polish nobles had vast estates in the Ukraine. Many Jews worked for them as agents. In order to be able to fulfill their obligations to the landlords, the agents had to make heavy demands on the serfs.

The Catholic Polish noble held the Greek Orthodox Ukrainian peasant in contempt. He considered him a slave belonging to an inferior race and treated him with relentless brutality. The Ukrainian peasant reacted to this attitude with a deadly hatred. But the Polish *pan* was far away, while his representative, the Jew, was always before his eyes. It was only natural that the farmers' hostility should be directed primarily against the alien, unbelieving Jew.

The first signs of the approaching storm were already felt in the 1630s, when local uprisings broke out in various places. In one of them, in 1637, about three hundred Jews were killed and many synagogues were destroyed. But the general revolt occurred in 1648, when the Cossack leader Bogdan Chmielnicki, who had formed an alliance with the Khan of the Crimean Tartars, assumed command of the rebels. A large army of Tartars and Cossacks marched against the kingdom of Poland, joined by masses of Ukrainians. The Polish troops were defeated. In their advance, the rebels burned Jewish houses and savagely murdered men, women, and children. Thousands of Jews who tried to save themselves by flight died by the wayside.

The Cossacks and Ukrainians knew no mercy and wildly maltreated the Jews. Fortunate were those who fell into the hands of the Tartars. They were taken to Turkey where they were ransomed by local Jews. For the purpose of ransoming the captives, money was collected in other Jewish communities which accounts of the horrors had reached.

Rabbi Nathan Nata Hannover of Zaslav, who was an eyewitness of the events and succeeded in escaping to Western Europe, wrote a gripping description of all the atrocities committed against the Jews, in his chronicle of 1653, *Yeven Metsulla* (Deep Mire).

There was no deception which Chmielnicki did not stoop to in his "holy war." When he learned that several hundred Jews had found refuge in the town of Nemirov, he sent troops carrying Polish flags there. The Jews thought these were Poles coming to their rescue and opened the gate of the fortress for them. They were all massacred. In Tulchin, the Poles and Jews pledged to defend the city together and stay loyal to one another. But, in the end, the Poles betrayed the Jews when the Cossacks promised to spare their lives if they laid down their arms. About fifteen hundred Jews died a martyr's death there. Then the Poles who betrayed them were also slaughtered. Tens of thousands of Jews were massacred in Polonnoe,

Konstantinov, Pinsk, and many other places. In Lwow, where the mayor of the city refused to abandon the Jews, Chmielnicki was satisfied with receiving a ransom.

In November, 1648, when Chmielnicki's troops advanced on Warsaw, the Poles entered into negotiations with them and persuaded them to return to the Ukraine. However, that did not put a stop to the catastrophe which overwhelmed the Jewish people. The agreement between Poland and the Cossacks did not go into effect until the end of 1651; meanwhile, fighting broke out a number of times. Even after the peace treaty was concluded, Chmielnicki did not remain inactive. He came to an agreement with Czar Alexis of Russia with respect to the annexation of the eastern Ukraine to the Muscovite empire, and in 1654 he once more invaded Poland, this time together with a Russian army. Now, too, the Jews were the principal victims. Some of them fled for their lives, and the rest were massacred in Mohilev, Vitebsk, Minsk, Vilna, and elsewhere.

To further compound the horrors, the Swedes in 1655 also invaded Poland. The fact that the Swedes did not discriminate against the Jews was interpreted by the Polish patriots as proof of the charge that the Jews had collaborated with the enemy. They attacked the Jews and carried out atrocities which equaled those committed by Chmielnicki.

It was not until 1657, after Chmielnicki's death, that the Russian army withdrew and the Swedes also returned home. This marked the end of a period of indescribable suffering which had lasted eight years. More than seven hundred Jewish communities were wiped out or severely damaged. The number of victims was estimated to have run into the hundreds of thousands. The Jewish communities in all of the eastern Ukraine had been annihilated. Polish Jewry had been crushed for good. The refugees who escaped the slaughter were scattered all across Europe and, wherever they came, they brought accounts of the destruction of Polish Jewry. A heavy grief settled on the Jewish communities, and the profound impression left on everyone by the unprecedented disaster found expression in various works—in penitential prayers

Brocade Ark curtain with floral designs, hanging in front of the Ark of Law from Conegliano Veneto. The inscription in the cartouche at the bottom of the curtain was added in 1841. Roman Synagogue Collection, Jerusalem

and in lamentations. Many considered the horrors which had wracked Polish Jewry as the agonies preceding the advent of the Messiah. Cabalistic doctrine found fertile soil everywhere. People indulged in frequent fasts and recited special cabalistic passages. Anticipation of imminent redemption mounted.

Magnificent Passover dish from Poland, 18th century. The lower part of the dish, divided into three compartments for each of the three ceremonial matsot, is enclosed by an ornamental copper grill. In the upper part of the dish are containers for the haroset, the bone representing the Paschal lamb, an egg representing the daily Temple sacrifice, and parsley used as a bitter herb to recall the bitterness of Egyptian bondage. The upper part of the dish is ornamented with three crowns borne aloft by six lions. The inscription under the crown refers to the practice of eating matsa and bitter herbs together at the Passover ceremony, introduced by the Talmudic scholar Hillel in the 1st century B.C.E. The custom of ornamenting Passover plates and dishes was widespread in all the Jewish communities of Europe, but the use of magnificently designed dishes like this one developed only in Germany and Poland. Jewish Museum, New York

ITALIAN JEWRY IN THE SIXTEENTH CENTURY

Many of the Jews who had been expelled from Spain had found a haven in Italy. Everywhere, their coming strengthened the Jewish communities and stimulated the Jews to greater activity in the country's spiritual and economic life. In addition to refugee Jews, Marranos fleeing from Spain and Portugal also came to Italy to escape the talons of the Inquisition and return openly to Judaism.

At this time, Italy was an important center of Jewish learning, especially thanks to scholars coming from Germany and Poland. The *yeshiva* at Padua was headed by Rabbi Jacob Muenz, a native of Mainz, Germany, an outstanding Talmudic scholar, and later, by his son, Rabbi Abraham Muenz (died 1540), and by Rabbi Meir Katzenellenbogen (until 1565), who was also the leader of the Venetian community. At Mantua, there was a *yeshiva* which had become famous under the direction of Rabbi Joseph Colon (died 1480). Spanish scholars who made their homes in Italy brought cabalistic as well as Talmudic learning to Italy. Italian Jews also engaged in secular sciences and in philosophy and poetry, and took part in the dynamic spiritual life of the Renaissance period. The Spanish refugees, too, became part of this cultural atmosphere.

From the period of the Renaissance until the end of the eighteenth century, the culture of the Jews of northern Italy was immersed in general Italian culture. More than anywhere else in the art of Italy's Jews, this influence is apparent in the art of synagogues and their appurtenances. Arks of the Law carved in wood recall in their ornamentation Italian furniture of the Renaissance and Baroque periods. The Ark curtains, Torah scroll mantles, scroll binders, and reading-desk covers were made of rich brocade embroidery in typical Italian style. The front ornamental plates, crowns, and finials of the Torah scrolls suggest, as do the other ritual objects for everyday use and for holidays, contemporary Italian work in silver and gold.

DAVID REUBENI AND SOLOMON MOLKO

In 1523, a strange visitor, who aroused a great deal of excitement among the Jews, arrived in Venice. He was a man by the name of David, who claimed to be the brother of King Joseph, ruler of the Jewish tribes of Reuben, Gad, and Manasseh living in the desert of Habur. Hence the origin of his name, Reubeni, i.e., "the Reubenite." He demanded that the Jews of Venice help him reach Rome, since he was on an errand to the Pope for his brother. He found Jews who believed what he told them and helped him. David Reubeni then went to Rome mounted on a white horse. He was received by Pope Clement VII, to whom he proposed an alliance between the Jewish kingdom and the Christian states of Europe for the purpose of fighting the Turks.

The Roman-Jewish community generally regarded the strange visitor with skepticism, but he found many supporters there, especially among women in Jewish high society.

After much hesitation, the Pope gave him a letter to the king of Portugal, and David Reubeni left for Lisbon to conduct negotiations with King João III on the establishment of a military alliance. He spent about five years in Portugal, but the negotiations with the king brought no results. Ultimately, he fell into displeasure at court. His contacts with the Marranos, among whom his presence aroused a tense anticipation of the advent of the Messiah, angered the authorities, and he was requested to leave the country.

A Portuguese Marrano, Diego Pires, was so impressed by David Reubeni that he decided to adopt Judaism at once. He had himself circumcised, adopting the name of Solomon Molko, and at Reubeni's advice went to Turkey. At Salonica, he studied cabala with Rabbi Joseph Taytazak, then he journeyed to Palestine where he spent some time with the cabalists of Safad. From there, he traveled to Italy to announce the imminent advent of the Messiah. At Ancona, Rome, and Venice, his sermons and prophecies made a tremendous impression. His personal charm also influenced many Christians, including the Pope, who defended him against his persecutors. In Venice, Molko again met David Reubeni, who had returned to Italy after his unsuccessful trip to Portugal. The two of them decided to try interesting Emperor Charles V in the plan to mobilize world Jewry for a war against the Turks. In 1532, they appeared at the Reichstag in Regensburg, where they were received by the emperor. They were arrested, however, and handed over to the Inquisition. Solomon Molko was burned alive at Mantua and David Reubeni was taken to Spain where he apparently died or was killed. Shortly afterward, a story began circulating that Molko had not perished at the stake and would appear shortly as the King-Messiah. His standard and other possessions were reverently preserved at the Altneuschul Synagogue in Prague as hallowed souvenirs.

THE INQUISITION AND THE GHETTO IN ITALY

In the middle of the sixteenth century, the condition of the Italian Jews began to deteriorate precipitously. In 1553, Talmud manuscripts were burned at Rome and Venice. As the consequence of a ritual-murder accusation, the Jews of Rome were in danger of expulsion. The community was saved from this disaster literally at the last moment when the murderer was apprehended and the Jews' innocence was proved.

In 1555, Cardinal Caraffa, a fanatic Jew-hater, became Pope as Paul IV. During his pontificate, all the restrictions which the Church had decreed against the Jews in the Middle Ages were strictly reintroduced. The very year of his coronation, the Jews of Rome were crowded into a special quarter on the left bank of the Tiber, in the Roman ghetto, which was sur-

A Jewish wedding by the Venetian painter Pietro Longhi (1701–1785). The tendency to dramatization and exaggerated splendor in Longhi's paintings is quite apparent here. The rabbi conducting the marriage ceremony reads the marriage contract standing in front of the couple sitting on an interior platform, as the groom extends his hand to the bride. The mother of the bride or groom is placing her hands on the heads of the newlyweds in a gesture of love and protectiveness, while the guests and relatives look off in different directions. The boys on either side of the platform are standing about freely, with no interest in the proceedings. These are some of the typical ingredients of genre pictures of the 18th century. To the left, a troupe of musicians are visible in a box. Israel Museum, Jerusalem

rounded by a wall to separate it from the rest of the city. In the other cities of the Papal States, the Jews also had to live in ghettos. In Venice, where the term "ghetto" originated, the institution had been in existence since 1516. Pressure was exerted on the rulers of the rest of the Italian states to act in accordance with the example of the papal domains, and by the end of the sixteenth century all the Jews of Italy were living in ghettos. This law was not abolished until the middle of the nineteenth century; and in Rome itself only in 1870, at the cessation of papal rule.

Nevertheless, the spiritual activity of the Italian Jews did not stop even in the ghettos. At Ferrara, at the end of the sixteenth century, Azariah dei Rossi wrote *Me'or Einayim* (Light of the Eyes), the first attempt to study Jewish tradition in accordance with a scientific, critical method. He has justifiably been credited with inaugurating the modern period in Jewish scholarship. Jews in various places continued to study mathematics, the natural sciences, medicine, and philosophy. Rabbi Judah Leone Modena, a scholar, preacher, poet, and versatile writer, was chiefly associated with Venice. His contemporary, Samuel David Luzzatto, wrote apologetic works in Italian. Deborah Ascarelli in Rome and Sarah Copia Sullam in Venice wrote Italian poetry. From the beginning of the eighteenth century, special mention should be made of the poet and cabalist Moses Hayyim Luzzatto, who wrote poems, plays, books on ethics, and other works during his short lifetime. He moved to Acco, where he died of the plague at the age of forty. In Ferrara, Rabbi Isaac Lampronti compiled the Talmudic encyclopedia, *Pahad Yitzhak,* in which halakhic material is alphabetically arranged.

At the end of the eighteenth century, i.e., during the period of the French Revolution, when a large part of Italy was conquered by the French, all restrictions against the Jews were abolished in these areas and they were granted civil rights. But they enjoyed these rights only for a short time, for in 1814, after Napoleon's defeat, the previous state of affairs was restored and the Jews returned to the ghettos.

THE LOW COUNTRIES

In the second half of the sixteenth century, the Low Countries freed themselves from both Habsburg rule and the power of the Church. The new Republic promised its inhabitants freedom of religion. After the persecutions and expulsions of the fourteenth century, a very small Jewish community remained in the Netherlands; but now Jews persecuted in other countries and Marranos dreaming of returning to Judaism began to turn their eyes to this land of freedom. They were also attracted by the economic prosperity of the Low Countries, which afforded them opportunities of productive activity. At the end of the fifteenth century, the emigration of Marranos from Portugal began. After a lengthy journey full of adventures, the first group reached Amsterdam in 1593. This was followed by other groups, and in 1597 they were granted permission to live openly as Jews. Rabbi Moses Uri ha-Levi came from Emden, Germany, followed several years later by Rabbi Joseph Pardo from Venice, for the purpose of instructing and guiding Marranos returning to the fold. By 1608, there were already two congregations in Amsterdam, Beth Jacob and Neveh Shalom.

Despite the fact that freedom of religion was assured by law to all the inhabitants of the Netherlands, relations between the Jews and the authorities were not always idyllic. In response to complaints presented by Catholic and Armenian merchants, the Amsterdam municipality restricted the number of Jews entitled to live within the city's limits to only three hundred families. Restrictions were also introduced with regard to the professions in which they were permitted to engage. The merchants' guilds refused to take in Jewish members, and the universities made it difficult for Jewish students to enroll.

Nevertheless, Jews in time succeeded in entering all the branches of economic life, as well as the liberal professions and even the army. The Dutch army which left to conquer Brazil in 1624 had numerous Jewish volunteers.

The center of the Jewish community was in Amsterdam, but, in the course of the seventeenth century, Jews scattered throughout the country and introduced more dynamic economic activity wherever they went. The Jews made a major contribution to the development and expansion of Dutch trade. They also played an important role as bankers. The wealth of Dutch Jewry was reflected in the palaces built by leading Jews, and especially in the great Sephardic Synagogue in Amsterdam, which was consecrated in 1675 in a magnificent ceremony.

The Spanish and Portuguese Jews of Marrano extraction, who constituted a sort of proud, rich Jewish nobility, were joined by another kind of Jewish immigrant coming to the Netherlands to seek a livelihood and freedom. These were Ashkenazic Jews from Germany and the Slavic countries. In the middle of the seventeenth century, they already had a separate congregation with a synagogue and cemetery as well as a rabbi and school of their own. The Ashkenazis were modest people with limited means, unable to engage in international commerce and financial transactions. They were for the most part petty traders and craftsmen.

The Jews in the Netherlands lived a respected, free life unlike that of their coreligionists in any other country, and the rulers of the House of Orange treated them well after having many times become convinced of their loyalty toward them and the country which had become their adopted homeland; but they were not granted full civil rights until after the French conquest in 1795 and the establishment of the Batavian Republic.

The Jewish communities in the Netherlands were conducted in a most conservative spirit. The rabbis and community officials were ready to suppress any manifestation of free thought, which they regarded as heresy, with a strong hand. A famous instance was the case of Uriel Acosta, a Portuguese Marrano who joined the Amsterdam community in 1618. He expressed criticism of Talmudic traditions, which to him did not seem to suit the spirit of Judaism as he understood it. The rabbis excommunicated him, and for fifteen years he lived under the ban. Finally he recanted, but he soon incurred the wrath of the rabbis again when he expressed doubts about the Pentateuch. He was excommunicated once more. Seven years later, he recanted again and agreed to do penance publicly. However, the terms for his penance were so degrading that he committed suicide after the ceremony. He left a horrifying autobiography.

Another instance with less tragic results was the case of the philosopher Baruch (Benedict) Spinoza. He was a native of Amsterdam. Besides Jewish studies, including the works of medieval Jewish philosophers, Spinoza learned Latin, which served as the key to the natural sciences and the philosophy of Descartes. He began to adopt a free, critical attitude toward Judaism. The rabbis and community leaders tried in vain to restore his faith in the Jewish religion or at least persuade him to keep public observances. Finally, they had no choice but to excommunicate him in 1656. Spinoza reconciled himself to the ban, went off to live by himself at The Hague, and devoted himself to the philosophical research which gained him worldwide fame and immortality in the history of human thought.

However, such shocks were unusual. Generally, the Jews of the Netherlands adhered to the traditions of their fathers and maintained internal discipline. The communities, headed by rabbis famous as scholars, teachers, and preachers, saw to it that the younger generation was educated in the traditional spirit.

The famous men of learning of the seventeenth century included Rabbi Saul Levi Morteira, Spinoza's teacher, Rabbi Isaac Aboab de Fonseca, Rabbi in Pernambuco, Brazil, in the years 1642–54, during the Dutch occupation, and, especially, Rabbi Manasseh Ben-Israel, scholar, writer, and stirring preacher, the man who devoted himself to the restoration of the Jewish community in England.

The Small Amsterdam Haggadah *is the name of this Passover* haggadah *printed for the first time in Amsterdam in 1662. The text is accompanied by illustrations, and the opening page is also highly ornamented. Moses and Aaron are depicted on either side of the title page, with a picture of the sacrifice of Isaac on the altar at the bottom. The* haggadah *was reprinted in 1756 in Fürth, Germany, the opening page being colored by hand*

ENGLAND

After the expulsion of the Jews from England in 1290, only isolated individuals were to be seen in the country. But, following the abolition of the monarchy in 1649 and the establishment of a Puritan republic under the leadership of Oliver Cromwell, a new mood came into being in England. The Puritans, whose entire spiritual world was based on Scripture, tended for religious reasons to agree to the re-establishment of the Jewish community in their country. For similar reasons, Rabbi Manasseh Ben-Israel, the most brilliant of the rabbis of Amsterdam's Jewish community, attributed great importance to the return of his people to England. He was imbued with an abiding faith in imminent redemption, but he believed that a condition of redemption was the dispersal of the Jews to all the countries of the entire world. The book *Tikvat Yisroel* (Israel's Hope), in which he explained his ideas, the Latin edition of which was dedicated to the British Parliament, made a strong impression on the Puritans.

167

A platter from England. Sets of porcelain, specially prepared as wedding gifts, were common in both Ashkenazic and Sephardic communities of the Netherlands. Dutch Jews emigrating to England brought this custom with them. This platter depicting a wedding ceremony bears the inscription, "Thy God shall rejoice over thee as the bridegroom rejoiceth over the bride." The dotted letters in the inscription correspond to numbers indicating the date: 1769. The material and glazing indicate that the platter was made in Staffordshire. Jewish Museum, New York

In 1655, Manasseh Ben-Israel traveled to London and opened negotiations with Cromwell. A convention of clergymen, merchants, and jurists, convoked to discuss the matter, established that there was no legal obstacle in the way of the return of the Jews to England; however, strong opposition appeared in business circles, which feared Jewish competition, and Cromwell preferred to avoid coming to a decision. Manasseh Ben-Israel left England in 1657 in disappointment and died on his way back to Amsterdam. However, his efforts had not been in vain. Although the opposition from merchants continued, the English authorities tacitly agreed to the establishment of a Jewish community in London, for the time being consisting of Marranos who had previously come to England as Christians and now openly returned to Judaism.

They were allowed to open a synagogue and acquire a cemetery. Slowly, Jews from the Continent, both Ashkenazis and Sephardis, began immigrating to England. Even after the Restoration (1660), attempts by the merchants of London to secure the nullification of the policy of tolerance toward Jews were of no use. The English monarchs protected them and did not permit their rights to be violated. In 1690, an Ashkenazic synagogue was consecrated in London, and, in 1701, the Sephardis dedicated the beautiful synagogue at Bevis Marks in London.

Nevertheless, the Jews were still tolerated aliens who paid the special tax levied on foreigners. Only gradually and by means of a struggle which lasted throughout the eighteenth century and the first half of the nineteenth did the Jews secure equal rights. The Jewish struggle was aided by English thinkers such as John Toland, who demanded civil rights for them. In 1718, Jews born in England were permitted to acquire land.

In 1753, Parliament passed a law permitting every Jew to be naturalized after having been in the country three years. To be sure, the law was rescinded the following year because of the antagonism of the Opposition, but the Jews did not let the matter rest and the Jewish Board of Deputies, which had been founded in 1760, henceforth conducted an organized, systematic struggle. The Jews were rooted in the country's life, and a number of families attained not only great wealth but also a respected position and considerable influence in public life. At the end of the eighteenth century, it was already clear that victory was no longer in doubt and that the achievement of the desired goal, civil rights, was to be only a matter of time.

HASKALAH,

SABBATIANS,

MASKILIM,

AND HASIDIM

For the Jews of Germany, the sixteenth century was a period of persecution and expulsions—a sort of extension of the darkest days of the Middle Ages. The hackneyed libels did not cease. Jews were accused of the murder of Christians for the purpose of using their blood in baking *matsot,* and charged with desecrating the Host. Any pretext sufficed to stage a show trial, torture Jews with investigations, burn them at the stake, and drive from their homes all those who had not been killed. The Jews were expelled from Nuremberg (1499), all of Brandenburg and Colmar (1510), Regensburg (1519), various towns in Saxony (1537), Bavaria (1551), and again from Brandenburg twenty years after being permitted to return.

To a certain extent, a direct appeal to the emperor to alleviate the suffering of the Jews and abolish a number of their disabilities helped. Most successful on behalf of his people during the entire first half of the sixteenth century was the German-Jewish leader and writer Joselmann (Joseph) of Rosheim, a native of Alsace. He represented the interests of the German Jews before Emperors Maximilian I and Charles V, who respected and appreciated him, granting him official recognition as "Warden and Leader" of the Jews.

During the reign of Maximilian I, Joselmann succeeded in securing nullification of the order to burn the Talmud which was issued as a consequence of the activity of the apostate Johann Joseph Pfefferkorn. The latter, a former Jew from Moravia with a criminal past, had adopted Christianity in Cologne and agreed to serve the Dominicans in their war on the Jews. In the years 1507–9, he published works full of savage lies about the Jews. He even succeeded in securing an order from the emperor to confiscate and destroy the Talmud and any Hebrew book the contents of which contradicted Christianity. However, in view of the numerous protests which the order evoked, and under the influence of Joselmann, the emperor postponed its implementation and summoned the opinions of experts, including the Christian humanist and scholar Johann Reuchlin. Reuchlin, who knew Hebrew and was familiar with Jewish literature, defended the Jews and clearly proved Pfefferkorn's ignorance and the falseness of his accusations.

In many other instances, too, Joselmann was successful in warding off attacks. He defended the Jews of Alsace during the Peasant Revolt (1525), secured the acquittal of Jews who had been falsely accused, worked for the return of the Jews who had been expelled from Brandenburg and Bohemia, and the like. However, despite his indefatigable efforts for half a century, the fate of the Jews in Germany was still intolerable.

Fortunately for them, Germany was at the time divided into a goodly number of large and small states and free cities, each of which conducted a different policy toward the Jews, according to the interests or caprices of whoever happened to be the ruler. As a result, Jews who were expelled from one place generally found refuge somewhere else in Germany, occasionally not far from their original homes. Thus, for example, Jews expelled from Nuremberg settled in nearby Fuerth, and those driven out of Cologne were accepted in neighboring Deutz. While some communities were being liquidated by expulsions, others were coming into being, and existing communities were strengthened. For instance, the community in Frankfurt-am-Main grew as a result of taking in refugees from other cities. In Hamburg, too, an important community was formed by German Jews and Marranos from Spain and Portugal.

Martin Luther's reform movement did not change the stifling anti-Semitic atmosphere prevailing in Germany. At the beginning of his activity, Luther hoped that the Jews would join his reformed church (Protestant), but when his hope did not materialize he launched a violent attack against the Jews and stirred up hatred against them in his writings and sermons. Joselmann succeeded in preventing the publication of one of his works at Strassburg. However, Luther encountered no difficulty in having it published else-

Spicebox in the form of a tower surmounted by a dome. It is made of partly pierced beaten silver. There are birds and animals among the leaves and flowers. A squirrel cracking a nut can be seen in the lower left panel. The early spiceboxes date back to the Second Temple period, when it was customary to burn spices on a small incense altar on the evening following the Sabbath, for the purpose of preserving the fragrance of the holy day. This is apparently the origin of the vessel's traditional structural form. The custom of smelling myrtle leaves in a glass container dates from 13th-century Germany, and the practice of decorating the vessel is known from the 14th; however, the earliest such container extant, also in the shape of a tower with a tapering roof, is of the 15th century. The spicebox in the illustration was apparently made in Frankfort, Germany, at the end of the 17th century. Israel Museum, Jerusalem

where, and the poisonous seed which he assiduously sowed fell on fertile soil. In the German states which joined the Reformation, no changes for the better occurred in the oppressive regime against the Jews.

This regime continued throughout Germany in the seventeenth century as well. In 1614, gangs led by the vicious Vincent Fettmilch attacked the Jews of Frankfurt. Despite the fact that Emperor Matthias used the full weight of his authority in their behalf, the Jews were expelled from the city. Two years elapsed before the emperor succeeded in arresting and executing Fettmilch and his comrades and allowing the Jews to return home.

Similar events happened in Worms at the same time.

During the Thirty Years' War (1618–1648), the Jews suffered much more than the Christian population. The armies maltreated them, and the rulers, both Protestant and Catholic, in need of large sums of money, levied heavy taxes on them.

In 1670, the Jews were expelled from Austria on the charge of having set fire to the royal palace in Vienna.

COURT JEWS

Nevertheless, an interesting development began in the seventeenth century that was to some extent to mollify the harsh fate of the Jews. The financial condition of most of the German states was very bad, and their rulers needed large sums of money. Under the circumstances, kings and princes who were in no way sympathetic to Jews nevertheless condescended to do them a favor and utilize their financial talents. When the Jews were expelled from Austria in 1670, Emperor Leopold permitted the Jew Samuel Oppenheimer, a supplier of the imperial army and the court banker, to remain in Vienna with his family and a number of useful officials. Later, this group was joined by Samson Wertheimer, who inherited Oppenheimer's position after the latter's death in 1703. Around these two men, the Vienna community was gradually revived, with the tacit agreement of the emperor.

Other rulers of German states followed suit, and the "Court Jew," as such a man was called, became a common phenomenon. There was scarcely a court in Germany without its Jew. These Court Jews served

(Opposite page) Ornamented Torah scroll in gold-embroidered mantle, surmounted by a partly gilded silver crown, Italy, 1742. Pair of finials from Padua. The mantle, crown, and finials which together ornament the scroll were originally patterned after the raiment of the high priest in the Temple. The gilded decorations around the crown represent parts of the apparel of the high priest, such as the mitre, the breastplate, and the ephod *(apron), and several of the vessels of the sanctuary and the altar, i.e., the Ark of the Covenant and the golden altar. Israel Museum, Jerusalem*

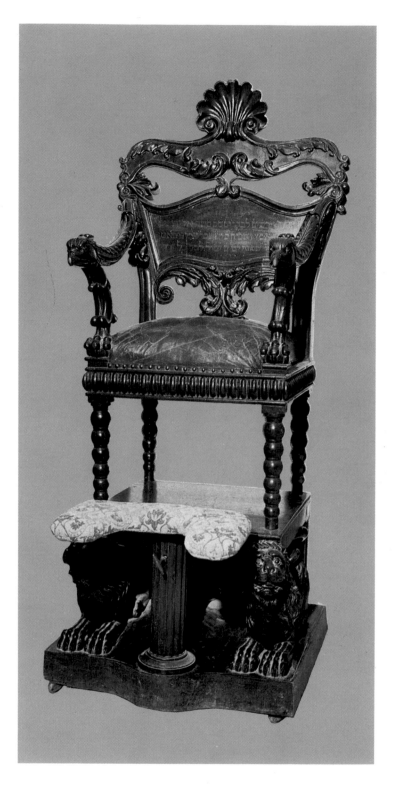

The chair on which the newly born infant was circumcised was called the Chair of Elijah, as he is considered the patron of babies, zealously protecting them, particularly after the circumcision ceremony. Chairs for this purpose, fashioned of carved wood with a footrest for the godfather holding the infant on his knees, were to be found in Jewish communities in Germany and Italy. This one is from Italy. Roman Synagogue, Jerusalem

their masters faithfully and contributed toward the recovery of the economies of various states and the development of commerce and industry to create

sources of revenue for the rulers. They had access to high society and were exempted from the disabilities which applied to other members of their community. Most of them had warm Jewish hearts, continued to be interested in the fate of their fellow Jews, and employed their influence on their behalf. Many of them acquired prominence as philanthropists and patrons of Jewish scholars or Jewish institutions.

However, by the nature of things, Jews who attained such high positions aroused envy and hatred among Christians. Numerous rivals worked hard to make their masters suspicious of them and lead to their dismissal, and sometimes the Court Jew met a bitter end. Some also brought disaster to the Jewish communities in their countries when their careers came to an end. Such was the case, to name only two of the most tragic and best-known instances, with Leopold in Brandenburg and Suess Oppenheimer in Wuerttemberg.

In Brandenburg, from which the Jews had been expelled in 1510 as a consequence of a charge of Host desecration, the elector, Joachim II, agreed in the middle of the sixteenth century, at the urging of Joselmann of Rosheim, to permit Jews to re-establish their community in his domain. Although an enthusiastic supporter of the Reformation, the elector paid no attention to the anti-Jewish sermons of Luther, and he appointed a Jew, Leopold of Prague, as finance minister. Leopold's devotion to his master, and his skill in collecting taxes for the treasury, made the population hate him and increased the general animosity toward Jews which the Protestant clergy constantly kept stirring up. After Joachim's death in 1572, Leopold was accused of having poisoned him. In Berlin, a mob attacked the Jews, robbed their houses, and tore down the synagogue. Under torture, Leopold admitted all the crimes attributed to him, and was executed in an extremely cruel fashion. The Jews of Brandenburg were expelled once more, not to return for more than a century.

Joseph Suess Oppenheimer was a member of the wealthy, renowned family to which the agent of Emperor Leopold, Samuel Oppenheimer of Vienna, mentioned above, also belonged. In 1732, Joseph Suess was appointed agent of Charles Alexander, heir apparent of the Duchy of Wuerttemberg. After his accession to the throne, Duke Charles Alexander confirmed Joseph Suess' appointment as finance minister. Oppenheimer enjoyed the duke's confidence in all matters. He carried out a general reform of the Duchy's entire financial system, established a state monopoly over the trade in various commodities, and developed the country's industry.

Despite the fact that his activities had greatly benefited the Duchy's economy, his high office and influence over the duke aroused strong hatred in court circles and among the populace. The life of luxury which he permitted himself, and a certain amount of favoritism which he displayed toward Jews, increased the feelings of hatred. Joseph Suess Oppenheimer felt that he could not maintain his position any longer,

Jewish wedding, by an anonymous artist of the Bohemian School in Eastern Europe, 18th century. The splendor of the Baroque costumes and the artist's style reveal the locality and period of this wedding ceremony. Israel Museum, Jerusalem

despite the duke's support, and he requested permission to resign. It was just at this time that the duke died suddenly. Joseph Suess was arrested at once, tortured, and put on trial. He confessed to all the crimes with which he was charged; the court sentenced him to death, and he was hanged. Before he mounted the scaffold he was offered his life if he adopted Christianity. Joseph Suess rejected the proposal and bravely went to his death. At this time, the Jews of Stuttgart were expelled and not permitted to return until the end of the eighteenth century.

The existence of the Court Jew was thus a doubtful blessing for the Jews of Germany. Nevertheless, from the long-range point of view, it made its contribution toward improving relations between Jews and Germans and paved the way for emancipation, i.e., the abolition of disabilities and the acquisition of equal civil rights.

TURKEY IN THE SIXTEENTH CENTURY

On being expelled from Spain in 1492, many Jews found a haven of refuge in the Ottoman Empire. Sultan Bayazid II welcomed the refugees, for he realized that these Jews, who were highly educated and experienced in various fields, would make important contributions to his country's development. He was once supposed to have said, "How can you call Ferdinand a wise king when he impoverished his own country and made ours wealthy?"

During the sixteenth century, Marranos who succeeded in leaving Spain and Portugal continued coming to the Ottoman Empire, where they could return to Judaism openly.

The reigns of Sultans Suleiman the Magnificent (1520–1566) and Selim II (1566–1574) may be regarded as the Golden Age of Turkish Jewry. A Jew by the name of Shealtiel was appointed to represent the Jews of the Empire, and he was accorded the right to come and go as he pleased in the royal court. The walls of Jerusalem and Tiberias were rebuilt. The physician and adviser of Suleiman the Magnificent was the Jew Moses Hamon, son of Joseph Hamon the Elder, a native of Granada, who had been the physician of the sultans Bayazid II and Selim I. Moses' position of court physician to Selim II was passed on to his son Joseph. Moses Hamon had a great deal of influence which he used on behalf of the Jews. When Greeks and Armenians in Anatolia tried to eliminate their Jewish competitors by framing a ritual-murder charge, Moses Hamon secured a *firman* (order) which stated that, henceforth, the right to try ritual-murder cases would be reserved only for the sultan himself and not for ordinary judges.

Suleiman's sympathetic attitude towards the Jews was also known outside of Turkey. When he conquered Hungary and entered Buda, the capital, in 1543, the population thought it necessary to place a Jew, Joseph ben Solomon, at the head of the delegation receiving the conqueror to hand him the key to the city.

During Suleiman's reign, Doña Gracia Mendes and her family settled in Constantinople (*q.v.* chapter 9).

After the death of Selim II, the Ottoman Empire began to decline and with it, the prestige of Turkish Jewry. As the central authority weakened, the power of the provincial governors grew and they issued decrees for the purpose of extorting money from the Jews and harassed them in various ways. The attitude of the sultans toward their Jewish subjects also changed. Sultan Murad III (1574–1595) once even ordered the destruction of all the Jews in his kingdom, apparently in anger against incidents of excessive elegance displayed by Jewish women in Constantinople. The decree was rescinded through the intercession of the Jewish physician Solomon Ashkenazi, the confidant of the Grand Vizier Mohammed Sokolli, but the sultan forbade Jews to wear garments of silk and turbans.

In the sixteenth century, many mystics from Spain with profound knowledge of the cabala settled in Safad. These included Solomon Alkabez, author of the liturgical poem, *Lekha dodi* (Come, my beloved), welcoming the Sabbath, Joseph Caro, author of the code *Shulhan Arukh*, Elijah de Vidas who wrote *Reshit Hokhma* (The Beginning of Wisdom), Moses Cordovero, author of *Pardes Rimmonim* (Pomegranate Grove) on the cabala, and others. Thanks to these scholars, Safad became a cabalistic center. In 1569, a Jerusalem-born cabalist, Isaac Luria, came to Safad. During the few years he lived in the city (he died there in 1572), disciples who enthusiastically welcomed his doctrines on theoretical and practical cabala gathered about him. His cabalistic system is permeated with a yearning for redemption and hope for the advent of the Messiah. Luria himself wrote nothing, but his doctrines were spread after his death by his pupil Hayim Vital, and found willing ears throughout the Jewish world. They prepared the ground for the mass Messianic movement associated with the name of Sabbatai Zevi which was to appear in the middle of the seventeenth century.

THE MESSIANIC MOVEMENT OF SABBATAI ZEVI

Sabbatai Zevi was born in Izmir in 1626. As a youth, he was already deeply absorbed in the study of the mystical *Zohar* and Lurianic cabala. Handsome, with a passionate character, he attracted a coterie of friends and admirers who studied cabala under his guidance and participated in the life of prayer and asceticism which he taught. They basked in the glow of their yearning for redemption. The cabalists had no doubt that redemption was near, in accordance with the *Zohar's* view of the verse of Leviticus 25:13, "In this year of jubilee ye shall return every man unto his possession." The second word in the verse is the Hebrew *ha-zot*, bearing the numerical equivalent of 408 in the fifth millennium since the Creation, which corresponded to the year 1648. Actually, the *Zohar* refers to personal redemption and "the return of every man to his soul, which is his possession," but in their impatience the cabalists went wide of the plain text and interpreted it to mean the advent of the Messiah.

When news of the massacres of Jews in the Ukraine precisely in the year designed for redemption reached Turkey, Sabbatai Zevi regarded the sanguinary events as constituting the agonies preceding the coming of the Redeemer. A belief ripened in his heart that he had been chosen to be the Savior, and he decided to take action. His first symbolic act was publicly to pro-

Portrait of Rabbi Sasportas, oil on canvas by the Dutch painter Izaak Luttichuys. Jacob Sasportas was a rabbi, cabalist, and unrelenting adversary of Sabbatianism. He was born in Oran, North Africa, in 1610, and died in Amsterdam in 1698. He officiated as rabbi in Tlemcen (at the age of 24), Fez and Salé. In 1649, he was arrested at the order of the Moorish king, but succeeded in escaping to Amsterdam with his family three years later. Here he stayed until the disorders in North Africa subsided, and then returned at the king's invitation. The king then sent him on a special mission to the Spanish court to seek assistance against rebels. On his return (1664), he was invited to serve as the rabbi of the Portuguese community in London. In 1673, he served as rabbi in Hamburg, after which he was again called to Amsterdam, where he officiated as rabbi of the Portuguese community until his death. Izaak Luttichuys (1616–1673) was noted for his portraits, landscapes, and still lifes. Israel Museum, Jerusalem

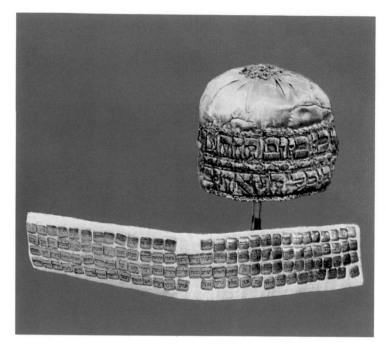

Patriarchs in the Cave of Machpelah in Hebron, and devoted himself to numerous ascetic practices. Many people from Jerusalem flocked to him, especially after he had helped the local community out of a serious difficulty. When the Turkish governor levied an enormous tax on the Jerusalem community, Sabbatai Zevi traveled to Cairo and had the order withdrawn, with the help of the tax farmer Raphael Joseph Chelebi, one of his adherents.

nounce the Tetragrammaton—the name of God, represented by the letters YHWH, traditionally too sacred to be enunciated as they are written and formerly articulated only on the Day of Atonement in the Holy of Holies of the Temple by the high priest. For this bold act, which was considered blasphemy, he was excommunicated by the rabbis of Izmir. Sabbatai Zevi left his home town, spent some time with the cabalists of Salonica, and then went to Constantinople where he met the cabalist Abraham Jakini who encouraged him in the belief that he was the Messiah. Eventually, Sabbatai Zevi reached Palestine, where he visited hallowed tombs, prayed near the Tombs of the

that he had left to perform an errand and had returned as the Messiah. On a second visit to Cairo, Sabbatai Zevi married a girl named Sarah, who was originally from Poland and whose parents had been killed in the massacres of 1648. She had been taken in by a convent, where an attempt was made to bring her up as a Christian, but she had run away. After wandering through the Netherlands and Germany, she had arrived in Leghorn, Italy, where she had announced that she was fated to marry the Messiah. On learning of this, Sabbatai Zevi sent messengers to Leghorn to bring her to Cairo, where a wedding was held in great pomp.

At Gaza, Sabbatai Zevi met a young man called Nathan Benjamin Levi, who acknowledged him as the Messiah and became his faithful prophet. Thanks to the energy and enthusiasm of Nathan of Gaza, a large-scale, systematic propaganda campaign for the Messiah got under way. In 1665, letters were sent to numerous Jewish communities in many countries in which Nathan made eloquent, fervent prophecies that soon the Messiah, Sabbatai Zevi, would remove the crown from the head of the sultan and place it on his own and gather all the Jews in the Holy Land.

While the letters were preparing the ground for the Messianic movement in Europe, Sabbatai Zevi returned

(Above left) Ornamental collar of tallith *(prayer shawl) and skull cap for Day of Atonement. The cantors in a number of communities were in the habit of putting on a special cap for the Day of Atonement service and even a* tallith *with a specially ornamented upper border to suggest the apparel of the high priest in the Jerusalem Temple on the holiest day. In a number of East European countries, it was customary to wear a long white robe resembling a shroud on the Day of Atonement, as an indication of accepting the divine verdict to be handed down regarding the future, and as a symbol of the soul's purity. There were communities in which all the men in the congregation used to wear special caps on the Day of Atonement and also to ornament their prayer shawls. The ornamental collar and cap in the picture date from the end of the 18th century in Poland. Israel Museum, Jerusalem*

(Below left) Eighteenth-century Hanukkah lamp decorated with the two-headed Polish eagle and the figure of Judith brandishing the sword with which she cut off the head of Holofernes. These motifs, like the filigree ornamentation, are basically Polish Baroque. Only the traditional form of the candelabrum and its use are typically Jewish. Israel Museum, Jerusalem

Laver for washing hands, built into the exterior wall of the synagogue at Conegliano Veneto near Venice in 1710. Roman Synagogue, Jerusalem

to Izmir. The ban under which he had been placed had long been forgotten, and the Jews of his native town welcomed him as the King-Messiah with boundless enthusiasm. Representatives came from Jewish communities in Europe to accord him honor. Sabbatai Zevi dismissed the rabbi who opposed him and installed one of his followers in the position. At first, he introduced ascetic practices for purposes of penance, then he held banquets and processions in which songs and religious poems were chanted. He also abolished fasts and converted them to festive occasions.

In Europe, Nathan's prophecies fell on willing ears among Jews who had experienced their fill of horrors and among Marranos hungering for redemption. Particularly enthusiastic were the communities of Spanish and Portuguese Jews in the Netherlands and Hamburg. In Amsterdam, Jews bearing the Torah scrolls danced in the synagogue, and the news of the advent of the Messiah was told to Christians. Many Christians were interested in the movement, for, according to certain interpretations of the Gospel according to John, a belief had gained wide currency that in 1666 important events connected with the Jews would take place. Some people thought that, in that year, the Jews would accept baptism; others held the view that the kingdom of the Messiah would come into being and the Jews would return to their own country. Even scholars displayed interest in the events, and one man even wrote to Baruch Spinoza for an opinion. Among the Jews of the Netherlands, such celebrated scholars as Rabbi Isaac Aboab, Rabbi Raphael Moses d'Aguilar, the physician and thinker Benjamin Mussafia, and many others were swept up in the movement. Among the few who were not carried away was Rabbi Jacob Sasportas, who was then rabbi in Hamburg. But his call for clear thinking fell on deaf ears. The people believed in redemption because there was an emotional need for it.

The atmosphere in Hamburg was very picturesquely described by the woman writer Glueckel of Hamelin, a native of Hamburg, who wrote her memoirs in Yiddish. Every letter from Turkey was read aloud in the synagogue. Young Portuguese Jews would come dressed in festive attire wearing green ribbons, Sabbatai

Hanukkah lamp of silver and gilt, Poland, 19th century. The Jews of Poland scrupulously observed the practices connected with the lamp and used it to adorn the house. From A. Burstein Collection, Lugano. Israel Museum, Jerusalem

Zevi's color. Many people sold their houses and prepared provisions for a journey in order to be ready to leave for Palestine when the day came. In Italy, France, Hungary, Bohemia, and Poland, as well as in the towns of North Africa, the agitation and anticipation mounted as the Messianic year of 1666 came closer.

And when 1666 came around, Sabbatai Zevi left Izmir for Constantinople to remove the crown from the sultan's head. Before his departure he divided the government of the world among his closest adherents, appointing them as kings, ministers, and dukes. The Turkish authorities considered the much-publicized journey of Sabattai Zevi bordering on open rebellion. It is no wonder then that they took action, and the Grand Vizier, Ahmad Kiuprili, issued an order for his arrest. When the ship on which Sabbatai Zevi was traveling reached the Dardanelles, he was taken into custody by the Turkish authorities and taken to Constantinople. Asked the purpose of his trip, he replied that he had been sent by Jewish scholars in Jerusalem to collect money for poor people in the Holy City. For the time being, he was incarcerated in the capital; but, when his followers began making pilgrimages to the prison to gaze upon the countenance of the Messiah, the authorities transferred him to a place of detention at Abydus, near Gallipoli on the shore of the Dardanelles. His adherents called this jail *migdal oz,* i.e., "Tower of Strength."

Strangely enough, the "Messiah's" arrest did not shake the faith of his followers in him. On the contrary, failure of the Turkish authorities to execute Sabbatai Zevi was interpreted as a miracle from heaven by them and as proof of the uniqueness of the man. The "Tower of Strength" prison now became the center of the Messianic movement. Sabbatai Zevi lived there with his wife and secretary, and, from all over the world, individual believers and official delegations representing various communities came to pay their respects. Even the Council of Four Lands sent a delegation to inform him of the suffering of Polish Jewry, and he promised its members that the day of reckoning was near. The ferment continued throughout Europe, and everyone impatiently waited for new developments. They did not have to wait long, although what occurred was not what Jews hungering for redemption had been looking forward to.

At Sabbatai Zevi's invitation, the Polish cabalist Nehemiah Cohen came to Gallipoli to see what the Messiah was like. After a discussion lasting three days and nights, the cabalist came to the conclusion that Sabbatai Zevi's claims to being the Messiah were groundless. He stated this explicitly, and then, in order to escape attempts on his life by Sabbatai Zevi's followers, Nehemiah Cohen announced his intention to adopt Islam. The apostate cabalist informed the Turkish authorities that Sabbatai Zevi was a fraud, inciting the Jewish people to rebellion.

In view of this new turn, the authorities decided that the time had come to put an end to the matter. Sabbatai Zevi was brought to Adrianople to appear before Sultan Mohammed IV. There are no reliable details concerning what took place between Sabbatai Zevi and the court council. He was apparently presented with a choice between a death sentence as a rebel and saving his life by becoming a Moslem. The sultan's physician, an apostate Jew, may have influenced him and persuaded him to yield. At any rate, in the presence of the sultan, Sabbatai Zevi donned a turban to indicate that he had adopted Islam. He took the name Mehemet Effendi and was given the honored position of sultan's doorkeeper, *Kapici Pashi*. His wife and a number of his adherents became Moslems together with him.

When news of the "Messiah's" conversion reached Jewish communities everywhere, it caused bitter disillusion. Many immediately dropped their faith in the disappointing Messiah. Others could not accept such a disgraceful end to the Messianic movement on which they had pinned all their hopes; they found or invented all kinds of explanations. One story had it that the conversion was only for appearances and that the royal crown had been wrapped inside the turban Sabbatai Zevi had put on. There was another version in which, while a reflection of Sabbatai Zevi's image was accepting Islam, he himself had ascended to Heaven, from where he would appear to redeem his people when the time came. Nathan of Gaza continued to believe in him and sent letters to a number of Jewish communities in which he endeavored to give them encouragement and asked the believers to be patient.

Meanwhile, in Adrianople, Sabbatai Zevi maintained close ties with his followers and even went to synagogues. Although he argued that he was doing this for the purpose of spreading Islam among the Jews, and despite the fact that a number of his disciples had begun to wear turbans in public, the sultan regarded him with suspicion. In 1673, he was banished to the citadel of Dulcigno in a small Albanian town. He died there two years later at the age of forty-nine. Nathan of Gaza died four years after that, at the age of thirty-five.

THE AFTERMATH OF THE SABBATIAN MOVEMENT

After Sabbatai Zevi's death, the popular Messianic movement which aspired to the restoration of a Jewish kingdom in Palestine became quiescent. However, cabalistic circles in various places continued to study the significance of the great, strange events of the previous years. They developed theories to explain the cosmic function of Sabbatai Zevi and the reasons for his failure and even hoped for his return to complete the process of redemption.

A handful of his followers, those who had been close to him, remained in Salonica and Adrianople. Their faith had not been affected by the "Messiah's" conversion and death. In 1683, two hundred and fifty families decided to follow in their leader's footsteps and adopt Islam, thus giving rise to the *Dönmeh* (Turk-

Hanukkah lamp of filigree silver, Ukraine, 18th century. The Jews of Russia also observed the traditional uses of the Hanukkah lamp. The ornate style is characteristic. Presented by the late J. Pnini. Israel Museum, Jerusalem

ish for "apostates") sect. Outwardly they were Moslems, but, among themselves, they clung to the belief that Sabbatai Zevi was the Messiah, and observed a number of Jewish practices as well as special customs. The sect is still in existence, although it has divided into a number of factions; it is now threatened by assimilation into the Turkish environment after the dissolution of the center in Salonica at the city's annexation to Greece and the dispersion of the sect's adherents throughout Turkey. The *Dönmeh* marry chiefly members of their own group.

The agitation stirred up by the Messianic movement did not easily subside in Poland either. Cabalists continued to maintain ties with *Dönmeh* circles in Salonica, and spread the belief that forty years after his conversion—in 1706—Sabbatai Zevi would reappear and redeem his people. This movement was headed by Hayim Malak and Judah ha-Hasid ("The Saint"). Their followers called themselves "Hasidites" (Pious Ones) and devoted themselves to prayers and penance.

Despite the secrecy in which the members of the sect shrouded themselves, the rabbis leading Polish Jewry were aware of the connection between it and the Sabbatian movement. They regarded it as a serious danger to Judaism, and sought to combat it. To escape this persecution, the Hasidites decided to go to Palestine and wait there for the imminent advent of the Messiah. In 1700, about fifteen hundred persons set out on the journey. The Hasidites reached Palestine by various routes after a long, weary journey in the

Common Hanukkah lamps in Poland, made of brass alloy, were not inferior in ornamentation to the more magnificent lamps of silver and gold. The symmetrical motif of pairs of animals is one of the traditional characteristics of such ornamental lamps. The Hanukkah lamp apparently originated in the period of the Mishna and Gemara, but only a small number of early specimens are extant and most of them are of clay or stone. The oldest known metal lamp with a back plate dates from 14th-century France. Private collection

course of which about five hundred of them died. Unfortunately for them, Judah ha-Hasid died several days after their arrival in Jerusalem. The Hasidites were on the verge of starvation; in agony and want, they waited for the year of redemption. But 1706 came and went without their hope coming true. A number of the disappointed Hasidites adopted Islam and joined the *Dönmeh,* and others in desperation became Christians. Part of them returned to Poland. Among those going back to Poland was Hayim Malak. He is said to have maintained his faith in Sabbatai Zevi to the end of his life, and even continued his efforts to spread it.

In Western Europe, too, there was to be an epilogue to the Messianic movement. The Palestinian cabalist Nehemiah Hiya Hayun came to Italy in 1710, stayed in Leghorn for a while, and then continued on to Germany and the Netherlands. Everywhere he met scholars and spread clandestine propaganda on behalf of his Sabbatian beliefs. In Amsterdam, Rabbi Zevi Ashkenazi and Rabbi Moses Hagiz, two determined opponents of Sabbatianism, unmasked him and accused him of heresy, but his supporters were so numerous and powerful that both accusers were compelled to leave Amsterdam. Only the intervention of the rabbis of Izmir and Constantinople, who excom-

municated him, forced Hayun to abandon his activities in Europe. However, there were repercussions to his European trip about thirty years later, when Rabbi Jacob Emden, the son of Rabbi Zevi Ashkenazi, accused Rabbi Jonathan Eibeschütz, who in his youth had maintained ties with Hayun, of belonging to the Sabbatians. Rabbi Eibeschütz denied the charge and the controversy between the two rabbis lasted for many years.

MOSES MENDELSSOHN

In the eighteenth century, a new spirit originating in England and France also appeared in Germany. This was the spirit of Enlightenment, aspiring to freedom of thought, a better society, and the search for solutions to man's problems by means of reason and intelligence. By the nature of things, this spirit could not fail to affect the attitude of European peoples toward the Jews living among them. But it also influenced the Jews and their attitude to the Christian environment.

Until the eighteenth century, the Jews generally still lived in almost complete social and cultural isolation. This was the period of the ghetto. Relations with the Christian surroundings were limited to the economic sphere and were accompanied by the hostility of the Christians and characterized by a lack of trust on the part of the Jews. The synagogue and school stood at the center of Jewish life. Above all, the Jews esteemed devotion to sacred studies. Acquaintance with books and even thorough familiarity with them were more widespread among Jews than among other peoples. Although their erudition differed completely from that of their neighbors and their knowledge of secular disciplines was quite meager, the Jews had no inferiority complex. Their feelings of self-esteem were affected neither by the negative opinions of their Christian neighbors about them not by the discrimination which they suffered.

As mentioned above, the religious Reformation which started in Germany had thus far brought no practical improvement in the condition of the Jews. Nevertheless, it was a historical event of great importance, for part of the German states freed themselves because of the Reformation from the power of the Catholic Church, which still fanatically advocated the principles of anti-Jewish discrimination. This provided opportunities for bettering the condition of Jews in the future as a consequence of the spread of the humanistic ideas of the Enlightenment among writers and thinkers in Germany by way of English and French texts. These factors slowly prepared the atmosphere which, at least in theory, made a new approach to the problem of Jewish-Christian relations possible.

The wish to come closer to the German people and become acquainted with its culture became more intense among the Jews. Naturally, this desire was especially felt among the wealthy, among the Court

Jews, their families, and agents who because of their businesses were in closer contact with the upper level of German society. Knowledge of the German literary language and even of other foreign languages began to penetrate into the Jewish world. In the 1740s, it was possible to find German books and newspapers in Jewish houses. However, Enlightenment (*Haskalah*) as an organized movement with defined aims only began among German Jews with the activities of Moses Mendelssohn. His work belongs to the eighteenth century, though its fruits ripened in the nineteenth, during the period of emancipation.

Moses Mendelssohn was born in Dessau in 1729 and was given a traditional Jewish education. But when he followed his teacher, Rabbi David Fränkel, to Berlin, the capital of Prussia, in 1743, a new world opened before him. He learned German and other languages, acquired a broad general education, and devoted himself especially to philosophic studies. His friendship with the German poet Gotthold Ephraim Lessing and the writer and publisher Christoph Friedrich Nicolai opened the way into German and, in general, European intellectual society for him. A whole series of books and articles on philosophical subjects written in highly polished perfect German which appeared during the years 1755–70 brought him fame throughout Europe. Particularly successful was his book *Phädon,* in which he tried to prove the immortality of the soul. This work, translated into many languages, was considered the loftiest expression of the idea of humanism characteristic of the Enlightenment movement.

Phädon marked a major turning point in Mendelssohn's life. Because of it, a correspondence developed between him and the Swiss theologian Johann Kaspar Lavater, who discovered an affinity between Mendelssohn's philosophical ideas and Christianity, and invited him to change his faith. Mendelssohn answered that his philosophical studies had created no doubts in his mind about the truth of the Jewish religion and that it was his intention to cling to it. From then on, Mendelssohn devoted his entire activity to his own people. His work centered around a translation of the Pentateuch into German. The translation, printed in Hebrew script, to make it possible for every Jew to read and learn German from it, was accompanied by a commentary (the *Bi'ur*) which tried to clarify the simple meaning of the text on the basis of logic and grammar. In compiling the commentary, Mendelssohn had the assistance of his friends Solomon Dubno, Naphtali Herz (Hartwig) Wessely, and Herz Homberg. The book appeared in 1783 under the title *Netivot Shalom* (Paths of Peace). Numerous Jewish circles received the translation and commentary with great enthusiasm as the herald of a new period. On the other hand, Mendelssohn's achievement unleashed a storm in conservative Jewish circles. The rabbis foresaw the dangers of assimilation and disintegration lying in wait for the Jewish people in the paths taught by Mendelssohn, and they regarded it as their duty to declare war against the "German Bible" and the "Torah of Moses of Dessau." They forbade reading the work, and threatened those violating the prohibition with excommunication; in some places, the volumes were burned publicly.

The rabbis' wrath stemmed from a profound concern for the fate of their people, and subsequent developments proved to what extent their fears had been justified. However, they were unable to hold back the historical process which had got under way. Mendelssohn's Pentateuch and the accompanying commentary gained wide currency, not only in Germany but also in Poland and Russia, and gave the key to European culture to generations of young men hungry for knowledge.

There were times when the acquisition of an alien culture was accompanied by a disparagement of Jewish traditional values and a readiness to merge completely with the Christian environment by baptism. A conspicuous example of a lamentable development of this sort was provided by Mendelssohn's family itself. While Mendelssohn himself observed traditional Jewish practices, proudly defended Judaism, and found a philosophical basis for its precepts, his sons and daughters abandoned their ancestral faith after his death.

Of course neither Moses Mendelssohn nor the circle of Berlin intellectuals intended such results. They wished not to destroy but to build, and this point was

Passover seder *plate. Glazed plate depicting the members of the household walking around the table set for the* seder *ceremony, their staves in their hands, their bags on their backs, and their loins girded as the Book of Exodus describes the Israelites' departure from Egypt. The plate was made in Liverpool, England, in 1788. Jewish Museum, New York*

Burial society beaker, Bohemia, 1713. This was formerly in the synagogue at Unterberg-Eisenstadt, Hungary. The large beaker was apparently used by the burial society for collective drinking, a custom common to all professional guilds of the period. Made of glass and painted in black and gray enamel, it is one of the few such extant. Besides the dedication at the top, the beaker bears the painting of a funeral procession in which all the members of the society are shown participating in their various tasks. The family of the deceased and his son reciting the kaddish *(prayer for the dead) are also depicted. It was salvaged by the late M. Narkiss who found it in fragments in Germany after World War II. Israel Museum, Jerusalem*

emphasized in the periodical *Ha-Me'assef* (The Gatherer), the organ of *Hevrat Doreshei Leshon Ever* (Society for the Hebrew Language), which was founded in 1783 by Mendelssohn's friends and disciples. Its aim was to enrich the Jews' spiritual life by publishing scientific articles and translations from French and German literature in good Hebrew. However, as knowledge of the German language spread, Hebrew became superfluous as an instrument for acquiring knowledge, and *Ha-Me'assef* suspended publication in 1797.

Three years after Mendelssohn's death in 1786, the

French Revolution broke out. Where the Jews were concerned, its standard-bearers came to the logical conclusion arising from the principles of the Enlightenment movement and granted them civil rights. In their triumphal march across Europe, the revolutionary armies everywhere brought the Jews salvation from the restrictions of the Middle Ages and threw the gates of the ghettos open. In many places, periods of reaction came in the wake of Napoleon's defeat, but the Jews no longer relaxed their struggle for their rights. The rulers slowly came to the realization that they could not check historical development. By the middle of the nineteenth century, the emancipation of German Jewry had become an accomplished fact. The Jews were now free citizens, integrated into the life of the country. And, at the time, no one dreamed that, in less than a century, a period of horror would return, unparalleled even in the darkness of the Middle Ages.

POLISH JEWRY IN THE EIGHTEENTH CENTURY

Polish Jewry, which had suffered so much in 1647–48, and had been shaken to its foundations by the hopes aroused by the Sabbatian movement and its subsequent disappointments, did not easily find its way back to normalcy. The external conditions under which the Jews of Poland lived during the period of the Saxon kings also increased their distress. In 1698 and 1710, trials of Jews were staged in Sandomir on the basis of a ritual-murder charge. Innocent Jews were sentenced to death and executed, and the king was hard put to prevent the expulsion of the Jews from the city. Ritual-murder charges increased in various places. In the wars between Poland and Sweden, Jewish communities were alternately robbed by the armies of both sides. In the Ukraine, tens of thousands of Jews were massacred by the Haidamaks. The communities were heavily in debt, and their authority grew lax. Institutions of Jewish learning which had formerly been the pride of Polish Jewry never recovered. Instead of the Talmud and its codifiers, books on ethics and the cabala now served as the people's spiritual fare. Yearning for speedy redemption beat in everyone's heart. Sabbatian circles continued to exist and their emissaries traveled around the country and won adherents to their cause.

The difficult crisis affecting Polish Jewry in the middle of the eighteenth century produced two mystical movements. One, the Frankist movement, was a sort of revival and continuation of Sabbatianism; once again, all the dangers inherent in attempting to bring on the Messianic Age prematurely by false methods became apparent, and Frankism ended up outside of Judaism. The second movement, the Hasidism of Israel Baal Shem Tov, was a sort of negative reaction to Sabbatianism, the search for a new approach to Judaism. It was a movement of renewal and recovery, which was to leave an indelible stamp on all of Jewish life, far from the borders of Poland and the period of its founding.

Spicebox, cup for sanctifying wine, and candle for havdala *(ceremony marking the end of the Sabbath), Germany, 18th century. Acquired by subscription in memory of the late M. Narkiss, for thirty-five years director of the Bezalel Museum, Jerusalem. The gold cup, decorated with scenes from the lives of Isaac and Jacob, was donated to a Frankfort synagogue in 1765 in accordance with a provision in the will of Michael, son of Rabbi Speyer, for the purpose of "sanctifying the wine in it each holiday and to serve as an eternal commemoration before God. And just as he specified in his will, so his heirs did, and the terms of his will were fulfilled on 2 Tevet 5585." The holder for the* havdala *candle is also from Frankfort and was made in 1741. The tower-shaped spicebox is of silver and partially gilt; of Austrian origin, it was made in 1810. Israel Museum, Jerusalem*

THE FRANKIST MOVEMENT

In the middle of the century an extraordinary man, despite his ignorance, appeared to assume leadership of the Sabbatian circles which had been operating clandestinely in various parts of Poland. This leader brought them out of hiding, turned the spotlight of history on them and himself, and once more agitated the hearts of Polish Jewry by arousing hopes of redemption and threatening the existence of traditional Judaism. But, when he left the stage, Polish Sabbatianism also departed with him for good.

Jacob Leibovicz, known as Jacob Frank, was born in Podolia in 1726, a century after the birth of Sabbatai Zevi. His father was a Sabbatian. Until the age of thirty, he made frequent trips to Turkey on business and came in touch with the leaders of the *Dönmeh*

sect. It was there that the revelation came to him, and he returned to Poland, where he claimed divine inspiration had instructed him to work and redemption would materialize. When he appeared in Podolia and Galicia in 1755, he was enthusiastically received as the personification of Sabbatai Zevi. Believers flocked to his side. He taught them his doctrine, which was based on the mystical *Zohar* and rejected the authority of the Talmud. Frank revealed to them the secret of the divinity which embodies three principles—the "Holy Ancient One" or the Creator of the Universe, the "Holy King" or the Messiah (Sabbatai Zevi or his personification Jacob Frank), and the "Supreme Lady" or feminine aspect of the godhead represented by the Divine Presence—and urged them to stop obeying the commandments and precepts of traditional Judaism. He insisted that only when the Jews cease to obey

183

Tablets with the Ten Commandments, Saluzzo, Italy. This panel of colored marbles was apparently embedded in the eastern wall of the synagogue—not, as is the usual practice, in the doors of the Ark of the Law. The style of ornamentation is typical 18th-century. Roman Synagogue, Jerusalem

Silver plate for the Pidyon ha-Ben ceremony held thirty days after birth to redeem the first-born in accordance with the Biblical commandment (a sum of money is given to a Cohen—a descendant of the ancient priestly family of Aaron—who generally contributes it to charity). This plate was made in Poland in the 18th century. Characteristic of the ornamentation of such plates is the scene of the sacrifice of Isaac on the altar, embossed in the center in a popular style. The father placed the coins for the redemption of his first-born son in the plate. Israel Museum, Jerusalem

these commandments would the God of Truth appear and complete the work of redemption.

Living by a doctrine which abolished all conventional standards, the Frankists engaged in extreme debauchery, especially in their ceremonies and feasts. Matters reached the stage of a public scandal, and the rabbis mustered their forces to stamp out the disease which was spreading among the people. In 1756, Frank and his followers were excommunicated and a campaign of persecution was launched against them. In their distress, Frank and his group appealed to Bishop Dembovski, an avowed anti-Semite, who was interested in the sect for its opposition to the Talmud. Dembovski agreed to protect them, and also ordered a public disputation between the Frankist "anti-Talmudists" and the representatives of traditional Judaism.

The disputation, which took place in June, 1757, at Kamenets-Podolski, was chiefly concerned with the problem of whether or not the Talmud was a dangerous work. Several months later, the bishop found in favor of the Frankists, imposed a heavy fine on the "Talmudists," and ordered the Talmud to be burned.

Unfortunately for the Frankists, Bishop Dembovski died that same year. Although they succeeded in receiving an edict from King Augustus III guaranteeing their safety, they clearly realized that they had no future as a sect within Judaism. Accordingly, Frank suggested changing the shell while preserving the fruit, i.e., adopting Christianity outwardly. At first, Frank and his followers made an attempt to join the Church under certain conditions; for instance, that they be permitted to dress like Jews, grow beards, intermarry with Jews, observe the Sabbath, etc. At the same time, they requested a second public debate with the "Talmudists" to prove, among other things, the truth of the ritual-murder accusation. The Church would not accede to their conditions, but a second disputation was held, from July until September, 1759.

In front of Christians, the Frankists raised the charge of ritual murder against all Jews, fully aware of the fact that they were lying. Even the priests serving as judges were not convinced of the blood libel, but the debate gave anti-Semites a weapon for attacking the Jews.

After this disgraceful incident, Frank and his adherents had no choice, and about a thousand of them, headed by their leader, adopted Christianity unconditionally. Many of his followers recoiled from this final step and preferred to remain Jews and conceal their aberrant faith; left without a leader, they or their children in time established closer ties with traditional Judaism and were absorbed back into it.

Since Frank continued to regard himself as the Messiah and was revered as such by his followers, he was arrested at the request of the Inquisition and imprisoned in the first partition of Poland. Released by the Russians, Frank settled first in Brno, Moravia, and later in Offenbach, Germany. Until his death in 1791, he maintained a magnificent court paid for by his followers in Poland. After his death, his pretty

Scroll of Esther illuminated on parchment, Netherlands, 17th century. The custom of painting scrolls of the Book of Esther apparently began in the 15th century in a number of German and Italian communities, but the oldest manuscript extant is from the 16th century. The scroll in the picture is open to the section illustrating Haman and his ten sons hanging from a scaffold at Mordecai's order and the Jews killing their enemies. Charles Feinberg Collection, Detroit

daughter Eve tried to assume leadership of the sect but became involved in debt and died in 1816 while creditors were attacking the rest of her property. After her death, the movement fell to pieces, and the Frankists who had adopted Christianity were absorbed into Polish society. Many of them married into the Polish nobility and they or their descendants attained high positions in commerce and industry, the liberal professions, and public life.

HASIDISM

Entirely different from the Frankist movement was Israel Baal Shem Tov's Hasidism. Israel Baal Shem Tov was also a native of Podolia. He was born in 1700 in the town of Okup. Until the age of thirty-six, he lived in great poverty, secretly studied cabala, and earned a living from modest jobs. He was considered an ignoramus, even by his brother-in-law, Rabbi Gershon Kuttower of Brody. In the mid-1730s, he began spreading his doctrine, based on Lurianic cabala. He taught the need of inner devotion in observing the commandments and of communion with God in prayer, the importance of joy in worship, love of one's fellowman, and simple faith without attempts to seek the support of traditional arguments. The common people, who saw nothing to attract them in the dispassionate erudition of the rabbis and who found satisfaction of their spiritual needs in Baal Shem Tov's teaching, flocked to him by the thousands. Baal Shem Tov also succeeded in winning over a number of scholars who came to him for inspiration, among them Rabbi Dov Baer of Mezdyrzecz and Rabbi Jacob Joseph Cohen of Polonnoe.

In 1740, Baal Shem Tov settled in the town of Miedzyboz in Podolia, which became the center of the new movement. He lived there until his death in 1760, but also traveled a great deal in the area in order to keep in touch with his followers. After his death, leadership passed to his disciple Dov Baer, the *Maggid* (preacher). Under him, the movement organized and spread to new regions — the Ukraine, Lithuania, and central Poland. The idea of the *Zaddik,* the saintly rabbi mediating between the material and spiritual worlds, the guide, holy man, and intercessor between the believer and God, the nucleus of which already existed in Baal Shem Tov's teaching, crystallized in the doctrine of the *Maggid* of Mezdyrzecz.

As Hasidism spread, secondary centers with their own *Zaddikim* (plural of *Zaddik*) came into being. As long as the *Maggid* was alive, these secondary centers were subservient to Mezdyrzecz, but after his death in 1772 the movement split into groups, each centered around its own *Zaddik*, since there was no longer a leader capable of maintaining control of all the Hasidim.

In the generation after the *Maggid,* there were a number of important *Zaddikim* who were active in spreading and strengthening Hasidism. Among them, mention should be made of Rabbi Levi Isaac of Berdichev, Rabbi Menahem Nahum of Chernobyl, Rabbi Israel of Ruzhin, Rabbi Nahman of Bratzlav, Rabbi Aaron "the Great" of Karlin, Rabbi Shneor Zalman of Liady, founder of the intellectual Habad movement, Rabbi Elimelech of Lizensk, Rabbi Jacob Isaac of Przysucha, and others. Around each one, a circle of varying size of pupils and disciples came into being. The Hasidim regarded the resettlement of Palestine an outstanding deed of merit. Israel Baal Shem Tov set out for the Holy Land but changed his mind on the way. His brother-in-law, Rabbi Gershon Kuttower, did manage to reach Palestine, and settled first in Hebron and later in Jerusalem. Rabbi Menahem Mendel of Przemyslany and Rabbi Menahem Mendl of Vitebsk settled in Tiberias. A group of followers accompanied each one of them. The Hasidim in Europe supported the members of their group in Palestine, and for a long time Rabbi Shneor Zalman of Liady directed this activity.

At the very outset, while Israel Baal Shem Tov was still alive, the rabbis regarded Hasidism with hostility. Rabbi Hayim Rappaport of Lvov, who headed the Jewish side in the second disputation with the Frank-

ists, proclaimed Baal Shem Tov a quack, and in 1772 a number of communities excommunicated the Hasidim. Among their most outspoken opponents was Rabbi Elijah, the Gaon of Vilna. In the 1740s and 1750s, the opponents of Hasidism organized and the controversies between them and the Hasidim grew more acrimonious. The Hasidim were accused of deviating from religious customs, neglecting study of the sacred books, and withdrawing from the body of the Jewish people. But the controversy was still an internal struggle. It assumed a more disgraceful form when both sides began running to the authorities with slander. Rabbi Shneor Zalman was arrested after the opponents of the Hasidim (called *Mithnaggedim,* i.e., "Opponents") had told the authorities that he was disloyal to the government. He was acquitted and released. On the other hand, the Hasidim slandered the leader of the Vilna community.

Thus, the eighteenth century ended in a bitter struggle between the Hasidim and the *Mithnaggedim*. In this contest, neither side displayed excessive fastidiousness in the choice of means for attacking the adversary, although, for the sake of fairness, it should be pointed out that the conflict was started by the *Mithnaggedim* and they were generally the attackers.

However, no attack or persecution, no mockery or contempt, and no ban succeeded in expelling the Hasidim from the Jewish people, as was the case with regard to the Frankists. They clung to Judaism with all their might and would not relinquish it, until their approach came to be accepted as one of the ways of traditional Judaism and exerted a profound influence even on the *Mithnaggedim*.

Toward the end of the eighteenth century, the first attempts were made by the friends and disciples of Moses Mendelssohn to introduce the principles of Enlightenment, first into Galicia, and later into Poland and Russia. In Galicia, which belonged to Austria at the time, Emperor Josef II encouraged these attempts, and in Poland, too, the authorities and various Christian intellectuals sought ways to solve the Jewish problem by merging the Jews into Polish culture. However, both Hasidim and *Mithnaggedim* believed that the Enlightenment movement was undermining the foundations of Judaism and vigorously fought it. That struggle and the developments which it produced belong to the history of the nineteenth century.

THE NINETEENTH CENTURY

One of the panels from a folding sukkah (booth erected for the Feast of Tabernacles) from Fischach, southern Germany. The entire sukkah is shown on the pages following

The Jewish community in France which came to an end in the general expulsion of 1394 was gradually renewed in time, in part surreptitiously and partly by the annexation of new areas with their Jewish populations. After the expulsion of the Jews from Spain and Portugal at the end of the fifteenth century, Marranos from both countries began coming to settle in the towns of southern France. Outwardly, these immigrants were loyal sons of the Catholic Church, but the mask was quite transparent. Only the great benefit which their commercial activity brought to the country's economy moved the French government to shut its eyes, and even protect them. Slowly the population became accustomed to them and, in the first half of the eighteenth century, they were permitted to return to Judaism openly. They were joined by Jews from the areas under papal rule (in Avignon and the Comtat Venaissin) who had come to all parts of France. Meanwhile, the districts of Alsace and Lorraine were added to France in 1648. There was a large community of Ashkenazic Jews there, differing from the Sephardic Jews of southern France in language, customs, and economic situation. The well-to-do among them were moneylenders, and the poor made a living from peddling and animal trading. In both regions, which had previously been German, the Christian population intensely hated Jews as a matter of tradition.

Special taxes were levied on all the Jews of France, their freedom of movement was limited, and there were restrictions on their economic activity. However, the government's attitude was not consistent and differed from place to place. The most difficult situation prevailed in the two districts of Alsace and Lorraine, where three-quarters of all the Jews in France lived. Even before the Revolution, an urgent need for remedying the situation was felt. A Catholic priest with liberal tendencies, Abbé Henri Grégoire, who later joined the revolutionaries, published *An Essay on the Physical, Moral, and Political Rehabilitation of the Jews,* in which he attributed the Jews' "degeneration" to their suppression, and recommended their recognition as citizens with equal rights as the way to bring about their normalization. Count Mirabeau, the liberal nobleman who later became one of the leaders of the Revolution, also published a book on *Moses Mendelssohn and the Political Reform of the Jews,* in which he appealed for the abolition of all discrimination and the opportunity to let the Jews prove that they were good citizens.

THE FRENCH REVOLUTION

The French Revolution, which broke out in 1789, marked the beginning of a new era for the nations of Europe, including the Jews dispersed among its peoples. The Jews of France were of course the first to benefit from the blessings of the Revolution and were recognized as full-fledged citizens in the country. However, emancipation was not granted to them as a gift free of pain. Mirabeau and Abbé Gregoire remained loyal to the views which they had voiced before the Revolution and endeavored to help the Jews in their speeches in the National Assembly. But the delegates from Alsace vigorously opposed their suggestions for a long time. When the Sephardic "aristocrats" saw that their redemption was being delayed because of their Ashkenazic fellow Jews, they decided to repudiate them and appealed to the Assembly separately, pointing to their special position and the charters which they had received in the past. Their appeals were crowned with success, and in January, 1790, their requests were granted. After this treacherous act, the Jews of Alsace continued their struggle alone, with the help of friends in the Assembly, until logic and justice overcame the opposition of their enemies, and the general emancipation of the Jews of France was proclaimed in September, 1791.

The Jews hastened to demonstrate their gratitude to their native land and their wish to be Frenchmen like all other Frenchmen. They made generous contributions to the funds of the Revolution and courageously and devotedly served in the National Guard and the army.

When the revolutionary armies crossed the borders of France and began to overrun the countries of Europe, they brought the new principles of *Liberty, Equality, Fraternity* wherever they went. One of the first acts of the conquerors was to open the gates of the

Folding sukkah. At the beginning of Jewish emancipation, a tendency quickly spread among Jews to introduce greater comfort into their home life. The wealth of many German Jews enabled them to build large country houses outside the closed community, and also indulge in pastimes uncommon until then among Jews of Germany, such as horseback riding and hunting. They generally continued observing Jewish traditions, sometimes even more strictly than their ancestors of a century before. This folding sukkah, made of a series of painted panels, was numbered for ready erection every year. It was especially manufactured for a rich Jew from Fischach, early in the 19th century. Many of the scenes painted on the panels depict the owner's house and way of life. Here, the house is painted in an idyllic landscape. Another panel (opposite page) shows the father with his son or a friend, hunting birds; in another, the wife awaits her husband's return (see close-up on page 187). In the central section, opposite the entrance, the owner had the artist paint an imaginative picture of Jerusalem and the Temple, along with scenes from the life of the community and from the life of the prophet Elijah. A close-up appears at the lower right of this page; in it, in the upper left portion, the Jews receive the Torah on Mount Sinai and the Levites participate in the Temple service. Gift of the Deller family through the late Dr. H. Feuchtwanger in memory of Abraham Deller, who died in 1938. Israel Museum, Jerusalem

ghetto and grant the Jews civil rights. The Jews of Italy were emancipated in 1797. One year before that, all the discriminatory laws against Jews had been abolished in the Netherlands. In the German states which they conquered, the French also tore down the walls of the ghettos, sometimes in a military ceremony, and proclaimed liberty for the Jewish population. Within a few years, the condition of the Jews in a large part of Europe underwent a radical transformation. It was not surprising that the Jews were grateful to their liberators, and many of them joined the French army.

NAPOLEON AND THE JEWS

Of the occupied territories, there were two which successfully opposed the introduction of the new spirit, Bavaria and the Duchy of Warsaw. In Bavaria, many of the disabilities were gradually abolished, but the Jews were not granted equal civil rights. The Duchy of Warsaw established by Napoleon in 1807, which expired in 1815, adopted the principle of full civil rights in its constitution; however, in view of the opposition of the aristocracy and the burghers, it was decided in 1808 to postpone the implementation of this paragraph for ten years.

Thus, the devotion of the Jewish military hero, Berek Joselowicz, to the cause of Polish freedom in Kosciusko's rebellion (1794) did the Jews no good. Later, Joselowicz fought with distinction in Napoleon's armies. In 1807, he returned to serve the Duchy of Warsaw and was killed in battle leading a cavalry charge.

It is noteworthy that, in the Duchy of Warsaw, part of the Jews also opposed emancipation. The Hasidim under the leadership of Rabbi Jacob Isaac ("The Seer") of Lublin and Rabbi Israel of Kozienice regarded it as a first step to assimilation and the abandonment of traditional Judaism and joined the forces of reaction to prevent its implementation.

In 1804, Napoleon Bonaparte was crowned Emperor of France. Before gaining the throne, he displayed interest in the Jewish people while he was directing the war against the Turks and English in Palestine in 1798–99. After the conquest of Gaza and Jaffa, he issued a call to the Jews of the Orient to join his struggle and promised to restore the Kingdom of Jerusalem. There was no response to his appeal, and it is difficult to gauge the seriousness of his promise. In Europe, he insisted on granting civil rights to Jews in every coun-

try under his authority as part of the principles of the Revolution which were to be universally applied. In France itself, the emperor treated the Jewish problem in a most original fashion.

In 1806, complaints against the financial transactions of the Jews of Alsace increased. Napoleon disliked this Jewish community because it constituted a cohesive ethnic and cultural group which impressed him as a "nation within a nation." He made up his mind to break up Jewish solidarity and crack down on the Jews without, at least openly, violating their rights. And all this he decided to do in a magnificent fashion which could be interpreted by naive Jews as according respect to their people and enhancing its prestige.

An assembly of Jewish notables was convoked in Paris in July, 1806, and requested to answer twelve questions. The questions were concerned with laws regarding personal status (the attitude of the Jews to polygamy, divorce, and intermarriage), the relations between the Jews and their native land according to Jewish law (whether or not they regarded the French as brothers and France as their homeland, and whether or not they were prepared to defend their country and obey its laws), the authority of the rabbis, and prac- the emperor's satisfaction. Their answers expressed question of intermarriage, to which a vague answer was given, the notables replied to all the queries to the emperor's satisfaction. Their answers expressed loyalty to France and a readiness to place respect for the country's laws above any other obligation.

In order to endow the replies of the assembly of notables with a solemn official religious stamp, Napoleon convoked a Grand Sanhedrin in 1807. The revival, as it were, of the supreme authority of the Jewish people made a powerful impression in France and the rest of Europe. The splendor of the name "Sanhedrin," which awakened hallowed memories, concealed the

189

fact that actually it was a spectacle designed solely for the purpose of serving the emperor's ends. The Sanhedrin met in great pomp under the presidency of Rabbi David Sinzheim of Strasbourg and did what the emperor expected from it, i.e., it confirmed the answers of the notables and gave them the force of "Jewish laws."

After he attained his purpose, Napoleon revealed his true intentions, and in 1808 issued a set of rules which regulated the economic activities of the Jews for a period of ten years. The rules, which applied not only to the Jews of France but also to those in the conquered territories, restricted the Jews' freedom of movement and limited their freedom of action in various spheres.

This discriminatory code which struck the Jews as a degrading affront and a bitter disappointment was called by them *le décret infâme* (the infamous decree). Later, certain harsh aspects of the rules were relaxed, but most of the restrictions remained in force until the fall of Napoleon. They were abolished in France in 1818 by the Restoration government. It was one of the ironies of history that it was the Bourbon reaction which restored to the Jews of France the rights that the French Revolution of 1789 had granted them.

EMANCIPATION IN GERMANY

In the period of the Napoleonic wars, Prussia was the the center of German opposition to the French conqueror. It was defeated on the field of battle and its territory reduced, but it was neither conquered nor subdued.

In the matter of the status of its Jews, Prussia did not take dictation from the French, as the other German states had done. Shortly before the French Revolution, in 1787, representatives of the German-Jewish communities directed an appeal to the new king, Frederick William II, to abolish a number of the most irritating and degrading discriminatory laws. Officials of the Prussian government discussed the problem for two years. When in 1789 they finally announced a number of insignificant reforms which the government was prepared to introduce, the Jewish representatives had the courage and honor to reject the patronizing favor.

Under the impression of France's proclamation of emancipation, the king ordered a re-examination of the condition of the Jews and the preparation of a basic reform. However, this time, again, no noteworthy progress was achieved. The problem was now further complicated by the fact that the number of Prussian Jews increased as a consequence of the annexation of former Polish territories during the partitions of Poland in 1793 and 1795. Meanwhile, the wars with France broke out and, under the circumstances, the Prussian government had more pressing concerns than rectifying the condition of the Jews.

The problem became more immediate after the defeat of the Prussian army at Jena (1806), when an urgent need was felt for reorganizing the state and uniting the entire population, including the Jewish minority, for a supreme effort in the war against Napoleon. The implementation of this plan was entrusted to the Ministers Stein and Hardenberg, two statesmen whose liberal tendencies also extended to the question of the Jews. At Hardenberg's recommendation, King Frederick William III published his "order concerning the civil status of Jews in the state of Prussia," which abolished all the discriminatory laws, granted Jews full civil rights, and imposed all civil duties, including military service, on them. Only in connection with the Jews' fitness to serve in the government apparatus did the king reserve the right for himself to decide at a later date. The Jews of Prussia were overjoyed. In order to demonstrate their gratitude, they joined the Prussian army and enthusiastically gave their lives for the country's liberation.

After Napoleon's defeat (1814), the representatives of the European powers met in Vienna for the purpose of re-establishing order out of the chaos which had taken possession of the Continent in the wake of the French Revolution and the protracted wars. Among other things, the discussions at the Congress of Vienna also touched on the problem of Jewish rights. Partisans of the "old order" regarded the emancipation of the Jews as one of Napoleon's achievements and wanted to abolish it. At the Congress, however, there were also liberal statesmen, especially Hardenberg and Alexander von Humboldt, the Prussian representatives, who favored maintaining the rights which had been granted to the Jews, and even Metternich, the conservative Austrian prime minister, tended to side with them, although not when it came to his own country. But, in the end the reactionaries gained the upper hand. The section in the Treaty of Vienna dealing with Jewish rights was formulated in an extremely cunning fashion: it established that Jews should enjoy all the rights granted to them by the various states (instead of the proposed original version, "in the various states"). Since no German state, with the exception of Prussia, had granted the Jews any rights of its own free will, but only under pressure of the occupying forces, emancipation was everywhere abolished, and the original situation was restored. In Prussia, too, the rights of the Jews were whittled down. The prophets of German patriotism, especially university professors, flooded the country with anti-Jewish literature, and the students translated their doctrines into action. Under their leadership, mobs attacked Jews in the streets in many cities, broke into their houses, and plundered or destroyed their property. This outbreak of violence against the Jews in 1819 is known as the *Hep, Hep* riots because of the slogan shouted by the mobs bent on destruction. The word *hep,* said to be of Crusader origin, is an acronym of *Hierosolyma est perdita* — Jerusalem is lost.

After the Congress of Vienna, France and the Netherlands were the only countries in which Jews continued to enjoy full civil rights.

Close-up of folding sukkah, from Fischach, southern Germany, shows details of painted panels

Naturally, the Jews of Germany did not accept the return to their previous status, particularly since, in the meantime, important changes had taken place within Jewish life.

REFORM JUDAISM

In the period of the Napoleonic wars, a number of Jewish financiers achieved fame, particularly the Rothschild family from Frankfurt-am-Main, and exerted a growing influence on the economic life and, thus, also on the political life of Europe. The sons of Meyer

Amschel Rothschild, the loyal Court Jew of the landgrave of Hesse-Cassel and founder of the Rothschild bank in Frankfurt, financed the wars against Napoleon and became the associate of statesmen, princes, and kings. Besides the Rothschilds, other Jews at that time also attained positions of power as respected and influential financiers. This entire rich society was rooted in German culture. Many of them acquired a broad European education, and the salons of beautiful, intelligent Jewish women such as Rachel Varnhagen von Ense and Henrietta Herz in Berlin and Fanny von Arnstein in Vienna were centers of literary life. Aris-

One of the first Jewish artists in the emancipation period was Isaac Ilyitch Levitan of Lithuania (1860–1900). Levitan was justifiably considered the greatest Russian landscape painter of his time. During the last four years of his life, he served as professor of landscape art at the Moscow Academy. This picture is entitled Russian Village. *Israel Museum, Jerusalem*

tocrats, statesmen, writers and thinkers, Germans and foreigners, enthusiastically flocked to their homes. The Jews, or at least part of them, became more polished, assuming an appearance less alien and distasteful to Germans.

In the field of religion, there occurred changes designed to narrow the gap between Jews and Germans. As the spirit of Enlightenment preached by the friends and disciples of Moses Mendelssohn spread, an aspiration appeared to adapt the principles of Judaism to the rationalist philosophy in vogue, to abolish customs and beliefs which seemed outdated and backward, and to give the synagogue service a more aesthetic and

modern form. David Friedländer, a disciple of Mendelssohn, was the first theoretician of Jewish religious reform. After the failure of his attempt in 1799 to persuade the Protestant Church to take in a group of Jews without requiring them to accept Christian dogma, he concentrated on reforming Judaism in accordance with the spirit of the times. He demanded that the Jews give up their belief in Messianic hopes and exchange the Hebrew language for German in the synagogue worship. Part of his demands were implemented by Israel Jacobsohn, who shortened the prayers in Hebrew and added German prayers and congregational singing as is customary in Protestant churches. In

1886), called *Wissenschaft des Judentums* (Science of Judaism). Zunz and his companions and pupils systematically and critically studied the history of Judaism and its literature, according to the established principles of the science of history. Publishing the results of their research in German, they afforded access to the treasures of Judaism to German scholars as well.

THE "NEW JEW"

Many Jews now distinguished themselves in the field of German literature as well as in philosophy and science. Ephraim Moses Kuh wrote poems in the German rococo style. Ludwig Borne, who changed his religion and moved to Paris in 1830, was one of the leaders of the "Young Germany" group of writers. Heinrich Heine, also an apostate, but a Jew deep in his heart until the end of his life, developed new ways in German lyric poetry and greatly influenced its development. Salomon Maimon was one of the severest critics of Kant's philosophy. Lazarus Ben David distinguished himself as a philosopher and mathematician. Thus, the Jew became a common figure on the German cultural scene.

A new type came into being in Germany in this period—a Jew who no longer differed from the German in language, education, and behavior, who considered himself a German of the Mosaic religion, and was even ready to give up the increasingly tenuous bond with that religion in order to identify himself completely with the Germans and become assimilated among them. Even Jews whose ties with traditional Judaism had not weakened began drawing a line between the religious sphere, in which they remained loyal to their ancestral tradition, and the secular domain, in which they made an effort to be as German as other Germans.

The new Jew no longer wanted to bear the injustice of discrimination and vigorously demanded the recognition of his full civil rights. In order to attain emancipation, the Jews sided with the liberal forces whose program included equal rights for Jews.

Jews played an active part in the revolution of 1848, and when Parliament convened in Frankfurt, there were four Jews in it. The most brilliant of them was Gabriel Riesser who belonged to the moderate Liberal Party and was one of the vice-presidents of the assembly.

Riesser, who was born in Hamburg in 1806, and had studied law, found doors closed to him when he tried to practice his profession or teach at a university. From then on, he saw it as his mission to struggle for emancipation. In fervid articles, Riesser debated with the critics of Judaism, denounced the injustice done to the Jews, and demanded equal rights for them. In Parliament, he delivered a passionate address in favor of emancipation which made a strong impression on the deputies. And the constitution which was framed in the spring of 1849 did contain a paragraph promising equal rights to the members of all faiths. However,

1810, organ music was introduced into the service. Orthodox circles of course opposed these reforms, which they regarded as an imitation of Christian services and a deviation from the hallowed Jewish tradition. However, their opposition was of no use. In various forms, bringing more or less extreme changes in opinions and customs, Reform Judaism spread throughout Germany. Rabbis with university educations headed the Reform communities and brought them prestige in German intellectual circles. Many of them, such as the extremist Abraham Geiger and the moderate Zechariah Frankel, brilliantly represented the new science founded by Leopold Zunz (1794–

Self-portrait by the Dutch painter Jozef Israels (1824–1911). Israel's Jewish romanticism is steeped in the spirit of French realism of the Barbizon school. His self-portraits reveal the mature style of the last years of his life, when he was already under the influence of the Impressionists. Israel Museum, Jerusalem

Parliament was dissolved by force in June, 1849, and its decisions remained on paper.

In the years following the failure of the revolution, Riesser continued his struggle for emancipation. In the economic progress of the 1850s and 1860s, the Jewish middle class also strengthened its position. The wars between Prussia and Denmark in 1864, between Prussia and Austria in 1866, and between Germany and France in 1870–71 gave the Jews opportunities to demonstrate their patriotism on the battlefields as well.

In the year before the outbreak of the war with France, in 1869, the North German Federation already granted emancipation to the Jews in the territories belonging to it. When the German Reich was established after the victory over France, this law was introduced into the entire area of the Reich. Thus, the long Jewish struggle was victorious.

At that time, no one could imagine that it would be a transitory victory which would end in devastating tragedy after the passage of only seventy years.

Self-portrait by Jozef Israels. 1824–1911. Israel Museum, Jerusalem

AUSTRIA

At the end of the 1760s there were a number of Jewish families in Vienna, several communities in Bohemia and Moravia, and some tens of thousands of Jews in the towns and villages of Hungary. All the discriminatory laws and restrictions inherited from the Middle Ages were still in force against the Jews in the lands of the Habsburg emperors.

A new problem was created in 1772 when in the first partition of Poland a large part of Galicia, with a quarter of a million Jews, was added to Austria. It was a community which differed socially and culturally from the rest of the Jews of Austria. At first, Jewish self-administration continued as it had operated in the kingdom of Poland. However, this state of affairs changed when Emperor Josef II ascended the throne in 1780. The new emperor certainly had many good intentions. In the Edict of Tolerance which he published in 1782, he revealed his wish to transform the Jews into useful subjects by introducing changes in the educational system, spreading knowledge of the crafts, and giving Jews freedom in the choice of an occupation. He also abolished the badge of shame and the head tax, and at the same time, expanded the authority of the communities, made it obligatory for the Jews to use the German language, and required them to serve in the army.

The advocates of enlightenment approved of the reforms. Naphthali Herz Wessely, a close associate of Moses Mendelssohn, wrote *Divrei Shalom ve-Emet* (Words of Peace and Truth), in which he appealed to the Jews to comply with the Edict of Tolerance. Herz Homberg, also a member of Mendelssohn's circle, even became an agent of the Austrian government. As chief inspector of schools and censor for books, he attempted to force the blessings of enlightenment in the emperor's spirit on the Jews of Galicia. However, the Jews of Galicia considered the reforms an attack against the foundations of Judaism. They opposed them vehemently and finally forced Homberg to leave the region in disappointment. At the death of Josef II (1790), the Edict of Tolerance also expired, together with the wish of the authorities and the emperors to improve the Jews' legal position.

In the period of the French Revolution and the Napoleonic wars, Austria was one of the principal strongholds of conservatism in Europe and persisted in this position after Napoleon's defeat as well. During the Congress of Vienna, the Jews appealed to Emperor Franz II for equal rights, but received no answer. Prince Metternich, the Austrian prime minister, was not an anti-Semite and maintained friendly relations with the Rothschild family and other Jews, but, fearing a liberal revolution, he was in principle opposed to reforms and anxious to preserve the existing regime. The result of course was that many Jews joined the revolutionists.

Whatever the Edict of Tolerance did not succeed in doing by coercion from above meanwhile occurred as a natural development. At Vienna and Prague, the gradual assimilation into German culture continued. The Jews began occupying more and more important positions in the economic as well as the spiritual life. In Galicia, the stronghold of the Jewish conservatives, where a bitter struggle was being waged between the Hasidim and *Mithnaggedim*, both adversaries were prepared to form a united front against any inroads of the "heretical" Enlightenment. Here, too, however, the supporters of enlightenment slowly paved a road for their new ideas. Solomon Judah Loeb Rapoport studied the literature of the Gaonic period and published the result of his research in articles which appeared in the Hebrew literary and scientific annual *Bikkurei ha-Ittim* (First Fruits of the Times) and its successor *Kerem Hemed* (Vineyard of Delight). The thinker Nahman Krochmal spread his philosophic and historical doctrines chiefly by word of mouth. Fear of the fanatical elements prevented him from publishing his important work *Moreh Nevokhei ha-Zeman* (Guide to the Perplexed of the Time), which appeared only posthumously. Judah Leib Mieses, Joseph Perl, and Isaac Erter attacked Hasidism in their writings.

1848 AND ITS AFTERMATH

When the revolution broke out in March, 1848, many Jews participated in it. There were Jews among its leaders and its first victims. For the minorities in Austria, the revolution was both liberal and national; this fact was bad for the Jews. In Bohemia, the Czechs attacked the Jews for allegedly siding with the hated Germans. In Hungary, the nationalist revolutionaries demanded that the Jews give up their individuality and assimilate among the Hungarians. In Galicia, the

Self-portrait by Leonid Pasternak (1862–1945). The style of the father of the writer Boris Pasternak was chiefly influenced by German Expressionist painting. Israel Museum, Jerusalem

Jewish community was divided into persons loyal to German Austria and the supporters of the Polish movement of liberation. The revolution was suppressed before the end of the year, but its principal aim had been achieved, at least as far as the Jews were concerned. The new Emperor, Franz Josef II, inserted a paragraph promising the Jews equal rights, in the constitution which he gave the people in 1849. All the disabilities were not yet removed, but it was nevertheless an important step forward.

Austria's military defeats in the war with Italy in 1859 and against Prussia in 1886 proved to the emperor that something had to be done to strengthen the kingdom internally. Accordingly, Franz Josef II issued a new constitution in 1867 granting full rights to all the minorities in his realm, including the Jews, who

A deeply romantic painter was Maurycy Gottlieb (1856–1879), born in the city of Drohobycz, a center of the Jewish Enlightenment movement in Galicia. At the age of sixteen, the talented youngster reached the Academy of Painting at Cracow and studied under one of the greatest Polish painters, Jan Matejko. His works include this Young Woman, *painted in 1877. Israel Museum, Jerusalem*

now were to receive complete emancipation with no restrictions whatsoever.

Although anti-Semitism was not entirely eliminated from the hearts of the Austrian people, with the authorities still occasionally continuing to display a lack of good will, and Jews of Austria still encountering obstacles in their paths, they regarded the constitution of 1867 as the fulfillment of their aspirations, and their reaction was boundless loyalty to their land and emperor.

The process of cultural assimilation continued. While in Galicia proponents of the Enlightenment movement such as Abraham Krochmal (author of *Ha-Ketav veha-Mikhtav*—Script and Writing), Isaac Hirsch Weiss (who wrote a history of the development of the Oral Law down to the Middle Ages in his five-volume *Dor Dor ve-Doreshav*), and others continued to use the Hebrew language to spread their ideas, writers and scholars in the rest of Austria wrote in German. Learned rabbis such as Adolf Jellinek and Moritz Gudemann published important studies on Jewish topics. Poets like Ludwig August Frankl and writers like Karl Emil Franzos, who later moved to Germany, enriched German-Austrian literature.

ITALY

In 1796, northern Italy was conquered by the French army under the command of General Napoleon Bonaparte. In 1797–99, the rest of Italy also came under French rule. The country was divided into a number of republics. In 1804, when Napoleon became Emperor of France, the republics were abolished and two kingdoms established, the Kingdom of Italy in the north with Napoleon himself as king, and the Kingdom of Naples in the south ruled by his brother, Joseph, and later by his brother-in-law, Joachim Murat.

Wherever the French army came, the walls of the ghettos were opened and the Jews granted full civil rights. The Jews of Italy enthusiastically welcomed the change in their status and actively participated in the new government, even joining Napoleon's army. When the emperor convoked the assembly of Jewish notables in 1806 and the Grand Sanhedrin a year later, delegates from the Kingdom of Italy came to take part.

After the fall of Napoleon, the previous rulers again assumed power all over Italy and the former condition of the Jews was restored, but not all the achievements of the Napoleonic period were abrogated. In the Lombardo-Venetian kingdom under Austrian rule, as well as in the Duchy of Tuscany, various restrictions were reintroduced, but Jews were not required to return to the ghettos, and the special taxes were not imposed again. On the other hand, the reactionary forces demonstrated all their brutality and ugliness in Piedmont, where there was strong Jesuit influence, and in the Papal States; Jews were herded back into ghettos and the gates were locked at night. They were not permitted to employ Christian servants. Once more they were compelled regularly to listen to conversionist sermons. Jewish children were kidnaped, baptized against the wishes of their parents, and educated as Christians.

An uprising by the Italian liberation movement in 1831, in which Jews also took part, was quelled by the intervention of the Austrian army. But the revolt broke out anew in 1848, again with the active participation of Jews. Daniele Manin, a leader of the revolution from Venice, was of Jewish extraction, and one of the first acts of the Venetian Republic was to grant its Jews equal rights. Charles Albert, King of Sardinia, went to war against Austria for the purpose of liberating and uniting all of Italy. After a number of early defeats and a tense pause of ten years, the war of liberation was renewed by Victor Emanuel II in 1859, and finally ended in a victory over Austria and the establishment of a united Italian kingdom in 1861. Jews participated in all these wars. Many of them fought devotedly and bravely in the ranks of the patriots. Jewish bankers, including the Rothschilds, provided the means for the struggle. Isaac Artom was

The most famous German-Jewish painter of the 19th century was Moritz Daniel Oppenheim (1801–1882). Under the influence of his Parisian teacher Jean-Baptiste Regnault, he painted numerous historical pictures, especially on Biblical subjects. His traditional Jewish education and the four years he spent in the Roman ghetto left their mark on the Jewish genre paintings in which he specialized and which were to make him famous. His Return of a Jewish Volunteer from the Wars of Liberation, executed in 1883, appeared at a time when the enfranchisement of German Jews was being hotly debated and greatly influenced the struggle for Jewish rights. Immediately afterwards, he painted a series of twenty-three genre pictures of Jewish family life in costumes of half a century before. The canvases, depicting Sabbath observances, Bar-Mitzvah celebrations, weddings, circumcision ceremonies, and the like, executed in a sentimental, romantic atmosphere, were very popular in Jewish circles during the past century. In order to be able to issue good photographic reproductions of them, a publisher asked Oppenheim to repeat the oils in grisaille and the painter did them over with great precision. This Sabbath Afternoon is one of these reproductions. Israel Museum, Jerusalem

Winter's Day in Berlin *by Lesser Ury (1861–1931), one of the most important of German–Jewish Impressionists. Another of his works appears at right. Israel Museum, Jerusalem*

protection of Napoleon III, the French emperor. Garibaldi's attempts to take Rome in 1867 failed.

Pope Pius IX, who had displayed liberal tendencies in 1848 and had even ordered the walls of the ghetto demolished, completely reversed his policy in 1850. All the anti-Jewish decrees were renewed and strictly enforced.

While the Italians were preparing for a decisive war against Austria, and emancipation was still waiting at the doorsteps of Austria and Germany, an incident occurred in the Papal States which shocked public opinion throughout the world. In the city of Bologna, in the Pope's territory, a Christian nurse declared that she had secretly baptized a Jewish child by the name of Edgardo Mortara. On the basis of this declaration, the papal gendarmes kidnaped the child from his home and handed him over to the Church to be brought up as a Catholic. The press in Italy and throughout Europe protested, and the rabbis of Germany complained to the Pope. The English philanthropist and intercessor on behalf of his fellow Jews, Moses Montefiore, traveled to Rome, but Pius IX refused to receive him. The Pope even refused the requests of Emperor Napoleon III of France and Franz Josef, Emperor of Austria. The child was brought up as a Christian and in time became a Catholic priest.

The Jews of Bologna were emancipated in 1860, but the Jews of Rome had another ten years of suffering and degradation in an atmosphere resembling that of the Middle Ages. Finally, in September, 1870, Rome was captured by the army of Victor Emanuel II and became the capital of united Italy. This conquest brought the Jews of Rome civil rights equal to those of other Italians and freedom from a regime of terror.

Italy was perhaps the only country in which, together with discriminatory laws, all anti-Jewish feeling vanished. An atmosphere of friendship, understanding, and close cooperation prevailed between Jews and other Italians. In all the fields of endeavor — politics, the army, commerce, industry, and the spiritual life — Jews were able to act freely and aspire to the highest posts. In such an atmosphere, assimilation of course increased. Simultaneously, however, a dynamic Jewish cultural life developed in the Jewish communities, which fostered their ancient traditions and established magnificent synagogues, elementary schools, and rabbinical seminaries.

an assistant of Count Cavour, Italy's prime minister in the wars of the Risorgimento. Giuseppe Finzi was the friend and assistant of the Italian national hero, Giuseppe Garibaldi. In accordance with the liberal spirit of the leaders of the Italian rebirth, the new Italian government granted full rights to the Jews in actual practice.

THE JEWS OF ROME AND NATIONAL UNITY

For a decade, the city of Rome remained outside the Kingdom of Italy and was ruled by the Pope under the

ENGLAND

At the end of the eighteenth century, there were more than twenty thousand Jews in England. Part of this community, especially the Sephardic aristocracy in London, was swept by a wave of desperation after the abolition of the naturalization law of 1753. Numerous families joined the Anglican Church for the purpose of removing the last obstacle to their complete integration into English society. However, most Jews remained loyal to Judaism, entertained hopes for at-

Ury did most of his work in Berlin, where he lived and died, a modern descendant of the French Impressionists. He gave powerful expression to his deep emotional sensitivity in scenes of city cafés and windswept streets, with cars and people rushing by. Lesser Ury sketched his cityscapes in the open air and later completed them in his studio, giving great thought to their composition from the point of view of color and feeling. He came from a poor family and suffered from poverty all his life, dying destitute, locked in his studio as a recluse. The painting shown here is titled A Broad Avenue on a Rainy Night. *Israel Museum, Jerusalem*

taining its aims in the future, and meanwhile reconciled themselves to the situation, which was better than in other European countries. Judaism demonstrated its attraction for non-Jews when a member of the English nobility, Lord George Gordon, adopted the Jewish faith in 1787; Gordon had previously represented Protestantism in its fanatic struggle against Catholicism.

Generally, an atmosphere of tolerance prevailed in England, and no one troubled Jews engaged in a craft or in a trade. Big merchants and wealthy bankers in the City of London were accepted by upper-class English society and occupied highly respected positions in their country's economic life.

The French Revolution and the Napoleonic wars did not bring the Jews of England the transitory emancipation which they had been granted on the Continent. But these events did give them a chance to

199

Landscape *by Isaac Levitan expresses the melancholy of the broad Russian horizon. Israel Museum, Jerusalem*

strengthen their economic position and improve their social status. Jewish financiers supported the war effort, contributing towards the victory over Napoleon. Particularly outstanding in this activity was Nathan Meyer Rothschild, the son of Meyer Amschel Rothschild of Frankfurt, who during his father's lifetime had already moved to England and opened a branch of the family bank in London. In 1814, he loaned not only England but her allies as well vast sums of money for financing the war. In the same period, other Jewish financiers such as Moses Montefiore and the Goldsmid brothers also became famous.

The situation was paradoxical. On the one hand, the Jews of England lived as all other normal citizens, subject to no discrimination in the economic, social, or religious sphere; but, on the other hand, they were deprived of precisely that privilege to which they aspired and which they justifiably considered their formal recognition as citizens with equal rights—the right of active participation in the municipal and national political life. The principal stumbling block was the text of the oath which any Englishman assuming public office had to take. The wording of this was clearly Christian. Apostates such as the economist David Ricardo, who was elected to Parliament in 1819, or Benjamin Disraeli, who was sent to the House of

1855, Salomons was the first Jew to be elected Lord Mayor of London. However, his attempts to break through the barriers against Jews in Parliament failed after his election as a member of the Liberal Party in 1851. He was prevented from taking his seat in the House of Commons because he declined to take the Christian oath and was even fined for voting illegally.

Victory in the parliamentary arena was achieved by Lionel Nathan Rothschild, Nathan Meyer's son. Lionel was elected to Parliament to represent the Liberals in 1847, but could not take his seat because he rejected the text of the oath. The House of Commons was prepared to alter the text, especially after an inspiring speech delivered on this occasion by Benjamin Disraeli; but the matter again encountered the opposition of the House of Lords. The Liberals in London stubbornly elected Lionel over and over again. Finally, Parliament had no choice. In 1858, the Jewish M.P. was permitted to take his seat after taking a special oath, and in 1860, a law changing the text of the oath was passed.

This in effect marked the official attainment of complete emancipation in England. Lionel's son, Nathaniel Meyer, first Baron Rothschild, was made a lord in 1885 and thus became the first Jewish member of the House of Lords.

BENJAMIN DISRAELI AND MOSES MONTEFIORE

To a great extent, the positive attainment of emancipation was made possible by Benjamin Disraeli, Earl of Beaconsfield. Despite the fact that he was baptized in childhood, he remained full of sympathy and admiration for the Jewish people all his life, not concealing his feelings and even expressing them in his writings and speeches. After some difficult beginnings to his parliamentary career, not lacking in references by his opponents to his Jewish origins, Disraeli, thanks to his talents as orator and statesman and his bold vision and personal charm, became the leader of the Conservative Party, the party of the British aristocracy. He was prime minister twice, the second time for more than six years. With the help of the Rothschilds, he acquired a dominant holding in the Suez Canal Company. Disraeli honorably represented his country at the Congress of Berlin in 1878, brought the Island of Cyprus under British rule, secured the title of Empress of India for Queen Victoria, winning her confidence and friendship, and added a romantic note to British imperialistic policy. He gave the Jewish struggle for equal rights his unqualified support and, at the Congress of Berlin, also utilized his influence for the benefit of Jews in the Balkan countries.

Among the Jews of England of the period, Sir Moses Montefiore was one of the most interesting personalities. He was a member of a distinguished family of Italian origin and the brother-in-law of Nathan Meyer Rothschild. After amassing a fortune as a broker in partnership with Rothschild, he retired from business in 1824 at the age of forty and devoted the re-

Commons in 1837, were sworn in as loyal Christians and encountered no difficulties. But Jews who had not adopted Christianity could not take the oath of office in Parliament, as that body refused to alter the official text. Beginning in 1830, numerous bills were presented to Parliament with a view to opening the way to public office for Jews. Generally, the bills were passed in the House of Commons but rejected by the House of Lords.

The way to municipal office was initially opened by David Salomons who was elected alderman in London in 1837 and succeeded in taking office after a vigorous struggle without taking the Christian oath. In

Self-portrait by Max Liebermann (1847–1935) shows the great contribution of this German artist of the late 19th century and early 20th. He successfully struggled against the established academic style steeped in sentimentality. As the value of the French Impressionists was rising in the 1920s, Liebermann emerged as one of the masters of the German Impressionist school. Israel Museum, Jerusalem

maining sixty years of his life to activities on behalf of the Jewish people. For forty years he headed the Board of Deputies of British Jews.

He first demonstrated his talent for interceding on behalf of Jews in the so-called Damascus Affair. In 1840, the Jews of Damascus were accused of the murder of a Catholic priest for religious purposes. The French consul in Damascus had a hand in pinning this charge on the Jews. Jewish dignitaries were arrested and tortured. Two of them died from the torture, and the rest were threatened with the death sentence. The anti-Jewish agitation put the Jewish community of Damascus in serious danger. Montefiore traveled to Egypt and Turkey with the French-Jewish statesman Adolphe Crémieux to intercede on behalf of the accused Jews. He not only secured their acquittal but also persuaded the Turkish sultan to issue an order forbidding charges of ritual murder in the future.

Moses Montefiore was always ready to travel anywhere that Jews were in trouble and to render assistance without concern for his money or his health. He journeyed to Rome to use his influence to try to secure

the release of the child Edgardo Mortara, and in other cases to Morocco and Russia. But his greatest love was reserved for the Jewish community of Palestine. He visited the country seven times and expended considerable efforts to improve the living conditions of the old, settled community. He strengthened it by establishing opportunities for productive work. Politically, even then, Moses Montefiore dreamed of Palestine restored to its people.

THE RUSSIAN "PALE OF SETTLEMENT"

For centuries Russia tried to prevent the establishment of a Jewish community in its territory. To the extent that there were nevertheless Jews in Russia, the Czars oppressed them and plagued them with all kinds of restrictions. Twice during the eighteenth century, they were ordered expelled. However, the number of Jews in the vast Russian empire was not large and, actually, the problem was more a pathological hatred of all Jews than the existence of an anomalous Jewish minority.

This situation changed at the end of the eighteenth century. The partition of Poland brought to Russia, in addition to large territories, a compact Jewish population of more than seven hundred thousand persons. At first, the authorities had no idea how to deal with this huge minority which had become their responsibility. The first policy was to establish by decree a "Pale of Settlement"—approximately coinciding with the new provinces—as the only area in which Jews were permitted to reside and work. Thus, a huge ghetto was set up along Russia's western border. Jews from the villages were herded into this ghetto for the purpose of "preventing their harmful influence from affecting the Russian farmer," and were compelled to crowd together in the towns with no concern for where they might find sources of livelihood. In theory they were granted limited municipal rights, from which they never actually benefited; extremely heavy special taxes were collected from them.

The Jews pinned certain hopes on Czar Alexander I (1801–1825), who was considered a liberal. Their loyalty to Russia during Napoleon's invasion of the country in 1812 gave them the right to hope for an improvement in their condition after the Russian victory. But their hopes did not materialize. The Czar saw the solution of the Jewish problem in spreading Christianity to the Jews, yet he was not prepared to lift a finger to better their condition. On the contrary, the spirit of reaction mounted during the last years of his reign.

Immeasurably worse was the condition of the Jews under the successor of Alexander I, his brother Nicholas I (1825–1855), who embodied traditional Russian opposition to the liberal spirit of the West. He was determined to force the Jews to relinquish their individuality and become assimilated into the general population, with respect to both religion and culture, and he did not hesitate to adopt any means he deemed suitable for achieving this end. About six hundred orders and regulations concerning Jews were promulgated during the reign of this czar, and each one brought new repressive measures. Their few rights were further reduced, they were forbidden to employ Christian servants, they were not permitted to build new synagogues, books in Hebrew and Yiddish were censored, unauthorized works were ordered burned, and the like.

But the worst and most inhuman of all the decrees was the law creating the "cantonists." Children of twelve were mustered for military service for a period of twenty-five years. The Jewish communities were required to supply the recruits, and the rich men heading them were accused by the poorer elements of favoritism in carrying out the order. In the barracks, the officers did everything possible to break the spirit of the boys and force them to adopt Christianity. Many of them broke down under the torment, but most of them held firm during the horrifying ordeal and remained loyal to Judaism.

All the protests of the Jews in other European countries against the persecution of their coreligionists in Russia were of no avail. Even the visit of Moses Montefiore in 1846 brought no practical results, despite the fact that his personality made an impression on the Czar.

Meanwhile, the Czar tried another way to overcome the Jews' opposition to assimilation. With the help of a young German Jew, Max Lilienthal, who was unaware of the Czar's real purpose, and with the consent of a limited circle of Jews favoring Westernization, a plan was drawn up for the establishment of a network of government schools for Jews. The plan was designed to remove their children from the influence of the elementary Jewish religious schools and educate them in the spirit of Russian culture. An attempt was made to win over the parents by exempting the pupils of government schools from military service. However, the efforts were in vain. Nothing could persuade the Jews, with the exception of a negligible minority, to send their children to a school which they regarded simply as the beginning of a road leading to conversion.

THE "LIBERATING CZAR"

When Nicholas I died in 1855, not only did the Jews breathe more freely. The Russian masses, who had had enough of tyranny and were deeply ashamed of the disgraceful military defeats in the Crimea, also felt relieved. All of Russia, including the Jews, hoped for better days under the new Czar, Alexander II (1855–1881), regarded as a man with liberal ideas. Alexander justified the title of "Liberator-Czar" when he freed more than forty million serfs. Russian intellectuals under Western influence now dared raise their voices and demand a change in the attitude toward the Jews. Abolition of the cantonist system in 1856 was enthusiastically received as a sign of better times to come. Certain classes of Jews—big merchants, university graduates, and the members of certain professions—were permitted to settle in Russian cities outside the Pale of Settlement. Jews were granted limited rights in district administration and permitted to practice law. While all this hardly touched the wretched life of the masses of Jews in the Pale of Settlement living from hand to mouth, well-to-do Jews took advantage of the easing of the law, and in a short time a class of Jews came into being which had been educated in Russian schools and adapted itself to the Russian environment. It seemed that Russia, too, was making progress toward a satisfactory solution of the Jewish problem, although the advancement was slow and late.

However, the Polish revolt of 1863 put an end to all these hopes. Once again reaction had the upper hand. Hatred of Jews once more increased among the population and in government circles. The press agitated against the Jews and warned against the "Jewish peril." The authorities even made use of informers of the caliber of the apostate Jacob Brafman, who published sensational "revelations" of a Jewish plot against Russia.

THE POGROM

In 1881, Alexander II was assassinated by Nihilists and, unfortunately for the Jews, the group responsible for the murder included one Jewess. Naturally this fact was exploited to the hilt by anti-Semitic propagandists. The fruits of the agitation ripened in a short time. The new Czar, Alexander III (1881–1894), did

Portrait of a Young Woman *by the Dutch painter Isaac Israels (1865–1934), son of the famous Jozef Israels. Like his father, he, too, was noted for his unmistakably Impressionistic portraits. Israel Museum, Jerusalem*

The genre painter and portraitist Isidor Kaufmann (1854–1921) took great pains with the details of his work. He was careful to endow his canvases with realistic vitality and expression. The Portrait of a Rabbi on this page reveals Kaufmann's love of minute detail and vitality. From photograph in archives of Massada Ltd.

not conceal his hate of the Jews, and his position was interpreted as allowing a free hand for practical steps against the "enemies of the fatherland." In the spring and summer of 1881, a wave of pogroms swept over many cities—Elizavetgrad, Kiev, Berdichev, Odessa, Balta, Warsaw, and others. The pogroms were repeated a year later. With the encouragement and active assistance of the authorities, mobs wounded and murdered Jews, plundered and razed dwellings and synagogues, and destroyed much property.

In London, New York, and other cities protest meetings were held, in which Christian personalities also expressed their outrage at these atrocities. But these denunciations had no effect on the Russian government, and the pogrom was thereafter one of the established techniques for handling the Jewish problem in Russia, employed again and again when the occasion arose.

On the recommendation of Minister of the Interior Ignatiev, a sworn Jew-hater, the Czar in May, 1882, approved regulations known as the "May Laws" governing the life of Jews in Russia, which remained in force until the collapse of the Czarist regime in the 1917 revolution. Jews were now forbidden to dwell outside the towns, even within the Pale of Settlement. Local authorities could expel Jews from areas under their jurisdiction even without any prior notification. Secondary schools and universities were almost completely closed to them. In the economic sphere, too,

restrictions were tightened. Jews who had settled outside the Pale of Settlement were driven back with great cruelty. The Jews were expelled from Moscow in 1891, and the expulsions from St. Petersburg, Kharkov, and other cities were sadistic operations.

MODERN HEBREW LITERATURE

Despite the regime of horror and mounting impoverishment, the spirit of the Russian Jews was not broken. In the Pale of Settlement, a dynamic Jewish life went on chiefly centered around the synagogue and the rabbi or Hasidic Zaddik. Nor had joy ceased to exist in Jewish homes, especially in Hasidic circles. Sabbaths and holidays were accompanied by singing and dancing.

The Jews were greatly concerned with the education of their children. In elementary schools, the children industriously studied the prayer book and the Pentateuch and took their first steps in the study of the Gemara. In the *yeshivot*, boys imbibed the Talmud and halakhic codes.

This appeared to be a closed little world, insulated against winds blowing from the outside. However, actually, the spirit of Enlightenment had already penetrated it, at first surreptitiously, and had gradually spread despite the opposition of conservative circles, both Hasidic and *Mithnaggedic*. In Russia, the Enlightenment movement did not take the road of assimilation into the Russian environment, but expounded the new values in Hebrew, thus laying the foundation for a modern Hebrew literature. Isaac Beer Levinsohn in his writings, *Te'uda be-Yisroel* (Mission in Israel) and *Beit Yehuda* (House of Judah), advocated the ideals of the Enlightenment and tried to prove that there was no contradiction between Judaism and a secular education. Abraham Mapu created the Hebrew historical novel with *Ahavat Tsiyon* (Love of Zion); Judah Loeb Gordon started his literary career as a romantic poet and then turned to barbed satire which contains overtones of revolutionary pathos. Moses Loeb Lilienblum fought for the crystallization of a new philosophy of Judaism, both positivist and secular. Perez Smolenskin moved to Vienna, where he published the monthly *Ha-Shahar* devoted to literature and current affairs, and created the realistic story in Hebrew.

Mendele Mocher Sforim (Solomon Jacob Abramovich) wrote his first tales in Hebrew; but, later on, he went over to the vernacular, the Yiddish spoken by the Jews of Eastern Europe, and laid the foundation of the modern literature in this language. Whereas a satirical tone predominates in his works, Sholom Aleichem (Solomon Rabinowitz), a younger contemporary of his, depicted the Jews of the Pale of Settlement in humorous stories full of warmth and love for his people. After them, writers like Isaac Leib Peretz, Sholem Asch, and others assured Yiddish literature an honored position in the world's literary endeavors.

BETWEEN NATIONALISM AND ASSIMILATION

Maurycy Gottlieb. Head of a Jewish Woman, *Israel Museum, Jerusalem*

The nineteenth century brought Jews in the civilized countries of Europe victory at last in their lengthy struggle for equal rights. It could apparently be hoped that the twentieth would bring them complete integration into the life of the countries which had granted them civil rights and that, at least in these lands, the painful "Jewish problem" would be solved once and for all. However, it cannot be said that the skies of the Jewish world in Western and Central Europe became brighter the day the new century began.

THE "NEW ANTI-SEMITISM"

Memory of the storms which had passed had not yet faded away when other ominous clouds began gathering on the horizon. The powerful outbreak of anti-Semitism with which the civilized peoples had reacted to the termination of the historical process of emancipation was not yet forgotten. Its aftermath was still creating unrest and did not allow the Jews to find peace easily. In France, the "Jewish traitor" Alfred Dreyfus was amnestied, it is true, after five years of imprisonment on Devil's Island, but six more years had to pass before the judges would publicly admit that an innocent man had been punished. In Germany, the medieval charge of ritual murder was revived in 1900: the Jews of Konitz (Chojnice), then Prussia, were accused of having murdered a German young man for the purpose of using his blood in a religious rite. The accused persons were acquitted for lack of evidence, but the anti-Semitic press published inflammatory articles, and pogroms were carried out in Konitz and in a number of other places in the summer of 1901. In 1903, the cry of agony and wrath engendered by the pogrom at Kishinev burst out of Eastern Europe.

Nevertheless, a general air of optimism prevailed among the Jews. In Germany there were about six hundred thousand Jews at the turn of the century. Most of them were engaged in commerce and industry, but they also played a large part in banking, the liberal professions, the press, literature, the theater, music, and the plastic arts. There was hardly a cultural sphere in which they did not leave an appreciable mark. Their economic condition was generally sound, and some of them had become rich. Jews were active in politics, belonging chiefly to the Liberal and Social-Democratic parties, and here and there they were elected to the Reichstag or the parliaments of the various German states. These deputies considered themselves the representatives of all the German people and faithfully served the interests of their constituents. On the other hand, they generally did not feel obligated to say anything special in connection with problems specifically concerning Jews. The Jews of Germany were rooted in German culture, felt themselves Germans in every respect, and demonstrated fervid patriotism. However, the sincere willingness of the Jews to be like all other Germans evoked no corresponding response among their fellow Germans to consider them brothers.

Immediately after the attainment of emancipation, reaction made itself heard. The Germans looked upon the Jews as aliens endangering the purity of their culture and perverting its spirit. The German historian

Amedeo Modigliani (1884–1920) was already considered a genius as a boy in his native city of Leghorn, Italy. After studying classic academic art in Venice, Modigliani began developing an original style, far from accepted academic realism. His early works were influenced mostly by African sculpture and Cubism. The elongated human forms which he created reveal the unique style of one of the great painters of our time. During the thirty-six years of his life, Modigliani suffered from sorrow, hunger, and poverty; he died of tuberculosis in a Paris hospital in 1920. It was not until about a decade after his death that he was recognized as the most human and sensual artist of the School of Paris. This figure of a girl—the daughter of his concierge in Paris—was painted in 1917. Joseph H. Hazen Collection, New York

Treitschke openly proclaimed, "The Jews are the misfortune of the German people." The German economic crisis of the 1870s prepared the soil for anti-Semitic propaganda which pointed to the Jew as scapegoat. The anti-Semitic movement was headed by the Protestant clergyman Adolf Stoecker, the Kaiser's court preacher. He founded the Christian Socialist Union which soon secured seats in the Reichstag and even induced the Conservative Party to follow its anti-Semitic line. Chancellor Bismarck, the all-powerful prime minister for many years, did not share

the anti-Semites' ideas, but he encouraged them clandestinely as a counterweight to the Liberals, whose Jewish leaders angered him with their sharp criticism of his policies. The scientific basis for anti-Semitism was supplied by a talented English-born writer, Houston Stewart Chamberlain, in his work *Foundations of the Nineteenth Century,* which appeared in 1898. He claimed the Jews were the most despised representatives of the inferior Semitic race and were conducting an uninterrupted war against the civilization of the Aryan race, exemplified in the highest degree of purity and brilliance by the German people. The counterpropaganda of the "Society for Fighting Anti-Semitism," founded in 1890 by people of good will, both Christians and Jews, was not very effective.

At the beginning of the twentieth century, anti-Semitism, it is true, became less vociferous, but it did not grow one whit weaker and showed its full power in various spheres. In admissions to the bar and appointments of judges, Jewish candidates were discriminated against, and questions raised in Parliament, protests, and petitions did no good. The military was closed to Jews. An insignificant number were employed as government officials or as teachers, especially at universities. Celebrated scientists were granted professorships only in extraordinary instances. Socially, the negative attitude was clearly felt.

"CITIZENS OF THE JEWISH RELIGION"

To many doors still locked to Jews, there was a magic key as long as racial theories did not gain currency in governing circles. If a Jew agreed to adopt Christianity, no one bothered to check his credentials. Even superficial conversion opened new possibilities. Many Jews accepted baptism to clear their paths of stumbling blocks. Others married German women and raised their children as Christians. However, despite the fact that the number of apostates was not negligible, this phenomenon remained limited to individual instances. Most of the Jews of Germany remained faithful to Judaism, scorned the hypocrisy of changing one's faith for a material aim, and clung to the hope that progress and common sense would ultimately be victorious.

Meanwhile, the Jews who rejected total assimilation as a solution to the Jewish problem organized to defend their rights. In 1893, an organization was formed in Berlin with the characteristic name of "Central Society of German Citizens of the Jewish

Leopold Gottlieb (1883–1930)—brother of the painter, Maurycy—was born four years after Maurycy's untimely death. His parents encouraged him to follow in his brother's footsteps in the hope of restoring the genius' honor to the family. Leopold Gottlieb excelled chiefly in sketching and succeeded mainly by Impressionistic means in expressing figures of great intensity such as the portrait shown here. Israel Museum, Jerusalem

Religion." In 1904, the "Society of German Jews" was founded. The principal activities of these societies were in two directions: a large-scale propaganda campaign to extirpate anti-Jewish prejudices, and pressure on the authorities for the purpose of securing legal recognition of the Jewish group as a religious denomination with the same rights as the Catholic and Protestant churches. Both societies demonstratively stressed loyalty to the German Reich and culture and advocated this principle among their members. This position was sharply expressed in 1897, after the First Zionist Congress, when the German Rabbinical Association published a declaration denouncing the Jewish Nationalist movement.

The war of the Central Society against Zionism did not succeed in suppressing the Nationalist movement. And it was particularly in Germany that enthusiastic supporters of the movement appeared, including such spiritual leaders as Martin Buber and political leaders and men of action such as David Wolffsohn, Otto Warburg, Arthur Ruppin, and others.

Despite the tendency of many German Jews to remain apart from the rest of the Jewish community and regard themselves as part of the German nation, life forced upon them the awareness that all Jews are willy-nilly responsible for one another. Because of the difficult condition of the Jews in Eastern Europe, a steady stream of emigrants flowed from there to Germany. From the Jewish point of view, these immigrants rooted in Judaism were a blessing for the communities in Germany. They strengthened Jewish self-consciousness in Germany and introduced a spiritual ferment into community life. At the same time, however, the *Ostjuden* (Eastern Jews) were a thorn in the flesh of the older Germanized population, and they also added fuel to the fires of anti-Semitism. Both for humanitarian reasons and out of their feeling of responsibility (and also because they wanted anti-Semites to be less aware of this immigration), Jewish organizations were eager to help these immigrants and make their adjustment easier. "The Aid Society of German Jews," established in 1901, extended help to the victims of the pogroms of 1903 and 1905, and also conducted negotiations with the Russian government to improve the condition of the Jews.

Among the Jewish communities of Germany, the struggle between Conservative and Reform Judaism continued. In the Reform congregations, attempts were made to carry through radical changes such as shifting the Sabbath to Sunday, reducing the number of precepts to circumcision and the observance of Jewish holidays, elimination of the Hebrew language from the synagogue service, and the determination of a minimal creed. Most of the Jews anxious for religious reforms rejected such extreme innovations for fear they would lead to a split in German Jewry. But, nevertheless, it was impossible to prevent the schism. The Reform Jews and the Orthodox could no longer live under the same roof. In the 1870s, Orthodox Jews under the leadership of Samson Raphael Hirsch, Rabbi of Frankfurt-am-Main, already founded separate communities in various places. And it was German Orthodox Jews of the school of Samson Raphael Hirsch who in 1912 established the world Orthodox organization Agudath Israel, perhaps without being aware of the fact that this widened still more the breach in the "absolute Germanism" of Germany's Jews.

CENTRAL EUROPE

The Austro-Hungarian monarchy quickly attached itself to the new German anti-Semitism of the 1870s. Anti-Jewish agitation fell on fertile soil here and was not long in bearing fruit. In 1882, a ritual-murder charge was framed in Tisza-Eszlar, Hungary, and the suspects were cross-examined by methods used in the Inquisition, with all the pertinent implements. It is true that the accused were finally acquitted and, in the verdict, emphasis was laid on the fact that the charge of ritual murder was a lie, but in the meantime the atmosphere had become poisoned, and in a number of places events reached the stage of violence against Jews. One of the "experts" who had revived the heritage of the Middle Ages and spread false accusations against the Jews, including the charge of using blood for religious purposes, was August Rohling, Professor of Theology at the University of Prague. Pitted against him was Rabbi Joseph Bloch, a member of the Austrian Parliament, who in a series of articles proved the professor's ignorance and denounced his forgeries. Rohling filed a libel suit against Bloch. But the trial did not go in his favor, and only withdrawal of the suit saved Rohling from a verdict which would have brought him complete disgrace. In any case, he had to resign from the university.

However, this defeat of one of its major spokesmen did not weaken the anti-Semitic movement, which had deep roots in large parts of the population. Karl Lueger, a lawyer by profession, who headed the movement in the 1890s, was elected mayor of Vienna a number of times. Emperor Franz Josef confirmed his election in 1897 only after much hesitation.

In Austria-Hungary there were more than two million Jews, of whom about nine hundred thousand were in Hungary, about eight hundred thousand in Galicia, and some one hundred thousand in little Bukovina. This constituted a large Jewish population concentrated in a single territory, most of whom were Orthodox and nationalistic Jews, speaking Yiddish and rooted in Jewish culture. This population might have succeeded in securing official recognition as a nationality (like the Czechs, Poles, or Rumanians) within the monarchy, if it had been united and had worked energetically toward such a goal. An opportunity presented itself in 1906 when the electoral system was changed in order to assure all the nationalities in the monarchy fair representation in Parliament. However, the chance was missed because of the discord among the Jews of Austria-Hungary.

In Austria itself, that is, the German states of the dual monarchy, the Christian Socialist Party, an out-

Max Liebermann, Garden in the Summer. Liebermann was a son of the generation which strove toward a synthesis of Jewish, German, and European cultures (see page 202)

growth of the anti-Semitic movement, achieved predominance, and its influence was felt to a marked degree in the social and economic life. Anti-Semitism was most severe in the capital, Vienna, where one hundred and fifty thousand Jews lived.

A considerable portion of the Jews of Austria, especially those whose families had been there a long time, were assimilated on the German pattern and regarded themselves as an inseparable part of the German nation. The community leaders, all of them assimilationists, had faith in the protection of Emperor Franz Josef, who was not influenced by the anti-Semitic movement, and hoped that hatred of the Jews was nothing more than a transitory phenomenon. Many believed its source to be the emigration of *Ostjuden* from Galicia, Hungary, and Bukovina to the capital and other Austrian cities. So great was their fear of "what the Gentiles would say" that prominent, influential Jewish personalities issued declarations publicly repudiating any bond of national solidarity between cultured, progressive Austrian Jews and the alien, backward Jews from Eastern Europe.

Nevertheless, there was in Vienna a handful of nationalistic Jews, many of them students, who were influenced by the theories of Nationalist writers such as Perez Smolenskin, Leo Pinsker, and Nathan

Portrait of the writer Beschewiss. *The humanist in the School of Paris was Benzion Rabinowitz, born 1884, known under his pseudonym of "Benn." The dignified human expressions in his work bring it close to modern Italian "metaphysical painting." Israel Museum, Jerusalem*

Birnbaum. They rallied around the Jewish students' association "Kadimah" and Pinsker's pamphlet *Auto-Emancipation*. After Theodor Herzl, himself a Viennese (although born in Budapest), began his political activity on behalf of Zionism, quite a strong Zionist movement, which influenced the political and community life of Austria's Jews, came into being.

In Galicia, most Jews were Orthodox. Since the 1880s, the *Hibbat Zion* (Love of Zion) Nationalist movement had been growing there, and at the end of the century the first Zionist societies were formed. However, leadership of the communities was generally in the hands of the assimilationists, who identified with the dominant Poles and supported Polish candidates in elections. By waving the threat of the danger of more anti-Semitism, the leaders of the communities also influenced the Orthodox, especially the Hasidim, to support the demands of the Poles and oppose the Jewish Nationalist movement. However, this self-effacement was of no assistance in influencing the Poles, who boycotted Jewish merchants and systematically squeezed them out of every branch of economic life. The condition of the Galician Jews deteriorated rapidly and, at the end of the first decade

of the twentieth century, reached a distressing low point. It is accordingly only natural that the Jews of Galicia constituted a large proportion of the emigrants to Vienna, to the rest of Europe, and across the Atlantic.

In Hungary, the assimilated Jews were Hungarian patriots passionately supporting the native language and culture. The Orthodox Jews, too, emulated them in their loyalty to the Hungarian nation. Here, the Orthodox and the Reform congregations maintained separate communities. Assimilation increased from the end of the nineteenth century on. Intermarriage became more common and the incidence of conversion became much greater; nevertheless, the Jewish Nationalist movement gained supporters in Hungary also, albeit in a more limited circle.

In view of the disunity among Jews, an insignificant representation in Parliament was to be expected. Most of the Jewish deputies were elected as representatives of non-Jewish parties and served interests which were not always best for the Jewish people. Yet, despite the discord and uncertainty among the Jewish population in the Austro-Hungarian empire, the general situation was not always bleak. Jews occupied important and respected positions in commerce, banking, and industry. There were many Jews in the liberal professions, including journalism. Jews worked in the civil service, as teachers at all levels, and even made careers in the army, although there was no lack of serious obstacles here, too. In intellectual life, literature, the theater, and music, they made a very marked impression.

To be sure, many people were well aware of the basic weakness of Jewish life in the Diaspora—for political Zionism had come from Vienna and its organizational center was located there for years—but the great majority ignored the dangers and threats. Brimming vitality, optimism, and cheerful complacency characterized Austro-Hungarian Jewry.

FRANCE AND THE DREYFUS CASE

In France, the natural reaction to the military defeat in the war of 1870–71 with Germany was an upsurge of fanatical nationalism and the placing of blame on "traitorous elements," including the Jews, of course. A tone of rabid anti-Semitism was heard in the nationalist press and literature. In 1886, there was published a sensational book by the journalist Edouard Drumont, called *La France juive* (Jewish France), which claimed to prove that the Jews had joined forces with the Freemasons to take over France. The book had an unprecedented success. Tension mounted, and it found its release in the world-shaking spy trial known as the Dreyfus Case.

In 1894, a Jewish officer, Captain Alfred Dreyfus, was arrested and accused of spying for Germany. A court found him guilty on the strength of a forged document, stripped him of his rank, and sentenced him to life imprisonment on Devil's Island. When the forgery was discovered and the real offender, Major

View of St. Paul, *by Adolphe Milich (1886–1964) was a Swiss painter born in Poland who painted in a post-Impressionist style. His paintings contain much poetic feeling, even though their subjects are generally landscapes and still lifes from nature. This landscape was painted by Milich in 1920. Israel Museum, Jerusalem*

Esterhazy, brought to justice, a military court acquitted him, because the army refused to tarnish its reputation by admitting that a miscarriage of justice had taken place. The anti-Semitism involved in its position was all too apparent. The affair became a public scandal. Not only Jews but leading French personalities such as the noted politician Georges Clemenceau and the famous writer Emile Zola demanded a retrial. Reactionary circles, however, stubbornly opposed this. The entire country was split into two camps, for and against Dreyfus, which violently attacked one another. In a number of places, particularly in Algeria, there were serious physical outbreaks against Jews. In 1899, public opinion forced the government to bring Dreyfus back to France and hold a new trial. Once more he was convicted, but his sentence was commuted to ten years' imprisonment. Again tempers on both sides flared. Dreyfus' supporters demanded absolute justice and were not satisfied with a pardon by the President of the Republic. They did not rest

211

until Dreyfus was exonerated in 1906 and his rank in the army restored.

The journalists who covered the developments of the Dreyfus Case in its early stages included Theodor Herzl, the correspondent of a Viennese newspaper. His work *The Jewish State,* which was written in 1896 and marks a decisive turning point in Jewish history, grew out of the profound impression which the affair made on Herzl.

Dreyfus' acquittal was a serious blow for the anti-Semitic movement, but its supporters did not give up. A group of writers advocating hate of the Jews gathered around the monarchist newspaper *L'Action Française.*

There were about one hundred and sixty-five thousand Jews in France, of whom roughly a hundred thousand lived in Paris. The anticlerical atmosphere prevailing in France, which led to the complete separation of Church and State (1905), was reflected among the old established Jewish population by considerable indifference to religious matters. The Jewish Nationalist movement also elicited only a slight response in France. Jews who had been living in France for some time were generally assimilated; intermarriage and conversions were a common occurrence. However, about fifty thousand of the Jews in France were refugees from Eastern Europe who had fled from Russia in the first decade of the century to seek freedom from persecution. All of them settled in Paris and stimulated the emergence of a new Jewish national and religious awareness in the anemic body of French Jewry. The end of the Dreyfus Case brought the Jews of France a period of peace and a complete feeling of self-confidence. They no longer encountered discrimination in receiving appointments as university professors. Jewish scholars became members of the French Academy. Jews could be found in top government posts, in the judicial system, in the army (as high as the rank of general), in all spheres of culture and art, as well as in commerce and industry. They were rooted in French civilization and active in the various political parties.

ENGLAND

In England there were about sixty thousand Jews in 1880, most of them in London. This settled population had long been participating in the life of the country. Many of them had attained high positions in society and politics. However, integration into British society had weakened the ties with Judaism in numerous circles. Masses of Jews fleeing the death and destruction of the Russian pogroms abruptly broke into this complacent world. In the period between 1881 and 1914, when World War I began, more than two hundred thousand East European Jews came to England. From the Jewish religious and nationalist point of view, this migration was a blessing for stagnating British Jewry, to which it brought new life.

However, such mass immigration naturally gave rise to numerous difficult problems, especially since the immigrants were destitute and had to begin a new life under disagreeable circumstances in a strange environment. On the one hand, their absorption was a heavy burden on the Jewish community and its charitable institutions, and, on the other, their willingness to work for any amount in order to eke out a subsistence aroused the antagonism of organized British labor. An anti-Semitic tone appeared in the press and in Parliamentary debates. Generally, the genteel British avoided using the word "Jews" and spoke of "aliens," but everyone knew to whom the term referred. Acts of violence and anti-Jewish boycotts were not lacking. In 1905, Parliament passed a new immigration law which laid down strict rules for the granting of immigration visas. Through the intercession of the Jewish Board of Deputies these rules were relaxed for the victims of political or religious persecution. But, nevertheless, the law achieved its end and, after it came into effect, immigration slackened considerably. East European Jews who succeeded in settling in England, however, established themselves rather quickly.

RUSSIA AND THE POGROMS

In Russia, Nicholas II, destined to be the last Czar, ascended the throne in 1894. The new Czar did not conceal his hatred of the Jews and his intention to continue the brutal repressive policies of his father, Alexander III. All the restrictions on the freedom of domicile, movement, and economic activity in the Pale of Settlement, in which about three million six hundred thousand Jews were living, and for Jews living outside it—about another one million six hundred thousand—were rigorously enforced. The process of impoverishment and proletarianization proceeded at a horrifying speed. There were no Jews whatsoever in the government service, and obstacles were placed in the path of Jewish lawyers and doctors. Jewish young people were kept out of secondary schools and universities. The unequivocal position of the government encouraged the savage anti-Semitism of the masses. In 1897–99, there were still pogroms, and in 1900 a ritual-murder charge was raised. In Vilna, a Jewish barber, David Blondes, was charged with attempting to wound his Christian maidservant for the purpose of extracting her blood for use in

Camille Pissarro (1830–1903), The Woman with the Red Kerchief. *Born in the Antilles, the son of Jewish parents of Portuguese extraction, Pissarro was educated in Paris. He is considered one of the fathers of Impressionism and was perhaps the most articulate among the painters of this school. Private collection*

baking *matsot*. The court sentenced Blondes to imprisonment for wounding the servant, without mentioning the blood libel, but his lawyer, Oscar Grusenberg, did not rest until a retrial was held and Blondes was acquitted on all counts.

Under such circumstances, one readily understands why many Jewish young people were sympathetic toward revolutionary movements and a number actively joined in them. In 1902, Sipyagin, the Minister of the Interior, was killed and was succeeded by Von Plehwe, a former head of the police and a sworn anti-Semite of German extraction. The new minister made up his mind to wipe out the revolutionary movements by placing the blame on the Jews as the enemy of the Russian people. The slogan was "Drown the revolution in Jewish blood." A campaign of lies and incitement in the press inflamed mob passions and led to a large-scale pogrom in Kishinev in April, 1903.

Today, after the horrors of the Nazi period, the Kishinev pogrom, in which forty-seven were killed and more than six hundred wounded, seems quite a modest occurrence; but in 1903, the world was not yet quite so inured to atrocities, and news of the savage massacre aroused indignation and anger not only in other countries but even within progressive circles in Russia itself. In Europe and America, mass meetings were held in which both Christians and Jews participated. Famous personalities expressed their shock and vigorous protest in speeches and articles. Kaiser Wilhelm II of Germany, Emperor Franz Josef of Austria-Hungary, and President Theodore Roosevelt of the United States appealed directly to the Czar. The shock to Jews throughout Russia was also profound. At this time, the Hebrew poet Chaim Nachman Bialik wrote his poems *Al ha-Shehita* (On the Slaughter) and *Be'Ir ha-Hariga* (In the City of Killing).

The Russian government took some superficial steps to restore order, but actually world public opinion had no effect on Von Plehwe and his methods. At the end of August, the Jews of Gomel were attacked and successive pogroms were carried out in various parts of White Russia and the Ukraine. Fortunately for the Jews of Russia, war broke out between the Czar's empire and Japan in February, 1904. For a year, the government was busy with other concerns, and meanwhile Von Plehwe was assassinated.

Russia's setbacks in the war with Japan strengthened the revolutionary movements. Throughout 1905, acts of terror were carried out, demonstrations were conducted and strikes and uprisings broke out. The authorities tried repressive measures and did not hesitate to shed blood, but ultimately, the Czar was compelled to promise a constitution and agree to elections to a national assembly, the Duma. Jews played a conspicuous role in the revolution. A Jewish convention which met in Vilna in April demanded not only complete equal rights but far-reaching national and religious autonomy. An attempt by the government to crush the revolution by a wave of terror in October, 1905, which primarily affected the Jews, caused numerous casualties (three hundred dead in Odessa alone), but the revolutionaries, including the Jews, continued the struggle. Despite the terror and the fact that the members of the Jewish Socialist Party— the *Bund*—boycotted the elections, twelve Jewish deputies were sent to the Duma. But even before the Duma was able to pass the law on equal rights for Jews, a new pogrom occurred in Bialystok (June, 1906), and when the Duma placed the blame on the authorities and demanded the government's resignation, it was dissolved by the Czar.

Once more, pogroms were organized. Trials were also conducted in which numerous Jews were sentenced to death and executed by military courts. In the Second Duma, which met in February, 1907, and was dissolved four months later, there were only three Jewish deputies, and they did not dare open their mouths. In the years that followed, the government harassed the Jewish population with systematic cruelty. Jews from towns outside the Pale of Settlement were driven into the area. All disabilities and repressive measures were reinstituted and strictly enforced. Again young Jews were not permitted to acquire secondary school or university educations.

In the medieval atmosphere which prevailed in those years, new charges of ritual murder appeared as a matter of course. In 1911, Mendel Beilis, an official in a brick factory in Kiev, was accused of the murder of a Russian boy for ritual purposes. The anti-Semitic press began to incite the population. Professors of medicine testified that the blood had been taken out of the boy's body while he was still alive, and the prosecution did its best to secure the conviction of the accused Jew. Catholic and Greek Orthodox priests as well as "scholars" declared that the Bible and the Talmud require the use of blood in baking *matsot*. But, on the other hand, there were in Russia itself scholars, intellectuals, and even honest clergymen who protested against the attempt to revive a calumny which had long before been proved meaningless. Outside Russia, too, negative opinions by famous scientists and church leaders were published. The accused was brilliantly defended by Oscar Grusenberg, who a decade before had been the lawyer of David Blondes, charged with a similar crime. This defendant, too, was acquitted.

THE UNITED STATES

Most Jews saw only one way to save themselves from the terror regime in Russia—flight from this hell to the free world. Mass emigration, which had already begun in the 1880s, continued uninterruptedly during the early years of the twentieth century until the outbreak of World War I. About a million five hundred thousand Jews left Russia in the first fourteen years of the current century, in addition to about half a million who had departed in the last twenty years of the previous one. Most of the emigrants were headed for the land of freedom, the United States of America.

Jules Pascin (1885–1930), born in Bulgaria of a Sephardic family named Pincas, studied in Munich and traveled through Spain, Belgium, the Netherlands, America, and North Africa, before finally settling in Paris. In the course of his numerous travels, he made a very large number of sketches which reveal his special interest in the realistic human figure. His sketches abound in exotic events and figures, and particularly in women. Gift of the painter's brother, Joseph Pincas, Paris. Israel Museum, Jerusalem

215

A relatively small proportion settled in transit in other lands—Germany, France, and England—and remained there. The colonization project of Baron de Hirsch in Argentina absorbed about thirty thousand persons. Emigrants from Russia also reached South Africa and various countries in South and Central America. Beginning with the 1880s, emigrants with a nationalistic consciousness turned toward Palestine.

The United States of America was, for oppressed Jews, a dream of liberty, security, and unlimited opportunities. But the way there was strewn with obstacles. The generous assistance of Jewish organizations and charitable institutions in the way countries eased the agonies of the refugees only slightly, for, generally, they were destitute on leaving Russia. When they finally reached their destination, other difficulties began—adjustment pangs in a strange environment and their exploitation as cheap labor.

When the first immigrant Jews from Russia arrived in the United States in the 1880s, they already found a settled Jewish population there which numbered nearly a million persons.

A first group of twenty-three Sephardic Jews fleeing from Brazil, which the Dutch had returned to the Portuguese, settled in New Amsterdam in 1654. Ten years later, the city was captured by the English, who changed its name to New York. The initial group was followed by others, Sephardis and Ashkenazis, which settled in other English colonies in North America. It is true they were not granted civil rights, but they enjoyed freedom to practice their religion, and no one interfered with their economic activity. On the eve of the American War of Independence (1775), there were a little over two thousand Jews in the thirteen English colonies. Most of them supported the Patriots and many of them joined George Washington's armies. The Declaration of Independence assured them equal rights and, after the war, the promise was kept.

In the first half of the nineteenth century, many Jews came to the United States from Germany, Austria, Hungary, and Galicia, fleeing Europe's stifling reaction and seeking freedom in the new land. All the immigrants arrived penniless and for many years they were hard put to make a living. But they brought a rich cultural tradition from Europe and left their stamp on the life of the American Jewish community.

In the period of the Civil War (1861–65), in which about ten thousand Jews served on both sides, there were many communities in the northern and southern parts of the country. In many new towns, Jews were among the early pioneers.

In the religious field, a proportion of the Jewish immigrants brought the idea of Reform Judaism with them to their new homes. Reform synagogues were founded by rabbis from Germany such as David Einhorn and Gustav Gottheil. Deserving special mention is Rabbi Isaac Mayer Wise, a native of Bohemia, who unified the various factions in Reform Judaism into one large, national organization and also founded the seminary for Reform rabbis, the Hebrew Union College, in Cincinnati. Not all American Jews followed

the daring reformers; Conservatives found an outstanding leader in the person of Isaac Leeser, also a native of Germany. They, too, established their own institution for preparing rabbis, the Jewish Theological Seminary of America, in New York City.

The German immigrants were still struggling to adjust themselves to their new country when mass Jewish emigration from Russia began in the 1880s. For these refugees, too, the first encounters with life in the United States were extremely difficult. Many of them worked for a meager wage in factories and infamous "sweat shops," where the working day seemed endless. Others made their livelihood from peddling, small business, or various crafts.

The charitable institutions of the early Jewish communities worked hard to help the new immigrants adjust to their new life and to ease their burdens. Patiently and stubbornly, the refugees succeeded in time in establishing themselves. Some of them even became rich. Many of them acquired a higher education and went into the liberal professions. These achievements came as the result of a long struggle; but there were other gains which the immigrants secured immediately, as matters to be taken for granted—physical security, equal rights, and hopes for their children's futures. Even after they learned English, the immigrants from Eastern Europe continued to cling to and cherish their language, Yiddish. In a short time, a press developed in Yiddish, theater companies began performing in the language, and writers and poets created in it.

But, at the same time, the immigrants did everything possible to adjust to their American environment and become integrated into its life. Many Jews became active in public life and entered both local and national politics; they devoted themselves to cultural activities and the labor movement, and achieved important high positions.

Naturally, the immigrants continued to maintain ties with friends and relatives still remaining in Russia, and sympathized with them in all their difficulties. The pogroms of 1903–5 aroused strong protests among the Jews in the United States. Among Christians and in American government circles, the manifestations of Russian brutality caused a deep shock. Mass meetings were held, money was collected to help the victims of the pogroms, and the American Jews organized to take in increased numbers of immigrants. Even when certain circles in the United States became frightened in 1913–14 by the size of the immigration (not only of Jews) and demanded its restriction, they agreed to special consideration for the victims of religious persecution. But, in the meantime, World War I had broken out and temporarily stopped all immigration.

Generally, the immigrants from Eastern Europe strengthened the Orthodox wing of the American Jewish community. But, as the immigrants struck roots in the soil of their new country, many of them drifted away from Orthodoxy and joined the Conservative or even Reform movements. The institutions

As one of the leaders of the School of Paris painters and a close friend of Chaim Soutine, Michel Kikoïne (born 1892) painted numerous canvases of landscapes and portraits. This picture of a garden pool is typical of Kikoïne's impression of nature's organic life. Israel Museum, Jerusalem

of the various trends flourished. Particularly, the Jewish Theological Seminary of Conservative Judaism became one of the most important schools in the world for the study of Jewish culture, after its staff was joined by the Rumanian-born scholar Solomon Schechter in 1902. Schechter, who distinguished himself by his studies of ancient manuscripts discovered in a ninth-century Cairo synagogue (the Cairo Genizah), headed the Theological Seminary until his death in 1915. The Russian pogroms led to the founding of the American Jewish Committee, for the purpose of defending the civil and religious rights of all Jews.

Together with the Jews' integration into the economic life of the United States, in which they succeeded in achieving respected major positions, their active participation in the intellectual life of their new homeland grew steadily—in literature, the theater, the press, and in every branch of science. In addition, a specifically Jewish intellectual life flourished. Scholarly projects—special mention should be made of *The Jewish Encyclopedia*—enriched and disseminated Jewish learning. The fundamental Jewish consciousness also expressed itself in a lively participation in the Nationalist movement.

THE

RETURN

TO

ZION

Boris Schatz (1867–1932), self-portrait. Brush sketch on canvas. Israel Museum, Jerusalem

In the middle of the nineteenth century, when many German Jews considered assimilation the only solution to the Jewish problem, an assimilated German Jew conceived a revolutionary idea. In his book *Rome and Jerusalem,* which appeared in 1862, Moses Hess, one of the founders of Socialism, argued that the Jews are a nation and have the right to renew their national life in their historic homeland. However, his appeal elicited no response in his generation. A similar call was made twenty years later, in 1882, in the anonymous pamphlet bearing the title *Auto-Emancipation* which appeared in Germany. Its author was a physician and writer on public affairs from Odessa, Leo Pinsker; he had written in white heat in response to the 1881 pogroms. In Pinsker's opinion, there was only one way to put an end to the painful phenomenon of anti-Semitism—restoration of the Jews' national independence in their own country. Perez Smolenskin in Vienna and the reviver of the Hebrew language, Elieser Ben-Yehuda, also advocated the Nationalistic theory in their articles, and the bloody events in Russia created fertile soil for their ideas. In Russia and Rumania, *Hovevei Zion* (Lovers of Zion) societies were formed for the purpose of establishing a spiritual and political center in the Jewish ancestral homeland and a new society based on agriculture and physical labor. In January, 1882, a group calling itself *Bilu* (acronym of the verse from Isaiah, *Beit Iaakov, Lekhu U-nelkha*— "O House of Jacob, come ye and let us go") was organized in Kharkov for the purpose of settling in Palestine as pioneers and working to make their ideals come true.

The first *Bilu* members reached Palestine that same year, and others followed, despite difficulties created by the Turkish authorities. In 1882, the foundation of Jewish agricultural colonization in Palestine was laid. The settlements of Rishon le-Tsiyyon, Zikhron Ya'akov, and Rosh Pinna were established, and Petah Tikva, which had been founded in 1878 and abandoned, was resettled. In 1884, members of *Bilu* founded Gedera. However, the situation of the new settlements was extremely disheartening because of a lack of means, the settlers' inexperience, and difficult conditions in the country. A redeemer, Baron Edmond de Rothschild of Paris, known as the "Celebrated Philanthropist," then appeared to help the settlers in their distress. He took the colonies under his protection, furthered their economic recovery, and helped expand colonization. Despite the numerous complaints against the Baron's agents and their methods—some of which were undoubtedly justified—his intervention was a blessing. At the end of the century, there were about thirty agricultural colonies in Palestine with about six thousand settlers.

Meanwhile, a new leader appeared who in a few years succeeded in focusing all constructive forces among the Jewish people on a single goal — the establishment of a Jewish State in Palestine. The publication of the work *The Jewish State* by Theodor Herzl in 1896 began a new era in Jewish history.

(Opposite page) Nahum Gutman (born 1898), Huts in Neveh Sha'anan. Gutman, who is outstanding both for oils and watercolors, is the painter of the romantic early days of Tel Aviv's beginnings. In this painting, there is the same optimistic atmosphere and touch of poetry. Private collection

218

THE WORLD ZIONIST MOVEMENT

At the First Zionist Congress, which met in Basel in 1897, the World Zionist Organization was founded and henceforth it directed all activities for the realization of the aims of the Jewish Nationalist movement. The overwhelming majority of the *Hovevei Zion* societies joined it and acknowledged Herzl's leadership. At the outset, the Zionist Organization opposed continued surreptitious colonization in Palestine. Herzl wanted Zionist settlement to be based on the explicit consent of the Turkish government, which would grant the Jews a charter to that effect. But all his efforts to secure such a charter were in vain.

Nevertheless, important steps were taken to proceed with colonization in the future by the establishment of two institutions, a bank, the Jewish Colonial Trust, in 1889, and the Jewish National Fund in 1901 for the purpose of purchasing land in Palestine as the property of the entire Jewish people.

The first political proposal presented to the young movement indicating that it was being taken seriously created its first crisis. In 1903, the British government offered to establish an autonomous Jewish colony in British East Africa. Herzl considered the "Uganda Scheme" an opportunity for rendering immediate aid to the Jews of Eastern Europe until large-scale colonization became possible in Palestine on a firm foundation, and he presented it to the Sixth Zionist Congress convening in Basel. His words unleashed a storm in the hall. In vain Herzl protested that he regarded this plan as a temporary solution, a way station to Zion. A large proportion of the delegates opposed the suggestion in principle, considering it a betrayal of the Zionist ideal, and the movement was in serious danger of being split. Peace was restored with difficulty, and it was decided to send a delegation to Uganda to make a study of conditions on the spot. About a year after the controversial Congress, Herzl died in the prime of life, and Jewish people throughout the world were plunged into deep sorrow.

The Seventh Congress meeting in 1905 permanently removed the Uganda Scheme from the agenda and even decided that in the future no colonization plan dealing with any area other than Palestine would be considered.

After Herzl's death, David Wolffsohn, his successor to the leadership of the Zionist Organization, continued

Professor Otto Warburg, a famous botanist and enthusiastic supporter of "practical Zionism."

In 1908, the Palestine Office was opened in Jaffa and the pioneers of the Second *Aliya* (wave of immigration), who entered Palestine between 1904 and 1914, established a number of *kevutsot* (collective settlements), including Deganya, Kinneret, and Merhavya.

In the period between 1901 and 1914, the total number of Jews in Palestine increased from seventy to one hundred thousand. In 1907, there were twenty-seven agricultural settlements with seven thousand inhabitants in the country; by 1914, farm settlements numbered forty-three with a population of twelve thousand. Most of the immigrants who came with the Second *Aliya* had Socialist ideas and intended to lay the foundation of a new society in the country based on social justice. Practical experiments were made with various kinds of cooperative settlements. Many considered their spiritual leader to be Aaron David Gordon, who advocated the idea that physical labor, especially agriculture, should be the basic element of the Jewish national renaissance in the ancestral homeland. The new immigrants fought for the right to engage in productive manual labor in the early Jewish colonies, which had hired Arabs for such work, as well as for the right to guard Jewish property, for which Arabs were also employed. In 1909, the *Ha-Shomer* (Watchman) organization was formed for the latter purpose. In the same year, Jews from Jaffa founded a garden suburb called Tel Aviv (i.e., "Hill of Spring," the Hebrew title of Herzl's second book on the realization of Zionism, which he had called *Old-New Land*). Hebrew now became the predominant vernacular of the new Jewish community and the language of instruction in the schools. A bitter controversy which broke out in 1913 over the language of instruction to be used in the newly founded Haifa Technical Institute ended in a victory for Hebrew.

WORLD WAR I (1914-18)

The date on which World War I broke out —June 28, 1914—also marked a turning point in Jewish history.

In all the countries which participated in the war, Jews demonstrated their loyalty and even patriotic.

Reuven Rubin (born 1893). Rider with Bouquet (1923). One of the Israeli painters best-known abroad, Rubin expresses in his idealized landscapes the emotions evoked by the spiritual climate of the land of Israel. His Romantic style is characterized by simplicity and its adaptation to the visual world around him. Collection H. Richter, New York

the political activity for the procurement of a charter from the Turkish government. However, after a number of years had passed, it became obvious that acquisition of a charter was a false hope. The influence of circles which demanded immediate practical work to further colonization in Palestine steadily mounted, until it dominated the Tenth Zionist Congress in 1911, when Wolffsohn resigned and was succeeded by

The greatest Jewish painter of the School of Paris is undoubtedly Marc Chagall (born 1887). He achieved renown while still a young man in Russia and today is one of the world's leading artists. His work is regarded as the principal representative of contemporary Jewish painting from the point of view of both subject matter and style. The subjects and characters of his work are drawn chiefly from the world of Chagall's childhood in Vitebsk, and consist of a mixture of imagination and reality, humor and sorrow, cruelty and nightmare. This illustration, The Tribe of Asher, *shows one of the stained-glass windows of a Synagogue of the Medical Center, Jerusalem.*

221

Max Band (born 1900) was influenced by German Expressionist painting. His realistic portraits of circus scenes, clowns, and puppets were acclaimed for their strong color contrast and their depth of perception. Max Band painted this Portrait of a Boy *in 1935. Israel Museum, Jerusalem*

enthusiasm. About one hundred thousand Jews served in the German army and about three hundred thousand with the Austro-Hungarian forces. At least six hundred thousand Jews were in the Russian army and about three hundred thousand in the armed forces of other countries (England, France, the United States, Rumania, Turkey, Bulgaria). More than a hundred thousand Jewish soldiers were killed on both sides, and there were large numbers of wounded. Many became officers, and numerous Jews were decorated for bravery in action.

Jews also made valuable contributions to the war effort of both sides on the scientific front. The converted German Jew Fritz Haber put the German chemical industry on a war footing, and Walter Rathenau organized the supply of raw materials for war industries. In Great Britain, Chaim Weizmann headed the research laboratories of the Admiralty and discovered a new method for producing acetone.

Not all the belligerent powers appreciated the Jewish contribution to the war effort in the spheres of science, economics, and actual combat. There was a considerable amount of anti-Semitism in the German army, especially in Prussian units. In the summer of 1916, a special census was carried out for the purpose of determining the degree of Jewish participation in front-line units and in the auxiliary services. The stastical data were falsified and the distorted results of the "Jewish census" were utilized after the war by anti-Semitic agitators. Extremely distressing was the condition of Jewish soldiers in the Russian army; and the Jewish civilian population suffered in Russia more than in any other country. Some of the most violent military operations occurred in the Jewish Pale of Settlement and they caused much death and destruction to the dense Jewish population. In addition, the Russians distrusted the Jews behind the front lines and compensated for their military defeats by vengeful acts against them.

In 1917, the Czar's regime was toppled by revolution. The Jews' legal disabilities were abolished. Many Jews held important posts in the new government, and all of them hoped that their troubles were at an end. However, the civil war and attendant chaos in the country claimed a shocking number of Jewish victims. Both the reactionary White armies and the Communist Red Army devastated Jewish communities. In addition to large numbers of Jews who died of disease and starvation, about fifty thousand were killed in pogroms.

THE BALFOUR DECLARATION AND THE LIBERATION OF PALESTINE

At first, World War I halted the activities of the Zionist Organization, since its members and leaders were split between the two warring camps. Part of the leadership favored neutrality in the European struggle; for the purpose of demonstrating this position, a central office of the movement was opened in Copenhagen, the capital of neutral Denmark, in 1915. However, after Turkey's entrance into the war on the side of Germany and Austria-Hungary, other Zionist leaders began to feel that active participation on the side of the Allies, especially in the Middle Eastern theater, and the military conquest of Palestine could strengthen the national demands of the Jewish people.

From the outset, the war brought much suffering to the Jews of Palestine. Turkey abrogated its treaty agreements, thus depriving Jews who were foreign nationals of the protection of their native lands. The subjects of enemy countries were compelled either to adopt Ottoman nationality or to leave Palestine. Thousands of refugees went to Egypt and took up temporary residence in camps. At the initiative of Vladimir Jabotinsky and Joseph Trumpeldor, the first battalion of Jewish volunteers was raised from among the refugees. The British authorities did not want a Jewish

Visit to the Artist's Workshop *by Alfred Aberdam (1894–1965), the second generation of the School of Paris. Like many of his Jewish friends, Aberdam liked to paint pictures with a gloomy atmosphere. His elongated thin figures add to this typically Romantic portrayal. Israel Museum, Jerusalem*

The most harmonious of the Jewish painters of the School of Paris was George Kars (1882–1945). Kars' lyrical and optimistic attitude to life, despite his unhappy fate, is clearly expressed in the landscape Village on the Rhône *(1939). The vivid color harmony of his work places him in the foremost rank of the School's painters. Israel Museum, Jerusalem*

combat unit. They proposed the activation of a mule corps to serve as a supply force in the Gallipoli campaign. Trumpeldor agreed to this modest task, and the Zion Mule Corps devotedly carried out dangerous, vital missions. But Jabotinsky, who did not give up the idea of establishing a fighting unit, propagandized it among Russian Jews in England and also appealed to the British authorities. Finally, in 1917, the British decided to recruit Russian subjects living in Britain for the British army, and that same year the first Jewish combat unit, the 38th Battalion of Royal Fusiliers, was activated. This unit, which also contained volunteers from the United States, participated in the fighting in Palestine and eastern Transjordania in 1918.

Meanwhile, the Turkish authorities under the leadership of Djemal Pasha rode roughshod over the Jewish community in Palestine. Djemal Pasha hated the Zionists, whom he regarded as the potential allies of Turkey's enemies, and persecuted them mercilessly. Actually, the Turkish governor's suspicions were not unfounded. Many Palestine Jews saw that the Ottoman Empire was on the brink of collapse and would lose its control of the country. Some of them believed they should not remain inactive. A group headed by the agronomist Aaron Aaronson of Zikhron Ya'akov organized an espionage ring called *Nili* (Hebrew acronym of the Biblical verse "The Glory of Israel will not

lie"), which worked for the British and transmitted important military information to British headquarters in Egypt. However, the organization was discovered in 1917, and a number of its members paid with their lives for their devotion to the future of the Jewish community in Palestine.

During the same period, an event of decisive importance in the history of the Jewish people occurred. A story is told that the British Zionist leader, Chaim Weizmann, was once asked by Prime Minister Lloyd George what he wanted in recognition of his services for the war effort; Weizmann replied that he desired nothing for himself, only a land for his people. In any case, indefatigable efforts were involved in the behind-the-scenes activity which led the authorities to the act that was to be known to the world as the Balfour Declaration. On November 2, 1917, British Foreign Minister Arthur James Balfour published a document stating that the British government favored "the establishment in Palestine of a national home for the Jewish people." A month later, in December, a British force commanded by General Edmund Allenby entered Jerusalem.

POSTWAR EUROPE

After the defeat of Germany and her allies, national leaders gathered in Paris to draw up a treaty which

224

would assure the world lasting peace. Out of the conquered states and Russia, new countries—Poland, Czechoslovakia, Hungary, Lithuania, Latvia, Esthonia, and Yugoslavia—were carved, and other countries, such as Rumania, increased their area considerably. In most of these countries, there were large Jewish populations concerned with securing civil rights and cultural autonomy in the new states. The struggle for these aims was carried on in Paris by the leaders of American Jewry organized in the American Jewish Congress. They succeeded in securing the support of President Wilson and leaders of the other Allied powers. All the new states were required to recognize the Jews as a national minority and grant them equal rights.

Zionist leaders were also active at the Peace Conference. The Balfour Declaration was confirmed by the Allied governments and by the League of Nations, which was established in 1920. The mandate for Palestine was awarded to Great Britain, thus made responsible for keeping the promise made in the Balfour Declaration. After the nightmare of the World War, hope appeared among Jews that in the Diaspora they would henceforth be able to live in peace and honor without always being in fear of violence and persecution, while in Palestine pioneers could prepare the National Home.

THE SOVIET UNION

The dark cloud still lingering in the skies which seemed to be clearing was the fate of Russian Jewry, numbering about three million persons. After the horrors of the civil war ended, the Jews began adjusting to the new conditions. The law assured all citizens equal rights, irrespective of race or religion, but it could not uproot the deepest anti-Jewish feelings of the Russians overnight. Despite the fact that anti-Semitism was henceforth a criminal offense, it continued to exist in various forms. The leadership and rank-and-file of the Communist Party included Jews, and many members of the community accommodated to the new regime and became part of it. However, those wishing to remain faithful to their Jewish heritage quickly discovered that they had no place in the Communists' society. Observance of Jewish tradition as well as belief in the Zionist ideal were considered serious offenses by the authorities. In addition, the Communists mistrusted the Jews, who were largely members of the middle class.

In the 1920s, attempts at Jewish agricultural colonization were made in various parts of Russia with the encouragement of the government and the financial support of American Jewry. However, the settlements which were founded did not develop properly and ceased to exist after a short time, chiefly because of the opposition of the local population. In view of this failure, the government decided to establish a Jewish territorial unit in Birobidzhan on the Manchurian border, in the hope that the Jews would regard it as a substitute for the National Home in Palestine. The idea was to create there a secular society, cut off from Jewish tradition and speaking Yiddish rather than Hebrew. The plan aroused no enthusiasm. It is true that a Jewish community was established there which at one time consisted of as many as fifty thousand people, but their numbers later declined, and in 1959 less than fifteen thousand Jews remained, most of them in the regional capital. The idea of a Jewish national home in the Soviet Union failed. Most of the younger generation became assimilated in the anti-religious atmosphere, while a remainder made an effort to preserve a minimum of continuity.

Simplicity and monumentalism are the characteristic marks of recognition of Moïse Kisling (1891–1952). His use of contrasting colors to bring out light and shadows typifies his work in the Paris School, to which most Jewish artists in the first half of the century belonged. Although Kisling never belonged to any one artistic faction, his Man with a Pipe *(1923) reflects the influence of Cubism. Israel Museum, Jerusalem*

MINORITY RIGHTS IN THE SUCCESSOR STATES

Of all the new states, Czechoslovakia was the only one that strictly honored its obligation to the Jewish minority (about three hundred and fifty thousand). Jews there enjoyed complete rights and cultural autonomy. The Jewish national movement operated freely, and its administrative and spiritual center was in the capital, Prague. This idyll lasted until 1939, when Czechoslovakia was engulfed by Nazi Germany.

The situation was entirely different in Poland where there were more than three million Jews. It was not long before the Jews of Poland realized that their government's consent to grant minority rights had been only a deception. Actually, traditional Polish anti-Semitism reigned in the country. In universities, Christian students prevented Jews from entering lecture halls, and professors displayed sympathy for such acts. In the economic sphere, hatred of Jews assumed the form of a well-organized anti-Jewish boycott, which led to impoverishment of the Jews.

In Rumania, too, where about nine hundred thousand Jews were living, the matter of minority rights became a tragicomedy. Part of the Jews had no civil rights whatsoever, and all were the target of an extremely venomous anti-Semitic campaign.

In Hungary, six hundred thousand Jews lived under similar conditions, as did two hundred thousand in Lithuania and Latvia. After a brief period of delusion, the Jews in all these countries awoke to a bitter reality—a foreshadowing of greater evils to come.

THE UNITED STATES AFTER WORLD WAR I

The absolute contrast to the condition of the Jews in the Soviet Union and most of the countries of Eastern Europe was to be found in the United States. Here, there was a Jewish community of more than three and a half million enjoying full rights and complete cultural and religious freedom, and the Nationalist movement was able to develop without hindrance.

To be sure, the number of immigrants permitted to enter the United States every year had been restricted, and in the postwar years a certain amount of antagonism toward foreigners was evident. This mounted further in the depression period following the end of the 1920s, but it was directed less specifically against Jews than against foreigners in general, i.e., Italians, Slavs, Greeks, and the like. Nevertheless, the Jews did not accept this phenomenon without fighting back. The American Jewish Congress and the Anti-Defamation League of the Order B'nai B'rith courageously exposed and opposed every manifestation of discrimination. As economic conditions improved, the agitation subsided, and the anti-Jewish movement declined. The return to a more liberal atmosphere was hastened as the consequence of the negative reaction which the rise of the Nazi Party in Germany aroused among non-Jews.

American Jewry now led the Zionist movement. The Jews had earlier secured proclamations from President Wilson and Congress endorsing the Balfour Declaration. In 1921, Chaim Weizmann was accorded a royal welcome. In the period from 1921 to 1929, the *Keren ha-Yesod* (Foundation Fund—the financial arm of the Zionist Organization) collected about $10,000,000. The combining of all the various funds created the United Jewish Appeal, which accomplished so much for the rebuilding of Palestine. In the struggle carried on in Palestine against British policy which opposed Zionist interests, Jews of the United States gave full political support to the Jewish community of the Holy Land.

JEWISH COMMUNITIES IN OTHER NON-EUROPEAN COUNTRIES

Because of the restriction on immigration into the United States, Jewish emigrants from Eastern Europe turned in ever-increasing numbers to other countries after World War I. In the 1920–40 period, the number of Jews in Argentina doubled—from one hundred and sixty to three hundred and twenty thousand. In other parts of Latin America, the communities also increased in number, size, and importance.

In the lands of the British Commonwealth—Canada, South Africa, and Australia—the Jewish communities grew considerably in the period after World War I. In all these countries, the immigrants became integrated into their environment in a short time and attained respected positions in the economic and public life.

FRANCE, ENGLAND, AND ITALY

In Europe, France was one of the countries of refuge for Jews fleeing from the Ukraine and the destruction brought on them by the war between Poland and the Soviet Union in 1920–21. About fifty thousand refugees made their way to France and settled there, mainly in Paris. Together with approximately one hundred thousand refugees from the prewar Russian terror, the new arrivals from Eastern Europe constituted about one-half of the Jewish population of France. In the atmosphere of freedom and tolerance which prevailed in that country, the process of adjustment was quite rapid. After overcoming the unpleasant initial difficulties, the immigrants established themselves economically, and the younger generation enthusiastically adopted the values of French culture. The social gap between the old community, assimilated and with roots going back for generations, and the new arrivals grew smaller. Both considered themselves entirely French in every way, and took an active part in the public and political life. Jews were elected to the Chamber of Deputies and the Senate, attained

Jewish Villagers Greeting the Messiah *(1937). The atmosphere of folk Hasidism in Poland was introduced into the Jewish painting of the School of Paris by the caricaturist Ezekiel David Kirszenbaum (1900–1953). A poetic feeling impelled Kirszenbaum to paint the ancient Hebrew Prophets as the Jewish folk figures he had been familiar with during his childhood in a Polish town. In gay colors, almost in a carnival atmosphere, Kirszenbuam here depicts an imaginary scene of the Messiah's arrival in the town. According to the popular conception, the Messiah, who seems clearly to be a Hasid, is mounted on a white donkey; he is holding a phylactery bag in his hand, and his saddlebag contains the 613 commandments. As a representative of authority, the Messiah naturally arrives at the railroad station, which is guarded by a non-Jew. The reception party includes some of the Hasidim of the Rabbi of Kotsk and members of an association for reciting Psalms* (Hevra Tehillim), *both groups carrying signs to identify themselves. Israel Museum, Jerusalem*

ministerial rank, and even rose to the post of Prime Minister. They made a brilliant contribution to the intellectual life. It is enough to mention such names as those of Henri Bergson, philosopher and member of the French Academy, who was awarded the Nobel Prize for literature, Salomon Reinach the archaeologist and his brother Théodore Reinach the historian, the sociologists Emile Durkheim and Lucien Lévy-Bruhl, Joseph Halévy the orientalist, the poets Gustave Kahn, Léon Blum, André Spire and Edmond Fleg, the playwright Henri Bernstein, the composer Darius Milhaud, the painters Modigliani, Kisling, Pascin, Soutine, and Chagall, among others.

In England, the years following the end of World

227

War I were a period of internal consolidation of the Jewish community. Russian immigrants, who were still crowding together in the East End before the war and differed in their ways from both the members of the old community and the English population, strengthened their economic position, learned English, adopted local customs, and became integrated into every aspect of the country's life. In commerce, industry, and banking, Jews had for a long time been occupying highly respected positions. In all these spheres, the oldtimers were soon also joined by the sons of immigrants, and many of them were awarded titles for their part in advancing the economy. In the civil service, there were no obstacles in the way of talented Jews. Lord Reading became the Viceroy of India, Herbert Samuel was a member of the cabinet, and later first High Commissioner for Palestine. In Parliament and in the government, in the courts and in the rest of the country's institutions Jews acquitted themselves honorably in important jobs. It was the Jewish economist Harold Laski who laid the theoretical foundation for transforming England into a welfare state. As in France, so in England, too, Jews achieved distinction in all the branches of science, literature, and the plastic arts.

In Italy, the Fascist Party of Benito Mussolini seized power just a few years after the end of the war, in 1922. The exchange of a democratic regime for a Fascist totalitarian government did not affect Jewish rights nor the good relations between Jews and Italians. The government recognized the Jewish communities and their institutions. Jews were members in the Fascist Party and even occupied high positions in it. In all levels of the government service, in the army, and in the teaching profession, Jews continued to serve their country. The harmonious coexistence between Italians and Jews also continued after the Nazi accession to power in Germany, and a number of German refugees found asylum in Italy. The situation changed only in 1938, when the Italian government decided to establish close ties with Nazi Germany, and Mussolini introduced anti-Jewish legislation comparable to the Nuremberg Laws.

GERMANY AFTER DEFEAT

The military defeat which Germany suffered in World War I put an end to the imperial regime, which was supplanted by a democratic parliamentary government. The first National Assembly met in the city of Weimar, dear to German hearts from the period of Goethe and Schiller, and moved to Berlin in 1919 after the situation there had calmed down. The constitution of the so-called Weimar Republic assured complete equal rights for Jews, and serious efforts were made to eliminate anti-Jewish prejudice with which the administrative apparatus was still ridden. In all spheres, a liberal policy in the full sense of the word was introduced. Jews actively participated in political life. In

Bavaria, the Jew Kurt Eisner headed a revolutionary government, and a number of Jewish intellectuals took part in the government which was formed after his assassination (in February, 1919). Walter Rathenau was Minister of Reconstruction and later Foreign Minister of Germany; he did more for the recovery of the German economy and the country's re-entry into the European family of nations than any other man. Many Jewish scientists studied and worked in universities and research institutions. Albert Einstein and others brought worldwide praise to German science. Jewish poets, writers, and critics enriched German literature and endowed it with a new glory.

In the field of Jewish culture there was also much activity in Germany in the period following World War I. These were the years in which Martin Buber advocated a Jewish humanism, a deepening of religious perception, and a new attitude to the Bible and the Hasidic movement. With his friend Franz Rosenzweig, he began a new translation of the Bible, in which the translators tried to preserve the character and spirit of the Hebrew original in the German rendition. In 1920, Franz Rosenzweig founded the *Freies Juedisches Lehrhaus* (Free Jewish School) in Frankfurt-am-Main. In the few remaining years of his life (he contracted a serious illness in 1922 and died in 1929), Rosenzweig expounded a new approach to Judaism, which combined strict observance of the commandments with untrammeled freedom of thought. In rabbinical seminaries, many scholars furthered research on Jewish topics in the spirit of modern science. The Zionist movement was also very active, despite the fact that most German Jews tended toward full integration into the life of the German people.

It was precisely the desire of the German Jews to be like all other Germans, their participation and influence in all aspects of the political, economic, and cultural life, which aroused a mounting negative reaction. After the defeat it had suffered on the field of battle, the German people looked for a scapegoat and found it in the Jewish minority.

In 1919, the National Socialist German Workers' Party was organized in Munich. Its first members included a former corporal in the German army, of Austrian origin, at the time completely unknown to the public at large, Adolf Hitler. This party announced its intention to destroy not only the Jews of Germany but all of Jewry. All means were justified for the purpose of increasing hatred of the Jews and stirring up fear among Germans of the dangers threatening them. Wide circulation was given in those days to a libelous work, *The Protocols of the Elders of Zion*, translated from a fabrication invented by a Russian writer at the beginning of the century. The book claimed to have discovered a plot by Jewish leaders to take over the world by means of Zionism and Communism. The fact that in 1921 the *Protocols* had been demonstrated to be a crude forgery did not lower their prestige in German eyes.

A wave of terror broke out in Germany, and in 1921–22 a number of the leaders of the Republic,

Mané-Katz (1894–1962), Jewish Folk-musicians (1959). Mané-Katz, a painter who concentrated mainly on Jewish themes, was an outstanding member of the School of Paris. He settled in Haifa in 1958. Private collection

including Walter Rathenau, were assassinated. In 1923, Hitler attempted to seize power in Munich and failed. As a consequence of this abortive *Putsch,* he spent a year in prison. For the time being, his party was dissolved. In 1925, however, Hitler reorganized the party with himself as its head.

The German economic recovery of 1924–29 was a transitory phenomenon. In 1930, the condition became most serious again.

Cases of bankruptcy increased and unemployment reached huge proportions. In 1933, the number of unemployed reached about six million. The economic distress and fear of Communist revolution impelled President Paul von Hindenburg and his entourage to adopt drastic measures. On January 30, 1933, Adolf Hitler was named *Reichskanzler,* i.e., Prime Minister. The National Socialist Party became "the sole bearer of the political will of the German people." The swastika, which until then had been the emblem of the Party, became the state symbol, and Adolf Hitler became the almighty *Fuehrer* (leader) of the Third Reich. This decided the fate of Germany's six hundred thousand Jews. Concentration camps, discriminatory legislation (the Nuremberg Laws), destruction of property, wholesale arrests, complete elimination from Germany's social, cultural, economic, and political life, physical violence, and indiscriminate murder typified the day-to-day existence of the German Jew. Half of Germany's Jews saved themselves by flight; the rest were systematically killed off.

POSTWAR AUSTRIA

In Austria—the German part of the Austro-Hungarian Empire, which was established as an independent state after World War I—there were two hundred thousand Jews, some one hundred and seventy-five thousand of whom lived in the capital, Vienna. During the economic crisis with which the small, impoverished country had to contend, traditional Austrian anti-Semitism came back to life. Jewish participation in the activities of the Social-Democratic Party, which attempted to improve the situation, increased the blind hatred of Jews in clerical and conservative circles. With the rise of the Nazi (National Socialist) Party in Germany, anti-Semitism also increased in Austria. Gradually, the Jews were eliminated from public life and excluded from all economic activity. Nevertheless, Austria's Jews still felt a certain amount of security as long as the dominant Christian-Socialist Party opposed surrender to Nazi Germany and rejected the idea of Austria's annexation to the German Reich. However, after the murder in 1934 of Austrian Prime Minister Engelbert Dollfuss, who exemplified a combination of virulent anti-Semitism and proud anti-Nazism, Austrian Jewry was doomed.

THE GROWTH OF THE JEWISH COMMUNITY IN PALESTINE

The Balfour Declaration was a small remedy which to a slight degree anticipated the overwhelming disaster that would all but crush the Jewish people. After the Palestine mandate had been officially awarded to Great Britain, the Anglo-Jewish statesman Herbert Samuel was named first High Commissioner in 1920. This appointment had propaganda value. The British government wished to demonstrate that it intended to keep its promise and help establish a Jewish national home in Palestine. However, it soon became obvious that a home of this sort could not be built overnight.

From the beginning, Arab leaders opposed the idea of a Jewish national home. Early in 1920, even before the arrival of Herbert Samuel, attacks were carried out against various Jewish settlements. In the defense of Tel Hai in the northeastern corner of the country, seven Jews were killed (February 29, 1920), among them Joseph Trumpeldor, who had been active in organizing the Jewish Legion during World War I and in founding the pioneering organization *He Haluts.* In 1921, Jews were attacked in Jaffa and in Petah Tikva and other colonies. Many were killed, including the writer Joseph Chaim Brenner.

Despite the high commissioner's good will and his personal belief in the Zionist ideal, British officialdom showed no understanding of the interests of the Jewish community, while displaying great sensitivity to the position and reactions of the Arabs. Actually, part of the representatives of the mandatory government encouraged Arab opposition to the Balfour Declaration and its promise to the Jews. Under Arab pressure, Transjordania was removed in 1922 from the area to which the Declaration applied.

Despite all these difficulties, the Jewish community in Palestine grew considerably in the five years in which Herbert Samuel served as High Commissioner. In the period 1920–25, the Jewish population was doubled (from fifty-five to one hundred and eight thousand), as was the number of agricultural settlements (from forty-four to one hundred). Development also continued during the term of the second High Commissioner, Lord Plumer, who also more or less knew how to preserve order in the country. The Jewish National Fund acquired and developed new tracts of land which had previously been covered with swamps and plagued by malaria; in these areas new agricultural colonies were established. Tel Aviv became a dynamic Jewish city; its population grew from thirty-six hundred in 1919 to forty thousand at the end of 1929. The Jewish community had numerous schools. Newspapers and periodicals multiplied. In 1926, the *Ohel* Theater began presenting plays; in 1927, *Ha-Matatei,* a satirical theater, opened. A year later, the *Habima* Theater, which had been founded in Moscow in 1916 and had already achieved renown in Europe and the United States, established its permanent headquarters in Tel Aviv. Chaim Nachman Bialik, who was admired as a national poet, settled in Tel Aviv in 1924. The philosopher of Jewish nationalism, Achad Haam, had already been living there since 1922.

The Jewish community in Haifa also grew considerably. The Technical Institute (Technion) was opened in 1925. Important industrial enterprises were founded, and the mandatory government began building a modern port designed to be Palestine's principal harbor. In Jerusalem, the Hebrew University, the cornerstone of which Chaim Weizmann had laid in 1918, was opened on Mount Scopus in 1925.

The situation took a turn for the worse with the arrival of the third High Commissioner, Sir John

Kaete Ephraim Marcus (1892–1970), Merry-Go-Round (1960). Through the medium of vigorous color and true to life rhythms, the paintings of K. E. Marcus speak an urgent language. The painter was also a highly regarded sculptor. Private collection

Chancellor. During his term, the influence of those mandatory officials who had neither understanding nor sympathy for Zionist aspirations increased. The Arabs sensed the change in the political climate and in the summer of 1929 launched a large-scale attack against the Jewish community. In Jerusalem, Hebron, Safad, and many colonies 133 Jews were killed and 339 wounded. Instead of adopting drastic measures against the Arab rioters which might have prevented a repetition of the disorders, inquiry commissions were sent in to determine whether or not in general there was still room for expanding Jewish agricultural colonization in Palestine.

The conclusion reached by the commissions was negative, and as a consequence restrictions were imposed on further settlement and on Jewish immigration into the country. The Jewish community did not accept the change in the mandatory government's position. The *Haganah* (i.e., defense organization), which had been formed in 1920 and had demonstrated its strength in the 1929 disturbances, continued to grow and make preparations for all eventualities. One of its functions was to circumvent the restrictions imposed on immigration and to help prospective immigrants who were not granted entrance certificates to come into the country in a roundabout way. Those years marked the beginning of the so-called "illegal immigration," which subsequently assumed vast proportions and became one of the greatest harassments of the mandatory government. At the same time, considerable diplomatic work was done in London, which yielded some results. In 1931, Sir Arthur Wauchope, an honest, energetic man who revealed understanding for the Zionist undertaking and the aspirations of the country's Jewish community, succeeded Lord Chancellor. He served in the post until 1938. During his term, it was quiet in the country, and numerous refugees from the Nazis settled in Palestine. Up to 1939, fifty-five thousand immigrants from Germany had entered the Holy Land.

231

THE PRESENT

The seven-branched candelabrum, or Menorah, traditional symbol of Judaism and now the emblem of the State of Israel, stands proudly before the new Knesset (Parliament) Building in its capital, Jerusalem

Before Germany unleashed World War II with a sudden attack on Poland on September 1, 1939, she had already been waging war against the Jews for six years. During that period, the Germans had completely disrupted Jewish life in Germany, Austria, and Czechoslovakia. The Nuremberg Laws of 1935, which deprived Jews of their citizenship, cut them off from their non-Jewish neighbors, and brutally eliminated them from the economic and cultural life of the lands in which they had been living for centuries, were but the initial phase of Germany's war against the Jews. It was not until the Nazi occupation of Poland that Germany's rulers began methodically to implement what they euphemistically called "the final solution to the Jewish problem." In specially constructed death camps, the Nazis fiendishly proceeded to exterminate the Jewish people.

As German forces thrust into Poland from the West following the signing of a non-aggression pact between the government of Adolf Hitler and the U.S.S.R., Soviet troops swept in from the East. The tens of thousands of Jews who fled into the Soviet zone seeking to escape the Nazi machine of destruction were soon overtaken by the advancing German armies when the Nazis invaded the Soviet Union in 1941.

In areas occupied by the Nazis, whole Jewish populations were herded into congested ghettos, which they were allowed to leave only to work in Nazi forced-labor camps or to make the final journey to mass gassing chambers and crematoria. No one was spared; infants, women, old people were all snuffed out. In many instances, the Germans executed hundreds of Jews and buried them in mass graves.

With diabolical ingenuity, the Nazis took great pains to keep their plan for annihilating the Jewish people a secret so they could lead the victims to their destruction more easily. The clothing, hair, eyeglasses, and even false teeth of the murdered Jews were carefully classified and distributed for subsequent processing. Jewish property went to the German authorities. In many instances, the local population—Lithuanians, Poles, Ukrainians—gleefully helped the Nazis. A list of place-names few had ever heard of before came to represent the embodiment of evil—Auschwitz, Treblinka, Belzec, Maidanek, Sobibor, Chelmo, Buchenwald, Dachau, Bergen-Belsen.

But it took years of Nazi occupation completely to shatter Jewish life. Huddled in the ghettos, the Jews conducted lectures on various topics, presented plays, published newspapers, and risked their lives constantly to maintain contact with other communities and with the center of the Jewish renaissance in Palestine. Poets and prose writers put into words the turbulence in their hearts, the hopelessness of their existence, and the ultimate degradation of man by man. Scores of painters in the ghettos, concentration camps, and forest retreats left hundreds of visual expressions of the unspeakable horrors which they daily witnessed.

Slowly, as the accounts of the extermination of a people seeped through, Jews took up arms in last desperate attempts to stem the tide of destruction and let the world know what was going on. One of the greatest of such sagas occurred in the Warsaw Ghetto, where the Jews grimly fought the Nazis from April 19 to May 16, 1943, until tanks and artillery were brought in by the Germans. Only a handful escaped to join partisan groups fighting the Germans in the countryside.

Elsewhere in Europe, wherever the Jews turned on their murderers—at Bialystok, Tarnow, Vilna, Treblinka, Czestochowa—the result was always total destruction. In Poland and the occupied areas of the Soviet Union, in the French maquis and the Resistance movements in Belgium and the Netherlands, and among the partisans in Czechoslovakia and Italy, Jews played an important role in the war against the Germans. In addition, a million three hundred thousand Jews served in the armed forces fighting the Axis powers. Of this number, five hundred and fifty thousand were in the American services, five hundred thousand in the Soviet, sixty thousand in the British armies, seventeen thousand with the Canadian troops, and ten thousand with the South African forces. The Palestine Jewish community of four hundred thousand persons sent thirty thousand men and women volunteers to the various branches of the British army and eventually, when official permission was finally granted, to the Jewish Brigade Group, which saw action against the Germans in Italy and played an active role in rescuing the Jewish survivors of war-torn Europe and transporting them to Palestine.

Vital rescue work in Nazi-occupied Europe was carried out by members of a special parachute unit from Palestine dropped into enemy territory for the purpose of saving as many Jews as possible and organizing resistance activities.

After Hitler's accession to power in 1933, more and more Jews sought to save themselves in flight. However, there were few countries which agreed to give them refuge and an opportunity to rebuild their shattered lives. Since the League of Nations and private bodies were unable to do much to alleviate the homelessness of Jews fleeing Nazi persecution, President Franklin D. Roosevelt of the United States called a conference at Évian in 1938 to deal with the problem. Only the Dominican Republic agreed to accept any considerable number of Jewish refugees.

The British government, which was responsible for the administration of Palestine, refused to lower the barriers against immigration, despite the eagerness of the country's small Jewish community to take in all those fleeing Nazi persecution. In 1939, the London government issued a White Paper putting a halt to Jewish immigration and severely restricting the sale of land to Jews in most of Palestine.

Tora Mantel *by Yaacov Agam*

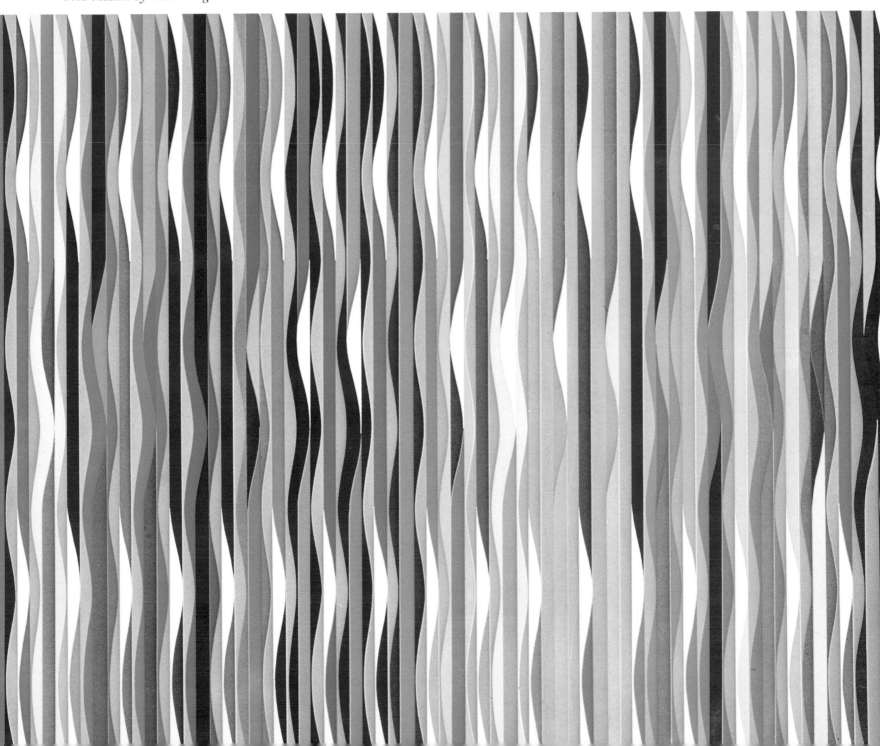

Jacob Wexler (born 1912), untitled oil *(1962). Under the influence of Braque and Picasso, Wexler developed a decorative and abstract style. Gallery Israel, Tel Aviv*

Michael Argov, untitled oil *(1962). Argov is a painter who gives his colors a new range of expression through imaginative use of texture. Gallery Israel, Tel Aviv*

Nevertheless, tens of thousands of Jews entered Palestine, whether legally or illegally, overland or in seagoing vessels of all kinds, in a vast movement organized by Zionist bodies for the purpose of running the British air, sea, and land blockade of the Jewish National Home. The dissolution of Jewish life in Europe was partly compensated for by a spurt of development in Palestine, where towns and villages grew, industries expanded, new enterprises came into being, a philharmonic orchestra was founded, museums were established in the principal cities and even in kibbutzim, and artists resumed their creative activity under new and stimulating conditions.

Many of the European artists who came to Palestine at this time had already established reputations in the art world. Isidor Aschheim, Jacob Steinhardt, and Miron Sima were familiar names in the Expressionist movement when they arrived in Palestine. Jacob Pins, Jonah Mach, and Ruth Bamberger developed a stylized Expressionism of their own in the country. A central figure among the painters who reached Palestine was Mordecai Ardon (formerly Bronstein), one of the pioneers in abandoning the visual representation of reality. Mordecai Levanon is an outstanding example of the impact of the Israeli landscape on a European artist. These artists found in the country a fertile soil for their activity and an art-conscious community eager for their work. Painters such as Marcel Janco, Nahum Gutman, Yosef Zaritsky, Reuven Rubin, Moshe Castel, Moshe Mokady, and Anna Ticho had already laid the groundwork for new trends in Israeli art. The Bezalel School of Art and its museum were world-famous and played a pivotal role in fostering public interest in the arts.

The Nazi treatment of the Jews impelled a number of Jewish artists to turn to purely Jewish motifs in their work. These include Ben Shahn in the United States, whose painting has achieved international prominence. During World War II, many Jewish artists such as the painter Adolphe Feder and the sculptor Moise Kogan were murdered by the Nazis after the invasion of France. Eminent figures like Marc Chagall, Jacques Lipchitz, and Mané-Katz succeeded in escaping from the Nazi-occupied area. A number of French-Jewish artists, such as Michel Kikoine, managed to hide out during the period of Nazi occupation. However, after the war, only a few survivors of the French-Jewish artists' colony returned to Paris.

When the smoke and stench of World War II began to clear away, the world suddenly became aware of the magnitude of the tragedy which had annihilated one-third of the Jewish people and made a shambles of Jewish life in Europe. Of three million Jews who had been living in Poland before the conflict, one hundred and twenty thousand remained; in Czechoslovakia, fifty thousand survived out of a community of three hundred and sixty thousand; thirty thousand Jews were left of the one hundred thousand in Belgium, and ten of the seventy-five thousand in Greece. This was the fearful pattern everywhere the German jackboot had trod. With no homes to return to and no close human being to go back to, four hundred and fifty thousand Jews in the displaced persons camps had no choice but emigration. The vast majority of them turned their eyes to Palestine, determined to seek peace and security among their own people. As the British redoubled their efforts to keep Jews from reaching Palestine, the opposition to their policies mounted, ranging from passive resistance to armed attacks against government installations and security personnel.

During the Hitler period and the critical years which followed, the five million Jews of the United States placed their organizational skills, economic resources, and cultural and social institutions at the disposal of the victims of Nazism. Agencies were set up for helping the new arrivals to the United States establish themselves and become integrated into the American Jewish community and the general American scene. Religious and cultural institutions extirpated from the European centers where they had functioned for generations struck fresh roots in the New World, from Canada down to Argentina. In the United States, the Jewish community lent its wholehearted support to the reconstitution of Jewish life in Palestine and, with the exception of a small, wealthy minority, endeavored to use its influence to persuade the British government to alter its restrictive policy.

The newly established pro-Communist states in Eastern Europe brought about the liquidation of Jewish organizational life. Zionism had been frowned upon, proscribed, or harshly persecuted in the countries taking their inspiration from the Soviet Union. With Jewish schools non-existent in hundreds of decimated communities, a sharp rise in intermarriage, the disappearance of Yiddish as a unifying factor, and the shortage of trained leadership, assimilation has been gathering momentum and threatens East European Jewry with extinction. In the U.S.S.R., the process has been exacerbated by a deliberate policy of blotting out the Jewish people as a cultural entity. Officially fostered anti-Semitism, assaults against the Jewish religion, the Hebrew language, and Zionism, and venomous attacks against Israel, coupled with large-scale financial, military, and political support of the Arab states vociferously proclaiming their intention to annihilate the Jewish State, have been making Jewish life ever more precarious in the Soviet Union and its satellites. The only exception to this was a brief period from 1947 to 1949 when the U.S.S.R. supported the establishment of a Jewish state in Palestine and lent it vital political and military support.

Aharon Giladi, Women *(1962). Giladi was a member of the ''New Horizons'' group which held its first exhibition in Tel Aviv in 1949. Without abandoning figurative art, Giladi's paintings are highly stylized. Gallery Israel, Tel Aviv*

Mordecai Ardon (born 1896), Scrolls *(1960). Ardon is one of the most remarkable living Israeli painters. After an Expressionistic period, he has developed a sort of Jewish Surrealistic symbolism. Private collection*

236

Léa Nikel, untitled oil *(1960). Léa Nikel is a very sensitive painter whose colors, rich in tone and texture, are forcefully emotive.*
Mrs. Zafrir Collection, Tel Aviv

The growing violence against the British regime in postwar Palestine led to the dispatch of various commissions seeking to reconcile the conflicting positions of Jews, Arabs, and the British government. During this period, the Arab League, founded by the British as an instrument for maintaining their power in the Arab world, assumed direction of the fight against Zionism. However, it was the British government which clashed openly with the Jewish community of Palestine. It refused to accept the recommendations of an Anglo-American commission for the transfer of a hundred thousand homeless European Jews to Palestine, and sent to detention camps all Jews caught attempting to enter the country without immigration certificates. In the wake of increasing violence, Britain in 1947 referred the Palestine problem to the United Nations. The recommendations of a majority of the members of a U.N. special commission, calling for the establishment of partitioned Jewish and Arab states in the country and the internationalization of Jerusalem, was accepted by the General Assembly on November 29, 1947. The Arabs in Palestine immediately made good their promise to fight the decision with bloodshed.

Widespread attacks against Jewish population centers and communications, by Arab gangs with the tacit and sometimes overt support of the authorities, were repulsed, and the Jews of Palestine prepared the administrative apparatus for governing their own state on the departure of the British on May 15, 1948.

Moshe Mokady (born 1902), Table and Picture *(1949). A master of color, Mokady manifests a great ability to dramatize apparently simple subjects. His work is essentially sensuous and impulsive. Private collection*

Yossl Bergner (born 1920), Landscape *(1961). Initially an Expressionist, Bergner started experimenting with abstract color values in the early fifties and his work took on a Surrealist bias. Mrs. Zafrir Collection, Tel Aviv*

Marcel Janco (born 1895), A Burning Village (1959). Born in Rumania, Janco spent the years of World War I in Switzerland, where he was among the founders of the Dadaist movement. His painting, sometimes abstract, sometimes figurative, always original, has achieved international recognition and has greatly influenced the younger generation of Israeli artists. Collection Jankelevici, Paris

On May 14, 1948, the leaders of the Jewish community proclaimed the establishment of the independent State of Israel. The following morning, the armed forces of Israel's Arab neighbors converged on the new country in a concentrated effort to throttle it at birth. Israel's fledgling army, an outgrowth of the *Haganah,* braced itself to fight back, and by the end of 1948 it had cleared the territory allotted to the Jewish state by the United Nations of all invaders and expelled them from some additional areas. In January, 1949, Israel's first general elections were held. Within the next few months, one Arab state after another agreed to an armistice, but not to permanent peace.

EMERGENCE OF ISRAEL AS A MIDDLE-EASTERN POWER

In the early years of the first Jewish state since Bar-Kokheva (132–135 C.E.), the entire Jewish communities of Yemen and Iraq were transferred to Israel. Subsequently, as the Jews of Israel tightened their belts and adopted a strict austerity regime to enable them to take in all who sought to enter the country, large numbers of Jews from North Africa and several Communist countries in Eastern Europe immigrated to the Jewish state. Contributions from the Jewish communities of North America and the Jewish centers in Latin America, Western Europe, South Africa, Australia, and other countries supplied Israel with the financial and moral backing to enable it to absorb the newcomers and develop the resources of the country and its people. Private investments, foreign loans, American grants, and German reparations all contributed to increasing Israel's economic capacities so that it could expand its exports.

American Jewry continued to play a central role in Israel's growth. At the same time, it developed its own institutions, which included nationwide fund-raising

239

Rachel's Tomb, Bethlehem, a shrine significant to world religions which have their roots in the Holy Land

agencies for local needs and Jewish-sponsored universities. The Jewish impact on general American culture, particularly on the literary scene and in the entertainment world, reached unprecedented dimensions.

In postwar Western Europe, France gradually rose to the forefront as the Continent's most important Jewish center. New communities, chiefly of North African Jews, were established in the western and southwestern parts of the country. In the Communist states of Eastern Europe, notably in the U.S.S.R., Czechoslovakia, and Poland, resurgent waves of anti-Semitism fostered by the authorities made it clear that Jewish life had no future.

While, in the Communist states, assimilation was being deliberately imposed by outside forces, in the countries of the West it increased as a natural development accompanying the Jews' growing identification with the lands in which they lived. However, a revival of traditional religious practices, and concern for Israel and pride in its achievements, accompanied this trend and counteracted it to some extent. Throughout the Jewish world, Jewish survival became synonymous with Israel's continued development.

During the two decades of its existence, Israel has never been able to relax its vigilance against the perennial attempts of the Arab states to destroy it. Unremitting attacks by marauders from across the border bent on robbery and murder drove her into a war with Egypt in 1956, when her troops drove through the Gaza Strip—a part of former Palestine under Egyptian domination since 1948—and the Sinai Peninsula in less than a week. Again, in 1967, she was forced to mobilize her citizen army, when Egypt moved large forces into the Sinai Peninsula and blockaded the Straits of Tiran. In a lightning six-day war, Israel's defense forces thrust through to the Suez Canal, taking all of Sinai and reopening the Straits of Tiran, moved eastward to reunite Jerusalem which had been rent asunder for nineteen years, and pushed up to the Golan heights, from which Syrian artillery had been shelling Israeli villages in the valley below.

The Six-Day War forged a feeling of unity among Jewish people all over the world which demonstrated to what degree Israel's survival is regarded as the backbone of Jewish existence by Jewry everywhere. With Israel threatened with destruction, every individual Jew, however remote he may have been from other Jews and Jewish life, saw himself as being personally affected, and acted accordingly, providing moral, financial, and political support far beyond what might have been expected. The spontaneous upsurge of desire to help Israel also gave rise to a movement of volunteers hurrying to the Jewish state to defend it with their lives, if need be. They prevailed. Israel lives.

240

An Israeli soldier writes the Hebrew name on a street sign, which had previously had only Arabic and English lettering identifying the location as Wailing Wall Road

Countless Israelis, both military and civilian, crowded to the Wailing Wall in the Old City of Jerusalem after its recapture from the Jordanians by the Israel defense forces during the Six-Day War. In the foreground, right, former Prime Minister David Ben-Gurion mingles with the joyous population

Accompanied by an Israeli soldier, Rabbi Shlomo Goren, head chaplain of the Israel defense forces, blows the shofar *(ram's horn) to signalize the recapture of the Wailing Wall from the Jordanians*

GENERAL BIBLIOGRAPHY

Baron, A., *Social and Religious History of the Jews, 2nd ed. rev. and enl., I–XIV, 1952–1970.*

Dubnov, S., *History of the Jews, I–III, 1967–1969.*

Finkelstein, L., ed., *The Jews, Their History, Culture and Religion, I–II, 1960³.*

Graetz, H., *History of the Jews, I–VI, 1891–1898.*

The Jewish People, Past and Present, I–IV, 1946–1955 (English transl.).

Roth, C., *Jewish Art, an Illustrated History, 1961.*

Roth, C., *A Short History of the Jewish People, New enl. ed., 1970.*

1. THE HEBREWS IN THE BIBLICAL PERIOD

Albright, W. F., *The Biblical Period from Abraham to Ezra, 1963.*

Holt, J. M., *The Patriarchs of Israel, 1964.*

Kaufmann, Y., *The Religion of Israel from its Beginning to the Babylonian Exile, 1960.*

Macalister, R. A. S., *The Philistines, their History and Civilization, 1914.*

Muscati, S., *The Semites in the Ancient Orient, 1959.*

Rowley, H. H., *From Joseph to Joshua, 1950.*

The World History of the Jewish People, 1st Ser. Ancient Times,
  1) Speiser, E. A. ed., *At the Dawn of Civilization, 1964.*
  2) Mazar B., ed., *The Patriarchs, 1970.*

2. THE ISRAELITE MONARCHY: FROM SAUL TO THE BABYLONIAN CONQUEST

Albright, W. F., *Archaeology and the Religion of Israel, 1953.²*

Alt, A., *Essays on O. T. History and Religion, 1966.*

Bright, J. A., *A History of Israel, 1959.*

Kenyon, K., *Jerusalem, Excavating 3000 Years of History, 1967.*

Mazar, B., ed., *Views of Biblical World, I–IV, 1959–1961.*

Thieberger, F., *King Solomon, 1947.*

Welch, A. C., *Kings and Prophets of Israel, 1952.*

3. FROM THE END OF THE BABYLONIAN CAPTIVITY TO THE DESTRUCTION OF THE SECOND TEMPLE

Bickermann, E., *From Ezra to the Last of the Maccabees, 1962.*

Bickermann, E., *The Maccabees, 1947.*

Cornfeld, G., *Daniel to Paul, Jews in Conflict with Graeco-Roman Civilization, 1962.*

Finkelstein, L., *The Pharisees, I–II, 1962³.*

Jeremias, J., *Jerusalem in the Time of Jesus, 1969.*

Russell, D., *The Jews from Alexander to Herod, 1967.*

Schalit, A. C. *König Herodes, 1969.*

Tscherikover, V., *Hellenistic Civilization and the Jews, 1959.*

Zeitlin, S., *The Rise and Fall of the Judean State, A Political, Social and Religious History of the Second Commonwealth, 1968.²*

4. PALESTINE AND BABYLONIA AS JUDAISM'S SPIRITUAL CENTERS

Finkelstein, H., *Akiba, Scholar, Saint and Martyr, 1936.*

Mantel, H., *Studies in the History of the Sanhedrin, 1961.*

Neusher, J., *A History of the Jews in Babylonia, 1965–1970.*

Neusher, J., *A Life of Rabban Yohanan Ben Zakkai, 1962.*

Strack, H. L., *Introduction to the Talmud and Midrash, 1931.*

5. THE JEWS IN THE EASTERN ROMAN EMPIRE

Moore, G. F., *Judaism in the First Centuries of the Christian Era, I–III, 1944–1948.*

Parkes, J., *The Conflict of Church and Synagogue, 1934.*

6. AN INDEPENDENT JEWISH KINGDOM IN CENTRAL ASIA

7. "COURT SLAVES" OF THE EUROPEAN KINGS

Blumenkranz B., *Juifs et Chrétiens dans le Monde Occidental, 430–1096, 1965.*

Dunlop, D. M., *The History of the Jewish Khazars, 1967.*

Fischel, W., *Jews in the Economic and Political Life of Medieval Islam, 1937.*

Kats, S., *The Jews in the Visigothic and Frankish Kingdoms of Spain and Gaul, 1937.*

Malter, H., *Saadia Gaon, 1921.*

Starr, J., *The Jews in the Byzantine Empire, 641–1204, 1939.*

The World History of the Jewish People, 2nd Ser., Medieval Period., 2) Roth, C. ed., The Dark Ages, 1966.

8. FOUR HUNDRED YEARS OF HORROR

Baer, F., *A History of the Jews in Christian Spain, I–II, 1961–1966.*

Grayzel, S., *The Church and the Jews in the XIIIth Century, 1933.*

Kisch, G., *The Jews in Medieval Germany, 1949.*

Parkes, J., *The Jews in the Medieval Community, 1938.*

Prawer, J., *Histoire du Royaume Latin de Jerusalem, I, 1969.*

Richardson, H. G., *English Jewry under the Angevin Kings, 1960.*

Synan, E. A., *The Popes and the Jews in the Middle Ages, 1967.*

9. ADAPTATION TO A NEW WORLD OF VALUES

Netanyahu, B. Z., *The Marranos of Spain from the Late XIVth to the Early XVIth Century according to Contemporary Hebrew Sources, 1966.*

Netanyahu, B. Z., *Don Isaac Abravanel, Statesman and Philosopher, 1968.*

Roth, C., *The House of Nasi: Dona Gracia, 1947.*

Roth, C., *The Jews in the Renaissance, 1949.*

10. EUROPE AT THE END OF THE RENAISSANCE
Dubnow, S., *History of the Jews in Russia and Poland, I,* 1916.
Katz, J., *Tradition and Crisis,* 1961.
Roth, C., *The History of the Jews in Italy,* 1946.

11. HASKALAH, SABBATIANS, MASKILIM AND HASIDIM
Dubnow, S., *Geschichte des Chassidismus, I–II,* 1931.
Goodblatt, M. S., *Jewish Life in Turkey in the XVIth Century as Reflected in the Legal Writings of Samuel de Modens,* 1952.
Hertsberg, A., *The French Enlightenment and the Jews,* 1968.
Meyer, M. A., *The Origins of the Modern Jew,* 1968.
Newman, L., *The Hasidic Anthology,* 1934.
Roth, C., *History of the Marranos,* 1959³.
Scholem, G., *Major Trends in Jewish Mysticism,* 1954³.
Stern, S., *The Court Jew,* 1950.

12. THE NINETEENTH CENTURY
Nachel, R., *Napoléon et les Juifs,* 1928.
Elbogen, I., *A Century of Jewish Life,* 1944.
Hanani, B., *L'émancipation des Juifs,* 1928.
Greenberg, L., *The Jews in Russia, I–II,* 1944–1951.
Philipson, D., *The Reform Movement in Judaism,* 1931.
Sachar, H., *The Course of Modern Jewish History,* 1958.
Szajkowski, Z., *Jews and the French Revolutions of 1789, 1830, 1848,* 1969.

13. BETWEEN NATIONALISM AND ASSIMILATION
Byrnes, R. F., *Antisemitism in Modern France,* 1950.
Cohn, N., *Warrant for Genocide,* 1967.
Davis, M., *Jewish Religious Life and Institutions in America,* 1913.
Dubnov, S. M., *History of the Jews in Russia and Poland, II–III,* 1918–1920.
Frumkin, J. G., ed., *Russian Jewry, 1860–1914,* 1966.
Handlin, O., *Adventure in Freedom,* 1954.
Janowsky, A., *The Jews and the Minority Rights, 1898–1919,* 1933.
Massing, P., *Rehearsal for Destruction, a Study of Political Antisemitism in Imperial Germany,* 1965.
Pulzer, P. G. J., *The Rise of Political Antisemitism in Germany and Austria,* 1964.

14. THE RETURN TO ZION
Bein, A., *The Return to the Soil: A History of Jewish Settlement in Israel,* 1952.
Goldberg, B. Z., *The Jewish Problem in the Soviet Union,* 1961.
Halperin, B., *The Idea of the Jewish State,* 1970².
Sokolov, N., *History of Zionism, I–II,* 1918.
Stein, L., *The Balfour Declaration,* 1961.
Zechlin, E., *Die Deutsche Politik und die Juden im Ersten Weltkrieg,* 1969.

INDEX